THE OLDEST CONSTITUTIONAL QUESTION

THE OLDEST CONSTITUTIONAL QUESTION

Enumeration and Federal Power

RICHARD PRIMUS

HARVARD UNIVERSITY PRESS

Cambridge, Massachusetts

London, England

2025

Publication of this book has been supported through the generous provisions
of the Maurice and Lula Bradley Smith Memorial Fund.

Library of Congress Cataloging-in-Publication Data

Names: Primus, Richard A., author.
Title: The oldest constitutional question : enumeration and federal power /
Richard Primus.
Description: First. | Cambridge, Massachusetts ; London, England : Harvard
University Press, 2025. | Includes bibliographical references and index.
Identifiers: LCCN 2024044482 | ISBN 9780674293595 (cloth)
Subjects: LCSH: Federal government—United States. | Implied powers
(Constitutional law)—United States. | Legislative power—United States.
Classification: LCC KF4600 .P76 2025 | DDC 342.73/041—dc23/eng/20241113
LC record available at https://lccn.loc.gov/2024044482

For my family

These cases implicate . . . perhaps our oldest question of constitutional law . . . the proper division of authority between the Federal Government and the States.

—*New York v. United States* (1992)

CONTENTS

PREFACE

For more than two decades, it has been my joy and privilege to teach constitutional law at the University of Michigan Law School. One of the central topics of the introductory course is federalism, and the biggest part of the course's investigation of federalism is about the reach of congressional power. When I began teaching, I more or less accepted the conventional view that the Constitution enumerates congressional powers in order to limit the federal government. I explained the Constitution's text, history, and structure to my students in ways that supported that view, much as my own teachers had explained them to me. But over the years, I found myself increasingly dissatisfied with the explanations I was giving. Federalism did not really work the way that I heard myself saying it did. Constitutional history was more complicated, and less supportive of the conventional view, than the story I was telling. And although the text of the Constitution could be interpreted to mean what I was saying it meant, that interpretation came to seem more forced and less natural than I had once believed. So I began to pull on the loose threads, asking here and there whether something about the conventional view might be not quite right. The more I pulled, the more I found that other threads came loose, until the entire garment unraveled.

The orthodox account of enumerated congressional powers, I came to think, is a story that constitutional lawyers tell themselves. It is a story that teaches its listeners—and its tellers—to understand the constitutional system in particular ways. And many of those ways are misleading. So it seemed worthwhile to try to understand where the story has come from, what work it has done, and whether a better account is possible—one that would offer a more complete and less distorted view and therefore better serve both the people who make constitutional law and the people who seek to understand it. This book is the result.

A practical note: at the end of the book, just after the conclusion, I have included a brief section called Frequently Asked Questions. It contains quick summary answers to questions that I was often asked about this project as I was writing as well as definitions of several terms that the book introduces. Feel free to consult it at any time if you think it might be helpful. That said, the book is written to explain its argument and its terminology along the way. So if you prefer simply to start at the beginning and read through, please do.

INTRODUCTION

ONE OF THE MOST fundamental ideas in American constitutional law is that the Constitution limits the federal government by enumerating its powers. Rather than writing a constitution that would give Congress the power to make whatever laws it believed to be in the public interest, the story runs, the Framers compiled a carefully circumscribed list of the things the federal government could do. Article I, Section 1, of the Constitution does not give Congress general legislative power; it vests Congress with the "powers herein granted." The eighteen clauses of Article I, Section 8, then specify—or, as the usual expression has it, *enumerate*—particular powers Congress may exercise. According to the traditional thinking, the Constitution's enumeration of specific federal powers indicates that the federal government may exercise those powers and no others.[1] Lest there be doubt, the Founding generation also adopted the Tenth Amendment, which provides that "[t]he powers not delegated to the United States by the Constitution . . . are reserved to the States respectively, or to the people." For all these reasons, the normal thinking runs, the federal government can do only what the Constitution's text affirmatively authorizes it to do.

It is hard to overstate the importance that constitutional lawyers ascribe to this view of federal power. In 1791, James Madison called the limitation of the federal government to its textually enumerated powers the regime's "essential characteristic."[2] The modern Supreme Court has called that limitation one of constitutional law's "first principles."[3] By confining the federal government to a set of defined activities and leaving everything else for the states, the enumeration of congressional powers is supposed to ensure a proper balance between central and local authority. In so doing, the standard thinking continues, the limitation of the federal government to its enumerated powers protects the rights of individual Americans, because it prevents any player in the system from exercising too much power.

The traditional thinking about enumerated powers is a bundle of related ideas rather than a single proposition. First comes the rule that Congress can act only on the basis of powers specifically listed in the Constitution. Call that the *enumeration principle*. Second is the rule that the enumerated powers, added together, amount to less legislative power than the federal government would have if it were a government of general jurisdiction—that is, if it were simply authorized to act in the public interest, in the way that state governments are. For reasons explained in Chapter 1, call that one the *internal-limits canon*. Then come a set of explanations and narratives about how the Constitution's text establishes those rules, why the Framers designed the system this way, and the functions that the enumerated-powers limitation performs for federalism and individual rights. For this bundle of rules, narratives, and explanations, I adopt the name *enumerationism*.[4]

Enumerationism

Like most bundles of ideas, enumerationism comes in different versions. It might be something that applies to the federal government as a whole, or it might apply only to Congress. On the latter way of thinking, Congress has only enumerated powers, but the president might have nonenumerated powers as well as enumerated ones.[5] In another vein, jurists take different approaches to the question of how literally the text of a power-granting clause must support exercises of the relevant power. But at a minimum, enumerationism insists that every law passed by Congress be authorized, expressly or at least implicitly, by specific power-granting words in the Constitution.

Enumerationism has enormous appeal. It is rooted in a skepticism and fear of remote central authority that has always been a powerful strain in American political thought. By demanding that every act of Congress have a specific textual warrant in the Constitution, enumerationism promises to confine the federal government to domains where the American people have deliberately authorized it to operate. In so doing, enumerationism offers to subordinate politics to the rule of constitutional law. And as long as the enumerationist model prevails, it can counteract or at least mitigate the natural tendency of powerful institutions to become more and more powerful over time—a tendency that, if not checked, could eventually yield a federal government that was imperious or even tyrannical. Enumerationism promises to stand against that danger, keeping federal governance within a limited domain and insisting that the will of Congress alone is never sufficient justification for federal law. Given the terrible consequences abusive governance can bring, these would be important virtues in any constitutional system. And generations of American lawyers have learned to read the Constitution as enumerationism directs.

What most American jurists have not recognized, though, is that reading the Constitution as enumerationism directs is not the only possible way of reading it. Similarly, enumerationism's account of constitutional history is a particular and problematic rendition of history. And its account of federalism is a stylized picture that is neither realistic nor helpful in the practical business of American governance. As a result, enumerationism has a paradoxical relationship to constitutional knowledge. One cannot understand— let alone participate in—the practice of constitutional law without knowing how to see the subject through an enumerationist lens. But one who mistakes that lens for unfiltered reality will misunderstand a great many things.

Put differently, enumerationism tells a particular story about the Constitution. It combines a set of anecdotes and images about American history, a set of propositions about how the world works, and a set of prescriptions for thought and action. It assigns specific meanings to constitutional clauses that could bear other meanings. It offers a lens through which constitutional lawyers understand (and misunderstand) not just the Constitution's text but also its history and the workings of federalism. But crucially, American jurists do not think of enumerationism as a lens through which they see constitutional law. They think of its claims as basic facts about constitutional law, more or less on par with the proposition that the Constitution is written in English.

Part of my aim in this book is to show that this conventional understanding is a mistake. Enumerationism is a way of thinking about the Constitution, not something an accurate understanding of the Constitution necessarily entails. Another part of my aim is to explain why enumerationism is a flawed and potentially damaging way of thinking about the Constitution—damaging enough that constitutional law would be better without it.

These sound like radical ambitions. In a way, they are: I hope to persuade people to change something fundamental in how they think about constitutional law. But in a different way, the ambition of this book is conservative, in the classical or Burkean sense. As I will explain, the constitutional law of congressional power has long featured a tension between official theory and actual practice. Official theory has been enumerationist, but actual practice has not been, most of the time. Learning to see the Constitution without the enumerationist lens would be a way of bringing our ideas into better harmony with traditional practice, not a way of rejecting experience in favor of some novel approach.

-<-+->--<-+->-

Enumerationism rests not on the text of the Constitution alone, not solely on an account of constitutional history, and not only on a proposition about the structure of federalism, but on a combination of all three, reinforced over time by judicial opinions. It makes sense that a fundamental aspect of constitutional law would unite these sources of authority. After all, the thinking goes, the confluence of text, history, and structure is not an accident. It exists because the Framers thoughtfully considered how to implement their vision of federalism, and they settled on the enumeration of powers as a crucial mechanism, so they wrote a constitution that puts that mechanism into practice. Text, history, and structure coalesce—three threads of a cohesive way of thinking.

Because each proposition within the overall enumerationist conception makes the other propositions seem intuitively correct, it would be difficult to unsettle the profession's commitment to any piece of that conception—enumerationism's account of history, or its vision of federalism, or its reading of the Constitution's text—so long as the other pieces remained in place. As a result, an argument questioning the claims of enumerationism is likely to be persuasive only if it induces doubts about *all* of enumerationism's major supports. The strategy of this book, therefore, is to explore the purported bases of enumerationism in each domain and to show the weaknesses in each one, and also to show that there are better alternatives.

So consider some preliminary problems with enumerationism's account of constitutional history, structure, and text.

History

Enumerationism has an origin story that is a canonical piece of American civic culture. According to the story, the delegates at the Constitutional Convention saw the enumeration of congressional powers as the Constitution's most important mechanism for limiting federal power. During the ratification debates, the Constitution's opponents charged that the Constitution would create an oppressive central government. The Constitution's supporters— Federalists, as they called themselves—replied that the limiting force of the Constitution's enumeration of federal powers would prevent the government from behaving oppressively. Indeed, leading Federalists cited the enumeration's power-limiting function to explain why the draft Constitution contained no bill of rights. According to their argument, a government limited to the powers enumerated in the Constitution would not be able to abridge the people's liberties in the first place.[6] In *The Federalist*, Alexander Hamilton wrote that the Constitution's enumeration of powers might even make the affirmative specification of constitutional rights undesirable, because affirmative prohibitions on federal power would undermine the idea that the Constitution authorized the federal government to do only a specific set of things.[7] Given the paramount status that modern Americans ascribe to the part of the Constitution we know as the Bill of Rights, the normal role of this story is to make the enumeration's role as a limiting mechanism seem essential.[8] After all, the reasoning runs, the drafters of the Constitution considered that approach to limiting federal power even more important than express guarantees of basic constitutional rights.

The trouble is that this story is a fable. As I will explain, there is no documentary evidence from the time when the Convention was working—none— indicating that the Framers omitted a bill of rights from the original Constitution because they expected the enumeration of congressional powers to do the necessary limiting work. Several leading Framers did defend the Constitution's lack of a bill of rights with that rationale during the ratification debates. But they were not explaining an approach they had developed and agreed on at the Convention. They were pitching a rationalization they invented after the fact, in an attempt to respond to the contention that the Constitution's lack of a bill of rights was a serious flaw. And the audience knew better than to buy what these Federalists were selling: there is no indication that any significant portion of the public believed that the enumerated powers obviated the need for a bill of rights. (Thomas Jefferson described the idea as a ruse that should not be taken seriously.[9]) In short, the ratifying public mostly recognized an ex post rationalization for what it was. Today, of course, constitutional lawyers commonly accept the enumeration-based rationalization as if it were fact. But that might simply mean that the Constitution's original supporters managed to fool future generations on this point, despite mostly failing to fool their contemporaries.

I am not arguing that the enumerationist approach to federal power is wrong because its origin story is a myth. Sometimes valuable practices have mythical origin stories. But it is worth noticing that enumerationism as a system of thought is powerful enough to have persuaded American constitutional lawyers—and also that part of the broader public interested in the Constitution—to accept a just-so story as if it were a historical account.

Structure: Enumeration and Federalism

According to the standard thinking, the enumeration of federal powers is a critical device for sustaining federalism because it limits the scope of what the federal government can do, thus preserving the state governments as autonomous policymakers in most areas of governance. But in practice, federal law is pervasively present throughout American life. Your house, your car, your job, your smartphone, your neighborhood's elementary school, the energy that powers the light you are using to read this sentence, the food you eat and the water you drink and the air you breathe—all are subjects of federal regulation enacted pursuant to Congress's enumerated powers. Enumerationism's account of a system in which federal law is confined to a limited set of domains is widely at variance with the reality of American life.

That reality does not mean that the federal government can do whatever it wants. Even in the exercise of an enumerated power, the federal government cannot establish an official religion, censor speech to enforce a political ideology, or authorize cruel and unusual punishments. Congress has used its power to regulate commerce among the states to ban the shipment of many disfavored items, from lottery tickets to marijuana. But Congress cannot use its power over commerce to attempt to stamp out Islam in the United States by banning the shipment of copies of the Qur'an. What prevents Congress from banning Qur'an shipments is an affirmative prohibition associated with the First Amendment, not the lack of a relevant enumerated power. So, there are many things Congress cannot constitutionally do. But as I will show later in depth, the enumeration of the federal government's powers is not a meaningful constraint.

Many constitutional lawyers—including several justices of the Supreme Court—see this state of affairs as a sign that something has gone wrong. On this view, a properly functioning system would be one in which the enumeration significantly limits federal power. The culprit, in the usual presentation, is the Supreme Court of the New Deal era, which adopted broad constructions of Congress's enumerated powers and especially its power to regulate commerce. On the theory that the New Deal constructions of congressional powers were too broad, the judiciary since the 1980s has grown steadily more committed to the view that those powers should be construed more narrowly—narrowly enough that the enumeration of powers would impose more meaningful limits on what Congress can do.

That trend has produced a small handful of landmark Supreme Court decisions. In *United States v. Lopez* (1995), the Court invalidated the Gun-Free School Zones Act on the grounds that the act was warranted by no enumerated power of Congress. It was the first time the Court had invalidated a federal law on enumerated-powers grounds since the 1930s. In *United States v. Morrison* (2000), the Court similarly invalidated a provision of the Violence Against Women Act. And in *National Federation of Independent Business v. Sebelius* (2012; *NFIB*), the Court came within a single vote of striking down Congress's most ambitious social legislation in half a century: the Patient Protection and Affordable Care Act, popularly known as Obamacare. Changes in the Court's personnel since 2012 have made the Court yet more enumerationist than it was when it decided *NFIB*. In short, the prevailing judicial view today is that the enumeration of congressional powers is an essential device for limiting the federal government. So if in practice it does not limit the federal government, that fact is a bug in the system rather than a feature.

But even in the Court's recent jurisprudence, nothing demonstrates that the enumeration of powers has the capacity to be a meaningful, federalism-reinforcing constraint on federal law. *Lopez, Morrison,* and *NFIB* demonstrate that the judiciary can deploy enumerationism as a basis for striking down federal statutes, and that matters a great deal.[10] But there is a difference between striking down statutory provisions here and there, on what amounts to an ad hoc basis, and coherently distinguishing things the federal government should be able to do from things that should be left to local authorities. *Lopez* and *Morrison* struck down particular laws, but they established no principles that would usefully sort national concerns from local ones. Indeed, they left Congress able to enact new versions of the invalidated laws differing only trivially from the original versions, thus reimposing essentially the same legal landscapes that existed before the original laws were invalidated. The same would have been true if the Court had invalidated the Affordable Care Act on enumerated-powers grounds. A decision striking down that law would have had massive practical consequences, but that is because the Congress that existed in and shortly after 2012 would not have reinstated the system, not because the Court's decision would have reduced the portion of the social world subject to federal regulation. So yes, the modern cases demonstrate that the Supreme Court can invalidate federal statutes on enumerated-powers grounds. But they do not demonstrate that the enumeration of congressional powers can be the basis of a coherent set of limits on Congress that, if enforced, would sensibly distinguish areas that are appropriate for national regulation from areas that are not.

Perhaps it really is the case that constitutional doctrine has been badly broken for nearly a hundred years. But there is another possibility. Perhaps the broad scope of congressional power that characterizes American governance in practice is not an error inexplicably insisted on by the generations of judges who served between 1940 and the end of the twentieth century. Perhaps it instead reflects a fact the official enumerationist lens has been unable to repress: the enumeration of Congress's powers is not a good device for limiting the scope of federal law. It is well designed as an instrument for *empowering* Congress, and that is the function it has mostly performed. But it performs poorly as an instrument of limitation.

That the enumeration of powers is not well designed for limiting Congress was not as visible in the eighteenth and nineteenth centuries as it became in the twentieth. Early in American history, it was easier to think of the enumeration as playing an important limiting role. The federal government had a small footprint, and an official story connected that fact to the

Constitution's enumeration of congressional powers. But in reality, what kept the federal footprint small was less the enumeration of Congress's powers than the preferences of American officials and the public to which they responded, as well as the federal government's meager practical capacities. Later on, Americans developed a stronger appetite for national action, and the federal government developed the practical capacity for active national governance. In the hands of a more ambitious and better-resourced Congress, the enumeration of powers was sufficient to underwrite more or less any regulation that Congress had the will to enact. That development might have distressed some of the Constitution's drafters, had they foreseen it. But it might have gratified others. As I will explain, some of the Constitution's key architects thought of the enumeration of powers as first and foremost a mechanism for empowering Congress, and that is what it turned out to be. So perhaps we should not think of the enumeration's failure to limit federal law as a problem. The problem, rather, is that many jurists expect the system of enumerated powers to do something it is not well designed to do. Maybe the idea that the enumeration of congressional powers is a crucial mechanism for limiting federal governance is mostly a fantasy.

I am not suggesting that *federalism* is mostly a fantasy. On the contrary, federalism is a robust and important feature of American government. Some things should be decided nationally, but many things should be decided locally. And fortunately, the constitutional system has mechanisms for maintaining the localist half of federalism. It must, or else it would be hard to explain why, more than two centuries after ratification, the United States continues to have a federal system—indeed, a federal system in which most governance happens at the state and local levels. (The long list of everyday subjects of federal law at the start of this section—your house, your car, your job, and so on—is also a list of subjects of state law.) But the mechanisms that maintain the localist half of American federalism do not include the enumeration of congressional powers. Some are affirmative prohibitions, like the rules that prohibit Congress from taxing a state's own tax revenue or from mandating what state officials must do in their governing capacities. Some are canons of construction by which courts err on the side of construing federal law not to displace state law. Some are built into the legislative and administrative processes of government and not enforced by courts. Some are matters of constitutional culture. And some are matters of the sheer practical imperatives of mass governance. Given the vast resources of local knowledge and local personnel state governments command, the federal government frequently finds it sensible to pursue its policymaking interests not by displacing state decisionmakers but by working with and through them in a rubric the scholarly literature calls "cooperative federalism."[11] To be sure, many of these mechanisms are not rules required by the text of the Constitution and enforced by courts wielding the power of judicial review. But that does not prevent them from being robust, consequential, and durable features of American government.

The foregoing mechanisms—some rooted in the written Constitution, some not—do not deliver the localist aspect of federalism *optimally*. Probably nothing could achieve that, even if people agreed on what optimal federalism would look like. But the fact that one might identify shortcomings in the federalism that results from these features of American government does not mean that these are not federalism's actual mechanisms. No matter how we assess the quality of the federalism these mechanisms deliver, it is they, and not the enumeration of powers, that do the work. So it is not only enumeration's origin story that is a myth. The normal account of why the enumeration of powers is valuable is also a myth.

Text

Just as the enumerationist lens shapes (and sometimes distorts) prevailing views about constitutional history and the workings of federalism, it shapes (and sometimes distorts) the prevailing reading of the Constitution's text. Here are three important examples. The first is about the Tenth Amendment. The second is about Article I's Vesting Clause. The third is about Article I, Section 8.

The Tenth Amendment

The Tenth Amendment reads as follows: "The powers not delegated to the United States by the Constitution, nor prohibited by it to the States, are reserved to the States respectively, or to the people." The dominant thinking reads "delegated to the United States by the Constitution" to mean "textually specified, in the written document that this Amendment amends, as belonging to the United States." The text will bear that reading. But both at the Founding and later, the text has also been read in other ways. To see the range of possible readings, it is necessary to notice two sources of ambiguity.

First, textual specification is not the only way that a constitution might delegate powers. Authority can be delegated implicitly as well as expressly. As I will show, some Americans in the Founding generation believed that the adoption of the Constitution delegated powers to the federal government both ways. Moreover, the Congress that proposed the Tenth Amendment specifically rejected two attempts to have the amendment speak of powers "expressly delegated" rather than just "delegated." To be sure, Congress's rejection of the formulation "expressly delegated" does not establish that "delegated" in the Tenth Amendment means "delegated, expressly or otherwise." But the attempt to include the word "expressly" indicates that a Founding-era audience understood that the amendment as written would bear a broader reading.

Second, and more subtly, "the Constitution" in the Tenth Amendment might not refer only to the written document we call "the Constitution." It could also refer to the broader system of government of which that document is an important part. As is well understood, Americans before 1787 regularly used the term "constitution" to refer not to a specific document but to a web of ideas, documents, practices, and institutions that constituted (note the word) a system of government as it actually operated. The British constitution, as early Americans knew it, was a constitution in that broader sense. And that broader sense of the word did not disappear upon the adoption of "the Constitution" in 1788. In 1789, when the Tenth Amendment was drafted, and in 1791, when it was ratified, the word "constitution" could mean either a specific document or a broader system.[12]

Modern theorists often use the difference between a capital C and a lowercase c to distinguish between the document we call "the Constitution of the United States" and the system of government that is "the American constitution" in the older sense. But that is a modern convention. In the eighteenth century, the capitalization of the word did not signal the difference between the system and the document. Reading "Constitution" in the Tenth Amendment to refer to the document rather than the system because the word appears with a capital C would accordingly be anachronistic. When the Tenth Amendment was written, "Constitution" was ambiguous.

That Americans at the Founding would sometimes have understood the word "Constitution" to mean a broader governing system rather than a specific document does not prove that that is the best way to read that word in the Tenth Amendment. But it does mean that it is a possible way to read it. All things considered, it is a reasonable way and perhaps even a good way. And if "the Constitution" in the Tenth Amendment can carry the broader meaning of "the constitution," then "powers delegated to the United States by the Constitution" need not mean "powers allocated to the United States by this document." It could instead mean "powers vested in the United States by the nature of this system of government, or by the logic of the decision to create this government." Some leading Framers believed that the United States derived important powers in those broader ways. What's more, constitutional doctrine has in fact followed that view. Although the point is usually pushed to the edge of the profession's consciousness, the Supreme Court has on several occasions held that Congress can sometimes legislate on the basis of inherent national powers rather than on the basis of enumerated powers only.

Again, the Tenth Amendment will bear the reading that enumerationism gives it. So I am not saying that the Tenth Amendment clearly indicates that the federal government is entitled to exercise powers delegated implicitly as well as explicitly or by the logic of the system rather than by the terms of the document. Without more, the text leaves those questions undecided. And that, of course, is the point. To read "delegated . . . by the Constitution" in the Tenth Amendment to mean "*expressly* delegated by the (capital-C) *Constitution*," and then to regard the Tenth Amendment as authoritatively establishing that the federal government may exercise only those powers enumerated in the Constitution's text, is to assume the thing that needs to be proved.

The Vesting Clause

Article I of the Constitution begins as follows: "All legislative Powers herein granted shall be vested in a Congress of the United States." Since the 1990s, interpreters across the ideological spectrum have endorsed an enumerationist reading of this language. Focusing on the words "herein granted," they read this text—commonly called the Vesting Clause—to mean that Congress can legislate only on the basis of specific grants of power articulated in the Constitution.[13]

But the text of the Vesting Clause does not speak the language of limitation. The enumerationist reading proceeds as if Article I began with the words "*Only* the legislative powers herein granted shall be vested in a

Congress of the United States." But the word "only" does not appear. The Constitution's language is as follows: "*All* legislative Powers herein granted shall be vested in a Congress of the United States." Granting an institution all powers of a certain kind is not the same as granting it only those powers, just as "all men are mortal" does not mean that *only* men are mortal. Similarly, the fact that Congress is vested with "all legislative powers herein granted" does not mean that it is not also vested with other legislative powers.[14]

Legal texts sometimes have meanings that differ from what ordinary-language interpreters would surmise. And some interpreters argue that Article I's Vesting Clause should be read, in context, as if it meant "only" where it says "all."[15] Later, I will explain in depth why the contextual arguments for reading the Vesting Clause that way are, at best, problematic. For now, the point is that the enumerationist reading of the Vesting Clause requires us to read the text to mean something other than what it most straightforwardly says. And as I will show, the enumerationist reading of the Vesting Clause was not a normal reading of the text for the first two centuries of the Constitution's existence. Perhaps that should not be surprising. After all, the text of the clause says something else.

Article I, Section 8

Finally, consider the idea that by including a list of specific congressional powers, the (capital-C) Constitution indicates that Congress can exercise only those powers. As Chief Justice John Roberts put the point in *NFIB*, "The Constitution's express conferral of some powers makes clear that it does not grant others."[16] The logic here is that of the canon of textual construction that states *expressio unius est exclusio alterius*: the expression of one thing excludes another thing not expressed. To invoke this idea in the context of the federal government's powers, constitutional lawyers often quote Chief Justice John Marshall, who wrote in the 1824 case of *Gibbons v. Ogden* that "[t]he enumeration presupposes something not enumerated."[17]

As it happens, Marshall in *Gibbons* wasn't saying what modern lawyers usually read him to mean. (He was making an argument about the enumeration of three kinds of commerce in the Commerce Clause—not the enumeration of federal powers throughout the Constitution—and, for reasons we will see later, his argument does not apply in the latter context.[18]) But the validity of the idea that the Constitution's enumeration of congressional powers implies that Congress can exercise only those powers does not depend on whether Marshall meant to express it on that occasion. What matters is whether the logic of expressio unius properly applies in this case. And crucially, the question must be posed that way—as a question about this particular enumeration, rather than as a question about whether enumerations are exclusive as a general matter. After all, expressio unius is not an iron law of logic applicable to all lists of specific items. Some lists are best read as exclusive, and others are not. (As the children's story about Frog and Toad illustrates, a list of Things I Need to Do Today is unlikely to mention *everything* I need to do today.[19]) Whether any list of specifics is best read as exclusive depends on particular facts about the function and context of that list. And given its most immediate context, there is something distinctly odd about the way conventional thinking applies the expressio unius canon to the Constitution's enumeration of federal powers.

To see the oddity, consider the statement with which Chief Justice William Rehnquist began his analysis in the landmark enumerated-powers case of *United States v. Lopez*: "We start with first principles. The Constitution creates a Federal Government of enumerated powers. See Art. I, § 8."[20] To anyone who has absorbed the standard thinking about enumerated powers, this statement is straightforward. Rehnquist states the enumeration principle, and he cites the section of the Constitution enumerating the powers of Congress.

Why, though, would pointing to Section 8 establish the principle that the federal government may exercise only its textually enumerated powers? Article I, Section 8, does not say that its list of powers is exclusive. If it establishes the principle, it does so implicitly, by being the sort of enumeration that should be understood as exclusive.

Here, then, is the oddity. Article I, Section 8, cannot be an exclusive enumeration of federal powers, because it does not articulate all of the powers the Constitution explicitly authorizes the federal government to exercise. Many important powers of Congress—the power to override state rules for congressional elections, the power to establish the line of presidential succession, the power to declare the punishment for treason, the power to admit new states—are specified elsewhere in the Constitution. Section 8 is a *partial* listing of congressional powers, not an exclusive one. It illustrates that a legislature can be given a longish list of particular powers and also be entitled to exercise other powers. And that is to say nothing of the fact that the powers of Congress do not exhaust the powers of the federal government, because the federal government also has two other branches.

Despite this basic fact about Section 8, Rehnquist's association of Section 8 with the idea of a limiting enumeration is conventional. Article I, Section 8, is the longest and most salient enumeration of federal powers in the Constitution, and in the shorthand language of constitutional lawyers, it stands for the idea of a limiting enumeration. But it is qualified for that symbolic role by virtue of its being associated with the idea of a limiting enumeration, not by virtue of stating or even illustrating the idea. It does neither of those things.

I am not suggesting that Rehnquist and others who have used Article I, Section 8, to stand for the idea of a limiting enumeration have engaged in deliberate distortion. It is more likely that lawyers and judges who make this move momentarily forget that there are congressional powers beyond Section 8. Or perhaps they regard the existence of those powers as details around the edges that should not prevent us from seeing the core workings of the system. We are socialized to see constitutional law through an enumerationist lens, so we tend to minimize, or not to notice, things that do not conform to enumerationism's picture.

That Article I, Section 8, is a nonlimiting list of congressional powers does not prove that Congress is entitled to exercise powers that do not appear in the text of the Constitution. Congress, or the federal government as a whole, might be limited to the powers enumerated in the Constitution even if the Constitution confers powers here and there throughout the document rather than with a single list (or a single list for each power-exercising branch). But the idea that a limiting enumeration is fundamental to the Constitution would be most easily maintained if the Constitution actually contained a single list of the things Congress (or each branch) is authorized to do. The Constitution contains no such list. That lawyers and judges often speak as if it does may seem like just an untidy detail, but it might be a detail that tells a tale—a sign that something about the dominant account does not fit the underlying material as well as the normal discourse pretends.

It is not my contention that the text of the Constitution cannot be read in the way enumerationism reads it. It can. As the old joke has it: I've seen it done. But that reading is a particular interpretation of the text, and in some ways a problematic one. Within the culture of constitutional law, it is an interpretation powerful enough to persuade jurists not just to read the text that way but, for the most part, to believe that there could be no other reasonable reading. But the strength of the enumerationist reading lies less in its ability to make sense of the text on its own terms—on that score it is at best contestable—than in the way it follows from enumerationist premises about history and structure. We know to read the text as enumerationism reads it because of the overall story of which that reading is a part. The story tells us why the Constitution was written as it was, how the public originally understood it, and how American federalism works. But on closer scrutiny, every part of that story is suspect.

Enumeration as Empowerment

I suggest a different approach. Rather than seeing the enumeration of powers as a device for constraining federal power, think of it as a device for ensuring an adequately empowered Congress. Yes, Congress needs to be both empowered and constrained, and yes, an enumeration of powers might in principle do both of those things. But in our actual constitutional system, the enumeration of congressional powers should not be expected to do the work of limitation. That work is done elsewhere, by structural devices like the system of checks and balances and by affirmative prohibitions like those in the Bill of Rights. Understood in its best light, the crucial function of the Constitution's enumeration is not to rule unspecified congressional powers *out*. It is to rule the specified powers *in*.

This view of enumeration as empowerment is at least as consistent with the Constitution's text and original meaning as enumerationism is. Indeed, I hope to persuade you that the model of enumeration as empowerment fits the best interpretation of the Constitution's origins better than the limiting-enumeration view does. But the text can be read either way, and I do not think that Founding-era history definitively decides between the two models. So I do not claim that the text or the original meaning of the Constitution compels the empowerment view. What makes the view of enumeration as empowerment superior is its strength along other important dimensions. The view of enumerationism as empowerment has a better account of the enumerated powers' role in federalism. It better supports democratically responsive governance. And as a matter of practice—albeit not of official theory—it is better rooted in constitutional tradition, because it reflects the way the constitutional system has in fact behaved over time.

⪻⟩⟨⪻⟩

The vision of enumeration as empowerment is rooted in the simplest answer to this basic question: Why was the Constitution written? The principal reason was that the Framers believed the United States needed a more powerful general government, one significantly more vigorous than existed under the Articles of Confederation. Under the Articles, Congress was too weak to provide the governance America needed. It was to solve that problem that the Framers convened at Philadelphia.

The enumeration of congressional powers was part of that project of empowerment in two different ways. First, it created a clear warrant for the general government to do many things it could not do under the Articles. Second, a big part of the Constitution's empowerment of the general government was its creation of an independent executive branch, which had to be both empowered and checked. Most of Article I, Section 8, was written not to allocate power between the federal government and the states but to check the president by allocating to Congress a set of powers that, given the British constitutional background against which the Framers worked, might have otherwise belonged by default to the president. In both respects, the enumeration of powers existed to empower Congress: once along the axis of federalism and once along the axis of the separation of powers.

The Framers wanted to check Congress as well as to empower it. But the enumeration of powers was not their major means to that end. The main strategies for limiting Congress were placed elsewhere in the constitutional machinery, in the system of checks and balances and in the structure of representative government itself. A bicameral arrangement in which legislation would need the approval of frequently elected popular representatives in one chamber and representatives of the state legislatures in another chamber could be counted on to reject oppressive measures, at least most of the time. That structural apparatus, and not a limiting list of powers, was supposed to be the chief mechanism for keeping federal legislation within proper bounds.

To be sure, an enumeration of powers could both empower and limit, if the list were exclusive. Some delegates at the Constitutional Convention—probably many of them—conceived of the enumeration as serving both functions. But there was no consensus on the question of whether the enumeration of powers had to be limiting as well as empowering. Some delegates did not believe it was possible to enumerate all of the powers Congress should have. And in the end, the Constitution's text did not declare the enumerated powers exclusive.

Indeed, if one substitutes a nationalist lens for the enumerationist one, Congress's enumerated powers could easily appear to state the floor, not the ceiling, of congressional power. The Preamble, for example, can be read as stating a set of ends the national government is both obligated and empowered to pursue. Or consider the Necessary and Proper Clause at the end of Article I, Section 8, which gives Congress the power "to make all Laws which shall be necessary and proper for carrying into execution the foregoing Powers, *and all other Powers vested by this Constitution in the Government of the United States.*" As noted earlier, "vested by this Constitution" can mean "vested by the nature of this system of government" rather than only "vested by the express terms of this document." On those more expansive understandings, the italicized language above might point to the existence of powers beyond those enumerated in the Constitution's text. Yes, the Preamble and the Necessary and Proper Clause can be, and usually are, interpreted to conform with enumerationist thinking. But if read through a different lens, they support a broader conception of the national government's power. Many Americans in the Founding era read them in that broader way.

The point is not that the more nationalist lens reveals the Constitution's true meaning. It is that the text conclusively establishes neither position. And not by accident. The Constitution was the work of many hands—it reflected a mix of ideas and agendas rather than cleanly embodying a single theory. The Framers agreed that the United States needed a more powerful general government, but they reached no consensus about just how powerful that government should be. They knew that whether the enumerated powers stated only the floor or also the ceiling was a crucial question of constitutional design. They could have said clearly that Congress could exercise only those powers enumerated in the text, had there been sufficient agreement on the issue. But there wasn't, and they didn't. The document they produced was a compromise, one that made it possible to argue both that Congress would have only its enumerated powers and that Congress would not be limited in that way.

The ratification debates of 1787–1788 repeatedly illustrated this ambiguity in the constitutional text. Famously, several of the Constitution's prominent supporters described the document in enumerationist terms—probably in an attempt to defuse opposition from Americans skeptical of a strong central government. The attempt to excuse the absence of a bill of rights by reference to the limiting function of the enumerated powers is a prominent illustration. But as the truth behind that story demonstrates, the fact that some of the Constitution's proponents offered a given interpretation of the Constitution does not mean that anyone was persuaded, much less that the proffered interpretation was a matter of public consensus. Many Americans during the ratification debates rejected the enumerationist reading. Some believed the Constitution would create a national government with something like general jurisdiction, or at least that it might. Some people opposed ratification for that reason. But others did not; they saw that the Constitution might create an enormously powerful national government and decided to vote in favor. In the end, it is impossible to know what proportion of Founding-era Americans read the Constitution in an enumerationist way, and it is impossible to know what proportion of the people who read the Constitution as creating a very powerful national government saw that as a reason to support the Constitution rather than oppose it. What seems clear is that at the time of ratification, the idea of the limiting function of enumeration was present and well known within constitutional discourse but not universally accepted as the correct reading of the Constitution. All the way through the ratification process, that idea existed alongside other conceptions on which national power under the Constitution would be more robust.

That a constitutional question remained open at the time of ratification does not mean that it is still open today. On some theories of constitutional authority—including my own—a way of implementing the law over time can become the law, even if it was not the law originally.[21] So even if the Founding generation left the question open, the consensus endorsement of enumerationism through the generations might have made that approach authoritative. Early in the nineteenth century, after Jefferson became president and the Federalist Party disappeared, enumerationism became a dominant way of thinking. The Supreme Court has many times endorsed enumerationism's basic principles: that Congress is limited to its enumerated powers and that those powers collectively give Congress less power than it would have as a legislature of general jurisdiction. Given the acceptance of the idea over time, enumerationism is part of the small-c constitution, even if it is not required by the big-C Constitution.

Crucially, however, enumerationism is only *part* of the small-c constitutional law of congressional power, because constitutional practice over time has accepted enumerationism as authoritative in only a partial way. Considered more completely, the authority of the small-c constitution—of tradition, or of practice over time—supports an unresolved combination of enumerationist thinking and nonenumerationist practice.

Officially, enumerationism has long been orthodox. Judges and others have said, repeatedly, that the federal government is limited by its enumerated powers. But those official statements have coexisted with two sets of contrary practices. First, and going back to the time of the early republic, federal officials have sometimes justified federal action on the basis of implicit or inherent national power rather than powers enumerated in the Constitution's text. In the First Congress, several leading members justified major legislation (including the creation of the Bank of the United States) on the basis of implicit or inherent national power. The Supreme Court through the nineteenth century and into the twentieth sustained federal laws on significant issues—slavery, greenback currency, territorial administration, federal elections, foreign affairs—by reference to historical understandings about the purposes of the Union, or the logic of federalism, or the inherent powers of national governments, rather than on the basis of textually enumerated powers. In other words, the official enumerationist position coexisted with a willingness, when the occasion called for it, to treat the enumerated powers as the floor but not the ceiling. Second, for nearly a century as of this writing, enumerationism has done very little to affect governance in practice, because the enumerated powers have been construed expansively enough to encompass more or less whatever Congress has the political will to legislate. Even while professing the principles of enumerationism, courts since the New Deal have permitted Congress to legislate pretty much as it sees fit, subject to affirmative constitutional prohibitions like those in the First Amendment.

The first of these realities is usually pushed to the margins of constitutional lawyers' professional consciousness because it does not conform to the enumerationist picture. The second is more widely acknowledged but often considered a sign that something has gone wrong. But both are part of the small-c constitutional order—that is, the workings of the American constitutional system as it has actually functioned. So an argument that regards acceptance over time as a form of constitutional authority cannot simply conclude that enumerationism's official story authoritatively establishes how constitutional decisionmakers must actually behave. Yes, enumerationism is a significant part of the constitutional tradition. But so are the contrary practices. To take both parts of that picture seriously is to see that the authority of tradition supports a system that lives with an ongoing tension. In practice, Congress can pursue pretty much any regulatory project for which it can summon the political will, subject of course to the Constitution's affirmative prohibitions. As a matter of our official story, we continue to affirm the principles of enumerationism. And our continued affirmation of the official story seems unable to make the realities of practice conform.

The Allure of Enumerationism

If what I have said so far is correct, then the fact that enumerationism remains our official story poses a puzzle. Why has this problematic way of thinking about constitutional law persisted, even though its account of how the system works is at odds with long experience? Indeed, why has it persisted so powerfully that most constitutional lawyers regard enumerationism not as a way of thinking about constitutional law but as a necessarily correct understanding of the Constitution? One partial explanation is inertia, or, more thickly put, the authority of the statements of prior interpreters in a constitutional culture that sees the past as a source of authority. Another is enumerationism's capacity to channel traditional fears about a remote central government. But to appreciate the full appeal of enumerationism, it is necessary to appreciate three of enumerationism's other functions. Instrumentally, it offers the opponents of federal action a possible basis for constitutional objection. Less obviously, and for the contrary constituency, it legitimates federal power by tying lawmaking to specific constitutional texts. And more diffusely, it helps legitimate the constitutional system as a whole by creating a sense of continuity with its heroic origins.

Enumeration's instrumental appeal is straightforward. Any new governmental initiative will have opponents, so it is always useful to have bases for attacking federal action as unconstitutional. Sometimes the Constitution contains affirmative prohibitions, like those in the Bill of Rights, that can ground arguments against federal action. But when some disliked federal initiative does not come within the terms of any particular prohibition, the claim that it also does not come within any enumerated power can function as a residual objection. Obviously, the viability of this strategy depends on constitutional lawyers' ability to argue, plausibly, that a given initiative is in fact beyond the enumerated powers. Over time, opponents of federal action have often found it possible to make that argument. Examples include the Bank of the United States, the Louisiana Purchase, the Fugitive Slave Act, greenback currency, and on and on through child labor laws, Civil Rights Acts, and the Affordable Care Act. In short, Congress has often legislated controversially, and one big part of enumerationism's appeal has been that it offers opponents of congressional action a way to argue against such legislation.

But enumerationism also has a more subtle appeal that runs in a contrary direction: it is an important tool for legitimating federal law. Indeed, over the sweep of history, the enumeration of congressional powers has done more to legitimate federal power than to limit it. (All of the challenged federal actions above were ultimately judged valid.) Perhaps this reality should not be surprising. The Constitution was written to create a strong national government. When leading Federalists presented the Constitution to the public in enumerationist terms in 1787–1788, their aim was to secure support for a dramatic increase in centralized power. They succeeded. And a reading of the Constitution motivated by a need to legitimate national power turned out to be useful for that same project on many later occasions. Once the new system was up and running, proponents of national action generally found that the congressional powers enumerated in the Constitution furnished sufficient bases for justifying the projects they wanted to undertake. Most of the time, therefore, the proponents of national action have had little incentive to fight enumerationism. On the contrary, by accepting the enumerationist paradigm and working within it, the supporters of any given piece of congressional legislation could present their proposal as consistent with the sound federal balance crafted by the Framers. As the federal government undertook increasingly ambitious projects over time, the fact that those projects could be presented as warranted by specific clauses in the Constitution could help defend those initiatives against opposition based on their novelty or their apparent (and often real) substantive departures from the modes of governance with which Americans had previously been comfortable.

Over the generations, arguments justifying federal law in enumerationist terms have been a significant legitimating force even when they have not

persuaded everyone. After all, the audience for an argument that some federal action is warranted by the enumerated powers is not only the people
who are strongly opposed. It also includes the noncommitted and the per-
suadable. Crucially, it also includes the proposal's own supporters. If we like
the idea of some proposal for national action but have the intuition that it is
not the sort of thing the federal government does, we can reassure ourselves
of the propriety of that action by noticing that the written Constitution,
with its ostensibly limiting enumeration of powers, makes the proposed action appropriate for the federal government. As is often the case with legitimating rationalizations, this one has had two audiences: the other and the self.

Enumerationism has also come to perform a more diffuse sort of legitimating function in constitutional law—one that supports not just the legitimacy
of specific federal actions but that of the system as a whole. For better and
for worse, constitutional legitimacy in the American system has always required a sense of fidelity to the Founding. Different schools of thought understand the nature of the required fidelity differently: it might be about respecting the past decisions of the nation as embodied by the ratifying public,
or it might be about implementing the wisdom of the Framers, or it might be
about a commitment to redeem a set of foundational promises.[22] Whether or not
they self-identify as originalists, most constitutional lawyers see current constitutional law as legitimate at least partly on the basis of its continuity, however defined, with a project that extends back to the Philadelphia Convention.

As time passes, however, the world in which the Constitution operates
becomes more and more different from the world in which it originated. The
more different the 1780s are from our own time, the less intuitive it is that a
set of decisions made then should have the authority to constrain our decisionmaking in the present. A sense of continuity with the moment of origin
helps defuse that problem by blunting our sense that we are radically different from our predecessors. So to maintain the sense of continuity that legitimacy requires, constitutional culture needs ways of closing the gap between
past and present. It needs ways of creating, among current constitutional
lawyers, a good-faith sense that even if the present looks different from the
past, they are operating fundamentally the same machinery that was put in
place long ago, subject of course to the changes made by constitutional
amendments. If constitutional lawyers (and the rest of the people who make
up what we can call the constitutional culture) can maintain that sense, then
they can preserve their sense of the legitimacy of the system over time.

Enumerationism is one of American constitutional culture's mechanisms for creating that sense of continuity. In 1787, leading Federalists presented the Constitution in enumerationist terms. As I will show, many Americans found that presentation unpersuasive, and at least some of the Federalists who offered it were probably arguing in bad faith. Overwhelmingly, however, constitutional lawyers consider the Federalists' enumerationist explanation of the Constitution authentic and authoritative. Even if undeservedly, it defines the dominant sense of how the system was intended to operate and how it originally functioned. As a result, modern Americans who recite that the federal government is a government of enumerated powers assert that the basic plan of American government remains what it was at the beginning. In so doing, they help persuade both themselves and their audiences that the constitutional law of the present is continuous with the constitutionalism of the Founding.

One might think that this assertion is an empty gesture. As I have noted, the enumeration of powers has in practice done almost nothing to limit federal governance in nearly a century, and even before that the system did not behave in quite the way enumerationism imagines. Reciting a traditional formula that does not correspond to any practically significant feature of the constitutional system might seem like a threadbare way of maintaining continuity with the system's past. We say that the federal government is a government of enumerated powers, and we thereby create an imagined connection between ourselves and our predecessors, but our assertion has little other impact on what we do. It certainly does not make American government in the present substantively like it was in the year 1900, let alone in the 1790s. So if continued assertion of the enumeration principle offers constitutional continuity, it does so in a formal and ritualistic way rather than a substantive one.

But it would be a mistake to underestimate the importance of form and ritual in shaping a community's sense of itself and in particular its sense of its relationship to its past. Rituals of continuity and reenactment are, along with storytelling, among a community's most powerful means of creating a sense of collective continuity with times long ago.[23] The assertion that the federal government is a government of enumerated powers is a ritual of continuity, and explaining the enumerationist approach to constitutional law by reference to things like the Framers' (mythical) calculus about why not to include a bill of rights in the Constitution is a practice of storytelling.

Measured by the standards of historical accuracy, the story is in some ways oversimplified and in some ways simply wrong. But a community's sense of fidelity over time is a function of its felt continuity with the past as it remembers that past, whether or not that memory captures history in all of its complexity. And the rituals and storytelling of enumerationism help create a discursive environment that links the constitutional present to the heroic constitutional past.[24]

Alternatives: Implied Powers and Cumulative Coverage

There is at least one other reason why enumerationism has had staying power in spite of its weaknesses. In the normal thinking, the alternative to a Congress limited by its enumerated powers is a Congress with what modern constitutional lawyers call a "police power"—that is, the general power to pass any law at all, except for laws violating affirmative constitutional prohibitions. (Think of the word "police" as a synonym for "policy" rather than as the name of a law-enforcement agency.) That alternative is unappealing, and not only because constitutional lawyers have learned as an axiom that Congress has no police power. It is also unappealing because the Constitution contains a long list of particular congressional powers, and reasonable people have the intuition that the Constitution would not bother to enumerate dozens of particular powers if it were designed to give Congress a general police power.

But even if it makes sense to think that the Constitution was not designed to give Congress a general police power, it does not follow that the Constitution requires enumerationism. There are at least two other—and better—approaches. The first one appeared frequently in constitutional jurisprudence prior to the New Deal. I will call it the model of *implied powers*. The second one has in practice been the dominant model since the New Deal, despite the official orthodoxy of enumerationism. I will call it the model of *cumulative coverage*.

The model of implied powers begins from the premise that the government of the United States is inherently or implicitly vested with the powers of a national government—whatever those might be. On the assumption that not every matter of public policy is a matter of national concern—that is, that some matters are of local concern only—then Congress would not have a general police power. But Congress could legislate on all matters of national concern. On that model, the enumeration of congressional powers does two things. First, it establishes that various powers belonging to the national government belong to *Congress* rather than the president or the courts. Second, the enumeration of powers makes clear that certain projects lie within the national domain. Where legislation comes within the enumerated powers, it is unnecessary to ask whether that legislation is sufficiently national in substance so as to be appropriate for congressional action—the constitutional text resolves that question in the affirmative. But Congress can also enact legislation that does not come within the enumerated powers, so long as it is in substance a kind of legislation it makes sense for a national legislature to undertake, rather than the sort of thing that should be left exclusively to local decisionmakers.

Another alternative—the model of cumulative coverage—has in practice been the dominant model since the New Deal. Unlike the model of implied powers, the model of cumulative coverage shares enumerationism's premise that Congress can act only on the basis of textually specified powers. And it concedes that the Constitution was not designed to give Congress a general police power. But what that means, on this model, is that the Constitution was not designed to *guarantee* Congress a police power. It does not mean that the Constitution is committed to *preventing* Congress from having the practical equivalent of a police power. The Constitution's concern is to ensure that Congress has many particular powers: to tax, to borrow money, to regulate commerce, and so on. If those powers collectively turn out to let Congress legislate as broadly as it could with a police power, then honoring the Constitution's enumeration of powers means letting Congress legislate that broadly. The conventional view that the enumerated powers must under no circumstances be construed as the practical equivalent of a police power is, on this view, a fallacy that arises from the misconception that the enumeration must be limiting. If the point of the enumeration is to rule things in, then the Constitution might be indifferent about whether the enumeration also rules things out.

I do not claim that the text or the original meaning of the Constitution necessarily establishes either the implied powers model or the cumulative coverage model. But both models are at least as consistent with the Constitution's text and history as enumerationism is. And as measured by other criteria for choosing among possibilities in constitutional law, these alternative models are superior. They have a more realistic and useful understanding of federalism. They are more able to deliver democratically responsive governance and less likely to leave important issues to be settled by the subjective views of judges. And they reflect the way the system has actually functioned. To be sure, constitutional law's official story has been enumerationist. But from the Founding to the early twentieth century, the model of implied powers better described constitutional law in practice. And as of this writing, the going model in practice for nearly a century has been that of cumulative coverage.

The long-running disjuncture between enumerationist theory and non-enumerationist practice could seem unsatisfying to someone who thought (perhaps reasonably) that a legal system should be transparent about its own functioning—that either the official theory should be discarded or the practice reformed to better match the official theory. But it is worth considering that the continued presence of both enumerationism and nonenumerationism in constitutional law is better understood as a reflection of the system's origins than as a subsequent corruption. From the beginning, the Constitution was ambiguous on the question of whether the enumerated powers were limiting. Rather than resolving the question, constitutional law maintained the ambiguity.

Moreover, from the New Deal to the end of the twentieth century, as official enumerationist theory coexisted with cumulative coverage in practice, the system functioned relatively well. Constitutional law had a robust jurisprudence of individual rights, predicated on affirmative prohibitions rather than the limiting force of the enumeration of federal powers. The national government was able to make national policy across a broad set of domains where modern life requires competent and coordinated governance. And the localist aspect of federalism lived on: the states remained meaningful players in American governance.

This claim that the system functioned pretty well while the tension between official story and actual practice lasted is a judgment about how well it delivered good governance for American society, not a judgment about how well it conformed to any set of putative legal requirements. It is a contestable judgment. But because my claim is practical rather than legal, a contrary judgment would need to be justified by a substantive account of what American federalism has failed to deliver, not by arguments about what the Constitution requires when seen through an enumerationist lens. To state an

objection to the practical claim, one must point to adverse practical consequences—to some respect beyond the value of (ostensible) rule-following in
which society would be better off if the enumeration did meaningful constraining work. And whether society would be better off in such an alternative regime is a question that must be answered by reference to our best
guesses about how a more constraining enumerationism would actually function, not by reference to eighteenth-century (or other) promises about how
it is supposed to function.

As I will explain, it is hard to understand why a more constraining enumerationism would improve things in practice: the enumeration of powers
identifies many powers that it makes sense for Congress to have, but it is not
well designed for identifying the things Congress should *not* be allowed to
do. Indeed, if history is a guide, pressing the enumeration of powers into
service as a tool of limitation is likely to invite or provoke judges to choose
which federal laws to invalidate largely on the basis of those judges' attitudes about public policy, even if the judges are trying in good faith just to
call the constitutional balls and strikes. In short, a more constraining enumerationism would in practice compromise democratic lawmaking at the national level without securing any real benefits as a matter of federalism.

As American government actually functions, neither the protection of individual rights nor the maintenance of robust local decisionmaking depends
on Congress's being limited by its enumerated powers. As long as that is true,
we are better off with a system where the enumeration does little or nothing
to constrain Congress than with a system where it constrains Congress capri-
ciously. It is not ideal to have a disjuncture between constitutional law's official enumerationist theory and its actual nonenumerationist practice. But
given the choice between that situation and one where a decent practice is
sacrificed to a bad theory, the former option seems preferable.

The Loaded Weapon

In the twenty-first century, however, the post–New Deal modus vivendi is
no longer stable. The judiciary has grown steadily more inclined to make
enumerationism do real work in constitutional law. As of this writing, it is
still the case that Congress can make law on pretty much any subject for
which it has the political will, so long as it does not violate affirmative

constitutional prohibitions like those in the Bill of Rights. But the Supreme Court of the present and the foreseeable future seems keenly inclined, and perhaps even eager, to curtail the work product of Congress on the grounds that it exceeds the scope of the enumerated powers. The near-death experience of the Affordable Care Act in *NFIB* was more than a shot across the bow, and changes in the Supreme Court's personnel since *NFIB* have made the Court yet more inclined to adopt a narrow view of Congress's powers. In the near term, it is not hard to imagine a jurisprudence that undermines a large swath of existing federal governance—or that prevents Congress from enacting new legislation needed to meet the problems of the present and the future. As long as enumerationism remains an official theory, it lies about like a loaded weapon.

Americans would differ about the merits of any particular law so invalidated. But the costs of the Court's striking down significant federal legislation on enumerationist grounds would go beyond the loss of whatever specific regulations disappeared. A constitutional jurisprudence that strikes down federal laws on enumerationist grounds would reinforce the story enumerationism tells about the Constitution. That story teaches Americans to think of the Founding of their republic as an exercise in skepticism about government, rather than as mostly a victory for confidence in the possibility of empowering government to serve the common good. If we accept the skeptical story, we misunderstand history, and we do so in a way that dampens our sense that we can and should use the government of the United States to address significant problems through collective action. Yes, many problems should be addressed locally rather than nationally. A judiciary that struck down federal laws on enumerationist grounds would say, and probably believe, that it was vindicating important principles of American federalism. But it would be wrong: the enumeration of powers is not a good tool for implementing the limits on national power that make for a federalism worth having. And to compromise the American capacity for national democratic action on the basis of a mistaken way of thinking would be little short of tragic.

If enumerationism were a requirement of constitutional fidelity—if the rule of law in our system required it—then perhaps the damage done when courts struck laws down on enumerated-powers grounds would be a cost that conscientious jurists would have to bear, absent some relevant constitutional amendments. But if we can see enumerationism as one particular theory about how to understand the Constitution, and indeed a theory with significant weaknesses, then the way should be open to better alternatives. So in this book, I show why the combined import of traditional sources of constitutional authority—text, history, structure, case law, and practice over time—provides better support for the models of implied powers and cumulative coverage than for enumerationism.

Chapters 1–5 deal with the Constitution's design, ratification, and early implementation. I focus on these early years not because I believe that original meanings are authoritative in constitutional law but because the conventional ideas about constitutional history that support enumerationism are overwhelmingly ideas about the eighteenth century. To unsettle the prevailing enumerationist thinking, it is necessary to present a different understanding of that time. Chapters 6–7 then look at judicial doctrine, showing constitutional law's long history of talking the talk of enumerationism while accommodating contrary behavior in practice. Chapter 8 deals with constitutional structure, explaining that enumerationism's purported contribution to federalism is illusory. Finally, Chapter 9 examines the text of the Constitution. With the enumerationist lens removed, the text of the Constitution is consistent with the model of implied powers, the model of cumulative coverage, or some combination of the two.

◄◄--►►--◄◄--►►-

Before closing this introduction, I offer two brief notes about this book's view of constitutional interpretation. The first is about the interaction between textual interpretation and things like history and structure. The second is about the significance of constitutional history. Both notes are descriptive rather than normative: they concern the way that lawyers and judges actually reach their views about constitutional issues, not the way that I or some other theorist might believe constitutional decisionmaking ought to work.

The Role of Text

Conventionally, when constitutional lawyers canvass arguments from text, history, and structure, they do so in that order: text first, history second, and structure third. That ordering reflects a deep commitment to the idea of written constitutionalism. Many a judicial analysis starts by saying, "We begin with the text." On the surface, that statement presents itself as a straightforward description of what the court is doing. But it is also more. It is the statement of a creed.

Because American constitutional culture generally regards the text as the highest form of constitutional authority, changing one's view of the text usually means changing one's view on the ultimate issue under discussion. As a result, interpreters are loath to abandon a familiar reading of the text unless they are satisfied that some other reading will yield better constitutional law. To enable interpreters to entertain unfamiliar textual readings and take them seriously, it is therefore necessary to explain why the unfamiliar readings would make substantive sense. And whether a reading makes substantive sense is, in significant part, a matter of whether it fits the relevant constitutional history and supports a sound conception of constitutional structure. So when constitutional interpreters evaluate a textual argument, they are usually also implicitly evaluating a larger argument—one that encompasses history, structure, and perhaps also other things, in addition to the words of the document.

In the end, every piece of the puzzle depends on every other. Constitutional interpreters generally (and reasonably) read ambiguous texts so as to render them sensible in light of considerations about history and structure, and they also form their ideas about constitutional structure and history partly by reference to their understanding of the text. But because the stakes are highest with the text, it is especially important, when inviting readers to see the text a particular way, to make clear why seeing it that way makes sense not just of the document's words but of history and structure as well. In the actual dynamics of constitutional interpretation, deciding how the text should be read is often the last step of the thought process, even if it officially comes first. That is why the analysis in this book alters the conventional sequence of arguments about text, history, and structure. Examination of enumerationism's historical grounding will come first, and then consideration of structure, and the text of the Constitution comes last. The aim is to enable readers to consider my analysis of the Constitution's text with a clear understanding of the historical and structural analyses that make that textual reading sensible.

The Role of History

Constitutional lawyers generally credit a view of the Founding on which the ratifying public understood the Constitution in an enumerationist way. That account is mistaken: it reads the evidence through the lens of enumeration-ism and finds what it expects to find. But it is not my view that the Constitution's early history, properly understood, authoritatively establishes any of the alternatives to enumerationism, either. In part, that is because I think the original meaning of the Constitution is ambiguous. And in part it is because I am skeptical, for reasons I have explained elsewhere, about most theories that purport to make original meanings authoritative in constitutional law.[25] So the point of this book's presentation of early constitutional history is not to show that the Constitution's original meaning, properly understood, makes enumerationism wrong and some alternative right. The historical analysis is intended to show problems with an existing way of thinking and to reveal plausible alternatives, not to prove what the law must be.

History matters in American constitutional reasoning in both official and unofficial ways. Officially, history can provide evidence of earlier understandings of a text, of prior practice, of the significance of a decision, of the background expectations underlying a rule, or of the problems with operating the constitutional system in a particular way. But the unofficial ways in which history matters are no less important. Even in an age when the family of approaches bearing the surname "originalism" has achieved substantial prominence, few constitutional decisionmakers adhere to clear theoretical views about how history should matter in constitutional law. But most of those decisionmakers—judicial and otherwise—are influenced by their sense of the constitutional past. Intuitive views about why the Constitution was written and ratified contribute to Americans' ideas about the content of constitutional law. So do intuitions about the nature and lessons of the Civil War, Jim Crow, the New Deal, the civil rights movement, and so on. Over the long run, successful constitutional arguments must usually be reconcilable with the decisionmaking class's intuitive sense of the national constitutional story.

The idea that historical intuitions matter requires some unpacking. As the term is used here, "historical intuitions" inhabit what some social theorists call the realm of "memory" rather than that of history conceived as an academic discipline. Memory in this sense is a partly historical, partly mythical space where complexities are smoothed out and past events acquire particular value-laden meanings.[26] Historical intuitions are not completely independent of facts, but neither are they strictly factual. They are complex products of disciplinary history, societal storytelling, and political imagination.

Most judges who look to historical sources for guidance in constitutional cases are not consciously trying to give force to the intuitions of memory. Their normal aspiration is to use history in the ways that history is officially supposed to matter. But in practice, and unofficially, the intuitions of memory do a fair amount of work in constitutional persuasion. Decisionmakers trying to make sense of a historical episode are more likely to read it to mean something they intuitively expect it to mean rather than anything else. And much of the time, historical intuitions rest on myths and simplifications that would not withstand careful analysis. Bringing historical complexity into the foreground can then encourage constitutional decisionmakers to think critically about propositions they have too easily taken for granted.

The historical chapters of this book are intended to challenge prevailing intuitions about enumerated powers. But I do not believe that the history I present authoritatively resolves questions about how constitutional law should operate in the twenty-first century. Partly for that reason, I do not engage certain methodological questions that feature prominently in debates among originalist theorists—questions like the relative importance of the intentions of the Framers of the Constitution and the understandings of the ratifiers, or the difference between the "original public meaning" of the text and what the actual public might have understood the Constitution to mean. Among sophisticated academic originalists, differences like these matter a great deal. But given my skepticism about this family of approaches in general, I have little reason to take sides or to present my account in the way one or another school of originalist thought would prescribe. As a normative matter, I do not think that the history establishes authoritative legal rules; as a descriptive matter, I suspect that the actual role of Founding-era history in shaping constitutional decisionmaking is more a function of the intuitions of historical memory than the application of any precise theory of interpretation. My aim, therefore, is to put pressure on some of the important historical intuitions that support enumerationism by showing that parts of the story undergirding that view of constitutional law are too simple—and other parts are simply wrong. To the extent that the effort succeeds, enumerationism should lose an important part of its support, and constitutional lawyers should become more open to considering alternatives.

We cannot do constitutional law without stories and simplifications. But if we can see them *as* stories and simplifications—that is, if at any given time we can see the lens we are looking through, rather than only being able to see *through* that lens—we can remain aware that a given approach is not the only way of looking at things. That might dispose us to be more willing, more often, to think about whether some perspective other than the one we are now using will best illuminate and support the things that make American constitutional law worth having.

CHAPTER ONE

MADISON'S ADVICE

S UPPOSE YOU NEEDED TO design a system of government for a new republic with an elected legislature. You would need to decide how many
houses that legislature should have, how large each house should be, and
how the members should be elected. You would also need to figure out what
powers the legislature should have. Governments need to get things done.
At the same time, a government with unconstrained power might do serious
damage. How, then, would you set about designing a legislature with the
right set of powers and the right set of constraints?

That was the problem confronting Caleb Wallace in the year 1785. Wallace was making plans for a constitution for a new government—the government of Kentucky. The region that is now Kentucky was at the time part of
Virginia. But the authority of Virginia's government was uncertain in the
western reaches of the territory it claimed. Given eighteenth-century technology and transportation, it was difficult for governments in Williamsburg
and Richmond to get things done beyond the Appalachian Mountains. By
1785, people could see the day coming when Kentucky would break off and
form its own government. When that happened, Kentucky would need a
constitution and a legislature of its own. What powers should that legislature have, and how should it be constrained?

Wallace, who lived in Kentucky, was thinking about those questions,
knowing that he would soon be called upon to help provide the answers. He
was a well-educated man—a Presbyterian minister and a graduate of the

College of New Jersey (now Princeton). He had relevant experience, having served in the Virginia legislature and also as a judge. But even so, Wallace thought that in his quest to figure out how a constitution should structure a new legislature, it would be useful to ask for expert advice. So Wallace wrote a letter to an old friend, a member of the Virginia legislature whom he had known since college at Princeton. The friend was James Madison.

In 1785, Madison did not yet have the national stature he would later acquire. But he was prominent within Virginia, and he had some experience in government. By the time Wallace wrote to him, Madison had spent four years in the Virginia House of Delegates and another three representing Virginia at the Continental Congress. As Wallace knew, Madison was an active and analytically minded legislator, someone who was constantly thinking about how government should be reshaped and improved. So Wallace asked if Madison would "be so kind as to favor me with such a Form of Government as you would wish to live under."[1]

Madison responded with a letter canvassing several aspects of constitutional design, beginning with how a legislature should be structured. First, he suggested dividing the legislature into two houses. Virginia had a two-house legislature, with a Senate and a House of Delegates, but bicameralism could not be taken for granted in America at that time. In Pennsylvania, for example, the legislature had only one house. One democratically responsive chamber acting alone, Madison believed, would be prone to acting recklessly.[2] A system in which legislation had to gain the assent of a second house would be steadier. Not that Madison was any great fan of Virginia's own Senate: "[A] worse one," he told Wallace, "could hardly have been substituted." Still, Madison wrote, the bicameral structure had some salutary effect. "[B]ad as it is," Madison wrote, the Senate "is often a useful bit in the mouth of the house of Delegates." Madison then made suggestions about the maximum sizes of the legislative houses, the quorum requirements for doing business, and the advisability of letting some nonlegislative body review, and if necessary invalidate, laws passed by the legislature. Madison also recommended employing a professional staff to write the bills the legislature would consider, rather than letting the elected officials themselves try to formulate their ideas into actual legislative proposals. The members of the Virginia legislature, Madison wrote, "give almost as many proofs as they pass laws of their need of some such assistance."[3]

After offering these recommendations, Madison discussed a possible approach to limiting legislation that might seem like a good idea but wasn't:

writing a constitution specifying affirmatively what the legislature was authorized to do. "If it were possible," he wrote, "it would be well to define the extent of the Legislative power but the nature of it seems in many respects to be indefinite." In other words, Madison saw the appeal, in principle, of enumerating legislative powers and saying that the legislature would be authorized to exercise those powers and no others. But he also feared that in practice, such a project would be unworkable, because it would be difficult to capture with verbal definitions all the things a legislature would need to do.

So Madison recommended a different approach. Rather than specifying what the legislature would be authorized to do, he explained, Kentucky's constitution should identify things that the legislature would *not* be authorized to do. After saying that the nature of legislative power does not lend itself to being captured by a set of specific authorizations, Madison wrote that "[i]t is very practicable however to enumerate the essential exceptions." As examples, he noted that "The Constitution may expressly restrain [the legislature] from meddling with religion—from abolishing Juries—from taking away the Habeas corpus—from forcing a citizen to give evidence against himself—from controuling the press—from enacting retrospective laws at least in criminal cases, from abridging the rights of suffrage [and] from taking private property for public use without paying its full Value," as well as "from licensing the importation of Slaves" and "from infringing the confederation"—that is, from failing in its obligations toward the United States as a whole.[4] These were all things that, in Madison's view, Kentucky should not want its legislature to do. So it would make sense for Kentucky to write a constitution saying, straightforwardly, that its legislature could not do those things.

In short, Madison took the view that an enumeration of powers was not a good mechanism for limiting a legislature. The better approach was to structure the legislative process in ways that might restrain and refine its outputs and to specify affirmative prohibitions on what the legislature could do.

Three Kinds of Limits

Madison's letter to Wallace considered three kinds of limits that a constitution might use to restrict a government's freedom of action. Using a helpful set of terms from modern constitutional theory, we can call them *internal limits*, *external limits*, and *process limits*.[5] In his advice about constitutional design, Madison recommended external limits and process limits but not internal limits.

Internal limits inhere in particular grants of power; they are the limits of grants of power taken on their own terms. For example, the United States Constitution gives Congress the power to govern the District of Columbia. Congress can use that power to promulgate a fire safety code for the District of Columbia. But Congress cannot use that power to promulgate a fire safety code for Michigan, because writing fire safety codes for Michigan is not part of governing the District of Columbia. That limit of the power to govern the District of Columbia is intrinsic to the power itself—hence, its classification as an "internal limit." In modern constitutional law, common questions about whether some federal law is within the internal limits on Congress's powers include "Is this a tax?" (because Article I, Section 8, clause i, gives Congress the power "to lay and collect taxes") and "Is this a regulation of commerce among the several states?" (because Article I, Section 8, clause iii, gives Congress the power to regulate such commerce). The idea that Congress is limited by the enumeration of its powers is an idea about internal limits.

External limits, in contrast, are affirmative prohibitions—thou-shalt-not rules—that block what would otherwise be valid exercises of power. To build on the previous example, Congress has an enumerated power to govern the District of Columbia, but Congress cannot make a law providing for whites-only elections in the District, because the Fifteenth Amendment forbids the federal government to deny voting rights on the basis of race. The Fifteenth Amendment rule against racial discrimination in voting is not inherently part of the power to govern the District. Before the adoption of the Fifteenth Amendment, Congress could use its power to govern the District to conduct racially restrictive elections there. The Fifteenth Amendment creates a separate constitutional rule that pushes back against the grant of power and thus limits that power "externally," meaning that the limit stems from something outside the grant of power it is limiting. In his letter to Wallace, Madison recommended that Kentucky constitutionalize external-limit protections for religion, jury trial, a free press, and so on. In modern constitutional law, common questions about whether a law violates some external limit on Congress's powers include "Does this law abridge the freedom of speech?" (forbidden by the First Amendment) and "Does this law take private property for public use without just compensation?" (forbidden by the Fifth).

The third kind, process limits, are features of the decisionmaking processes that are required for governmental action. For example, for the federal government to enact a statute, a bill must secure the approval of two different legislative houses and that of the president, or, if the president disapproves the bill, a two-thirds vote of each legislative house. The president and the members of both legislative houses must win elections in order to acquire and retain their decisionmaking power. These features of the process prevent the enactment of many laws that might be made if lawmaking required only a majority vote of one legislative body—or that of a small hereditary council. Process limits do not place particular outcomes wholly out of reach: if a crazy idea has enough political support, it can overcome the process limits and become law (assuming it does not transgress the other kinds of limits). But a well-structured process should reduce the likelihood of abusive legislation. Thus, a law requiring all Americans to pay 99 percent of their incomes to the federal government would be constitutional if enacted, but it could never be passed, because no Congress and no president would approve it. In his letter to Wallace, Madison began his recommendations with process limits: a bicameral legislature with maximum sizes and quorum requirements, professional staff to advise legislators about their bills, and an outside body to review legislation once adopted.

In American constitutional law, external limits and process limits both play important roles. The substance of federal law would be different if there were no First Amendment, and it would probably be even more different if Congress were a unicameral legislature. A central claim of enumerationism is that internal limits also play a critical role. In this book's introduction, I explained that two propositions lie at the core of enumerationism: that Congress can legislate only on the basis of enumerated powers and that those powers collectively give Congress less power than it would have as a legislature of general jurisdiction. The first one—that Congress can legislate only on the basis of enumerated powers—is the enumeration principle. The second one—that those powers add up to less than general jurisdiction—is the internal-limits canon. It maintains that Congress's legislative reach, taken as a whole, is constrained by the internal limits of those enumerated powers.

In fact, however, internal limits have not done much constraining work in nearly a century. And perhaps the failure of internal limits to do meaningful constraining work is not a century-long anomaly. Perhaps internal limits are not, in practice, a good technology for limiting legislatures. And perhaps the Constitution's designers, or at least some of them, understood that fact. After all, Madison's advice to Wallace was that enumerating a legislature's powers might seem like a good way to limit a legislature but in reality was not. The better ways were by structuring its decisionmaking process and by enforcing affirmative prohibitions.

Looking toward Philadelphia

Madison's advice to Wallace in 1785 likely sheds light on his thinking at the Constitutional Convention two years later. Unless Madison changed his mind about the relative efficacy of internal limits shortly after he wrote to Wallace, he would have been skeptical in 1787 that an enumeration of powers would be a good way to limit a legislature. Nonetheless, many people familiar with American constitutional law are likely to resist the idea that Madison at the Convention was skeptical about enumeration as a strategy for limiting federal power. That is partly because the prevailing understanding of Madison's ideas on this point has been shaped by arguments he made later in his career, when he described a limiting enumeration of powers as fundamental to the constitutional design.[6] But it is also partly because constitutional lawyers have internalized, as a matter of first principles, the idea that Congress differs from state legislatures precisely by being a legislature with a set of specific mandates rather than a legislature of general jurisdiction. If Congress and the state legislatures are fundamentally different in this respect, then Madison's views about how to limit Kentucky's legislature would not say much about his views about how to limit Congress. And because constitutional lawyers know to treat that difference between Congress and state legislatures as fundamental, there is a tendency to assume that Madison, too, always thought of Congress and state legislatures as differing in that way.

But in the 1780s, one could not simply assume that federal and state legislatures were inherently different in a way that would make a system of enumerated powers appropriate for one but not for the other. On the state side, it was possible to imagine a legislature with or without enumerated powers. Madison advised Wallace against enumerating the powers of Kentucky's legislature, but he entertained the possibility. On the federal side, there was no reason to think that a Congress of the United States by its nature had to be limited to a set of enumerated powers. Many people, Madison included, understood the Articles of Confederation to structure the existing Congress that way. But if the Articles created a Congress limited to a set of textually enumerated powers, it did so as a matter of choice rather than because no other arrangement was imaginable. As one writer put the point in 1787, the Articles of Confederation needed language limiting the general government to expressly delegated powers precisely because there was no inherent reason why it would be so limited.[7] In the absence of such an inherent reason, a constitutional reform could make a different choice. Accordingly, when the public noticed that the proposed 1787 Constitution contained no clause explicitly limiting the federal government to the powers expressly given to it, many Americans were skeptical about Federalist assurances that the new government's powers were limited to those enumerated.[8] So despite the later orthodoxy of the view that Congress differs from state legislatures because Congress is limited by enumerated powers and state legislatures have general jurisdiction, one cannot assume that Madison's advice about enumerated powers in 1785 was offered on the assumption that the two are necessarily or inherently different in that respect. Either kind of legislature could in principle be structured either way, and the question was about which alternative to choose.

Indeed, Madison's view about whether enumerations of powers could reliably limit legislatures might well have been informed by his experience of serving in Congress under the Articles of Confederation. Shortly after he arrived in Congress in 1781, Congress voted to charter the Bank of North America—essentially, a central bank for the United States. Madison had been ambivalent. He seemed to think that the bank was necessary as a policy matter but that Congress lacked the authority to charter it.[9] When Congress voted in favor of the bank, Madison seemed to regard the decision as reflecting a choice, on Congress's part, not to notice that it was acting beyond its authority.[10] "[T]he general opinion though with some exceptions," Madison wrote to a friend, "was that the Confederation gave no such power and that the exercise of it would not bear the test of a forensic disquisition & consequently would not avail the institution."[11] In other words, Congress had prudently or cagily avoided a full exploration of the question of its power, because the answer might have been unfortunate. Madison acquiesced in the vote, apparently hoping that the general understanding that Congress was acting beyond its powers would help prevent the decision to charter the bank from becoming a "precedent[] of usurpation."[12] But if Madison hoped that

Congress's chartering the bank would be its only act of overreaching, subsequent events disappointed him. Beginning in 1784, Congress passed several statutes providing for the sale of land in the Western Territories—statutes that Madison again understood to be authorized by no power delegated to Congress under the Articles.[13] So there is little reason to believe that when Madison told Wallace that enumerations of powers did not in practice confine legislatures, he thought he was describing a phenomenon applicable only to state legislatures. After all, the description fit his experience of Congress—indeed, a form of Congress significantly less powerful than the one he would soon help create.

Moreover, the reasons Madison gave for his skepticism about using an enumeration of powers to limit a legislature did not arise from any feature of state legislatures that differentiated them from the Congress that would soon exist under the Constitution. Madison's view was about the impossibility of anticipating and articulating all the things that a legislature would need to do. That concern would apply to Congress as well as to state legislatures. Congress might not do the full range of things state legislatures would do, but it would need to do many things, and there was no obvious closed list of what those things should be. And language is not more susceptible to clarity and precision when applied to a national legislature than when applied to a local one.

The problem was more acute in 1785 than people today might intuit, due to a difference between the constitutional cultures of the two time periods. In modern America, the text of the Constitution is routinely treated as the most potent source of constitutional authority, and everyone expects constitutional decisionmaking to include disputes about the precise meanings of specific words. Virtually all jurists make nontextual as well as textual arguments in constitutional law, but mainstream constitutional interpreters commonly assume that when the Constitution's text bears clearly on a question, the question is thereby settled. We have a strong intuitive understanding that the wording of constitutional clauses matters a great deal: if the clauses were worded a little differently, a markedly different set of results might follow. That expectation about close attention to language makes it seem feasible to confine a legislature by articulating its powers textually. For a modern lawyer, it is intuitive that the question "Is this something the legislature can do?" can be answered by proceeding exactly through a specific list of enacted clauses and asking about each one, "Do these words authorize the action?" with the understanding that if the answer each time is "No," the legislature has no such power.

But in an environment where officials were accustomed to thinking of text as just one of several sources of constitutional law, it would be less sensible to imagine decisionmakers answering a constitutional question by proceeding mechanically through a detailed text in that way. As historians like Mary Sarah Bilder, Jonathan Gienapp, and Daniel Hulsebosch have explained, American judges and lawyers prior to 1787 tended to regard the purpose or spirit of a constitution (say, that of Massachusetts or New York) as being as important as the particulars of enacted language.[14] American practice at the time was in this respect in keeping with British practice, in which the constitution was a complex matrix of traditions, ideas, and texts. That sort of interpretive environment is less hospitable than our own to the idea that questions about the extent of legislative power would be answered by close attention to the wording of an enumerated list. The text mattered, but interpreters would have been less quick to presume that it would decide contested questions. Presented with an issue to which the text did not speak clearly, they might easily proceed to questions about a constitution's overall purpose, rather than expecting the text to yield answers if read with sufficient care. Given that environment, and given that Madison had seen a Congress ostensibly limited to specifically delegated powers exercise powers beyond those delegated, it is no wonder that he thought an enumeration of powers a poor strategy for limiting legislatures.

Indeed, when Madison concluded that Congress had exceeded its powers under the Articles by chartering the Bank of North America and making laws respecting the Western Territories, he was reasoning from the general sense of a power-conferring instrument rather than from a close reading of its text. Like most American lawyers and politicians in the 1780s, Madison understood the Articles of Confederation to deny Congress the authority to exercise any powers except those specifically delegated in the Articles. But the text of the Articles did not say that Congress could exercise only powers enumerated in that instrument. What the Articles provided, in Article II, was that each state "retained its sovereignty, freedom, and independence, and every Power, Jurisdiction, and right, which is not by this confederation expressly delegated to the United States, in Congress assembled." As a logical matter, that is a different proposition. It announces what the states were entitled to do, not what the United States was prohibited from doing. If the exercise of a power by the United States would not deny the sovereignty, freedom, independence, power, jurisdiction, or right of a state, then on a strict reading the United States could exercise that power without running afoul of Article II.

This point was not idle abstraction. Indeed, it was the publicly articulated view of a Philadelphia lawyer who was, in 1785, of much greater stature than Madison: James Wilson. Wilson, who had studied law at several Scottish universities, was widely recognized as among the best legal minds in America. He was a signer of the Declaration of Independence, and he would go on to be a leading figure at the Constitutional Convention and one of the original justices of the United States Supreme Court. And in Wilson's view, the text of the Articles of Confederation indicated that the United States in Congress Assembled was entitled to exercise nonenumerated powers—including the power to charter the Bank of North America and to organize and dispose of the Western Territories. Proceeding on a careful reading of Article II, Wilson reasoned that if a state had wielded a certain power before the Articles went into effect, the state retained that power unless the Articles expressly relocated it. Article II was a declaration about what states "retained." But it did not follow from that declaration that the United States could exercise only powers expressly given to it in the Articles, because delegation from the states at the time of the adoption of the Articles was not the only possible source of congressional power.[15] Power could also accrue to the government of United States inherently, by virtue of its being the national government, or implicitly, in light of the decisions that constituted the Union as a polity.*

In 1785—the same year when Madison wrote to Wallace—Wilson articulated this argument in an essay defending Congress's decision to charter the Bank of North America. Wilson put the point this way:

> Though the United States in congress assembled derive *from the particular States* no power, jurisdiction, or right, which is not *expressly* delegated by the confederation, it does not *thence* follow, that the United States in congress have *no other* powers, jurisdiction, or rights, than *those* delegated by

---

*For a discussion of the distinction between inherent and implicit powers, see the "Frequently Asked Questions" section at the end of this book.

the *particular states*. The United States have *general* rights, *general* powers, and *general* obligations, not derived from *any* particular states, nor from *all* the particular states, taken *separately*; but *resulting from the union of the whole*. . . . Whenever an object occurs, to the direction of which no particular state is competent, the management of it must, *of necessity*, belong to the United States in Congress assembled. . . . It is no *new* position, that rights may be vested in a political body, which did not previously reside in *any* or in *all* the members of that body. They may be derived solely from *the* UNION *of those members*. "The case," says the celebrated Burlamaqui, "is here very near the same as in that of several voices collected together, which, *by their union*, produce a harmony, that was *not* to be found *separately in each*."[16]

In other words, the general government of the United States had certain powers simply by virtue of being the general government of the United States. For example, it might have implicit or inherent power to act in the interest of the Union as a whole. And because such powers had never been held by any state separately, Congress's wielding those powers without an express authorization did not contravene the rule that each state was to retain all the powers it previously had, except as expressly provided otherwise.

Wilson would carry this view with him when he helped draft the Constitution two years later. In that process, Wilson was no marginal figure. Though not a Virginian, Wilson probably participated in the small working group that drafted the "Virginia Plan" that structured the Convention's work. Later in the summer, his work on the five-member committee that wrote the first full draft of the Constitution would make him perhaps the single most important Framer in the shaping of the constitutional text's treatment of congressional powers.[17]

Madison's letter to Wallace was not nearly as prominent a document in 1780s America as Wilson's essay on the bank. But like Wilson's essay, Madison's letter can be understood as offering a way of coming to terms with Congress's behavior while the Articles were in force. In Wilson's view, the idea that Congress had exceeded its mandate was based on a mistakenly narrow conception of that mandate's scope. In Madison's view, Congress had in fact exceeded its mandate—but it was a mistake to give an institution like Congress a mandate of that kind. With the benefit of that experience, Madison recommended other ways of proceeding.

Madison's advice to Wallace in 1785 does not prove that he was skeptical about using an enumeration of powers to limit Congress two years later. Maybe he changed his mind, or maybe he saw the situations as dissimilar. But maybe not. Maybe he had a consistent view about what textual enumerations of power were or were not good for. Even if so, of course, Madison's view might not explain much about the enumeration of congressional powers in the Constitution. Madison was only one influence among several at the Constitutional Convention, and some features of the Constitution departed sharply from his vision. But if Madison wasn't everybody at the Convention, he also wasn't nobody. If he doubted that a textual enumeration of powers was a sound means for limiting a legislature, it is likely that other delegates shared his skepticism. After all, Madison was no extreme outlier in his willingness to contemplate nonenumerated legislative powers. Wilson's view that Congress had such powers even under the Articles was well known, and his colleagues respected him enough to put him on the committee that wrote the first draft of the Constitution.

Knowing Madison's view on this question in 1785 is also instructive for another reason. Wallace wrote to Madison because he considered Madison an insightful analyst. Most constitutional lawyers share that assessment. Not that Madison's views were always correct, of course. When he served in Congress after the Constitution was adopted, his colleagues sometimes dismissed his creative constitutional arguments as overly clever attempts to rescue his favored legislative positions by pretending that the alternatives were unconstitutional.[18] On some occasions, they were probably right. But even if Madison sometimes stretched constitutional logic when advocating particular causes, he was still a keen and active thinker on the subject of constitutional design. Accordingly, Madison's having held a view might at least signal that it is a view worth considering. And where the question of enumerating powers is concerned, Madison's skepticism has been borne out by subsequent events. Despite the orthodox principle that Congress is and must be limited by its enumerated powers, the enumeration has not in fact been the kind of limiting force that enumerationism insists it must be. Maybe Madison's advice to Wallace was right.

CHAPTER TWO

WHY ENUMERATE?

CONSIDER TWO CLAIMS THAT enumerationism makes about the Framers' decision to enumerate congressional powers in the Constitution's text.* The first is that the purpose of enumerating those powers was to limit the federal government. The second is that enumerating congressional powers was a good strategy for achieving that purpose. The first claim is an account of why the Framers did what they did, and the second is a judgment about the quality of their reasoning.

The first claim—that the Framers enumerated the powers of Congress in order to limit the federal government—is not false. But it is misleading, and in two different ways. First, it overstates the degree to which the enumeration of powers was designed for reasons of federalism, as opposed to the separation of powers. To a considerable extent, Article I, Section 8, was written not to allocate power between the states and the federal government but to allocate power between Congress and the president. Second, to the

---

* By "the Framers of the Constitution" or just "the Framers," I mean the group of men who attended the Constitutional Convention in 1787. In contrast, I use "the Founders"—short for "the Founders of the Republic"—to refer to the much broader group of Americans who participated in the Constitution-making events of 1787–1788, whether at the Convention or in the process of ratification. The difference in usage is rooted in the idea that the specific people at the Convention "framed" (that is, wrote) a *document*, but the *system of government* that document represents was "founded" (that is, established) by a wider process. Every Framer was a Founder, but only a few dozen Founders were Framers.

extent that the enumeration of congressional powers was meant to shape the balance of power between the federal government and the states, it was primarily meant to empower the federal government. To be sure, the Framers were many people thinking many things, and any decent answer to the question of why they enumerated congressional powers would recognize that they acted with a mix of purposes. So the present point is not that the Framers enumerated congressional powers in order to empower Congress—both against the president and against the states—and *not* to limit the federal government. It is that the balance of purposes lay more toward the congressional-empowerment end of the spectrum than the received memory of constitutional lawyers generally recognizes.

The second claim is problematic too. Like the first claim, it is not entirely wrong. Given the Framers' aims and the conditions they faced, enumerating congressional powers made some sense as a strategy for limiting the new federal government. But it made less sense for that purpose than the conventional wisdom assumes. By comparison, enumerating the powers of Congress made considerably more sense as a strategy for pursuing the other two purposes just described: empowering the federal government relative to the states and, within the federal government, empowering Congress relative to the president.

The two claims are distinct, but they are also mutually reinforcing. The idea that the Framers enumerated congressional powers in order to limit the federal government tends to encourage the idea that enumerating congressional powers was a good strategy for that end. Conversely, the belief that enumerating congressional powers was a good strategy for limiting the federal government makes it easy to believe that the Framers enumerated powers for that reason. By the same token, seeing the problems with each claim makes it easier to question the other. If we can recognize that the enumeration of powers made more sense as a device for empowering Congress than as a device for limiting the federal government, it will be easier to see that the Framers' choice to enumerate congressional powers was motivated less by a desire to limit the federal government, and more by a desire to empower Congress, than the conventional wisdom believes.

Showing that enumerating congressional powers made more sense as a technique of empowerment than as a technique of limitation does not prove that empowering Congress was the Framers' dominant motive. Sometimes people do things that don't make sense. But as long as we believe that enumeration was a well-crafted strategy for limiting the federal government, we will be disposed to credit the claim that the Framers acted for that reason. Recognizing that the enumeration was actually better suited for other purposes is accordingly a helpful step toward seeing that the normal story about why the Framers enumerated congressional powers might be flawed. It is also an important step toward realizing that the enumeration's failure to constrain Congress in practice might be a manifestation of something that was present in the nature of the enumeration from the beginning rather than a failure by subsequent generations to use the Constitution properly.

This book's discussion of the Framers' design occupies two chapters. In this chapter, I explain why the enumeration of congressional powers made more sense in 1787 as a device for empowering Congress—both against the states and against the president—than as a device for limiting the federal government. Then, in Chapter 3, I narrate the work of the Convention chronologically to show that the process from which the enumeration of powers emerged was considerably more nationalistic, and considerably less inclined to see the enumeration as a device for limiting federal governance, than the conventional thinking believes.

⤛⤜⤛⤜

The Framers' interest in limiting the power of what they called the "general government" had four major themes. First, many of them wanted to limit the general government in order to protect republican liberty as they understood it. Second, many of them wanted to ensure that the general government would not be able to interfere with or abolish the institution of slavery. Third, many Framers wanted to protect the status of the states as something more than geographic departments of a unified national government. Sometimes they spoke of this concern in the language of "sovereignty," albeit without always having a clear idea of exactly what sovereignty was. Fourth, at least some important Framers believed it necessary to limit the general government in order to preserve the authority of local governments to deliver day-to-day governance in an environment where a national government, no matter how powerful on paper, would lack the practical capacity to provide most of the governance society needed.

But the fact that the Framers wanted to limit the general government does not mean that it would have made sense for them to see Article I's enumeration of powers as a means toward that end. For each of the Framers' first three reasons for limiting the federal government, the enumeration of pow-ers would have been a poor choice of strategy. The fourth rationale is differ-ent; for that end, enumerating federal powers was a more fitting means. Cru-cially, however, that fourth rationale for limiting federal power rested on two premises that, though reasonable in the 1780s, are out of place in mod-ern America: that assigning a power to the federal government would block the state governments from acting in that domain, and that the federal gov-ernment would lack the capacity to provide adequate regulation on its own. After all, the fourth concern was—perhaps counterintuitively to modern Americans—that a too-empowered federal government would mean too *lit-tle* governance. If the general government turned out to have enormous ca-pacity, and if state and local governments could regulate where the federal government did not—both of which are now the case—then this worry would be substantially addressed. So in sum, enumerating congressional powers would in important ways not have been a good strategy for limiting the federal government—and to the extent that it *was* a good strategy, it made sense on a theory that, under modern circumstances, would not re-quire the enumeration to do any limiting work.

Below, I explain why the Framers wanted to create a strong central au-thority and why enumerating powers was a sensible means to that end. I then consider the Framers' major reasons for wanting to limit the federal govern-ment and explain why enumerating congressional powers was, for the most part, *not* a fitting means toward that end.

Enumeration as Empowerment

The Need to Empower

Beginning in 1781, the United States of America functioned under the agree-ment known as the Articles of Confederation. Under the Articles, Congress—or the "general government," as Americans often called Congress and the small collection of officials it directed—was a weak institution. By 1787, it was clear to many Americans that the general government's weakness was a serious problem.

Congress had trouble raising money, including the money it needed to pay debts incurred during the Revolutionary War.[1] Congress had no power to impose taxes. Instead, it was supposed to make requisitions of the states, meaning that Congress could identify an amount of money that each state was supposed to raise and contribute to the federal treasury. But Congress had no power to compel payment, and the states never paid their requisitions in full (if they paid them at all). As a result, the United States could not repay loans it owed to foreign countries, which made the new nation's international standing somewhat dicey. Nor could the general government reliably pay its own employees, including the members of the small US Army.[2] Organizing his thoughts in advance of the Convention, Madison described this problem as both fatal to and inherent in the existing structure of American government. It resulted, he wrote, "naturally from the number and independent authority of the States."[3]

The failure of the states to act as a union created many problems in foreign affairs. When Britain imposed trade restrictions on American ships, Congress could not order a unified American response. The same was true when Spain closed the Mississippi River to American shipping and when pirates seized American ships in the Mediterranean Sea. Moreover, several states took actions that violated the Treaty of Paris, which had ended the Revolutionary War. For example, the treaty provided that Americans who had remained loyal to Britain during the war would not be treated as criminals and that their remaining property would not be expropriated. But states violated those guarantees, and Congress could do nothing to make them comply. Given American noncompliance, Britain often refused to adhere to its obligations under the treaty, including its obligation to complete the withdrawal of its forces from the United States. So, even after the war was over, British garrisons remained within the borders of some American states. Congress could do nothing about it.[4]

Domestic affairs were difficult as well. Many states pursued protectionist economic policies, essentially treating other states like foreign countries for economic purposes. One state's actions to the detriment of another state naturally produced retaliatory measures. In some places, economic hardship led to violence. Most famously, in the 1786–1787 uprising known as Shays's Rebellion, several thousand western Massachusetts farmers tried to overthrow the state government by force.[5] And Congress could do little or nothing to bring economic stability or cooperation to the states. It had relatively little power, and the power it had was regularly flouted.

The domestic governance problems in the United States were not simply a matter of weakness at the center. The state governments were themselves often ineffective, even within their own boundaries.[6] Shays's Rebellion is again emblematic: the problem was not merely the adverse economic conditions that motivated the rebels but also the weakness of the Massachusetts government, which could barely maintain its own authority. Constitutional law's standard telling of the transition from the Articles of Confederation to the Constitution underplays this problem because it depicts the system under the Articles as one of "sovereign" states, and sovereign states are usually imagined as capable of internal governance. But the American states in the 1780s were not what modern social scientists would recognize as Weberian states—that is, governments enjoying monopolies on the legitimate use of force within geographically defined territories.[7] Much of the time, the state governments exercised their authority not as supreme authorities from which all other legitimate political power must flow but as important actors within a complex ecosystem of other power-wielding institutions: corporations, towns, churches, Native Nations, separatist movements, and so on. Shays's Rebellion was a particularly prominent episode in which the authority of a state to govern within its claimed territory was called into serious question, but it was by no means the only one.[8]

In that light, as Gregory Ablavsky has explained, the standard story on which the adoption of the Constitution relocated sovereignty from the state governments to the United States obscures a messier reality. In practice, the pre-1788 state governments could not easily exercise the kind of power that talk of sovereignty usually implies—power to which every other actor must yield. And contrary to the normal zero-sum presentation, the creation of a stronger national government was an opportunity for the state governments to become *more* powerful in practice. After all, the Constitution did not merely create a stronger general government. It created a political system in which the only recognized players other than that stronger general government were the state governments. With a robust general government at their backs, the state governments could clear the field of local claimants (towns, counties, corporations) to autonomy or quasi-sovereign power.[9] The Constitution's promoters clearly understood that their plan offered this benefit to the state governments. Hamilton's *Federalist* 9, for example, is an advertisement for the Union's ability to marshal overwhelming force to crush insurrections against the state governments. (Read next to its neighbor, Madison's argument in *Federalist* 10 that the extended republic would "break and control the violence of faction" looks like a peacetime version of the same argument.)

This understanding of the condition of the state governments in 1787 provides important context for reconstructing the Framers' senses of the relationship between a stronger general government and effective local government. If the state governments are imagined as firmly rooted and fully functional local sovereigns under the Articles, then it is natural to think that serious people in 1787 would have wanted to adjust the power of the general government only slightly—enough to improve coordination among the states but not enough to do much more than that. But if the state governments are understood as rickety, the field of possibilities looks different. In particular, it is then easier to understand why serious people would have been keen to vest extensive power in a national government—and to worry more about empowering the national government too little than about empowering it too much.

For all these reasons, the delegates who attended the Philadelphia Convention in 1787 went there to create a more powerful general government. Not that they were of one mind about how much more powerful the general government should be, of course. Some were enthusiastic about national power and favored transformative change, while others wanted a more modest species of reform. But the common problem that they faced was a deficit of effective governance, and their disagreements concerned the best ways to make their general government more powerful. As James Wilson put the point,

> Bad Governts. are of two sorts. I. that which does too little. 2. that which does too much: that which fails thro' weakness; and that which destroys thro' oppression. Under which of these evils do the U. States at present groan? [U]nder the weakness and inefficiency of its Governt. To remedy this weakness we have been sent to this Convention.[10]

The Utility of Enumerating Powers

In the conventional thinking of constitutional lawyers, a Congress with enumerated powers is the alternative to a Congress with the power to make law in general—what modern constitutional lawyers call the police power. That framing makes the Convention's choice to enumerate congressional powers seem like a choice to limit the powers Congress was granted. But the Convention did not really face a choice between enumerating congressional powers

and giving Congress a general police power. Giving Congress a general police power in the 1780s would have been a complete nonstarter, and for more
reasons than modern Americans intuit. The problem would not merely have
been that such a Congress would have been very powerful and many Americans were skeptical of strong central government. The further problem was
that according to the prevailing thinking, such a Congress could not coexist
with the state governments, because as a conceptual matter two governments
could not have the power to govern the same thing at the same time. In the
view of many Americans, the simultaneous operation of two such overlapping governments—of imperium in imperio, as the cognoscenti then said—
was logically impossible.[11] A Congress with general legislative power would
therefore have to be the exclusive legislature for all the territory it governed,
and that would mean two unpalatable things. First, the state legislatures
would have to go out of business or, at the least, be converted into something like local offices of a superior central authority, possessed of no power
except what the general government allowed them. Several leading Framers
were attracted to that idea (see Chapter 3), but neither the full Convention
nor the public as a whole would be willing to go that far. Second, the general government, which barely existed, would be solely responsible for all of
the necessary governance in a vast and diverse country. Few people thought
it was a good idea to try that, and for good reason. So a Congress with a general police power was never a realistic possibility. When the Framers thought
about enumerating congressional powers, a congressional police power was
not the alternative they were weighing.

A better way to think about the Convention's decision to enumerate powers is to consider the advantages of enumeration not relative to a police
power but relative to a statement of congressional power at the level of general principles. Imagine, for example, a statement like the one the Convention
adopted in July 1787, resolving that Congress should have the power "to
legislate in all cases for the general interests of the Union, and also in those
to which the States are separately incompetent, or in which the harmony of
the United States may be interrupted by the exercise of individual legislation."[12] Such a general statement would have been less useful than an enumeration of powers as a means of creating a sufficiently powerful general
government. To understand why, it is helpful to keep in mind three facts
confronting the Framers.

First, their envisioned government would function in a world where not everyone would be happy about the general government's exercising consequential powers. Objections might be rooted in general opposition to national governance, displeasure with specific measures taken, or both. But for one reason or another, the new government's actions were sure to be frequently opposed, and the question of its power to act would be frequently contested. People would argue about whether the government could do this or that thing. When that happened, a constitution that described congressional power in general terms would not be of much use. To keep with the example above, suppose the Constitution empowered Congress "to legislate in all cases for the general interests of the Union, and also in those to which the States are separately incompetent, or in which the harmony of the United States may be interrupted by the exercise of individual legislation." Objectors to congressional legislation would then predictably argue that this or that matter did not touch the general interests of the Union, was not beyond the competence of the states separately, and raised no issue related to the harmony of the United States. If the people empowered to adjudicate the question turned out to be skeptics about central power—and keep in mind that many decisions might be made in state courts—then those arguments would often be accepted, thus defeating the major purpose of holding the Philadelphia Convention in the first place.

On the other hand, if the Constitution spoke specifically about which powers Congress was entitled to exercise—say, the power to tax, to regulate commerce, or to make bankruptcy laws—then defenders of congressional action could establish their position by pointing to specific authorizations in the constitutional text. This greater specificity would not guarantee that claims of congressional authority would be accepted, because people can also argue about what constitutes a tax, a regulation of commerce, or a bankruptcy law. But over a broad range of actions Congress might take, the more specific authorizations set the boundaries of reasonable argument in a more Congress-friendly location. If government actors want skeptics to accept their authority to take a certain action, it is helpful not just to have the authority in writing but for the written warrant for their authority to state the relevant power in relatively specific language.[13]

A second background fact raised the premium on putting specific congressional authorities in writing.[14] Article IX of the Articles of Confederation enumerated a set of congressional powers. They included the power to bor-row money on the credit of the United States, to regulate trade with Indian tribes, to coin money and regulate its value, to fix standards for weights and measures, to establish post offices, to declare war, to grant letters of marque and reprisal, to make rules concerning captures on land and on water, to provide for the trial of piracies and felonies committed on the high seas, to build and equip a navy, and to make rules for the government and regula-tion of the land and naval forces. The Framers repeated those specific autho-rizations in Article I, Section 8, and it is not hard to see why. Omitting spe-cific mention of a power specified in the Articles would risk the inference that a power conferred by the Articles was not conferred by the Constitution.

Given a crucial difference between the Articles and the Constitution, the Framers could not solve this problem with a general statement like "All pow-ers vested in the United States under the Articles continue to be vested in the United States under the Constitution." Such a statement would not ex-plain *who*, under the Constitution, could exercise particular powers on be-half of the United States. Under the Articles of Confederation, all powers vested in the general government were held by a single institution: the United States in Congress Assembled. But under the Constitution, "Congress" would be just one of three branches of government. So it could not automatically be assumed that the powers held by the United States under the Articles would be powers of Congress in the new three-branch system. Indeed, some of the powers the Articles had given to the United States—like the power to send and receive ambassadors and the power to direct military operations—would under the Constitution be allocated to the president. To omit express instructions about who in the new government could exercise which powers mentioned in the Articles would therefore create uncertainty about which branch of government was authorized to exercise many important powers.

Worse still, a third background fact meant that if the Framers did not clearly specify who was to exercise which powers, future decisionmakers would likely allocate more power to one particular actor—the president—than the Framers thought desirable. That third background fact was William Blackstone's monumental *Commentaries on the Laws of England*, published in four volumes between 1765 and 1769. In the Framers' generation, Blackstone shaped many Americans' understanding not just of the common law but also of the British constitution. And in Blackstone's description of the British constitution, several powers the Framers wanted to assign to Congress were identified not as powers of Parliament but as powers of the king. Among others, Blackstone's list of Crown powers included the powers to regulate commerce, naturalize aliens, coin money, regulate weights and measures, establish courts, declare war, issue letters of marque and reprisal, and raise and regulate armies and navies.[15] These powers are allocated to Congress in Article I, Section 8, and modern Americans conversant with the Constitution associate all of these powers with Congress. But in the 1780s, the fact that Blackstone identified those powers as powers of the king in the British system made it likely that, in the absence of a contrary instruction, people would argue that those powers were vested in the president rather than in Congress. If the Framers wanted Congress to wield those powers, it would be prudent to say so explicitly. And the most straightforward way to communicate which Crown powers were to be congressional rather than presidential was to specify them with particularity—that is, to enumerate them as powers of Congress.[16]

Nothing about these rationales for expressly enumerating many powers of Congress required that *all* of the powers of Congress be enumerated. The point of the enumeration, understood this way, was not to rule out powers not mentioned. It was to rule *in* powers that were important to specify, lest Congress's authority to exercise those powers be doubted—either on the theory that the relevant powers were held exclusively by the states or on the theory that they belonged to the president. And if the point of the enumeration was to rule certain powers in, the considerations discussed here would supply good reasons for enumerating a list of powers that looked a lot like Article I, Section 8.

Enumeration as Limitation

The Framers wanted to limit the general government as well as empower it. But given their reasons for limiting the general government and given what enumerations of powers are and are not good for, there are reasons for skepticism about whether an enumeration of powers—let alone the actual enumeration of powers the Constitution contains—would be a sensible technology for doing the limiting work.

To begin to see why such skepticism is warranted, it is important to recognize that at least some of the Framers already knew, in the 1780s, that an enumeration of powers was not a particularly good way to limit a legislature.

Madison knew it, as he explained to Wallace in his 1785 letter. The better ways, Madison wrote, were with external limits (that is, affirmative prohibitions) and process limits (like bicameralism, executive presentment, and the requirement that legislators stand frequently for election). There is no reason to think that Madison was unique in holding these views. At the General Convention, other leading Framers like James Wilson and Roger Sherman also expressed doubts about the practicability of dividing national and local spheres of action by enumerating the powers of Congress.[17] Many of the Constitution's opponents in the ratification debates said that the Constitution's enumeration of powers would not limit Congress. They turned out to be right. Maybe the Framers were as discerning on this point as their opponents.

With that point as background, consider four leading reasons why delegates at the Convention wanted to limit the general government: to preserve republican liberty, to perpetuate chattel slavery, to protect the status of states, and to maintain local governments' authority to provide needed governance. To the extent that the first three reasons motivated the Framers' interest in limiting Congress, limiting congressional powers to those enumerated in the Constitution would not have been a particularly good strategy. And to the extent that the Framers were motivated by the fourth reason, there would be no contradiction between enumerating congressional powers and permitting Congress to exercise something close to general regulatory authority, so long as the federal government developed the practical capacity for comprehensive governance or the law permitted concurrent state and federal jurisdiction.

Liberty

Many Americans in the 1780s wanted to limit the general government because they feared that republican liberty could not survive in a polity as large as the United States. The central concern, boiled down, was that the country was too vast and the population too large for the people and the government officials who supposedly represented them to know and trust each other. The people would thus (correctly) come to perceive the government as alien rather than representative, and the government's authority would need to rely more and more on force rather than goodwill. Down that road lay tyranny.[18]

But would it have made sense to think that the Constitution's enumeration of congressional powers would solve that problem? It is hard to say yes. The powers Congress was affirmatively given, including to tax and to raise armies, seem like effective tools of oppression in the hands of a government inclined to wield them that way—as people recognized at the time.[19]

The sensible solution to the problem that a remote and unrepresentative government would likely become tyrannical over time would not have been to limit that government to a specific set of powers, including those powers most valuable to a tyrannical oppressor. It would have been either to make the government more representative or to take other steps to prevent the government from exercising its potentially tyrannical powers abusively. George Washington's one recorded substantive intervention in the Convention proceedings was likely a form of the first strategy: he persuaded the delegates to increase the potential size of the House of Representatives.[20] The work that occupied most of the Convention's attention—structuring a system of checks and balances—embodied the second strategy. But I know of no examples of Americans in the Founding generation who worried that the general government created by the Constitution would be sufficiently nonrepresentative to risk devolution into tyranny and also thought that the Constitution's enumeration of powers—including the power to tax and the power to raise armies—was anything like a satisfactory solution.

Slavery

For many Americans, the concern with protecting republican liberty coexisted—uneasily or otherwise—with a desire to perpetuate chattel slavery. Slaveholders in states where slavery was strong wanted to be certain that a powerful national government would not become a vehicle for emancipation. South Carolina's delegates were particularly clear on this point. More than once during the Convention, they said bluntly that South Carolina would support no Constitution that endangered slavery.[21] The three delegates who early on pushed most clearly for an enumeration of Congress's powers were from South Carolina.[22] During the ratification debates, southern Federalists promoted the Constitution in part by saying that the enumeration of Congress's powers would prevent the general government from interfering with slavery in the states that sanctioned it. So perhaps the enumeration of powers was motivated by a desire to protect slavery from federal interference.

At least in part, it probably was. But once again, it is worth asking whether the Constitution's enumeration of congressional powers would have been a sensible means to the relevant end. A Congress with the power to tax could tax the purchase or ownership of slaves or the sale of slave-produced commodities, thus undermining slavery by making it unprofitable. A Congress with the power to regulate commerce among the states could prohibit commerce in human beings or in the goods that enslaved people produced. Perhaps a Congress with the power to make rules of naturalization could make slaves into citizens. A Congress with the power to raise armies could conscript slaves, thus denying their labor to the slaveowners—and if certain precedents from the Revolutionary War were followed, military service could lead to emancipation.[23] Between the Framing and the Civil War, antislavery activists would point out all of these possibilities and more.[24] It is hard to imagine that talented proslavery lawyers at the Convention, on the lookout for threats to slavery, could not have seen the same possibilities.

Congress never passed such laws, of course, and the reason why not is best understood in terms of process limits, external limits, or a hybrid of the two. On the simplest reading, the sufficient explanation for Congress's not using its enumerated powers to attack slavery in the southern states is that most elected federal officials did not want Congress to pass such laws, either because they favored slavery or because they wanted to avoid the backlash and crisis that antislavery legislation would provoke. That explanation sounds straightforwardly in process limits, and it is not wrong. But it leaves out the fact that many federal officials thought of congressional noninterference with slavery less as a policy choice than as a constitutional principle. American officials in the early republic held a broadly shared understanding—following William Wiecek, historians call it the "federal consensus"—that the Constitution gave Congress no power to legislate against slavery in the states.[25] In its substance, that principle is an external limit rather than an internal one. Like the First Amendment's protection for free speech (except without a clause stating the point), it is an affirmative prohibition that blocks the exercise of congressional power. Because the rule against congressional interference with slavery was enforced by a shared understanding in Congress, we might think of the mechanism in terms of process limits or in terms of politically enforced external limits. But regardless of which of those classifications seems better, the purpose of protecting slavery would be better served by an external limit offering that protection directly, or by a political process that would block antislavery legislation, than by a system of internal limits.

The South Carolinians at the Constitutional Convention probably understood this logic. Indeed, as the Convention progressed, South Carolina's delegates insisted on two affirmative prohibitions on congressional power. One forbade Congress to block the importation of slaves.[26] The other banned the taxation of exports, thus preventing Congress from undermining slavery by taxing southern states' slave-produced agricultural products to the point of unprofitability.[27] Modern Americans may not immediately see the ban on taxing exports as intended to protect slavery, partly because we do not have an organic sense of the eighteenth-century economy and partly because the Constitution's final text listed its prohibition on interference with the slave trade and its prohibition on the taxation of exports separately, with other prohibitions in between. But at the Convention, the link between exports and slavery was well understood.[28] The Constitution's first draft linked them together in a section that, in its entirety, read as follows:

> No tax or duty shall be laid by the Legislature on articles exported from any State; nor on the migration or importation of such persons as the several States shall think proper to admit; nor shall such migration or importation be prohibited.[29]

That text in the Constitution's first draft (the substance of which survived into the final Constitution) was probably written by South Carolina delegate John Rutledge.[30] In writing that language, Rutledge was pursuing the eminently logical strategy of protecting an important interest with affirmative prohibitions on Congress, rather than by omitting relevant powers from Congress's arsenal. If one's goal is to protect a particular activity from national power, it makes considerably more sense to create an immunity for that activity than to pursue the indirect strategy of giving Congress twenty or thirty powers and calculating that none of them can be deployed to interfere with that activity. This is especially so if the powers given to Congress include, say, the powers to tax and to regulate commerce.

That being the case, one might well ask why South Carolina's delegates did not pursue their interest in protecting the institution of slavery by seeking a blanket prohibition on any national legislation touching *slavery*, as such. One reasonable answer is that they had a sense of what their fellow delegates would agree to. Partly to keep an explosive issue from bursting into the open and possibly scuttling the entire project of creating a system that all of the states would accept, the Convention delegates kept direct references to slavery out of their document. (Even the provision protecting the slave trade spoke in code: Article I, Section 9 of the Constitution protected "the migration or importation of such persons as any of the states now existing shall think proper to admit" before the year 1808.) As a result, external limits that would in effect protect slavery without naming slavery directly might have been the most effective options available—at least as far as external limits to be written into the Constitution's text were concerned. The external limit embodied in the "federal consensus" was something that could emerge as a matter of practical constitutional culture, given the prevailing constellation of understandings and interests, rather than something the Convention had the appetite for committing to paper.

Proslavery delegates also pursued strategies based on process limits. If the states wishing to perpetuate legal slavery could muster sufficient strength in the federal government's decisionmaking processes, they could protect slavery even if the government's powers on paper would be sufficient to end the practice. The Three-Fifths Clause contributed to this project by increasing the representation in Congress of states with large slave populations, and the Electoral College compounded that effect by making increased representation in Congress tantamount to increased influence in selecting the president. Indeed, there are indications that southern delegates expected these arrangements to protect their interests even more powerfully in the long term than in the short term, because they expected new western states to align mostly with the South. On that assumption, South Carolina could agree in 1787 to constitutional protection for the international slave trade only until 1808 partly because it was confident that by 1808 the balance of power in the general government would be such that Congress would not ban the slave trade then either.[31] History seems to have borne out the calculation that wielding decisionmaking power within the general government was more important to the future of slavery than anything in the Constitution's textual specifications of congressional power. Slavery lasted as long as proslavery politicians maintained control of the general government's elected branches, but it did not last much longer.

Sovereignty

Another possible reason for wanting to limit Congress was more abstract. The Articles of Confederation described the states as separately sovereign polities. Exactly what that meant was always contestable: sovereignty is a slippery concept.[32] But whatever it meant to say that states were sovereign under the Articles, the states would no longer be sovereign in that way under the Constitution.

That raised this question: if not sovereign entities, what would the states be? Would anything be left of their separate autonomy? Some of the Framers wondered whether the state governments would become "mere corporations," meaning something like administrative departments of the national government, carrying out tasks at their subordinate station.[33] Many delegates at the Convention wanted them to be more than that—to have some existence and decisionmaking authority independent of the general government. Whether it is helpful to describe that status in the language of "sovereignty" is a complex question, as the political theorist Don Herzog has made clear.[34] But whether or not they had an analytically coherent account of sovereignty, some delegates used the language of sovereignty (and of "mere corporations") to express their opposition to making the states fully subordinate to a national government. According to a commonly held view, one way to guarantee states a meaningful and not fully subordinate existence would be to provide that state governments would have exclusive authority over a broad swath of policymaking.[35] From the eighteenth century forward, the enumeration of congressional powers has been presented as a means to that end.

But there are at least two important ways in which the idea of enumerating congressional powers as a means for giving the states a status beyond that of "mere corporations" is more problematic than generally recognized. First, the idea of enumerating congressional powers does not seem to have figured in the Convention's major discussions of the status of states. When the delegates discussed ensuring that the states would enjoy some sort of quasi-sovereign status, the proffered solutions tended to address the structure of the general government rather than the list of projects that government could pursue. The Senate as the Framers designed it is a notable example: according to a number of delegates, letting state legislatures appoint one branch of Congress could preserve the states as something like sovereign entities within the Constitution's overall scheme of a robust national government.[36] On that way of thinking, guaranteeing states a status greater than mere administrative arms of the national government meant giving states seats at the table rather than limiting what could be decided there.

Second, there is a mismatch between the goal of guaranteeing domains of exclusive decisionmaking authority to the states and the description of congressional powers that the Convention actually drafted. For an enumeration of congressional powers to meet the state-status concern, it would have to be *limiting*. That means two things. First, the enumeration of powers must not be one that would in practice allow the national government to make law across all, or nearly all, of the important policy domains. Second, it must be unmistakable that Congress could legislate only on the basis of the powers enumerated. That principle—that Congress could exercise only a closed set of legislative authorities—would be at least as important as any particular substantive choice about what powers were and were not allocated to Congress.

It is not clear that the Constitution the Convention drafted satisfies the first criterion. For a long time, the enumerated powers of Congress have, in practice, authorized legislation on pretty much any topic. The conventional thinking today is that the Framers did not see things that way. But many Americans in the Founding generation—including both promoters and opponents of the Constitution—read the Preamble, the General Welfare Clause, and the Necessary and Proper Clause as plausibly vesting Congress with general legislative power, or at least something close to it.[37] Many of the Constitution's supporters publicly rejected that reading during the ratification debates. But the fact that that reading existed, and that it was prominent rather than merely marginal, makes it problematic to conclude that the Constitution clearly did *not* warrant congressional power that broad.

With respect to the second criterion, the mismatch between the idea of enumerating congressional powers as a means for preserving state sovereignty and the way the Constitution actually described congressional power is even more striking. If it had been important to the Framers that Congress be able to legislate only on the basis of the powers enumerated, it would have been easy for them to say so clearly in the Constitution's text. They did not. Most modern constitutional lawyers read the Tenth Amendment as such a statement, of course. But the Tenth Amendment is an *amendment*; it exists because the Framers, in the original Constitution, did *not* clearly provide that the textually specified powers of Congress were the only powers Congress would possess. Given the purported importance of the principle, it is a telling omission. To be sure, some of the Framers did want the enumeration to be limiting, and I am not suggesting that the omission of a clear statement to that effect proves that the enumeration of powers was not meant as exclusive. The point, rather, is that the absence of any such statement tells against the idea that the Convention as a whole regarded the enumeration as exclusive.

Some might suggest that the Framers did not clearly articulate the principle that Congress was confined to its enumerated powers because they took that principle for granted. But if the Framers took that principle for granted, they were puzzlingly obtuse. As soon as the draft Constitution was presented to the public, critics began to argue that the list of enumerated powers was not limiting, and they could make that argument because the document did not make the contrary principle clear.[38] As Jefferson put the point in a letter to Madison, one could say that the enumerated powers were limiting, but the document could just as easily support the opposite inference.[39] Perhaps the Framers understood their own text well enough to anticipate that point.

Similarly, it would be odd for the Framers to have thought that the principle that Congress could legislate only based on its enumerated powers would be taken for granted if they also thought that limiting Congress to a set of enumerated powers would prevent the states from being "mere corporations." Anyone paying attention at the Convention would know that several leading delegates—Hamilton, Wilson, Gouverneur Morris, Rufus King, maybe even Madison—affirmatively wanted a Constitution that would, in practice if not by declaration, reduce the states to administrative departments of the national government.[40] Not surprisingly, delegates who did not want to reduce the states to that status recognized the issue as live and contested: one delegate skeptical of central power said that the Convention's Virginia Plan, most of which was adopted as a basis for drafting the Constitution, would "absorb the State sovereignties & leave them mere Corporations."[41] Against that background, it would be odd for the Convention to have thought that it could enumerate powers, not specify that the enumeration was limiting, and trust that everyone would understand it that way.

None of this means that none of the Framers saw the enumeration of congressional powers as a means to preserve some aspects of state sovereignty (whatever that might mean) by limiting the scope of federal governance. Again, the Framers were many people thinking many things. But there are good reasons to think that this rationale for enumerating congressional powers was, at best, partial and contested. Indeed, whatever support there was at the Convention for protecting state sovereignty by giving Congress only a limited set of enumerated powers was insufficient to secure the thing such a strategy would most need: a clear statement that the enumeration of powers was limiting.

Capacity

Another reason the delegates had for wanting to articulate limits on the national government's legislative jurisdiction is less intuitive to modern Americans. Its root was a fear not of too much governance but of too little.

The United States in 1787 was an enormous country, with a growing population spread along more than a thousand miles of seaboard and hundreds of miles into the interior. It was not realistic, many Framers reasoned, for a single legislature to provide for such a diverse and extensive polity. The country needed governmental action: commerce had to be fostered and regulated, roads and canals had to be built, and so on. If Congress had the responsibility for all the necessary legislation, a great deal would be left undone. No single legislature could have the time and information necessary for attending to all these matters. Lacking real acquaintance with the needs of all of the country's far-flung localities, Congress would often fail to provide the governance America required.[42]

A comment at the Convention by Connecticut's Oliver Ellsworth exemplifies this concern. As Madison recorded the comment, Ellsworth said that "[w]hat he wanted was domestic happiness. The Nat[iona]l Gov[ernmen]t could not descend to the local objects on which this depended."[43] The rendering of Ellsworth's comment in Robert Yates's notes is even more suggestive:

> I want domestic happiness, as well as general security. A general government will never grant me this, as it cannot know my wants or relieve my distress. My state is only as one out of thirteen. Can they, the general government, gratify my wishes? My happiness depends as much on the existence of my state government, as a new-born infant depends upon its mother for nourishment.[44]

The concern here is not with limiting the power of government, lest too much power be a threat to liberty. The concern is with making sure that government is sufficiently active, attentive, and supportive to supply the conditions for a flourishing life. The language of "nourishment" and the analogy to an infant depending on its mother could hardly be more powerful on this point. The threat to be addressed is not intrusion but neglect.

To a modern constitutional lawyer, this concern does not call for limiting the powers of Congress. Modern Americans know that what Congress leaves undone can be done by state and local governments. The system operates, as a general matter, on the basis of concurrent jurisdiction, meaning that in most areas of domestic policy the state legislatures and Congress are simultaneously competent to regulate. So if Congress fails to attend to some important need particular to people in Connecticut, Connecticut can take appropriate measures by itself. But in 1787, many of the Framers either did not grasp or else actively were skeptical of concurrent jurisdiction. According to a commonly held view, Congress and the state legislatures needed to regulate separate and nonoverlapping policy domains.[45] Within that framework, assigning domains of legislation to Congress meant preempting state legislation. And on that understanding, giving Congress more responsibility than it could handle was dangerous, because whatever Congress failed to do would simply go undone.

Modern Americans often neglect this aspect of the Framers' worldview. Working from the premise that the primary role of the Constitution is to limit governmental action, many intuitively think that the point of confining Congress's powers to certain domains is to prevent Congress from overregulating. But the Framers were not primarily worried about overregulation. They were more worried about *underregulation*. The general government they knew was too weak, not too strong, and their project was to enable it to do more. And they needed to be careful, lest their design of a more powerful general government inadvertently compound the underregulation problem by stripping local officials of the authority they would need to manage all the public affairs that Congress, as a practical matter, would not be able to address. To the extent that the Framers envisioned only one government being responsible for any given policy domain, they needed to avoid assigning too many domains to Congress—not for fear that Congress would do too much but for fear it would do too little and that the states would be legally barred from picking up the slack. Enumerating specific domains of congressional legislation might have seemed like a way to address this problem.

If measured by this purpose, the Convention's choice to enumerate specific powers of Congress should be deemed a success. For more or less the Constitution's first century, the laws whose constitutionality the judiciary measured by reference to Article I, Section 8, were usually not federal laws. They were *state* laws, and the question was whether the relevant state had legislated in an area of congressional jurisdiction—most commonly under the Commerce Clause—and therefore, on the separate-spheres model, an area in which state law was preempted even if congressional power lay dormant.[46] By construing the Commerce Clause narrowly, nineteenth-century courts preserved the ability of state governments to regulate at a time when Congress lacked the will and the resources to do so in any comprehensive way.

But this approach to Congress's enumerated powers would also make it logical for courts to give congressional legislation a strong presumption of constitutionality. The problem to be solved, after all, is not that Congress might regulate things it should not. It is that Congress might fail to act in areas where it is the only authorized lawmaker. Where Congress has in fact regulated, thus obviating the risk that nobody will regulate, the courts can sustain Congress's regulation.

So consider what might happen over time if Americans became more interested in having an active national legislature and congressional capacity increased. As Congress gradually pushed its legislation into more and more areas, judicial willingness to sustain the things Congress did would yield a significantly expanded sense of what Congress's enumerated powers included. As judicial legitimations of federal laws multiplied, it would become harder and harder to articulate plausible distinctions between the purported sphere of Congress and that of the states, thus putting pressure on the idea that Congress and the states occupy separate regulatory spheres. That pressure could be relieved by adjusting to the idea of concurrent jurisdiction: why exactly, we now say, can Congress and the states not regulate in the same domains? And once we adjust to the idea of concurrent jurisdiction, preserving the states' capacity to regulate where needed would no longer require courts to articulate Congress's legislative jurisdiction as if it occupied only specific slices of the social world. Which is more or less what happened.[47]

⋖⋯⊱⋗⋖⋯⊱⋗

Enumerating the powers of Congress was a logical tool for some purposes and a less logical tool for others. It made sense as a means for empowering the general government. It also made sense as a means for ensuring that Congress rather than the president would wield an important suite of powers. It made less sense as a tool for limiting the general government as a whole. This is not to say that it was useless for that limiting purpose. But given the reasons why many of the Framers wanted to limit the general government, it fit less well than strategies based on external limits and process limits. And in the domain where enumerating congressional powers made the most sense as a way of articulating limits on federal governance—that of preserving the authority of state governments to provide needed regulation that Congress could not possibly provide—the relevant limits could be relaxed as the federal government's practical capacity for governance increased, and also as the legal system adjusted to the idea of concurrent jurisdiction.

That a tool is poorly suited for a given task does not prove that it was not in fact chosen for that task. So the fact that the enumeration of powers made more sense for empowering Congress than for limiting the general government does not prove that the Framers saw the enumeration as a technology of empowerment rather than one of limitation. In fact, the Framers thought about the enumeration of powers both ways, with different people among them emphasizing different aspects of what the enumeration might do—and sometimes with the same people emphasizing different aspects at different times. But even if considering what the enumeration of congressional powers was and was not well suited to do cannot answer the question of why that enumeration appears in the Constitution, it can reframe the inquiry. If we read the history of the Constitution's drafting through the assumption that the enumeration is a means toward limiting federal power, we are likely to construe the source material in ways that confirm that assumption. If instead we recognize that, on a logic available to the Framers, enumerating congressional powers made a lot of sense as a means toward a different set of ends, we will be more open to readings of the source material that place empowerment rather than limitation at the center of the project. This chapter's discussion of what the enumeration of powers was more and less likely to be useful for is thus an important bit of orienting context for Chapter 3, which narrates the Convention's work.

Understanding that the enumeration of powers made more sense as a means of empowering Congress than as a means of limiting federal governance is also important for a second reason—one that is separate from any attempt to establish the relative weights of the Framers' various motives in enumerating congressional powers. Enumerationism relies on an idea about what the enumeration of powers is *for*. Given how little the enumeration does in practice to limit the scope of modern federal governance, it is conventional to think that the enumeration, in the modern world, does not do the thing that it is supposed to do. But if we can see that even at the Framing it made sense to give a different answer to the question of what the enumeration was for, we will be able to see that in fact the enumeration does plenty of work in the modern regime and indeed that the work it does is broadly consistent with a set of purposes that were, in 1787, good reasons—indeed, the best reasons— for enumerating congressional powers. The enumeration authorizes the general government to exercise power, and within the general government it assigns particular powers to Congress rather than the president.

It would be wrong to think that the Framers enumerated congressional powers to empower Congress and not at all to limit the general government. But it is crucial to grasp the logic of the empowerment perspective. Whether or not we can say how much each perspective contributed to the shaping of the enumeration, we can notice that, as things have turned out, the enumeration has worked better as a technology for empowering Congress than as a technology for limiting federal power. The more we recognize that the enumeration always made more sense as a technology of empowerment, the more we will be able to see the way the system has operated in practice not as a pathology to be corrected but as a sensible playing out of the constitutional design.

―◂― CHAPTER THREE ―▸―

THE CONVENTION

WRITING ABOUT WHAT HAPPENED inside the "General Convention" of 1787 is a task to be approached with caution. There is no transcript of the proceedings. Unlike some public meetings of that era, the Convention did not have a designated shorthand reporter. There was an official journal, but it recorded events sparingly, making note mostly of votes taken. Most of the available evidence of what transpired comes from notes and diaries written by specific delegates.[1] Madison's journal—published more than half a century after the Convention—is the most famous source, and it has been influential. But neither Madison's journal nor any of the other diaries is close to comprehensive.[2] Nor is any of them fully reliable. Each source is the report of one interested party. Moreover, even delegates recording the proceedings in good faith were liable to mischaracterize the ideas of their fellow delegates from time to time, if only because people in large group conversations do not always thoroughly understand the complex thoughts other people are trying to convey.

In 1911, the historian Max Farrand published his *Records of the Federal Convention of 1787*, an impressive set of volumes that tried to compile the existing source material about the Convention into a single comprehensive whole. More than a century later, Farrand's *Records* remains a tremendously valuable resource. Indeed, as a matter of common practice, lawyers and others often treat Farrand's *Records* as if it were an official and reliable account of the body's proceedings. But Farrand's *Records* is simply a compilation of the Convention's journal and various surviving diaries, so it is only as reliable as its underlying sources. Moreover, the sources in Farrand's compilation only describe things that happened when the delegates sat as one general body. Much of the Convention's most important work happened in smaller committees, and what happened in those settings is even more elusive.

It does not follow that no responsible assertions can be made about what happened inside the Convention. But any claims should be tempered by an awareness of the limits of what the sources can demonstrate. It makes more sense to look for the larger themes of substantive arguments than to focus on particular words the sources attribute to delegates. It also makes sense to treat reports corroborated by other sources of evidence as more likely to be credible, as when the description of someone's argument is substantially similar in more than one delegate's recounting.

In this chapter, I present a perspective on the delegates' view of the enumeration of congressional powers, and I seek to do so in a way that respects the limits of what can be known about their deliberations. The perspective has both a critical argument and a constructive one. Critically, I seek to show problems with the standard enumerationist narrative of the Convention, on which the delegates saw the enumeration of congressional powers as a central mechanism for limiting the general government. Constructively, I seek to show that the Convention's orientation was considerably more nationalist and centralizing than the normal wisdom allows.

An appreciation for the delegates' nationalism makes it easier to see their enumeration of congressional powers as a mechanism for empowering Congress. It also makes it easier to see that at least some of the delegates expected Congress to be able to exercise powers not enumerated in the Constitution's text. To be sure, the text they adopted did not negate the possibility of an enumerationist reading. But it also did not demand such a reading. Indeed, it is likely that the Constitution was deliberately written to permit either interpretation. Once that ambiguity is visible, it is easy to see that the Convention wrote a Constitution that would support a more powerful general government than the standard enumerationist story admits. This is not to suggest that everyone at the Convention took the same view of congressional power, nor that everyone was equally enthusiastic about a robust national government. But the balance of opinion lay more toward the nationalist end of the spectrum than the received memory of constitutional lawyers generally recognizes, and the Convention's work product makes the most sense when understood against that background.

Below, I briefly describe the standard narrative about enumerated powers at the Convention, point out some of its problems, and sketch an alternative perspective. Then, at greater length, I canvass historical evidence from the Convention, working chronologically through the summer of 1787, to show that my perspective is well grounded in the primary sources.

The Standard Narrative and Its Problems

The standard narrative explaining how the General Convention arrived at its allocation of powers to Congress goes something like this:

The Framers were committed to creating a federal government that would pursue only a limited set of projects.[3] Early in the Convention's proceedings, the Virginia delegation called for a national legislature with the power "to legislate in all cases to which the separate States are incompetent," but that proposal did not mean that the general government would actually be authorized to legislate on the basis of so broad a principle. Virginia's proposal, known as Resolution VI, was a generally worded placeholder to be used until a more specific list of powers could be crafted.[4] From the beginning, it was clear that delegates wanted to limit Congress to a set of enumerated powers. The specification of those powers was deferred until the delegates could settle fundamental issues about the structure and composition of Congress. The work of specification fell in the first instance to the five-member Committee of Detail, which turned the Convention's agreed-upon principles and compromises into a draft for a written constitution. In keeping with the general understanding that Congress would have enumerated powers only, the Committee of Detail's draft duly replaced the broad language of Resolution VI with a list of particular powers.[5] With a bit of tinkering, that list became Article I, Section 8, as we know it. The delegates later emphasized the importance of having given Congress a closed list of specific powers when they overwhelmingly rejected proposals to include a bill of rights within the Constitution.[6] Including a bill of rights would imply that Congress had the power to act except where it was affirmatively restrained.[7] The deliberate omission of a bill of rights, the standard narrative concludes, reflected the importance that the Convention attached to preserving the principle—central to the system's design—that Congress could act only on the basis of its textually enumerated powers.[8]

This narrative has problems. Consider these four.

First, the surviving records of the Convention do not support the claim that Virginia's Resolution VI, when introduced and adopted, was understood as contemplating a limiting enumeration of congressional powers rather than a more broadly empowered national legislature. The resolution's language about power "to legislate in all cases to which the separate States are incompetent" is certainly open to the latter interpretation. Yes, some delegates responded to the introduction of Resolution VI by calling for—as Madison recorded the demand—"an exact enumeration of the powers comprehended by this definition."[9] But their doing so likely reflected an awareness that the resolution was most naturally read as calling for something else. Moreover, according to Madison's journal and the notes of Georgia's William Pierce, other delegates responded to the demand for enumeration not by saying that Resolution VI was just a temporary placeholder but by arguing that it would be difficult or even impossible to list all the powers Congress should have.[10] There is certainly no indication that the delegates voted to construe Resolution VI as calling for a limiting enumeration. Nor do the records suggest that the delegates reached an informal agreement to that effect before approving the resolution. So although it is plausible that some delegates understood Resolution VI as contemplating a limited enumeration—or wanted it to be understood that way—it seems unlikely that the Convention as a whole understood the resolution in that manner.[11]

A second problem concerns the Committee of Detail's mandate. The approved resolutions that the Convention charged the committee with turning into a draft constitution included not Resolution VI as originally introduced but an enhanced version adopted several weeks later. According to that enhanced version, Congress would be empowered to legislate not only "in those Cases to which the States are separately incompetent" but also "in all Cases for the general Interests of the Union."[12] Those formulas do not seem to call for a constitution that limits Congress to a list of specific projects. In the end, it is the Constitution rather than its drafting history that is the supreme law, so if the Constitution contradicts the resolutions given to the Committee of Detail, the Constitution prevails. But no scholar has produced a persuasive, evidence-based account establishing how and when (let alone why) the Committee of Detail discarded its instructions, nor why the Convention acquiesced and accepted a Constitution characterized by a limiting enumeration, rather than one enabling Congress to legislate in the broad national-interest way that the final version of Resolution VI envisioned.[13] The standard account of the limiting enumeration must say either that the approved resolution actually meant less than it seems to or else that the Convention reversed itself without leaving a record of when or why. Perhaps some such explanation is correct—the records of the Convention are incomplete, after all. But it will not do to say things like, "Well, the fact that they wrote a limiting enumeration shows that they must have changed their minds." Whether the enumeration was written to be limiting is precisely the question.

A third problem concerns the idea that the Framers omitted a bill of rights from their draft Constitution because they trusted the enumeration of congressional powers to limit the national government. As noted earlier, that story was invented after the fact. During the ratification process, the Constitution's critics charged that the lack of a bill of rights was a serious flaw. To defend the Constitution against that objection, some of the Constitution's defenders hit on the idea of arguing that the absence of a bill of rights was a *virtue*, if only one understood the genius of what the Convention had done. The public did not buy this argument: as often happens, the audience recognized an ex post rationalization for what it was, and the demand for a bill of rights continued unabated.[14] Today, of course, constitutional lawyers commonly accept the rationalization as if it were fact. But that just means that the Constitution's supporters managed to fool future generations on this point, despite failing to fool their contemporaries.

A fourth problem is a fact about what is missing from the Constitution that the Convention drafted. For several reasons, including their initial discussion of Resolution VI, the delegates knew that some among them affirmatively wanted a national government not confined by a set of enumerated powers.[15] They knew, therefore, that the question of whether the government would be confined to the enumerated powers was a live issue rather than something that could be taken for granted. Indeed, the delegates knew that the Constitution they approved contained an ambiguous clause that could easily be read to support the idea that the national government had powers beyond those enumerated.[16] So it is noteworthy that the delegates did not take the simple step of writing a clause that would settle the question. "This government shall have only the powers enumerated in this document" is not a hard sentence to formulate, and nothing like it appears in the document the Convention wrote. (Given the powerful impulse to make the Constitution enumerationist, many lawyers since the 1990s have argued that Article I's Vesting Clause is such a sentence. But it is not, and the Framers did not think it was.[17]) When the draft Constitution was presented to the public, people immediately recognized that the Framers had not included such a provision.[18] If the Convention had been intent all along on confining Congress to a set of textually enumerated powers, it is hard to fathom why they risked being misunderstood by leaving the point unstated.

None of these problems necessarily falsifies the standard account. Perhaps one could produce plausible arguments explaining each problem away, especially if the problems were taken one by one. But sometimes the accumulation of problems with a narrative is a sign that something about that narrative is wrong.

A better understanding of the Convention's attitude toward congressional power would begin with the point that the Framers' animating aim was the creation of a more powerful general government. Not everyone at the Convention was equally enthusiastic about that project, but many were strongly committed to it. Within that project, the enumeration of congressional powers was an important technology of empowerment. It empowered the general government relative to the states, and within the general government it empowered Congress relative to the president. Without a doubt, the Framers understood that the more powerful Congress they were creating would need checks. But the checking mechanisms on which they rested most heavily had nothing to do with enumerated powers. They were the process limits built into the checks-and-balances system that the Convention spent most of the summer working out.

Again, it is not my claim that the Framers uniformly understood matters this way. There was a fair amount of disagreement among them. Like many documents that are written to be acceptable to people with differing views, the Constitution left important questions undecided. One of the things the Constitution's text did not decide was whether Congress would be limited to its textually enumerated powers (or, in a softer version, its textually enumerated powers and such other powers as were implied by the textual enumeration).

But if the resulting ambiguity left the way open for an enumerationist interpretation, it also left the way open for nonenumerationist interpretations—and not by accident.

◄◄··►►◄◄··►►

The following discussion divides the work of the Convention into five chronological phases. During the first phase, from May 29 to June 19, the Convention operated as one large working group—in the relevant parliamentary terminology, as "the Committee of the Whole." At the end of that phase, the delegates approved as their "committee report" a set of resolutions based on the Virginia Plan, Resolution VI included. During the second phase, from June 19 to July 26, the delegates sat "in Convention"—that is, as the body empowered to approve, modify, or reject the report of the Committee of the Whole. During that time, they agreed to the (so-called) Great Compromise between large and small states and approved the enhanced version of Resolution VI. In the third phase, from July 27 to August 3, the Committee of Detail turned the approved resolutions into a first draft of a written Constitution. During the fourth phase, from August 7 until early September, the Convention debated and modified that draft. And during the fifth phase, from September 8 until the Convention's adjournment on September 17, the Committee of Style produced the near-final text of the Constitution, and the Convention rejected a proposal to draft a bill of rights.

Phase 1: "In the Committee of the Whole"— the Virginia and New Jersey Plans

The Convention was supposed to open on May 14, 1787. But there was no quorum yet present in Philadelphia. Travel was slow. As of May 20, only Pennsylvania and Virginia had fielded complete delegations.[19] So while those present waited for a quorum, several Virginia and Pennsylvania delegates formed a working group to prepare a proposal.[20] On May 29, in the Convention's first substantive working session, Virginia Governor Edmund Randolph presented that proposal, which came to be known as the Virginia Plan, in the form of fifteen resolutions describing a new system of government.

Those resolutions structured the delegates' conversation for the next two months, and the first draft of the Constitution would be written based on the Virginia Plan's vision.

A National Government

The Virginia Plan proposed to create a two-house Congress—Randolph called it a "National Legislature"—as well as a "National Executive" and a "National Judiciary." The National Legislature would have extensive powers. According to Resolution VI of the Virginia Plan, it would be authorized "to legislate in all cases to which the separate States are incompetent, or in which the harmony of the United States may be interrupted by the exercise of individual Legislation." Moreover, the National Legislature would have the power to veto state laws it deemed unconstitutional—in the words of the plan, "to negative all laws passed by the several States, contravening in the opinion of the National Legislature the articles of Union." And the National Legislature could "call forth the force of the Union against any member of the Union failing to fulfill its duty under the articles thereof."[21]

The Virginia Plan was a bold proposal to centralize governmental power. Indeed, some delegates seem to have wondered whether Randolph's proposal aimed at eliminating the state governments completely. According to both Madison and Maryland's James McHenry, South Carolina's Charles Pinckney on the next day asked Randolph whether his plan was intended to abolish the separate state governments.[22] Randolph said that it was not—just to empower the national one.[23] But it is not hard to understand why Pinckney and others might have thought it necessary to ask the question.[24] From their lived experience, modern Americans know that a vigorous United States government with the power to override state law can coexist with meaningful and permanent government at the state level. But such an arrangement was harder to imagine in advance. As noted earlier, many Americans in the 1780s found the idea of two governments exercising power within the same physical territory counterintuitive at best, unless one of those governments was merely the subordinate agent of the other. "[I]n all communities," Madison recorded Pennsylvania's Gouverneur Morris as declaring, "there must be one supreme power, and one only."[25] On the prevailing understanding of the then-operating Articles of Confederation, the states were sovereign entities, and the United States existed as a joint project among them, exercising only the powers granted by the states and subject to their authority. The delegates could imagine keeping that basic arrangement and delegating more powers to the general government, and they could also imagine flipping that arrangement and creating a sovereign national government that would dictate to the states. Harder for some of them to imagine was a system in which neither the states nor the general government would be fully the master of the other.[26]

Many delegates used the words "federal" and "national" to contrast the two visions of government just described. Thus, according to Madison, Morris told the Convention during the initial discussion of the Virginia Plan that he distinguished between a federal government, meaning one in which the states had only good-faith obligations to cooperate, and a national government, meaning one in which a supreme central authority could compel states to obey.[27] The Convention delegates did not always distinguish the terms "federal" and "national" in this way: fifty-five different people rarely all use the same terms for any set of concepts.[28] But to the extent that Virginia's delegates thought in these dichotomous terms, the Virginia Plan's use of the word "National" suggested which structure its authors preferred.

To Enumerate or Not to Enumerate?

The possibility of enumerating congressional powers came to the foreground the next day when the delegates, working methodically through the Virginia Plan's resolutions, reached Resolution VI. According to Madison, three South Carolina delegates expressed concern. Charles Pinckney and John Rutledge cautioned that the proposal to give the national legislature the power to legislate in all cases where the states separately were "incompetent" was vague, such that they could not decide whether to support it without seeing "an exact enumeration of the powers comprehended by this definition."[29] Pierce Butler worried aloud that Resolution VI would empower Congress too broadly: he feared, in Madison's rendering, that the Resolution was too "extreme in taking away the powers of the States."[30]

The South Carolinians who pushed here for an enumeration of powers were not, for the most part, hostile to powerful national governance. Rutledge was the least enthusiastic, but Pinckney would later move that Congress be given an unlimited power to veto state laws, and Butler would pronounce himself open to eliminating the state legislatures entirely, if a satisfactory system for representation in Congress were established.[31] So their interest in

greater clarity about what Congress would be empowered to do was probably not motivated by a general commitment to limiting national power. As
noted earlier, it is more likely that the South Carolina delegation was animated by a more particular concern: ensuring that Congress could not interfere with slavery.

The other delegates chose to duck the South Carolinians' probable (and
potentially inflammatory) motivation and instead continue the conversation
at the more abstract level. According to Georgia's William Pierce, several
delegates argued that for the time being the Convention should confine itself
to general principles, leaving further specification for later.[32] But some delegates also expressed views about what such further specification might ultimately look like. According to Madison, Randolph again gave assurances
about the status of state governments under the Virginia Plan, "disclaim[ing]
any intention to give indefinite powers to the national Legislature."[33] Several
other key delegates, however, expressed doubts about the feasibility of limiting the national government by enumerating Congress's powers. According to Georgia's William Pierce, Roger Sherman of Connecticut commented
that it would be "hard to define all the powers [of Congress] by detail";
Pennsylvania's James Wilson said that "it would be impossible to enumerate
the powers which the federal Legislature ought to have"; and Madison pronounced himself "convinced it could not be done."[34]

Madison's formulation of his idea is worth some attention. In line with
the perspective he had offered to Caleb Wallace two years earlier, Madison
recorded himself doubting the practicability of exhaustively enumerating
legislative powers:

> Mr. Madison said that he had brought with him into the Convention a
> strong bias in favor of an enumeration and definition of the powers neces-
> sary to be exercised by the national Legislature; but had also brought
> doubts concerning its practicability. His wishes remained unaltered; but his
> doubts had become stronger. What his opinion might ultimately be he
> could not yet tell. But he should shrink from nothing which should be
> found essential to such a form of Govt. as would provide for the safety, lib-
> erty and happiness of the community.[35]

Madison did not specify the reason for his initial "bias" in favor of enumerating and defining the powers of Congress. If we impute to Madison the

standard thinking in modern constitutional law, we would assume he meant to say that he was favorably disposed toward *limiting* Congress by enumerating and defining its powers. Maybe that is what he meant—but the assumption that he should be read that way might be too quick. Enumerating a legislature's powers can be a tool for empowering that legislature rather than (or in addition to) a tool for limiting it. As noted earlier, defining a legislature's powers (rather than stating them only at the level of general principles) can help prevent people opposed to that legislature's exercising power from construing its power too narrowly. If you know that your authority to do something will be challenged, you are better off if your power to act is stated with specificity.

For three reasons, it makes sense to think that Madison in the spring of 1787 was thinking of enumeration mostly as a technology of empowerment. First, Madison had cautioned Wallace against trying to use an enumeration of powers to limit a legislature. If Madison was skeptical of enumerating powers as a means limiting legislatures, it might not make sense to think that his "strong bias" in favor of enumerating congressional powers was motivated by a desire to limit that body. Second, Madison's major objective in 1787 was to invigorate the national government. So a bias in favor of enumeration would make sense if enumeration were a technology of empowerment. Third, the terms in which Madison articulated his remark make at least as much sense on the understanding that enumerating Congress's powers is chiefly a mechanism for ensuring that Congress is adequately empowered as on the understanding that enumerationism is chiefly a technology of limitation. A straightforward reason for having "a strong bias in favor of an enumeration and definition of the powers *necessary* to be exercised by the national Legislature" is to make sure that the powers Congress *needs* are clearly specified as belonging to Congress.[36] Perhaps Madison reasoned that the general government would need to do certain things and that if those things were not unambiguously within its authority, there would be a risk that a general statement like that in Resolution VI would be construed narrowly, thus depriving the general government of powers it would need. If that framework captures Madison's thinking, then the passage above should be understood like this: Madison wanted to ensure adequate power in the national government. He doubted that goal could be achieved by enumerating and defining the government's powers, because something necessary would always be left out. But he intended to remain open to any solution that would make the government adequately powerful, powerful enough to "provide for the safety, liberty and happiness of the community"—whether that involved an enumeration of powers or not.

I offer no firm view on whether Madison, in these remarks, conceived of enumerating congressional powers more as a mechanism of empowerment than as a mechanism of limitation. Given the limited evidence, it is hard to reach either conclusion with certainty. But in the course of the discussion, the delegates approved an amendment to Resolution VI that tracks the idea of enumeration as a mechanism for making sure that the general government could do the things it needed to do, rather than as a means of limitation. At the recommendation of Benjamin Franklin, the delegates added language to Resolution VI indicating that Congress should have the power to invalidate state laws violating treaties with foreign countries.[37] The problem of states violating treaties was one of the pressing matters that made the Convention necessary. On one reading of Madison's remarks, he had cautioned that even if a full enumeration of Congress's powers was impractical, it would be important to specify affirmatively those powers that Congress absolutely must have, lest those powers be denied to Congress through unduly narrow constructions of grants of power that were more generally phrased. The power to invalidate state laws contravening treaties with foreign countries was of the highest importance, and it concerned a matter on which the states would be unlikely to acquiesce in the national government's exercise of power unless it were specified clearly. So it would make sense to enumerate that power, lest its validity be denied.

To judge by the votes taken at the end of the conversation, the delegates were generally satisfied with the Virginia Plan's broad formulation of congressional power. South Carolina joined every other state but Connecticut in voting to approve the portion of Resolution VI that proposed a national legislature with the power to legislate in all cases in which the separate states would be incompetent. (Connecticut's delegation was internally divided and cast no vote.) With no recorded disagreement, the delegates also approved the portions of Resolution VI giving Congress the power to legislate where necessary to preserve the harmony of the Union and the power to invalidate unconstitutional state laws, including laws contravening treaties. In short, all of Resolution VI was adopted, with no state voting in opposition to any portion of it.[38]

The Status of States

The records of the delegates' conversations in the succeeding weeks do not reflect much discussion of particular congressional powers, nor of whether those powers should be enumerated. Having agreed to a national legislature empowered as described in Resolution VI, they turned their attention to the national executive and the national judiciary. When the discussion returned to Congress, the focus was not on what powers Congress would have but on how the institution should be structured and how its members would be chosen. But although those discussions did not directly address what powers Congress would have, they reveal a fair amount about the delegates' attitudes toward the underlying issue of the relationship between the general government and the states. And it is worth noticing the degree to which Convention delegates expressed strongly nationalist attitudes.

Consider a suggestion by Delaware's George Read. During a discussion about whether the lower house of Congress should be chosen directly by citizen voters or by the state legislatures, Read proposed that the election should be direct because the state legislatures should be completely dissolved.[39] The proposal was radical, but Read wasn't the only delegate willing to entertain the possibility. According to Massachusetts's Rufus King, Butler pronounced himself open to Read's suggestion, if the Convention could work out a satisfactory structure for representation in the national government.[40]

To be sure, even the Convention's strongest nationalists rarely went that far, and some may have thought it necessary to distance themselves from Read's suggestion. Consider Wilson, who was heart and soul for a strong national government. According to both Madison and King, Wilson spoke after Read and said he saw no reason why creating a strong central government should require the elimination of the state governments. On the contrary, he said, the state governments should be maintained, and he believed that the state and national governments could coexist without conflict. That could be done, Wilson said, so long as the state governments were limited to appropriate local purposes.[41]

Wilson's position was more moderate than Read's. Note, however, how far it was from the idea that would eventually become orthodox in constitutional law, according to which the appropriate domains of federal and state jurisdiction are preserved by limiting the *federal* government to a set of distinctively appropriate purposes. According to that orthodoxy, the federal government acts within its distinctively allocated sphere—that of its enumerated powers—while the states enjoy general and residual authority. Wilson seems to have offered the opposite picture: a national government with broad legislative power and state governments limited to particular concerns.

There is no record of an adverse reaction to Wilson's remarks among the other delegates. Hamilton recorded a relevant comment by Virginia's George Mason—who would eventually become one of the era's most stalwart defenders of state prerogatives—but Mason's point was not that Wilson had things backwards.[42] Instead, Mason (in Hamilton's rendering) noted that if a national government were formed, the natural course of events would shift the most important concerns to its decisionmakers, with the result that talent would flow to the national government rather than to the states. It would therefore make sense not to expect the state governments to do very much.[43] Like Wilson, Mason was contemplating an arrangement in which the states, not the nation, had the smaller footprint.

The next day, Mason explained that he did think the state governments would still have an essential role, even if the largest responsibilities moved to the center. His reason was practical. The United States was an enormous country, Mason reminded his colleagues, and he considered it impossible for one legislature to attend adequately to the needs of its far-flung parts. Madison rendered Mason's point as follows: "[W]hatever power may be necessary for the Nat[iona]l Gov[ernmen]t a certain portion must necessarily be left in the States [because it] is impossible for one power to pervade the extreme parts of the U.S. so as to carry equal justice to them."[44] State-level governance was needed to ensure that the work of government did not go undone. So, given that talent would naturally flow to the center, some measures had to be taken to prevent the state governments from withering away. To that end, Mason now argued that the upper house of the National Legislature—the Senate—should be selected by the state legislatures. That would keep the state legislatures relevant.[45]

Two things are worth noting about Mason's ideas here. The first is that his argument for maintaining the state governments tracked the limited-national-capacity rationale for enumerating powers. Mason did not argue that the existing states were sovereign or that governance from the center would be oppressive or corrupt. He argued that governance from the center would be inadequate because one central legislature could never have the information and capacity necessary to govern a country as large and diverse as the United States. Maintaining more localized legislatures would accordingly be crucial not as a way of checking national power but as a way of ensuring that the country would not suffer from being governed too little. In a letter to his son written from Philadelphia, Mason sounded the same theme: given the "difficulty in organizing a government upon this great scale," he wrote, a system implementing the Virginia Plan (which at that point Mason favored) would need to find a way of "reserving to the State legislatures a sufficient portion of power for promoting and securing the prosperity and happiness of their respective citizens."[46] The concern was not with preventing the national government from doing things that it could in practice do; it was with keeping the state governments alive to deliver what only they could deliver.

The second thing worth noting is that Mason's suggested method for preserving meaningful governance at the state level was a matter of structure and process, not a substantive limit on the powers Congress would exercise. That choice makes sense given the concern Mason was articulating: that localities' needs for governance might go unmet by a Congress too remote and too limited in capacity to address all of the country's concerns. If Mason had been concerned to limit the scope of national governance as such, he might have proposed either internal or external limits on the powers of Congress. He might have said that Congress should be able to do only a few strictly defined things, thus ensuring that state legislatures would remain the primary forums for governmental decisionmaking. Or he might have proposed that certain policy domains be off limits to Congress, thus ensuring meaningful business for the states to do. The available sources do not record his doing either of those things, and it makes sense that he would not have. Only the day before, Mason had noted that it would make sense for the national government to make most of the country's important decisions, because the national government would attract more talent than the state governments would. In that light, Mason's suggestion that the state governments be kept relevant through a process mechanism rather than by limiting what Congress could do makes a great deal of sense.

The Congressional Veto

The Virginia Plan proposed to give Congress the power to veto state laws that violated the Constitution. For some delegates, such a veto power would not go far enough. On June 8, Pinckney moved to expand the scope of the veto power so that Congress could nullify any state laws it thought improper, whether on constitutional grounds or others.[47] Madison vigorously seconded the motion. In his journal, Madison recorded himself reminding his colleagues that the states had a great propensity to act badly—toward the Union, toward each other, toward foreign countries, and toward weak parties within their own borders. That was why the Convention was necessary in the first place, and that was why Congress had to be able to veto state laws. And for the veto to be effective, Madison reasoned, it had to be general. If the veto were confined to specific cases—if Congress were authorized to veto unconstitutional state laws and laws contravening treaties but not other state laws—then every proposed congressional veto would become an occasion for disputing whether the state law in question was properly within the sphere of Congress's veto authority. States would insist that Congress had a mistaken interpretation of the Constitution or of the relevant treaties, such that the laws Congress purported to invalidate were valid despite Congress's disapproval.[48] In short, making the veto efficacious rather than simply inviting a further round of arguments about who had the authority to do what required giving Congress a general veto power, not one limited to a particular set of cases.

Madison's skepticism of a delimited veto cohered well with his skepticism toward enumerating Congress's legislative powers. In both instances, he resisted defining the cases in which Congress could act, because any enumeration of cases would leave out something that Congress should be able to do or, at the least, would be vulnerable to being interpreted that way. Others seem to have shared that perspective. According to both Madison and King, Wilson argued that it was better to give Congress discretion about when to exercise its negative than to empower states to insist that some of their laws were immune from congressional override.[49] That view would have been consistent with Wilson's earlier assertion that the state and national governments should be made compatible by confining the state governments—not the national government—to particular spheres of operation. Perhaps more interestingly, Madison's and King's notes suggest that Delaware's John Dickinson shared that view. When the Virginia Plan was first introduced, Dickinson had suggested that the Convention try to specify the particular powers the national legislature should have.[50] But by this point, he seems to have come to (or at least experimented with) a different approach. Supporting the

Pinckney/Madison motion to make Congress's veto general, Dickinson argued that it would not be possible to draw a line separating the legislative domains of the national and state governments. It followed that the Convention must take one risk or the other, lodging discretion with either the central authorities or the local ones. In keeping with the Convention's animating purpose of creating an effective general government, Dickinson reasoned that the greater threat was excessive state power, not excessive central power, and that discretion should lie with Congress. He understood, of course, that Congress was fallible and might exercise its discretion poorly. But that problem could be addressed with a process mechanism: given that members of Congress would be selected by the state legislatures in one house and by the people directly in the other, Congress would not be likely to act against the vital interests of the states.[51]

In the end, the delegates rejected the proposal to expand Congress's veto power over state laws.[52] But that decision may not have reflected the view that as a matter of principle the general government should not have broad power over the state governments. In substantial part, it may have reflected a concern among the small states that in practice, a veto would be wielded only against them, because the large states would be too powerful to be coerced. According to Hamilton, Delaware's Gunning Bedford expressed this point by saying that if South Carolina adopted a law, it wasn't going to give up that law except by force.[53] The example was surely not arbitrarily chosen. South Carolina was a rich state and, though not among the largest, not at all a small state, either. Its representatives had made clear that South Carolina had specific interests in slavery and in its export economy and that it would concede nothing on those matters. So Congress might in principle have the power to veto South Carolina's laws, but on any matter of importance South Carolina was not going to abide by such a veto, and the national government might not have the resources or the stomach to try to coerce it. Congress would understand that reality and, as a consequence, probably would not announce a veto against South Carolina in the first place. Where, though, would these dynamics leave a tiny state like Delaware, a state without the muscle or wealth or bellicose reputation that might deter a congressional veto? In light of that concern, it is not surprising that when the question was called, only the three largest states—Virginia, Massachusetts, and Pennsylvania—voted in favor of a general veto power.[54] Given the pattern of votes, it seems plausible that the proposal to expand Congress's veto power failed at least as much because of the concern about selective enforcement as because of any more abstract sense that the national government should not superintend local decisionmaking.

The New Jersey Plan

The scope of the veto was not the only issue that worried the small states during this phase of the proceedings. The greatest sticking point was the question of how to allocate representation in Congress. Delaware's representatives had instructions forbidding them to agree to any system in which different states would have different voting strength and early on informed the other delegates that any decision to the contrary might force them to leave the Convention.[55] And on the day after small-state opposition blocked the expansion of Congress's veto power, New Jersey's William Paterson argued against the Virginia Plan's proposal to allocate congressional representation based on population. According to Madison's notes, Paterson declared that any arrangement including proportional representation would make the United States a nation, not a confederacy, and was intolerable on that basis.[56] But a majority of the delegations apparently disagreed. On June 11, two days after Paterson's speech, the Convention approved the Virginia Plan's proposal to allocate representation in both houses of Congress on the basis of population.[57]

Different small-state delegates reacted to this setback in different ways. Delaware's Read once again argued for eliminating the states entirely.[58] Better to scrap the states, he may have reasoned, than to play the game as a weak one. Others set about a programmatic counteroffensive, drawing up a comprehensive alternative to the Virginia Plan—an alternative Paterson formally introduced to the Convention on June 15. Because Paterson represented New Jersey, that alternative is known as the New Jersey Plan. And the fate the New Jersey Plan would meet illustrates the commitment, among most of the delegations, to a robust national government. More specifically, it illustrates the understanding of at least some delegates that the national government proposed in the Virginia Plan would not be limited to enumerated powers.

Like the Virginia Plan, the New Jersey Plan called for strengthening the general government. But rather than speaking of a "national" legislature, executive, and judiciary, the New Jersey Plan called for what Madison termed a "purely federal" system.[59] In contrast to the Virginia Plan's broad Resolution

VI, the New Jersey Plan specified that Congress would be entitled to exercise the powers it had held under the Articles of Confederation and, in essence, just two others. First, Congress could raise revenue by imposing duties on imports, by a stamp tax on paper and related materials, and by postage fees for the services of the post office. There would be no general power of taxation. Second, Congress could make laws for the regulation of commerce. And crucially, the Congress invested with those powers would remain a one-house body in which each state would have one vote.[60]

At face value, the New Jersey Plan reflected a serious commitment to state sovereignty. Paterson had previously offered perhaps the Convention's strongest recorded paean to that idea, arguing, as he put it in his own notes, that "13 sovereign and independent States can never constitute one nation, and at the same Time be States."[61] Understood as an assertion of state sovereignty, the New Jersey Plan had two fundamental points, one about the scope of congressional power and one about voting power in Congress. On the former score, a Congress elected mostly by people outside New Jersey should not be able to bind New Jersey except on a limited set of questions New Jersey had expressly agreed to let Congress decide. On the latter score, in whatever decisions Congress was entitled to make, New Jersey should have equal dignity with every other represented entity.

That said, some delegates interpreted the New Jersey Plan less as a principled defense of state sovereignty than as a bargaining tactic aimed to extort concessions on the issue of representation. Dickinson—a small-state moderate—seems to have suggested as much privately to Madison. On the day the New Jersey Plan was presented, Madison recorded Dickinson's telling him that some of the small-state delegates were "friends to a good National Government" but could not agree to any system where they lacked equal voting power in at least one branch of the legislature, lest they "be thrown under the domination of the large states."[62] Pinckney put the point more acerbically. "[T]he whole comes to this," Madison recorded him as saying. "Give N. Jersey an equal vote, and she will dismiss her scruples, and concur in the Nati[onal] system."[63]

The records of the debate over the New Jersey Plan suggest that some and perhaps many delegates understood the Virginia Plan to call for a national legislature that would not be limited by a set of enumerated powers. Wilson, for example, gave a speech on June 16 in which, according to King's notes, he contrasted Resolution VI of the Virginia Plan's proposal for a

"Na[tiona]l Legis[lature] to legislate in national Cases" with the New Jersey
Plan's call for a Congress that would act only in "enumerated and partial Instances."[64] By describing the New Jersey Plan as an enumerated-powers-
only plan and pointing to that feature as a contrast with the Virginia Plan,
Wilson indicated his sense that Resolution VI was not merely a placeholder
for a set of enumerated powers to be named later. It was something genu-
inely different. The notes of several other delegates confirm King's account
of Wilson's speech. Hamilton, for example, recorded Wilson's contrasting
the Virginia Plan's vision of legislative power "in all matters of general Concern" with the New Jersey Plan's proposal for a Congress that would act only
on "partial objects."[65]

There is no record of anyone's disagreeing with Wilson on this point—no
one stepping forward to say that whatever differences there might be between the Virginia and New Jersey Plans, both envisioned a general government limited to enumerated powers. On the contrary, New York's John Lansing, who disagreed with Wilson about almost everything, described the
difference between the two plans in the same way. In a table written to track
Lansing's comparison of the two plans, King put "To possess enumerated
powers" in the New Jersey Plan's column.[66] The contrast, in Madison's rendering of Lansing's remarks, was with the Virginia Plan's proposal for a legislature that "absorbs all power except what may be exercised in the little
local matters of the States."[67] To be sure, the fact that Wilson and Lansing
described the contrast between the plans this way does not mean that everyone else saw things the same way. But Wilson and Lansing did not agree on
much. And the fact that there is no record of anyone's disputing their shared
characterization of the difference between the two plans, and on so fundamental a point, suggests that their views were not idiosyncratic.

On June 19, the delegates rejected the New Jersey Plan by a vote of seven
states to three. The only dissenting delegations were New Jersey, Delaware,
and New York—two small states and a medium-sized state whose one nationalist delegate (Hamilton) was outvoted by two of the Convention's most
extreme antinationalists (Lansing and Yates). By the same margin, the delegates adopted the Virginia Plan, as modified in the course of the debates, as
the official report of the Committee of the Whole.[68] That "national" plan,
characterized by people on both sides of the debate as calling for something
more than a Congress with enumerated powers, would be the basis for the
next phase of the proceedings.

Phase 2: "In Convention"—the Great Compromise and
the Bedford Resolution

With the adoption of the Virginia Plan as the official report of the Committee of the Whole, the delegates changed the procedural posture of their sessions and began to meet "In Convention"—that is, as the body empowered to make final decisions rather than as a preliminary working group.[69] Treating the report as if it were the product of any other committee, the Convention went through it from the beginning, debating and voting on each provision. That meant that everyone would get a second crack at each of the major issues, including the question of what powers Congress would wield and the question of how representation would be allocated.

Famously, the representation issue was readjudicated in this second phase. The defeat of the New Jersey Plan had not reconciled the small states to proportional representation. After weeks of wrangling, the Convention agreed to what Americans would later call the Great Compromise, by which representation would be based on population in the House of Representatives but each state would have the same representation in the Senate. The civic culture largely celebrates this arrangement. As the name "Great Compromise" suggests, the received impression is one of statesmanship, on which each side recognized the legitimate claims of the other. That impression bolsters the sense that the Framers thought of state sovereignty as a fundamental precept—one that small-state delegates insisted on for good reason and that large-state delegates accepted as deserving of accommodation. And the idea that the Framers took state sovereignty seriously helps support the enumerationist understanding of the Convention's project. After all, the more respect the Framers had for the idea of the states as separate sovereigns, the less willing they would have been to create a genuine national government whose powers might exceed a specific set of delegations from the states.

That line of thinking is badly flawed. By and large, the compromise did not reflect respect for the idea of state sovereignty. It merely reflected the ability of the small states, as a matter of hardball politics, to extort a concession that large-state delegates believed to be unjust, unprincipled, and secured in bad faith. Indeed, after the Convention acquiesced in the small states' demand for state-based representation, the states that had most insistently proclaimed the value of state sovereignty became strikingly nationalistic.

Once the small states secured their voting power in Congress, Delaware pro-
posed and New Jersey supported a modification to Resolution VI giving
Congress the power "to legislate in all cases for the general interests of the
Union."[70] The Convention adopted the change. Exactly what that language
might cover could be debated, but it is hard to read it as contemplating a
Congress empowered to legislate in enumerated cases only.

Skepticism about State Sovereignty

When the delegates began their deliberations "In Convention," the first order of business was to return to Resolution I of the Virginia Plan, which
called for a "national government." According to Madison, Yates, and King,
Wilson explained that he did not envision a national government that eliminated the states; he wanted the national and state governments to coexist.
But rather than seeing the states as quasi-independent entities, he analo-
gized them to administrative departments within an empire.[71] Madison recorded Hamilton as taking a similar view, on which the state governments
could helpfully continue as subordinate jurisdictions. What they should not
have, Hamilton explained, was the ability to make policy that the national
government could not overrule. The national legislature should have general
legislative authority, and the states would administer that authority and
perhaps fill in gaps where the vast extent of the country made it impracticable for the center to legislate as needed for local conditions.[72]

This vision of the state governments as regional outposts of the general
government may have discomfited some of the delegates, persuading them
that perhaps it was not such a good idea to call the new government "national" after all. On the next day, Connecticut's Oliver Ellsworth proposed to
amend Resolution I so that instead of speaking of "a national government . . .
consisting of a Supreme Legislative, Judiciary, and Executive," it would speak
of a "Government of the United States," consisting of those three institutions.[73] Not a "national government" and not a "federal" one—just this particular government, without the baggage that either adjective might carry.
According to Madison, "Mr. Randolph did not object to the change of expression, but apprised the gentleman who wished for it that he did not admit it for the reasons assigned."[74] In other words, Randolph—the official
sponsor of the Virginia Plan—was not inclined to fight about the wording,
but he wanted to make clear that in agreeing to a change in terminology he

was not making concessions at the level of substance. With Randolph's bless-
ing clearing the way, the Convention unanimously adopted the change.[75]
And consistently with Randolph's caveat, the delegates most leery of centralized power were skeptical that the change of labels would matter. According
to Yates, Lansing charged that the way that Wilson, Hamilton, and others
were describing the proposed arrangement illustrated only too well that a
government based on the Virginia Plan would have no place for real state
governments.[76]

The Virginia Plan's supporters offered a range of responses. Mason, who
had earlier explained why he thought it important to keep the state governments operating even if the most consequential decisionmaking was moved
to the center, asserted that it was no part of his thinking to annihilate the
states. But he did not back away from the view that a strong national government was essential, and he wanted to be clear—or at least Madison's notes
record him as wanting to be clear—that he regarded the republican creden-
tials of the general government to be as strong as those of the local governments. According to Madison, Mason emphasized that vesting power in the
national government was not taking power away from the people. It was merely
transferring power from one set of the people's representatives to another
set. Also according to Madison, Mason in his remarks continued to speak of
a "national Government," notwithstanding the Convention's agreement to
drop that term from the official resolution.[77] Madison himself seems to have
gone at least as far: according to his own notes, he was willing to entrust the
national government with the question of how much power it should exercise. A general government with "indefinite" (that is, general) legislative power,
he ventured, would not take away power from the local governments except
to the extent that doing so was good for the people, just as state governments
do not disable localities from acting except when doing so serves the public
good. So even a national government with the authority to take any and all
powers away from the states was not something to be feared.[78]

What's more, Madison recorded himself as saying, the principal objection
to abolishing the state governments was "that the General Government could
not extend its care to all the minute objects which fall under the cognizance
of the local jurisdictions."[79] That objection was not a concern about state sovereignty nor even about the possibility that the general government would
abuse its power. It was simply about the general government's limited practical capacity. If Congress turned out to have greater capacity than the delegates

predicted, such that it would become "practicable for the General Government to extend its care to every requisite object without the cooperation of the State Governments, the people would not be less free as members of one great Republic than as citizens of thirteen small ones."[80] Again, that prospect was too much for some of the delegates. According to Madison's notes, South Carolina's Charles Cotesworth Pinckney averred that he opposed both the formal abolition of the state governments and the functionally equivalent program of depriving them of meaningful agency.[81] But just as surely as Pinckney pushed back against Madison, Hamilton weighed in against Pinckney. The reality, Hamilton argued, was that the state governments might gradually fade away. Better to plan for that realistic possibility than to pretend it wasn't going to happen.[82]

In sum, leading delegates including Madison, Wilson, and Hamilton were willing to see the states become fully subordinate jurisdictions. Their views were not unique. According to Madison, King favored "preserving the States in a subordinate degree," to the extent that they were necessary for practical local administration, and Morris described the idea that the states should be regarded as important as "the bane of this Country."[83] Several delegates argued in favor of eliminating states, or combining or dividing existing states, or giving Congress the power to divide states even without the states' consent.[84] Others announced themselves willing to reconfigure the states if only it were practical.[85] Not everyone had those views, of course. But it is hard to conclude that the delegates held a shared commitment to any robust idea of state sovereignty.

The Great Ultimatum

In part because they did not regard state sovereignty as the sort of fundamental value that Paterson had asserted, many large-state delegates did not think of giving the small states an equal vote in the Senate as a way of accommodating a principled claim. It was giving in to an unjust one. When the system we know as the Great Compromise was proposed, Madison (in his own rendering) characterized it as "departing from justice in order to conciliate the smaller states."[86] Madison similarly recorded Butler as considering the compromise "a plan evidently unjust" and Morris declaring the small states simply motivated "by selfishness."[87] Madison's notes on the subsequent debate reflect more of the same. King asked rhetorically, "What reason can be assigned why the same rule of representation s[hould] not prevail in the 2d.

branch as in the 1st.?" and answered that "He could conceive none."[88] Wilson described "equality in the 2d. branch" as "a fundamental and a perpetual error."[89] And in Madison's own estimation, "substituting an equality in place of a proportional Representation" would mean that "the proper foundation of Governm[en]t was destroyed."[90]

There is no evidence that any delegate from any of the three large states (Virginia, Pennsylvania, and Massachusetts) considered the small states' demand for equal representation in one house to be in any way reasonable. That is not to say that none were willing to support the proposal. But those who were willing to go along do not seem to have done so because they thought the small-state position had merit. They simply recognized that the alternative to giving in would be the failure of the Convention to agree on a new form of government, and that alternative was unpalatable. "If no Accommodation takes place," Madison recorded Caleb Strong of Massachusetts observing, "the Union itself must soon be dissolved."[91] Gerry seems to have put the point more strongly. He had chaired the committee that recommended the "Compromise," and he had, as Madison recorded him, "very material objections" to the proposal. But the alternative was disaster: "If we do not come to some agreement among ourselves some foreign sword will probably do the work for us."[92]

With Gerry and Strong dividing the Massachusetts delegation on these realpolitik grounds, the Convention on July 16 approved equal representation in the Senate by a vote of five states to four.[93] It was a moment of crisis. Randolph regarded the vote as a serious breach that "embarrassed the business extremely" and suggested a temporary adjournment to allow the big states to determine how to proceed.[94] Pressing the small-state threat, Paterson suggested that an adjournment, if there were one, should be permanent rather than temporary. Reject this arrangement, he was saying, and there will be no new Constitution.[95]

At that point, Rutledge suggested the futility of a temporary adjournment, and in so doing—or at least as Madison recorded the intervention—made an instructive observation. In Madison's journal, Rutledge's remarks appear as follows:

> Mr. Rutlidge could see no need of an adjourn[men]t. Because *he could see no chance of a compromise* [emphasis added]. The little States were fixt. They had repeatedly & solemnly declared themselves to be so. All that the large States then had to do, was to decide whether they would yield or not.[96]

This is not the expression of a man deciding whether to make appropriate concessions in order to accommodate the reasonable claims of his colleagues. It is a recognition that the small states had issued an ultimatum. Indeed, if Madison captured Rutledge's remarks accurately, Rutledge did not understand the Great Compromise as a compromise at all. Instead, he saw the small states' position as demonstrating that compromise was impossible. The only question was what was worse: yielding to the demand or wrecking the entire Convention.

From the perspective of the large-state delegates, then, the Convention's decision (by just one vote, and without a single big state in the majority) to give each state the same representation in the Senate was not a Great Compromise. It was a self-interested power play by the small states. And the large states' acquiescence was not the recognition of some legitimate principle about state sovereignty. It was simply submission—for some of them, pointedly bitter submission—to a political reality they were powerless to overcome.

The Bedford Resolution

With the question of representation settled, the Convention turned back to the subject of congressional power. During the first half of July, as delegates wrestled over the representation issue, the language of Resolution VI provided that Congress would have power "to legislate in all cases to which the separate States are incompetent; or in which the harmony of the United States may be interrupted by the exercise of individual legislation," as well as to nullify unconstitutional state laws and state laws violating treaties with foreign nations.[97] On July 17, one day after the vote giving small states equal representation in the Senate, the delegates altered Resolution VI in two ways. First, they added language saying that Congress should have the power to legislate "in all cases for the general interests of the Union."[98] Second, they eliminated the power to nullify state laws.[99] The first of these changes indicated support for a broadly empowered Congress. The second change limited congressional power in an important way—but it also reflected confidence in the breadth of the power that the first change would authorize Congress to wield.

The first change, calling for Congress to be able to legislate "in all cases for the general interests of the Union," came on the motion of a delegate from the smallest represented state: Delaware's Gunning Bedford.[100] According to Madison's notes, Randolph described Bedford's proposal as "formidable," because it would empower Congress to override all manner of the states' own laws.[101] Also according to Madison's notes, Bedford demurred, saying that his language did not change the substance of Resolution VI. No state was separately competent to legislate for the Union's general interests, Bedford explained.[102] So a Congress empowered to legislate in all cases where the separate states were incompetent would necessarily have the power to legislate for the general interests of the Union. But regardless of whether Bedford intended to expand congressional power or merely to ensure that an already capacious vision of congressional power was properly understood, his resolution called for a broadly empowered Congress.

One day after securing their equal votes in the Senate, Delaware and New Jersey voted yes on this resolution, thus indicating that their insistence on representation by states in one house of Congress was not part of a commitment to limited national power.[103] (Recall Pinckney's prediction that New Jersey would dismiss its scruples if given an equal vote.) The change was adopted by a vote of six to four, after which the entire sentence—calling for Congress to have power "to legislate in all cases for the general interests of the Union, and also in those to which the States are separately incompetent, or in which the harmony of the United States may be interrupted by the exercise of individual legislation"—was approved by a vote of eight states to two.[104]

Then, by a vote of seven states to three, the Convention eliminated Congress's proposed power to veto unconstitutional state laws and state laws violating treaties.[105] That decision denied the national government a powerful weapon. But it would be a mistake to assume that it reflected opposition to robust national power among the delegates. The Convention had just approved the Bedford Resolution, after all. Nor did the defeat of the veto power reflect a broadly held view that as a matter of principle Congress should not be empowered to override the state legislatures. Some small-state delegates were skeptical of the veto not because it seemed problematic in principle but because as a practical matter they doubted it would ever be deployed against large and powerful states.[106] In the discussion on July 17, a further pragmatic argument for eliminating the negative came, according to Madison's notes, from Morris—a large-state delegate and an unquestionable nationalist. Morris argued that a congressional power to negate state laws was politically toxic and practically superfluous. The Constitution would need to be ratified by the states, Morris noted, and the states would hate a constitutional provision explicitly subjecting their laws to someone else's veto. An express veto power would therefore make ratification harder to achieve. Morris saw no reason to take on that challenge, because as a practical matter Congress could block state laws even without an express veto power. Any time a state legislature enacted an unconstitutional law or a law violating a treaty, Morris reasoned, Congress's powers under Resolution VI would be sufficient for overriding that law. Articulating a specific veto power would thus provoke resistance for no good reason.[107]

These discussions of Resolution VI were the Convention's last recorded substantial engagements with questions of congressional power before the appointment of the Committee of Detail nine days later. But one aspect of the discussion on the next day suggests something important about the way key delegates were thinking about the specification of congressional powers. On July 18, the Convention took up a resolution to guarantee each state protection against violent insurrections.[108] According to Madison's notes, Rutledge ventured that the resolution seemed unnecessary because Congress would obviously have the power to help put down an insurrection.[109]

Rutledge was among the Convention's leading supporters of specifying congressional powers with particularity. When Resolution VI was first introduced, he had asked that the powers of Congress be specified rather than left to the resolution's general formula.[110] According to Madison's notes, he renewed that request on July 16, when Resolution VI came back for discussion after the decision on representation.[111] (The Convention declined on both occasions.) But Rutledge's comment about a power to suppress insurrections suggests that his desire to enumerate congressional powers was not tied to a general view that Congress would have only the powers the Constitution affirmatively enumerated. On the contrary, if Rutledge expected Congress to have the power to suppress insurrections regardless of whether such a power were expressly specified, he necessarily expected that Congress would have some powers inherently or by implication.[112] There is no reason to think that he was alone in that view.

The following week, the Convention tasked the five-member Committee of Detail—Randolph, Wilson, Rutledge, Ellsworth, and Nathaniel Gorham of Massachusetts—with turning the approved resolutions into a first draft of a written Constitution. It is worth pausing to assess the attitude toward congressional power that the Convention articulated on the eve of that development.

The Bedford-amended Resolution VI called for a Congress able "to legislate in all cases for the general interests of the Union, and also in those to which the States are separately incompetent, or in which the harmony of the U. States may be interrupted by the exercise of individual Legislation." In explaining why Congress did not need a specific power to veto state laws, Morris had expressed the view that congressional power would be broad enough to override any state law. And Rutledge—generally regarded as a supporter of enumerating congressional powers and also as the strongest skeptic of national power on the Committee of Detail—had expressed the view that Congress would wield power beyond what the Constitution specifically enumerated. Against that background, it seems reasonable to think that the Committee of Detail would have set about drafting a Constitution for a government that included a powerful Congress—one empowered by, but probably not limited to, any enumeration of particular powers.

Phase 3: The Committee of Detail

The Committee of Detail worked in secret, and there are no known notes of its proceedings. The best scholarly guesses about how its draft took shape are based on surviving drafts in Randolph's, Rutledge's, and Wilson's handwriting.[113] On August 6, the committee presented the Convention with a draft that included an eighteen-clause section specifying powers to be vested in the legislature of the United States.[114] That section was, of course, the forerunner of Article I, Section 8.

The Committee's Enumeration and Resolution VI

What was the relationship between the committee's eighteen-clause enumeration of congressional powers and Resolution VI of the Virginia Plan? Scholars have given a range of answers to this question. According to one school of thought, the committee's draft substituted a narrower vision of congressional power for the one that the Convention had earlier agreed upon, and the Convention was persuaded that the change was a good idea.[115] According to a second theory, Resolution VI was always just a placeholder to be used until an exclusive list of enumerated powers could be written, and the committee faithfully implemented the Convention's program by writing a limiting enumeration.[116] These two ideas disagree about the meaning of Resolution VI: one sees it as calling for a Congress whose power goes beyond a specific enumeration, and the other does not. But they agree about the meaning of the committee's draft. On both conceptions, the committee enumerated the powers of Congress, and Congress was understood to be limited to the powers enumerated.

Each of these theories faces a significant problem. The problem with the first is that there is no indication that the Convention delegates detected a change in course. Perhaps the committee could have redirected the Convention: sometimes a small working group either hijacks the work of a larger body or else persuades the larger body to go in a different direction. But if that happened in this case, there would probably have been some discussion of the change. For example, when the committee presented its draft to the Convention, delegates who favored the broad vision of Resolution VI might have protested that what the committee had done was not what the Convention had agreed on. The surviving records contain no indication of any such protest or discussion, either in the Convention itself or in the private writings of the delegates. It is possible, of course, that there was some such protest, either within the Convention's proceedings or in informal conversations outside those proceedings, and that the surviving records simply do not reveal it. But the fact remains that there is no evidence that any Convention delegates thought the committee had departed from its instructions. Given the centrality of the point, it would be remarkable for a reversal to have left no trace in the record.

The problem with the second theory is that it demands a strained understanding of the language of Resolution VI. Yes, there is evidence that delegates expected the Committee of Detail to specify particular congressional powers rather than describing Congress's authority only at Resolution VI's broad level of generality.[117] But Resolution VI does not read like something whose content can be captured with a closed list of specific powers. A legislature empowered to make law in all cases for the general interests of the Union, and in all cases in which the states were not separately competent, would be a legislature empowered to do the various things the Committee of Detail's draft specified: tax, regulate commerce, establish a rule of naturalization, and so on. But there is little reason to think it would be a legislature *limited* to those specifically listed powers. Consider also that key delegates like Madison, Dickinson, Wilson, and Hamilton had expressed skepticism about whether the powers of Congress could be fully enumerated; that Wilson and Lansing, from their opposite perspectives, had identified a limiting enumeration of legislative powers as a trait that distinguished the rejected New Jersey Plan from the Virginia Plan; and that Rutledge, who was probably the committee member most keenly interested in limiting the national government, assumed that Congress would have the power to put down insurrections whether or not the Constitution so specified. In that light, the case for reading Resolution VI as a placeholder for a limiting enumeration becomes even less tenable.

It accordingly seems likely that both of the preceding approaches mistake the relationship between Resolution VI and the Committee of Detail's enumeration of congressional powers. On a better view, Resolution VI did not call for a limiting enumeration, and the Committee of Detail did not write one. Instead, Resolution VI called for a broadly empowered Congress, and the committee, in what eventually became Article I, Section 8, enumerated a set of powers that it was important to specify clearly, lest there be any doubt about Congress's authority to exercise them. The committee's report did not indicate that Congress would be limited to the powers thus enumerated; the enumerated powers might simply be a subset of the powers that Congress could exercise. Seen that way, there is no tension between the committee's list and Resolution VI.

Two features of the committee's draft testify to this conclusion. First, it is awkward to imagine that the committee's Article VII, Section 1—the forerunner of Article I, Section 8—was written or understood as an exclusive list of congressional powers, because Article VII, Section 1, did not include all of the congressional powers specified in the committee's draft Constitution. Instead, the committee's draft specified various congressional powers outside of Article VII, Section 1, just as the final draft of the Constitution specified various congressional powers outside of Article I, Section 8. As noted earlier, it is hard to see why a list of powers that is clearly not a complete list would implicitly embody the idea that there are no powers except those appearing on that list.

Second, the committee's draft contained a text that might be best read to negate any inference that the list of congressional powers was exclusive. That text, which Americans in the 1780s knew as the Sweeping Clause and which modern constitutional lawyers know as part of the Necessary and Proper Clause, was probably written to create a textual warrant for Congress to pursue the general interests of the Union even when doing so would go beyond the Constitution's more particular statements of power, just as Resolution VI directed. That warrant may have been written in a deliberately ambiguous way, such that more and less nationalist delegates could agree on a form of words to be adopted and each camp could claim that the Constitution reflected its vision. But if the Sweeping Clause was deliberately ambiguous, it was not *covertly* ambiguous. The ambiguity was out in the open.

The Sweeping Clause

The last clause of the Committee of Detail's Article VII, Section 1 declared that Congress would have the power "to make all laws that shall be necessary and proper for carrying into execution the foregoing powers, and all other powers vested, by this Constitution, in the government of the United States, or in any department or officer thereof."[118] This text has multiple components— so much so that, as John Mikhail has suggested, constitutional lawyers should perhaps speak of the Necessary and Proper *Clauses*, plural.[119] The first of those clauses, which we can call the "Foregoing Powers Clause," gives Congress the power to make laws for carrying into effect the powers specified earlier in the section. The second, which we can call the "All Other Powers Clause," gives Congress the power to make laws for carrying into effect whatever other powers the general government enjoys under the Constitution.

The two clauses appear to have separate drafting origins in the work of the Committee of Detail. The Foregoing Powers Clause first appears in an early draft, in Rutledge's handwriting,[120] and it seems to have been uncontroversial. The Framers broadly agreed that Congress needed latitude to choose the means for carrying its powers into effect and indeed that such power was necessarily implicit in the other grants of power. Madison thus later took the view that this clause actually gave Congress no power it would not have had otherwise, even without the textual specification.[121]

Matters are different with the All Other Powers Clause. Although we cannot know for certain, that clause seems to have been initially introduced not by Rutledge, whose support for a strong general government was tempered by a commitment to preserving slavery in South Carolina, but by Wilson, who was among the Convention's most fervent nationalists.[122] Indeed, Wilson believed that the general government even under the Articles of Confederation was inherently vested with certain powers simply because it was the government of the United States. His 1785 essay on the Bank of North America had made that case powerfully and publicly. And Wilson probably intended the All Other Powers Clause to affirm the existence of such "resulting powers," whether enumerated or not.

Because constitutional lawyers usually read the Necessary and Proper Clause(s) through an enumerationist lens, they do not notice the meaning that Wilson (assuming he was the author) likely intended. On the conventional view, the clause's reference to "the foregoing powers, and all other powers vested by this Constitution in the government of the United States" means "the foregoing powers, and all other powers *expressly* vested by this Constitution in the government of the United States." Understood that way, the purpose of the "all other powers" language is to give Congress the power to carry into execution the federal powers specified in the constitutional text but outside Article I, Section 8. But suppose, as seems likely, that the author of the clause was Wilson, who believed that the United States government had inherent powers and who did not think that an enumeration of powers could capture all the powers the general government should exercise. If Wilson wrote the clause, it is reasonable to think he intended "all other powers vested by this Constitution in the government of the United States" to mean "all other powers vested by this Constitution, *whether expressly or implicitly*, in the government of the United States." And on Wilson's view as articulated in his Bank of North America essay, the powers implicitly vested by the Constitution in the government of the United States would not have been only powers implicitly vested by particular pieces of constitutional text. They would have included whatever powers were inherent or implicit in the decision, announced in the draft's preamble and the language of its first two articles, to create a government of the United States of America consisting of "supreme legislative, executive, and judicial powers."[123]

As Mikhail has explained, two features of the clause's text point to this reading.[124] The first is the "all other powers" language, which identifies the clause as what Framing-era lawyers standardly called a "sweeping clause." A sweeping clause in a will, contract, corporate charter, or constitution was a clause inserted at the end of a list of particulars to negate the possible inference that the list was exhaustive. As the English Chief Justice Lord Mansfield wrote in 1774, "the use and object" of a sweeping clause was "to guard against any accidental omission" or to "take in every thing . . . which it was possible they might have omitted to enumerate precisely."[125] State constitutions at the Founding used sweeping clauses when describing the powers of their legislatures. The language of Wilson's own state constitution, for example, enumerated various powers of the Pennsylvania legislature and then said that the legislature "shall have all other powers necessary for the legislature of a free state or commonwealth."[126] The "all other powers" language was a standard sweeping-clause formula, and contemporary readers recognized it as such: Convention delegates and others in the Founding generation often referred to this text as the Constitution's "sweeping clause."[127]

The second relevant feature of the clause's text is its distinction between powers vested by the Constitution "in the government of the United States" and powers vested in "any department or officer thereof." As a general matter, the federal powers expressly vested by the Constitution are vested in specific "departments" (like Congress) or "officers" (like the president and the chief justice) rather than in the government of the United States as a whole. Nowhere does the Constitution say "The government of the United States shall have the power . . ." to do any particular thing. And if the Constitution does not expressly vest powers in the government of the United States as such, then it is problematic to read "all other powers vested by this Constitution in the government of the United States" to mean "all other powers *expressly* vested by this Constitution in the government of the United States." To read the language that way is to read it to refer to an empty set.

It is possible to resist this reasoning and read the language as the enumerationist lens directs. There is a sense in which every power vested in a department or officer of the United States is a power vested in the United States, so perhaps "all other powers vested in the government of the United States, or in any department or officer thereof" is two ways of saying the same thing. This reading has the vice of making either "the government of the United States" or "or in any department or officer thereof" superfluous, but the Constitution does contain superfluous text.[128] Alternatively, one could say that the Constitution does vest a power in the government of the United States as such, albeit without any text saying, "The government of the United States shall have the power . . ." The best candidate for a constitutional text vesting such a power is the Guarantee Clause, which provides that "[t]he United States shall guarantee to every state in this union a republican form of government." The Guarantee Clause is phrased as prescribing a duty rather than conferring a power, but if it implies a power—the theory being that a duty to guarantee every state a republican form of government makes sense only if it comes with adequate power to make good on the guarantee—then it is a power vested in the United States as such. If so, the set of powers to which this part of the Necessary and Proper Clause refers is not quite empty.

If the goal of an interpretation is to reconcile the text of the Constitution with enumerationism, these readings are serviceable. But that does not mean that they offer the most plausible reading of the text, let alone the only one. It certainly does not mean that they offer the best understanding of what Wilson, if he was the author, had in mind when he drafted the language. Wilson was not interested in confining the government of the United States to a set of textually enumerated powers. He believed that the Union had inherent powers even before the Constitution, and he wanted the Constitution to increase the general government's power. In the Committee of the Whole, he had argued that it would not be possible to enumerate the powers of the federal legislature. If he wrote a text that reads most easily as reflecting a belief in inherent and nonenumerated powers, it makes sense to think he meant it that way.

None of this is to say that the Committee of Detail unambiguously embraced inherent or implicit powers in addition to enumerated ones. Its draft did not expressly restrict the general government to the powers enumerated, but it also did not expressly assert the existence of nonenumerated powers. That said, the All Other Powers Clause seems to have been written to invite a reading that would give Congress the power to make laws necessary and proper for carrying into effect the inherent and nonenumerated powers of the United States. And if the clause did not state that proposition unequivocally, perhaps Wilson and his allies saw some advantage in the ambiguity. They were aware, after all, that not everyone wanted a Congress quite that powerful. A text that would support more than one reading might stand a better chance of getting adopted.

Phase 4: The Convention Debates the Draft

After the Committee of Detail reported its draft on August 6, the Convention spent ten days addressing other aspects of the proposal before discussing the powers of Congress. When the delegates did turn their attention to congressional power, their discussion was partly about ways of limiting that power. As had been true throughout the Convention, external limits and process limits held considerable appeal when delegates were serious about imposing constraint. Consider two examples. First, and as noted earlier, the

Committee of Detail had protected South Carolina's slavery-related interests in the way best calculated to get the job done: with affirmative prohibitions. According to the committee's draft, Congress would be expressly forbidden to tax exports or to prohibit or tax "the importation of such persons as the several States shall think proper to admit."[129] This language had teeth, and it occasioned two days of bitter debate. Second, southern delegates proposed that exercises of Congress's power to regulate commerce require approval by a two-thirds majority in each house—the rationale being that the northern states could outvote the southern states if a simple majority would suffice but that a two-thirds requirement would prevent commercial regulations from being enacted over the opposition of a solid South. In the Convention, however, a majority was sufficient to decide questions, and this proposal failed to carry.[130]

In terms of importance and potential explosiveness, these issues rivaled the question of small-state voting power in Congress. South Carolina had early and often made clear that it would never agree to a system in which the general government could tax exports or prohibit the slave trade. The gravity of the sectional conflict over laws regulating commerce is not as intuitive today as that of the slavery conflict, but the delegates in 1787 felt it keenly. The northern states had a strong orientation toward the Atlantic trade, and the southern states were vitally interested in the Mississippi River and the Gulf of Mexico. Southerners were acutely concerned that a government with a northern majority would make trade deals with foreign powers, sacrificing one set of interests to the other. Accordingly, the proposal to require a two-thirds majority to enact commercial regulations reflected not a heightened skepticism toward commercial regulations as a whole but a fear of one particular kind of commercial regulation—the kind benefiting the North at the expense of the South. A two-thirds voting rule would ensure that commercial regulation systematically hostile to southern interests could not be enacted, because northerners might make up a majority of the legislature but could never muster two-thirds without southern participation. Again, the stakes were high. When the proposal to require a two-thirds majority on commerce questions failed, Randolph—the sponsor of the Virginia Plan himself—declared that he might not be able to sign the Constitution.[131] And when he in fact declined to sign, he identified the majority voting rule for commercial regulations as one of the Constitution's two biggest flaws.[132] (The allocation of voting power in the Senate was the other.)

So it is perhaps telling that, as far as the sources reveal, neither Randolph nor his allies on this question tried to address their concerns by narrowing the language giving Congress the power to regulate commerce. Their interest in avoiding disadvantageous legislation under the commerce power was powerful enough to prompt the presenter of the Virginia Plan to say that he might not be able to endorse the Convention's work product if the concern were not adequately addressed. And where interests of that magnitude were concerned, delegates reached for the truly powerful tools of limitation—process limits and external limits. Indeed, it is hard to identify an issue that prompted any delegate to threaten to bolt the Convention, or to refuse to sign, for which the proposed solution was an adjustment of the enumerated powers of Congress rather than a structural device or an external limit.

This is not to say that the delegates put no stock in internal limits at all. But by this late stage of the Convention, some of the delegates who were inclined to think the Constitution should limit Congress by enumerating its powers had concluded that the draft before them did nothing of the kind, because its enumeration of powers was too generous to be limiting. According to Madison, Randolph warned that the Constitution's "definition of the powers of the Government was so loose as to give it opportunities of usurping all the State powers."[133] And two days after Randolph lamented the failure of a two-thirds process check on legislation regulating commerce, Mason announced that he could not sign the Constitution as it then stood.[134] He drew up a list of reasons, prominent among which was the charge that the Constitution failed to limit the uses to which national legislative power could be put. He sought a thoroughly revised Constitution, one in which "[t]he Objects of the National Government [would] be expressly defined." The existing draft, in his view, conferred on Congress "indefinite powers" under "general Clauses."[135] More particularly, he wrote that "[t]he sweeping Clause [that is, the "all other powers" language] absorbs every thing almost by construction."[136]

Phase 5: Wrapping Up without a Bill of Rights

On the last day of August, the Convention appointed an eleven-member committee, chaired by New Jersey's David Brearley, to make recommendations regarding a variety of still-unsettled matters.[137] A few concerned the powers of Congress. In early September, Brearley's Committee accordingly suggested language for what eventually became half a dozen sections of Article I, Section 8. The surviving records reflect contentious debate on some of the Brearley Committee's other recommendations, including its proposed system for choosing the president and its suggested prohibition on letting members of Congress hold governmental offices outside the legislative branch.[138] But where the powers of Congress were concerned, the records reflect little discussion.[139] If the delegates believed that the precise wording of the clauses enumerating congressional powers was a matter of significant importance, the surviving records do not reflect their concern.

On September 8, the Convention appointed another five-person committee, this one called the Committee of Style, to rewrite the existing draft in light of the changes the Convention had approved. The members of the committee—Hamilton, Morris, Madison, King, and Connecticut's William Samuel Johnson—skewed toward the nationalist end of the Convention's spectrum. The choice to give that group the pen for the final draft thus reflected a decision, or at least a willingness, to have the Constitution speak in a nationalist voice. To give one salient example, the Committee of Detail's draft had begun with the words "We the People of the States of New Hampshire, Massachusetts, Rhode Island and Providence Plantations, Connecticut, New York, New Jersey, Pennsylvania, Delaware, Maryland, Virginia, North Carolina, South Carolina, and Georgia. . . ." The Committee of Style returned a draft that began "We, the People of the United States. . . ."[140] The Convention made no further changes to the draft text describing the power of Congress after the Committee of Style presented its proposal.

On September 12, the same day when the Committee of Style presented its draft, the Convention considered a motion to appoint a committee to draft a bill of rights. A bill or declaration of rights, as those terms were generally understood in 1787, was a statement of fundamental principles about government and political authority, or asserting certain rights, or both.[141] The Virginia Declaration of Rights, for example, began by declaring that "all men are by nature equally free and independent," stated that all power is derived from the people, described the purposes of government and the right of the people to change their government, and asserted a series of principles about officeholding, elections, and the separation of powers. It then enumerated particular liberties with respect to subjects like jury trial, cruel and unusual punishments, and religious freedom. When the Convention sat, eight of the thirteen American states had bills or declarations of rights.[142] The Convention delegates seem to have been decidedly of the view that their new Constitution should not include one: the motion to appoint a committee to prepare a bill of rights was defeated, ten states to none.[143]

Within a short time after the Convention adjourned, the issue of whether the Constitution of the United States needed a bill of rights became a prominent part of the ratification debates, and it did so in a way that implicated the function of enumerating the powers of Congress. Several of the Constitution's supporters argued that a bill of rights would be superfluous because the enumeration of congressional powers sufficed to limit the national government—or even that a bill of rights would be affirmatively dangerous, because it would imply, incorrectly, that Congress was not limited to the powers enumerated. Those ideas would become staples of constitutional thought, and they are a deeply entrenched part of enumerationism's conventional wisdom. But these ideas seem to have developed after the Convention adjourned, as a rationalization of the Convention's failure to include a bill of rights, rather than being an accurate account of why the delegates did not include one. Indeed, if one looks only at sources from the time when the Convention sat rather than at things people said and wrote after the Convention adjourned, there is no evidence—none—that the delegates omitted a bill of rights because they trusted the enumeration of powers to limit the federal government.

Madison's Account

The only known account of the Convention's discussion about whether to draft a bill of rights is from Madison's journal, and, as Mary Bilder has shown, it is from a portion of Madison's journal that Madison composed more than two years after the Convention adjourned.[144] Madison's account is accordingly a source from the post-ratification period rather than a contemporary record of the Convention: it reflects what Madison remembered and chose to record two years later, after the ratification debates' discussions of a bill of rights. And it sheds little light on the Convention's thinking. Madison's entire account consists of short comments from three delegates: Mason, Gerry, and Sherman. According to Madison, Mason told the Convention that "[h]e wished the plan had been prefaced with a bill of rights." If someone were to move for the creation of a committee to draft one, Mason said, he would second the motion. Gerry "concurred in the idea" and made such a motion, which Mason duly seconded. Sherman then opposed the motion. A bill of rights was unnecessary, he said, because the state declarations of rights would still be in force. Mason responded that the state declarations of rights were insufficient, because "[t]he Laws of the U.S. are to be paramount"—that is, given the supremacy of federal law, a state declaration of rights would not protect against oppressive measures approved by Congress. Without further recorded discussion, the motion was defeated, ten states to none. And there Madison's description ends.[145]

If Madison's account is reliable, it raises tantalizing questions about how the Framers thought about bills of rights. Notably, the exchange between Mason and Sherman suggests a disagreement about whether a bill of rights would establish rights as a matter of positive law or recognize the existence of natural or common-law rights already in force. Mason's argument that federal law would override the state bills of rights makes sense on the first view: if constitutional rights would be valid against the federal government only if established as positive law in the federal Constitution, then state bills of rights would not block the operation of federal law. Sherman's point makes sense on the second view: the state declarations of rights would be relevant not because they established rights as a matter of positive law but because they would inform adjudicators of the existence of a preexisting authority superior to federal law.[146] But nothing in this account explains why the Convention rejected the proposal to draft a bill of rights. Perhaps Sherman voted no for the reason he gave, but it is impossible to know how many other delegates agreed with that rationale and how many voted against the proposal for other reasons. And nothing at all in Madison's account suggests that anyone voted against drafting a bill of rights on the theory that the enumeration of congressional powers made one unnecessary or inadvisable.[147]

Other Hypotheses, with an Emphasis on Slavery

Is there a better explanation for the Convention's overwhelming rejection of Mason's call for a bill of rights? Given the scant documentary evidence, it is impossible to know for certain why the proposal was rejected. Moreover, any attempt to answer the question should acknowledge that the Framers were probably motivated by a mix of concerns rather than by any single rationale. But their decision is not entirely mysterious. As a threshold matter, it is not obvious that a group of Americans in 1787 would have presumed that a constitution should include a bill of rights. Several states did not have bills of rights, after all. And where the Constitution the Framers were drafting was concerned, there were important reasons *not* to include a bill of rights—reasons that have nothing to do with the standard story about enumerated powers. Here are two. First, prefacing the Constitution with a bill of rights (as the Framers largely understood bills of rights) might have implied that, under the Constitution, the United States would fully displace the state governments as primary political entities. Second, and perhaps more importantly, trying to draft a bill of rights for the United States Constitution might have wrecked the Convention over the issue of slavery.

To see the force of the first consideration, recall that eighteenth-century bills of rights typically recited fundamental principles about the composition and purpose of government, rather than being composed only or primarily of specific entitlements like jury trial or freedom of religion. A typical bill of rights might say, for example, that all power is derived from the people, or that men leave the state of nature and enter society to better protect their natural rights. (Because they set out the fundamental justification for governments, such bills of rights normally functioned as prefaces to constitutions rather than as the sort of epilogue modern Americans are accustomed to.) According to one way of thinking, bills of rights were therefore appropriate in state constitutions, because the state governments were the ones formed, as it were, out of nothing, on the model of Lockean social compacts. (Not that any state government was ever actually formed by people who were not already under a government, but that is a different matter.) The Articles of Confederation, which composed only a second-order government, had no bill of rights. In this light, including a bill of rights with the new Constitution would have announced the proposal not merely as a reform of the existing system but as making the United States, rather than the state governments, into the primary political unit.[148]

That implication might not have been an insuperable obstacle, had enough delegates wanted a bill of rights. The Convention's decision to submit the Constitution to ratification by popular conventions rather than state legislatures could be interpreted as carrying a similar message about the primacy of the United States in the new system. So could the choice to begin the Constitution with the words "We the People of the United States" rather than with some formula indicating that the parties to the agreement were the existing state governments—as the Articles of Confederation had. Perhaps a Convention willing to adopt a Constitution beginning "We the People of the United States" had already taken on board whatever nationalist picture of government a bill of rights stating fundamental principles of government would imply, and, having done the first thing, should not have hesitated at the second. On the other hand, perhaps the Convention was willing to go only so far in that direction, either because its own members were uneasy or because they figured that every prominent announcement of such a change would intensify the opposition that the Constitution would need to overcome to be ratified.

That set of questions might well have been overwhelmed, however, by a different problem. As the delegates understood, an attempt to state fundamental principles of government and individual rights might break the Convention apart over the issue of slavery.[149] The existing state bills and declarations of rights differed radically from each other in ways that reflected the underlying conflict on that question. In Massachusetts, the state Declaration of Rights opened with the statement that "[a]ll men are born free and equal," and the state's Chief Justice had concluded on that basis that slavery was unconstitutional.[150] New Hampshire and Pennsylvania had state bills or declarations of rights announcing that "all men are born equally free and independent," and slavery was clearly on its way out in both jurisdictions.[151] But in Delaware, Maryland, North Carolina, and Georgia, where slavery was deeply embedded, the declarations of rights were more circumspect. Rather than speaking in terms of the freedom and equality of "all men," these state declarations of rights spoke of the rights of "Freemen."[152]

Against that background, imagine the problem that would have arisen if the Convention had tried to write a bill of rights for the whole United States. Some delegates hostile to slavery would likely have insisted on the language common in northern states. Other delegates would have objected strenuously to any language that might imply the invalidity of slavery under the new Constitution. South Carolina and Georgia had made clear that they would agree to no Constitution that did not protect slavery within their borders. Forcing the issue could jeopardize the entire delicate agreement.

No one understood that problem more intimately than the delegates from Virginia. Virginia had a large slave population. But uniquely among the southern states' declarations of rights, Virginia's declaration opened by asserting "[t]hat all men are by nature equally free and independent." That language had not been adopted without a struggle. At the 1776 convention at which Virginia approved its Declaration of Rights, two political factions fought bitterly about the relationship between the principled language of the opening clause and the reality of chattel slavery.[153] Several of Virginia's delegates to the General Convention in 1787 had been present at that Virginia convention eleven years earlier. Mason, who was personally critical of slavery, had been the principal draftsman of the Virginia Declaration of Rights. Randolph's father-in-law, Robert Carter Nicholas, had led the slavery-protective opposition. In Philadelphia a decade later, Mason and Randolph surely both understood how volatile a replay of that conflict would be. So did Madison, for whom the Virginia convention had been a formative political experience. So did probably everyone else in the room. (Consider that the following year, when Virginia's ratifying convention recommended several amendments, the recommendations were patterned on Virginia's own Bill of Rights—but without the statement that all men are by nature equally free and independent.[154] That one, Virginia thought, should not go in the national Constitution.)

Now consider the roles Mason and Randolph played with respect to a bill of rights at Philadelphia. Randolph sat on the Committee of Detail, playing a key role in reducing the Convention's vision to a first draft on paper. He knew that a bill of rights would occasion explosive controversy. The draft his committee produced did not contain one. When the suggestion to draft a bill of rights finally arose at the Convention, it came from Mason—who had by that point announced his intention not to support the Constitution and who would go on to be a determined opponent of ratification. It is not too much to wonder, then, whether Mason's proposal was a deliberate attempt to wreck the Convention's work by provoking a fundamental conflict that could not be resolved. Indeed, the broad mass of delegates who had sweated through the summer to make agreement on the Constitution possible treated the proposal for a bill of rights in just the way that one should expect them to treat a motion to blow up the whole project at the last minute: they voted it down, ten states to none.

The traditional enumerationist account of the Convention's decision to forgo a bill of rights hides this slavery problem. Rather than foregrounding the role slavery played in shaping the Convention's work, it pushes that uncomfortable topic out of view and substitutes a story about the Framers' talent for elegant design. That distortion contributes to two opposite but coexisting pathologies in the way Americans think about slavery and the Constitution:

the tendency to minimize the role that slavery played in Framing-era America and the countervailing tendency to imagine the Framers as uniformly proslavery or at least as untroubled by it. The key reality that underlay the Convention's decision to omit a bill of rights, on the account I am suggesting, was not the Framers' satisfaction with slavery but their deep disagreement about it. The enumerationist story about the Bill of Rights thus hides both the Framers' conflict about slavery and their decision to manage that conflict by tolerating the institution. It also supports an unwarranted sense that a limiting enumeration is crucial to the Constitution's design. Constitutional lawyers would think more clearly about each of these subjects if they thought of the omission of the Bill of Rights as rooted in the problem of slavery rather than as part of the design of a government of enumerated powers.

◄◄┄►►◄◄┄►►

Officially, few constitutional interpreters think that the subjective ideas or intentions of the Convention's participants are authoritative in constitutional law. Some are skeptical that original meanings should govern, and (at least as of this writing) those who consider themselves originalists generally say that authority lies in the public meaning of the adopted text rather than in the words or thoughts of the Framers. Nonetheless, it is a feature of American constitutional culture that an idea about the Convention and its purposes has persuasive weight. As long as we are confident that the Convention took an enumerationist approach to federal power, we will be close to unwilling to entertain the possibility that enumerationism is a flawed approach to constitutional law. Understanding that the Convention was a good deal less enumerationist than is generally supposed is accordingly an important step toward seeing that constitutional law today need not be, and ultimately should not be, enumerationist.

Early in this chapter, I identified four problems with the prevailing account of how the Constitutional Convention thought about enumerated powers. Here is one more. As every modern constitutional lawyer knows, the Constitution's enumeration of congressional powers does not, in practice, do much to prevent Congress from pursuing the projects for which it musters political will. The Constitution shapes Congress's ambitions through the structure of the lawmaking process—elections, bicameralism, presentment—and the courts have invalidated congressional legislation based on affirmative prohibitions like those in the First Amendment. But with exceptions around the year 1820 and for a few decades around the turn of the twentieth century, Congress from 1789 forward has been able to pursue pretty much any project for which it has the political will, subject only to affirmative prohibitions. This fact does not prove that the Framers did not intend the enumeration to be meaningfully limiting. But if they did intend it to be meaningfully limiting, then it must be accepted that the Framers were, in this crucial respect, quite bad at constitutional design, because a central part of the machinery seems to have failed, more or less from its inception.

The Framers cannot be rescued from this charge by saying that their design was good but the Constitution has been systematically misapplied. The correct anticipation of how real people in office will act is a necessary part of successful constitutional design. But there is another way to avoid the conclusion that the Framers' ideas about enumerated power were a colossal miscalculation. We could replace the conventional understanding, on which the Framers invested heavily and unambiguously in what turned out to be an ineffective mechanism, with a better understanding on which the Framers were not, as a group, committed to that mechanism in the first place. Not, of course, because modern Americans have a duty to make the Framers look good. The Framers had strengths and weaknesses. But in fairness to them, and for the sake of accuracy in our own understandings of the constitutional system, we should not overstate their commitment to a bad idea. Some of them wanted a limiting enumeration. But for others, the enumeration of congressional powers was fundamentally a means of empowering Congress, and Congress could have nonenumerated powers as well as enumerated ones, and the work of limitation was to be done elsewhere. The Constitution that the Convention wrote was crafted to leave the door open to that latter conception. As a result, we should understand the way things have turned out in practice not as a betrayal of the Framers' design but as the realization of a vision—not the only vision, but one of the visions—that was embedded in the Constitution from the beginning.

CHAPTER FOUR

RATIFICATION WITHOUT AGREEMENT

W HEN THE GENERAL CONVENTION adjourned in September 1787, it sent its proposed Constitution to the Confederation Congress, then sitting in New York, with a request that Congress send it on to the state legislatures for ratification. During the year that followed, Americans argued extensively not just about whether to ratify the Constitution but about what the Constitution meant. The question of how much power the Constitution would give the general government was central to those arguments. Americans in later generations have looked back to the ratification debates when making their own arguments about what the Constitution means.

According to the conventional thinking, the ratification debates of 1787–1788 demonstrate that the prevailing view of the Constitution at that time was enumerationist. The legal significance of that interpretation of the ratification debates depends, of course, on contested questions about the authority of original meanings. But even nonoriginalist interpreters are regularly influenced, to greater and lesser degrees, by the idea that the Constitution had a certain meaning when it was ratified. The prevailing understanding that the ratification debates reflect an enumerationist view of the Constitution is accordingly a powerful force supporting enumerationism. And that prevailing view is mistaken: the historical record of the ratification debates does not support the claim that the Constitution in 1787–1788 had the meaning that the conventional enumerationist view ascribes to it. What the ratification debates actually demonstrate is that in 1787–1788, the question of whether the Constitution established a federal government limited by and to its enumerated powers was a matter of deep and persistent disagreement. Some people read the Constitution in an enumerationist way, and others did not. The debates did not resolve the issue.

To show the different ways in which Americans read the Constitution during the ratification period, this chapter surveys a set of arguments from the year after the General Convention adjourned, beginning with the Constitution's reception in Congress in September 1787 and proceeding chronologically through the last ratification conventions of 1788. The chapter does not present a comprehensive narrative of ratification-era arguments about congressional power: the source material is simply too vast.[1] But the evidence presented here, drawn from several state conventions and also from some of the prominent essay writing of the period, should suffice to show that disagreement about the nature and extent of the power the Constitution would allocate to Congress was deep, common, and persistent.

◄◄‥►►‥◄◄‥►►

Throughout the year of ratification, Americans arguing about how much power the general government would have if the Constitution were adopted returned again and again to five issues of interpretation. First, what if anything was the legal significance of the Preamble? Was it merely an introductory sentence with no operative force? Or did the statement of the purposes for which the Constitution was ordained—union, justice, domestic tranquility, the common defense, the general welfare, and the blessings of liberty—mean that the government of the United States would have the authority to pursue those ends?

Second, what was the scope of congressional authority under the General Welfare Clause of Article I, Section 8? Under that clause, Congress would have the power "to lay and collect taxes, duties, imposts, and excises to pay the debts and provide for the common defense and general welfare of the United States." Endorsing what would eventually become prevailing judicial doctrine, some Federalists insisted that this language authorized Congress to tax and specified the purpose for which federal taxes could be imposed—that is, to raise money to pay for the common defense and general welfare.

But others thought the clause empowered Congress to do three separate things: to tax, to pay the government's debts, and to provide—meaning not just to fund but to *legislate*—for the common defense and general welfare. Needless to say, the second reading would give Congress far more power than the first.

Third, how broad was Congress's power under the Necessary and Proper Clause? More particularly, what was the meaning of the "Sweeping Clause"— embedded within the Necessary and Proper Clause—which spoke of a congressional power to make laws for executing not just the powers enumerated earlier in Article I but *"all other powers* vested by this Constitution in the government of the United States"? On a narrow reading, the clause gave Congress only the power to carry into effect other powers written expressly into the Constitution. But the Sweeping Clause could also have a broader reading, on which "all other powers" also referred to nonenumerated powers implicitly vested in the general government.

Fourth, what if anything was the relationship between enumerated powers and the Constitution's lack of a bill of rights? Some Federalists (like Wilson and Hamilton) took aggressive positions about a bill of rights being superfluous and dangerous. Others (like Madison) engaged more circumspectly. And leading Antifederalists (Mason, Patrick Henry, Samuel Adams, Richard Henry Lee) as well as less committed combatants (like Jefferson, writing from Paris) tended to treat the idea that the enumeration of congressional powers obviated a bill of rights with something between skepticism and derision.

Fifth and finally, what was the significance of the fact that the Constitution had no language analogous to the statement in Article II of the Articles of Confederation that the states retained all powers not "expressly delegated" to the United States? Antifederalists often pointed to this fact to challenge the Federalist claim that the government would be limited to those powers enumerated in the Constitution. Federalists pushed back, but in divergent ways. Some, like Pinckney, insisted that the Constitution did restrict Congress to powers expressly delegated to it, despite the absence of a clause so providing. Others, like Madison, embraced the idea that the federal government would exercise powers not "expressly" delegated but attempted to keep that idea within nonthreatening bounds by arguing that the "implied" powers available to the general government would only be those implicit in the Constitution's express grants of power. And others, like Wilson, seemed to leave open the possibility that Congress would have inherent "resulting powers" by virtue of its status as the national legislature of the United States.

There were Americans of considerable intelligence and prestige on both sides of these questions.[2] But among constitutional lawyers who recognize some diversity of ratification-era opinion, the orthodox wisdom is that whatever disagreement existed was resolved in favor of the answers given by prominent Federalists who represented the Constitution in an enumerationist way. Leading examples of such representations include a speech by Wilson in Philadelphia, popularizing the idea that the enumeration of powers made a bill of rights counterproductive; Madison's *Federalist* 39 and 45, describing the new government as having jurisdiction over "certain enumerated objects only" and its powers as "few and defined"; and Hamilton's *Federalist* 84, reprising the argument about enumerated powers and a bill of rights. Modern constitutional law treats these sources as authoritative. As one leading theorist has put the point, where the Constitution's original meaning was ambiguous or potentially ambiguous, public statements by leading Federalists that disavowed broad constructions of national power "clarify what the original public meaning" was.[3]

But why, exactly, are those statements more clarifying of the Constitution's original meaning than other statements made at the same time by people offering different views? The Founding-era Americans who read the Constitution as giving the national government more power were not systematically less intelligent or less skilled as readers of text than those who read the Constitution as giving the national government less power. People who attended the General Convention might have had special insight into the intentions behind the Constitution's drafting, but the claim that statements by people like Wilson, Hamilton, and Madison are especially probative of the Constitution's original public meaning cannot rely on their status as Framers. After all, different Framers endorsed both broad and narrow understandings of national power. Moreover, at least according to the currently dominant view, the thing that these views are said to clarify is the Constitution's original public meaning, not the Framers' intentions: the question is not what the drafters thought but what the audience should have understood. The views of the Framers are relevant data for answering that question, but they are not entitled to more weight than the views of other well-informed contemporary readers of the text.

The idea that the narrow readings of national power given by people like Wilson, Madison, and Hamilton are especially probative accordingly does not rest on their status as Framers. It rests on their status as prominent Federalists—that is, as prominent supporters of ratification. And the leading rationale for treating these Federalists' interpretations as authoritative is that those interpretations are a good guide to what the public would accept—or, more precisely, a good guide to what the last marginal voters whose support was necessary for getting the Constitution ratified would accept. If the leading Federalists described the Constitution in a certain way, the thinking goes, and if the ratifiers took those Federalists at their word when agreeing to the Constitution, then those descriptions define the Constitution as it was agreed to.[4] As a matter of the official conventions of twenty-first century thinking about original meanings in constitutional law, it is not clear that this argument works, because it is about the subjective understandings of the small group of people who voted to approve a text rather than the objective meaning that text should carry for the general public.[5] But regardless of how practitioners of any given strand of originalist theory would deal with that problem, the argument has an intuitive logic. It would not be fair, the thought runs, for the Federalists to persuade people to ratify the Constitution on the understanding that it created a government limited to enumerated powers and then for that Constitution to be interpreted as authorizing a government with nonenumerated powers too. Madison appreciated the persuasive force of this point. Arguing in Congress in 1791 against the creation of the Bank of the United States, he urged a narrow construction of the Necessary and Proper Clause on the ground that the "friends of the constitution" had explained it that way to the state conventions.[6] As a convenient shorthand, I will call this idea the "Ratifiers' Reliance" argument.

The Ratifiers' Reliance argument has a general form: one could think that the ratifiers, nationwide and as a whole, relied on what the leading Federalists as a group said to the public during the many months of ratification debates. But the idea can also have a more concrete and particular form. In Virginia, for example, the Constitution was ratified by only a narrow margin. On the second-to-last day of debate at the Virginia convention, Madison asserted a strong form of the argument that the federal government would have only its specifically enumerated powers. So perhaps some members of the Virginia convention voted for ratification on the understanding that they were agreeing to a government only as powerful as the one Madison had described. If the delegates at Virginia's convention (and perhaps those at other state conventions) reasonably relied on those assurances (and others like them) when they voted, then those assurances state the understanding of the Constitution those ratifiers agreed to—and therefore, on some theories of constitutional law, the legally authoritative meaning of the Constitution.

But the Ratifiers' Reliance argument has important weaknesses, even if one adopts the premise that some set of facts about how Americans in 1787–1788 thought about the Constitution settles its legal content. Yes, Madison and other Federalists addressed themselves to Americans who were hesitant about making the general government too strong and tried to persuade them that the proposed Constitution should not worry them. That leading Federalists in the ratification debates frequently described the Constitution in enumerationist terms does suggest that they thought the Constitution was more likely to be ratified if the public—or at least some important slice of the public—thought of it that way. But there is no reason to think those Federalists had a precisely correct assessment of what the ratifiers needed to believe in order to support ratification. Perhaps Madison and his fellow travelers were being more cautious than necessary. Moreover, it is not clear why anyone should think the ratifiers or the broader public understood the Constitution as Madison and his fellow travelers represented it. The fact that the Constitution got ratified does not prove that the public believed the enumerationist interpretations that Madison and his fellow Federalists offered, much less that the Constitution was ratified in reliance on those interpretations. We simply do not know why the thousand or so voters at the state conventions who voted in favor of the Constitution voted as they did. Perhaps some were persuaded by Madison's representations. But perhaps others found those representations unpersuasive or unreliable and voted for the Constitution anyway.

Indeed, we have good reason to think that some delegates felt that way. Consider Randolph, who at the end of the General Convention had declined to sign the Constitution and who was widely recognized as an important fence-sitter in the ratification process. At the end of the Virginia convention, Randolph acknowledged that the Constitution might create a powerful general government—even a dangerously powerful one—but explained that he would support ratification on the grounds that it was better than the alternative.[7] Or consider the Massachusetts lawyer Silas Lee, who would later represent his state in Congress. Shortly after Massachusetts voted to ratify, Lee wrote that he had "great doubts whether the Liberties of the People are not exceedingly endangered" by the power the general government would wield under the new Constitution. But he still favored ratification as "the safest of the Alternatives," because nonratification would be even worse.[8] Americans with views like these made calculated decisions to support the Constitution not because they believed Federalist assurances about limited congressional power but because they figured the Constitution was better for the country than the Articles of Confederation even if it would create a general government more powerful than Madison was letting on.

At the very least, the idea that Federalist assurances about limited congressional power moved the net vote count decisively in favor of ratification requires no small amount of speculation. And it seems especially unlikely if one thinks of the ratifiers as worldly and sophisticated actors who understood the dynamics of governmental decisionmaking. Why, exactly, should a Virginian who saw that the Constitution could be read to give Congress vast implicit power feel confident that he could rely on Madison's representation that it would not be read that way? After all, some Americans who favored the Constitution read it to create a more powerful general government than Madison was saying.[9] The Constitution's most nationalist supporters never authorized Madison to waive their right to interpret the Constitution to empower the national government more broadly—and once in a while, they publicly acknowledged their view that the Congress would have some powers beyond those expressly enumerated.[10] There was no reason to think that after the Constitution was ratified, Madison (alone or in combination with the others making similar arguments) would be able to prevent the general government from acting on a broader understanding of its powers, if the officials in control of that government had a mind to do so. Indeed, they turned out to have just such a mind through the 1790s, and Madison was unable to stop them; quite predictably, his protests that the state conventions had been promised a less-powerful government were brushed aside. So it might have been naïve for a skeptic of national power at the Virginia convention to think, "I read this Constitution to permit a deal-breakingly large amount of federal power, but Madison assures me that that is not the Constitution's meaning, and I will vote to ratify in reliance on his representation." To my knowledge, the historical sources do not record anyone's explaining his voting position on the Constitution in these terms.

To be clear, the narrow readings of federal power that Madison and other leading Federalists offered during the ratification process might be good guides to the Constitution, even if nobody relied on them. Another possibility is that these readings state the understandings of people with unusual insight into the composition and workings of the Constitution. But not everyone with special insight into the composition and workings of the Constitution was on the same side of the question. In the end, whether any given interpretation was especially insightful is a question to be examined on its merits.

When one assesses the insight on offer in ratification-era arguments, it is important to be willing to entertain the possibility that those arguments were not always made in perfectly good faith. Sometimes, Federalists and Antifederalists alike might have dissembled for the purpose of persuading their audiences. This is not to suggest that Founding-era Americans were an especially mendacious bunch. The advocates on both sides were trying to win elections. Corner-cutting, exaggeration, disingenuity, and even outright lying are known features of political campaigns. Almost nobody assumes that twenty-first-century politicians believe everything they say. The participants in the ratification debates were not categorically above this normal human behavior. Certainly people at the time regarded a fair amount of ratification discourse as untrustworthy: on the floor of Congress in 1791, Gerry said that nothing the Constitution's supporters said during ratification should be relied on, because people said whatever they thought they had to say in order to get the Constitution ratified.[11]

Gerry had opposed ratification through much of the process (though he came around by the end), so perhaps his statement itself had a partisan inflection, and in any case I am not advocating that readers be quite so dismissive.[12] Federalists and Antifederalists alike probably believed what they said a fair amount of the time, as most people generally do. But to assess the debate in a realistic way, and to avoid being misled about what it means that this or that Founder said this or that thing about the Constitution, it is important to be willing to ask, about any given argument, whether it might be a mistake to take it at face value. Recall, for example, that at the Convention, Wilson (in Madison's rendering) declared that letting each state have equal representation in the Senate was "a fundamental and a perpetual error"; to the ratifying public, Wilson described that arrangement as an admirable bit of compromise and professed his "astonishment, in beholding so perfect a system."[13] Madison at the Convention explained cogently that giving the House of Representatives sole power to initiate money bills was a meaningless gesture that would have no practical effect on federal legislation, given the Senate's power to propose amendments; to the ratifying public, Madison presented the House's distinctive power over the purse as "the most complete and effectual weapon with which any constitution can arm the immediate representatives of the people."[14] One could go on.

⊰⊶⊱⊰⊶⊱

I have two overlapping aims in this chapter, and neither is to demonstrate that most Americans (or most of the ratifiers) thought about the extent of federal power under the proposed Constitution in any particular way. On the contrary, my first aim is to present the discourse of ratification as a debate featuring multiple points of view, some of them nonenumerationist and reasonably so, and also as a discussion that did not settle the question of which views were best. My second aim is to raise doubts about at least some of the enumerationist views that leading Federalists endorsed. In service of both aims, I encourage readers to see the arguments of Madison, Hamilton, Wilson, and others not as authoritative explanations or reliance-inducing warranties but as arguments for understanding the Constitution in certain ways—arguments that not everyone at the time accepted, for understandable reasons.

Before proceeding, a word is in order about the historical source material. In many respects, the available sources for the ratification debates are more accessible and more reliable than the material for the General Convention. The Convention worked in secret; the ratification process featured massive amounts of public debate. Moreover, participants in the ratifying debates frequently published their ideas. That said, not all of the source material from 1787–1788 is in the form of published essays and speeches. The proceedings of Congress, like those of the Convention, are recorded mostly in individual diaries. The proceedings of the state ratifying conventions were generally public, and for some states the records are extensive. But the published records of the state convention proceedings might create, in modern readers, an unjustified confidence that we know exactly who said what. For example, a shorthand reporter took notes at the Virginia convention, and based on his notes the proceedings have been published at great length. But it seems unlikely that the published version exactly reflects what was said at the convention. Eighteenth-century shorthand was not stenography. Moreover, the reporter did not have a seat on the convention floor; he sat in the spectators' gallery, from where it was often hard to hear some of the delegates, especially delegates who tended to speak softly (like Madison).[15] That the published notes show all the delegates speaking in complete sentences pretty much all of the time probably reflects the reporter's augmentation of what he was able to hear, rather than an uncanny eloquence on the part of all the delegates. Many years later, John Marshall—who served as a delegate at the Virginia convention—averred that he never would have recognized what appeared in the published proceedings under his name as his own remarks.[16] Perhaps the chief justice was exaggerating or distancing himself from things said long ago that he preferred not to own. But the basic point is a caution well taken.[17]

Congress Considers the Constitution

When the General Convention adjourned, it sent a final copy of the draft Constitution to the Confederation Congress. Ten Convention delegates were also members of Congress. So when on September 26 Congress began to consider the proposed Constitution, the discussion included some people who had participated in the drafting process and others who confronted the document without that experience, as the general public would. Like the Convention, the Confederation Congress kept only a rudimentary journal, and our knowledge of the proceedings depends on notes taken by individuals who were present.

According to New York representative Melancton Smith, the second day of conversation featured a discussion of why the proposed Constitution had no bill of rights. It is not clear from Smith's notes who first raised the issue. The recorded conversation on the subject begins with two of the Convention's leading members—Madison and Gorham—defending their work product, presumably against someone's objection, by saying that in this Constitution no bill of rights was necessary. According to Smith's notes, Gorham explained that bills of rights were necessary in state constitutions but not in the proposed United States Constitution. In the state governments, Gorham explained, the legislatures had general authority, and bills of rights functioned "to retain certain powers"—that is, to mark some things the legislatures would not have the authority to do.[18] The available sources do not record Gorham's saying that Congress under the newly proposed Constitution would have a more limited grant of power. But whether or not he made that point explicitly, his argument seems to have been intended to draw that contrast between Congress and the state legislatures. And if Gorham left that part of the analysis implicit, Madison made it plain. In Smith's rendering, Madison argued that a bill of rights was not necessary in the new Constitution because Congress's "powers are enumerated and only extend to certain cases."[19]

Gorham and Madison did not persuade everyone in the room. In particular, they did not persuade Richard Henry Lee, the Virginia delegate who eleven years earlier had introduced the resolution declaring American independence. According to Smith's notes, Lee responded that a bill of rights had not been necessary for the United States under the Articles of Confederation "because it is expressly declared no power sh[oul]d be exercised, but such as is expressly given—and therefore no constructive power can be exercised." It was the prevention of such "constructive powers," Lee maintained, that was the "great use of a Bill of [R]ights."[20]

Smith's notes do not record Lee pointing out that the proposed Constitution contained no text declaring the federal government limited to its expressly granted powers. But the sense of his argument seems to have been that Gorham's and Madison's idea rested on an unwarranted premise: that Congress under the new Constitution would only be authorized to exercise those powers that were expressly given. What was the basis for that premise? Nothing in the proposed Constitution said so. Worse still, in Lee's view, the proposed Constitution's failure to state that Congress would be limited to the powers enumerated seemed particularly meaningful because it stood in contrast to the Articles of Confederation.

Lee might have been overreading the Articles. After all, that document did not expressly limit Congress to a set of enumerated powers. It declared that the states retained all powers not expressly delegated to the United States. As Wilson had pointed out in his Bank of North America essay, that was not the same thing: there might be powers inherent in the United States that had never belonged to any state, such that Congress's exercise of such powers would not violate the rule providing that the states "retained" all powers they previously enjoyed, except those that were delegated expressly. But the cogency of Wilson's point notwithstanding, Lee's view of the Articles was conventional. Most well-socialized American lawyers and politicians in 1787 understood the Articles' language about express delegation to do what Lee indicated. The proposed Constitution had no parallel language.

What's more, the essence of Lee's response to Gorham and Madison would have been just as cogent had Lee taken Wilson's more capacious view of national power under the Articles. On Lee's conventional view, the Articles provided that Congress could exercise no powers but those expressly delegated to it. On Wilson's view, the Articles provided that Congress could exercise no powers *previously held by the states* but those expressly delegated to it. The drafters of the Constitution had not said either thing. Given the contrast, it made sense to think that the Constitution contemplated Congress's exercising powers *beyond* those expressly delegated—including powers previously exercised by the states. To be sure, the text of the Constitution did not say "Congress may exercise more powers than are identified in this document." But the salient omission of any statement limiting Congress to the powers expressly delegated to it left the door open to the exercise of other powers. Given that state of affairs, Lee argued, a bill of rights was essential.[21] So he proposed to add a bill of rights to the Constitution before sending it on to the states for ratification.[22]

It is worth being clear about what Lee wanted. Given his premise—that the absence of language limiting Congress to expressly delegated powers was significant and a potential cause of trouble—Lee might have sought to amend the Constitution by adding language that would confine the general government to expressly delegated powers only. But that was not his agenda. Neither in Congress nor in his personal correspondence did Lee recommend such an amendment—and Lee was not at all shy about recommending amendments. In addition to a bill of rights with sweeping language about the principles on which governments are founded and a long list of specific guaranteed liberties, Lee recommended that Congress modify the Convention's draft by establishing a Privy Council, reducing the power of the Senate, eliminating the vice presidency, increasing the size of the lower house of Congress, raising the quorum requirements for both houses, and revoking the Great Compromise, such that both houses would be apportioned in proportion to the populations of the states. Needless to say, a man willing to push all of these changes would have had no reason to be shy about also calling for language about "express delegation" of powers—had he wanted to. So although we cannot know, it seems reasonable to infer that Lee did not particularly object to the idea that Congress might exercise powers beyond those expressly enu-merated in the Constitution's text. What he objected to, in a system with a Congress thus empowered, was the absence of a bill of rights and several as-pects of the constitutional structure that would, as a matter of process, shape what laws Congress would choose to enact.

A majority of Lee's colleagues opposed his proposal to revise the Conven-tion's work. In their view, Congress should send the Convention's draft as a whole to the states, rather than imagining itself as a sort of second Conven-tion that could tinker with the text. But on the merits of the bill of rights issue, Lee had a point. What justified the absence of a bill of rights? Gorham and Madison said that one was not necessary because Congress could only exercise its enumerated powers. But what supported that interpretation? What guarantee was there that Congress or other decisionmakers in the fu-ture would abide by that view, especially given the telling contrast with the Articles of Confederation?

Had he been in a mood to do so, Lee might have pointed to other argu-ments Madison made in Congress as a way of skewering Madison's claim that the enumeration of Congress's powers in the Constitution was inherently limiting. The delegates had skirmished that day about whether the General Convention had exceeded its mandate. According to Smith's notes, Lee pointed out that under the Articles of Confederation, Congress itself could not ap-prove a measure like the proposed Constitution without the unanimous con-sent of all thirteen states, but that the proposed Constitution purported to become effective on the ratification of only nine states. In Lee's view, that meant that the Convention had gone beyond what it was authorized to do. The Articles bound Congress, and the Convention was called by the author-ity of Congress, so the Convention's mandate could not possibly include a power to provide for the amendment of the Articles—let alone their whole-sale abrogation—with less than unanimous state consent.[23] In response to Lee, Madison conceded that the Convention had not stayed strictly within its limits, but he argued that any excess was justified by the necessity of the case and by the precedent of Congress itself. Congress too, Madison said, had "in many Instances exceeded their powers." He pointed to the laws or-ganizing and disposing of the Western Territories as an example.[24]

Madison's intention was to defend the Convention's work by saying that Congress's own example demonstrated the folly of expecting such a body to stay scrupulously within its official mandate. In reality, Madison knew, bodies

like Congress sometimes transgress the boundaries of the powers they have
been officially given. As a plea to excuse the Convention's excesses, Madison's point might have been reasonable. But it is noteworthy that Madison
offered this defense on the same day when he also argued that a bill of rights
was unnecessary because Congress would be limited by its enumerated
powers. After all, this defense undermined his claim that the Constitution's
enumeration of powers would constrain Congress. If Congress often exceeded
its expressly delegated powers even under the Articles, which were generally understood to have an explicit rule limiting Congress to those expressly
delegated powers, it is hard to see why anyone should have confidence that
Congress would not exceed its enumerated powers under a new Constitution
lacking any such explicit limitation.

We cannot know what was in Madison's mind when he made these remarks. But there are reasons to think he understood that enumerating a legislature's powers was not a reliable way to limit what that legislature would
do. Madison had observed that very day that Congress under the Articles
had often exceeded its enumerated powers, and he had warned Wallace two
years before that legislatures by nature do not lend themselves to being confined by enumerations of power. What's more, after Lee pushed back against
the claim, Madison seems to have abandoned the position. From that day
until the following June, as the ratification debates raged and Madison contributed dozens of essays to the conversation, he did not repeat the claim
that the Constitution's enumeration of congressional powers made a bill of
rights unnecessary. Perhaps he realized that Lee had a point.

Wilson on a Bill of Rights

The idea that the Constitution's limited grant of power to the general government made a bill of rights unnecessary burst onto the public scene a little more than a week later, on October 6, in a speech Wilson gave outside the
Philadelphia State House. Wilson's speech was a sensation. It was published
in the *Pennsylvania Herald*, republished there in the next day's edition to
satisfy the demand for copies, and reprinted in more than thirty newspapers.[25] Coming as it did at the opening moment of the ratification debates,
Wilson's argument about congressional powers and a bill of rights framed
much of the subsequent discussion of those topics. Two hundred years later,

when the Supreme Court in *United States v. Lopez* insisted that internal limits must do real work in constitutional law, the Court cited Wilson's speech as evidence of the Constitution's original meaning.[26]

Wilson argued from a premise familiar to modern constitutional lawyers: that Congress and the state legislatures face opposite default rules. The state governments, Wilson explained, were governments of general jurisdiction, and each state legislature possessed all legislative power except what was affirmatively denied to it. In contrast, Congress had only those powers it was affirmatively given. And Congress was given no power that endangered fundamental liberties. It followed, Wilson argued, that no bill of rights was necessary.

As reported in the *Pennsylvania Herald*, Wilson put the point this way:

> [C]ongressional authority is to be collected, not from tacit implication, but from the positive grant expressed in the instrument of union. Hence it is evident, that in the former case [i.e., that of the state legislatures] every thing which is not reserved is given, but in the latter [i.e., with respect to Congress] the reverse of the proposition prevails, and every thing which is not given, is reserved. This distinction being recognized, will furnish an answer to those who think the omission of a bill of rights, a defect in the proposed constitution.[27]

For example, Wilson continued, there was no need for a constitutional provision protecting the freedom of the press, because, with the minor exception of Congress's power to regulate within the district that housed the seat of government, Congress had no power to control the press in the first place.[28]

It is accordingly easy to read Wilson's speech as offering, in a strong form, the argument that the federal government would have no powers except those enumerated in the Constitution. The modern Supreme Court has invoked Wilson's speech for that proposition, and many of Wilson's contemporaries heard him that way at the time.[29] But on careful consideration, there are at least four ways of understanding the speech, and the conventional view is probably the least tenable of the four. The possibilities are:

1) The conventional interpretation: Wilson believed that the federal government would have no powers other than those enumerated in the text of the Constitution, and in his view that feature of the Constitution made a bill of rights unnecessary.

2) The sincere complexity interpretation: Wilson believed that the internal limits of the federal government's powers made a bill of rights unnecessary, but he also believed that the federal government would have nonenumerated powers in addition to its enumerated ones. He intended to communicate both parts of that more complex conception, but he failed to do so as clearly as he could have.

3) The deliberate ambiguity interpretation: Wilson believed that the internal limits of the federal government's powers made a bill of rights unnecessary, but he also believed that the federal government would have nonenumerated powers in addition to its enumerated ones. For political reasons, he intended to communicate the first of those ideas with unmistakable clarity and the second idea more hazily.

4) The hardball politics interpretation: Wilson did not believe that the internal limits on Congress's powers made a bill of rights unnecessary. He made the argument anyway, because he figured it would help secure political support for the Constitution.

The conventional interpretation faces two straightforward problems. First, the position it attributes to Wilson is a bad argument, and Wilson surely knew it. As previously discussed, Congress would have several powers sufficient for violating people's rights. (As a tool for restricting the liberty of the press, the copyright power comes to mind. Or perhaps Congress would use its power to tax to make the publication of certain materials prohibitively expensive or use its power to regulate commerce to ban the circulation of certain newspapers.) Second, crediting the conventional interpretation requires believing that Wilson had, in a short time, radically altered his core beliefs about the government of the United States.

Consider how curious it would have been for Wilson, of all people, to believe that Congress would have no powers other than those enumerated in the Constitution's text. Wilson was on record, in his Bank of North America essay just two years earlier, arguing that Congress had inherent powers even under the Articles of Confederation—powers resulting automatically from the fact that Congress acted for the Union as a whole. Did he now mean to say that the new Constitution would take a more restrictive posture toward national power than the Articles of Confederation had? If so, on what basis? Everyone knew that the Constitution would make the United States government more powerful, not less, than it had been under the Articles. Certainly nothing in the text of the Constitution purported to withdraw from the government whatever inherent powers it had previously enjoyed. What's more, in contrast to the Articles, the proposed Constitution contained no statement reserving to the states all the powers that the states had previously enjoyed except those expressly delegated to Congress. At the Convention, Georgia's William Pierce recorded Wilson taking the view "that it would be impossible to enumerate the powers which the federal Legislature ought to have."[30] And Wilson himself likely drafted the Sweeping Clause with the intention of authorizing the exercise of "all other powers" appropriate for the general government, including powers beyond those specifically mentioned in the text of the Constitution. So it makes sense to be skeptical about whether Wilson really meant to embrace the position that under the new Constitution, the federal government could exercise only those powers enumerated in the Constitution's text.

Consider next the sincere complexity interpretation. On this view, Wilson believed that Congress would have only the authorities it was affirmatively given and that that fact about Congress made a bill of rights superfluous, but he did not abandon his view that the national government would have resulting as well as enumerated powers. This possibility may not occur to most readers of Wilson's speech, because we tend to read through the lens of enumerationism. But if one sets that lens aside and reads Wilson's speech in the context of his previously expressed ideas, it is easy to understand his remarks as consistent with his earlier commitment to a national government with inherent powers.

Wilson said that "congressional authority is to be collected, not from tacit implication, but from the positive grant expressed in the instrument of union." If that statement is understood to mean that Congress would have no powers beyond those specified in the Constitution's text, then Wilson was turning his back on his previous ideas and embracing the enumeration principle. But "the positive grant expressed in the instrument of union" included the Sweeping Clause, which, on Wilson's understanding, pointed to a suite of federal powers beyond those enumerated in the Constitution's text. For Wilson, the Sweeping Clause probably meant that those other powers were not mere matters of "tacit implication." The text of the Constitution testified to their existence.

But if Wilson did not think that the federal government would be restricted to its enumerated powers, could he believe that internal limits on congressional power made a bill of rights unnecessary? He could. (Whether he *did* is a separate question. But clearly he could.) To say that a government has resulting as well as enumerated powers is not to say that it has general jurisdiction. Wilson did not think of the government's nonenumerated powers as an amorphous mass: he thought of them as a more or less catalogable set of powers logically arising from the purposes for which the government was formed. If Wilson thought of those powers as knowable and as no threat to fundamental liberties, then the fact that the government had nonenumerated powers would have been compatible with his argument that a bill of rights was unnecessary in light of the limited powers the government had been given.

That way of thinking about national power and a bill of rights is logically coherent, consistent with Wilson's previously expressed ideas, and reconcilable with the text of his speech. But this interpretation of Wilson's speech also has weaknesses. For one, there is still the fact that Congress's powers under the Constitution—even if one counts only the enumerated powers—seem more than adequate for oppressive behavior. But there is also more.

If Wilson was trying to persuade the crowd that a bill of rights was superfluous even though the federal government would have nonenumerated powers, he wrote a rather ineffective speech. The speech is consistent with the idea that the general government would have nonenumerated powers, but it is easy to miss that reading of the speech if one is not looking for it. And that is not only true of modern readers. In 1787, Wilson was widely understood as having endorsed the view that the general government would have enumerated powers only. So if it was his intention to communicate both that the government would have nonenumerated powers and that no bill of rights was necessary, he did so with too much subtlety for much of the audience. On the assumption that Wilson was a competent public communicator, we might accordingly doubt that he meant for his audience to understand that he believed the general government would have nonenumerated powers. If Wilson had wanted to make sure that his audience understood that part of his thinking, he probably would have communicated it more clearly.

So consider possibility 3 above, on which Wilson held the same combination of views as in possibility 2 but was content, for political reasons, to let the crowd hear him as endorsing the simpler view that the federal government would have only enumerated powers. Wilson's job that day was to motivate the public to support the Constitution. He needed to convince people that the absence of a bill of rights was not an important defect. Given his highly developed theory about the nature of the American Union and the resulting powers of the federal government, Wilson might have felt confident that the government had nonenumerated powers but that those powers could not be used in oppressive ways. But some of Wilson's audience might have been skittish about the idea that an undefined set of national powers could be counted on to be benign. So given Wilson's practical aim—to persuade people that the federal government would have no powers that would endanger their rights—he might have decided to make the argument without highlighting the prospect of a general government with nonenumerated powers. He might even have decided to speak in a way that encouraged his audience to think of the Constitution as limiting the general government to enumerated powers, if that was how they were inclined to hear him, as long as he could do it without actually contradicting his own view—and while sprinkling in enough affirmation of his resulting-powers view so as not to alienate the portion of the audience that shared his nationalist orientation and whose support might be vitiated if the Constitution had to be understood as restricting federal power too sharply.

If Wilson intended to speak ambiguously, he might well have known that he was either stretching things or counting on the limited discernment of his audience. But those possibilities are completely plausible. Wilson was a fancily educated and highly accomplished lawyer. He knew how to choose words carefully. (Wilson opened by protesting that he was "unprepared for so extensive and so important a disquisition," but perhaps this dean of the Philadelphia bar had not come to give a public address at a political meeting without giving some thought to his tactics.) In short, Wilson may have crafted an argument intended to allay one audience's concerns about the absence of a bill of rights without sacrificing his long-standing ideas about the government of the United States as the possessor of nonenumerated powers. If that involved a bit of studied ambiguity, it would be neither the first nor the last time that a politician avoided committing himself too clearly on a controversial topic.

All things considered, this interpretation seems more plausible than either of the first two. But it too has weaknesses. For one, there is still the issue of whether Wilson could really have believed that the scope of Congress's powers made a bill of rights superfluous. That question is shown in sharper relief in the context of this interpretation, which posits that Wilson was clever and careful in crafting the speech. The more we think that the speech was cleverly and carefully crafted, the harder it is to understand Wilson's assertion that a government with the power to tax, to regulate commerce, and to issue copyrights had no power that might endanger a free press anywhere beyond the seat of government.[31]

So consider, finally, the fourth option: that Wilson's speech was simply hardball politics. Maybe Wilson did not really think the internal limits of the federal government's powers would make a bill of rights unnecessary. Maybe he made an argument he did not believe in the service of securing political support for the Constitution. It is not a hypothesis that flatters Wilson's honor. But politicians sometimes say what they think their audiences want to hear, even when doing so requires taking liberties with the truth. It would be naïve to preclude the possibility that Wilson and other Framers were always above such behavior, especially with the stakes so high. Consider that in this same speech, Wilson spoke admiringly about the Great Compromise, after having declared at the Convention that equal representation in the Senate was "a fundamental and perpetual error."[32] To get the Constitution ratified, its partisans sometimes exaggerated its virtues.

The major disadvantage of this interpretation, of course, is that it portrays Wilson as insincere. That is problematic not just because it runs contrary to the civic culture to present Founding Fathers as liars but because as a matter of historiographical method it is usually better to figure out why an apparently strange set of statements made sense to the person who made them than to conclude that someone was just not making sense—or lying. But in this case, the hypothesis of insincerity has to be taken seriously. Each of the other interpretations has weaknesses, and this one makes a fair amount of sense.

I offer no definitive conclusion about which of these interpretations is the best way to understand Wilson's speech. But all things considered, some combination of the third and fourth interpretations seems most plausible. The first interpretation—the conventional one—has Wilson endorsing a view at war with one of his previous core ideas and using that view as the basis for a bad argument. The second interpretation solves the first problem but not the second. The third interpretation comes closer to solving both problems, and the fourth one clearly does, albeit at the price in both cases of portraying Wilson as less than completely transparent. Wilson was trying to get the Constitution ratified; he was probably not above cutting corners in his public speeches in order to make it happen. In any event, the possibility that Wilson was speaking with deliberate ambiguity and the possibility that he was simply dissembling both seem more plausible than the possibility that he had suddenly abandoned the view of government that he had held both at and before the Convention. And the claim that most people understood him to have made—that the Constitution obviated the need for a bill of rights by enumerating the powers of government—would soon be roundly disbelieved.

The Extension

Whatever might be said about Wilson's argument to this point, his speech soon added a more adventurous claim. As far as we can tell, Madison and Gorham had argued in Congress that the limited scope of Congress's powers under the Constitution made a bill of rights unnecessary. Wilson went further: he argued that declaring rights would be *dangerous*. After saying that there was no need to provide affirmatively for the liberty of the press because Congress had no power to regulate publications, Wilson ventured that a constitutional provision purporting to protect the liberty of the press would actually endanger that liberty, because it would imply that Congress had some power sufficient for abridging the liberty of the press in the absence of some protection. "[T]hat very declaration," Wilson warned, "might have been construed to imply that some degree of power was given, since we undertook to define its extent."[33]

Wilson thus presented the absence of affirmative guarantees of rights as a positive virtue of the proposed Constitution. That was a bold extension of the enumerated-powers argument, and it might have been attractive to some audience. After all, it suggests that the Constitution was the product of careful and even elegant design and that it embodies more wisdom than might initially meet the eye. It also suggests that, far from having been inattentive to the liberty concerns that prompted calls for a bill of rights, the Constitution's drafters had been keenly concerned with vindicating American liberties. They had simply gone about it in a more subtle and effective way than the people calling for a bill of rights had thought of.

But the idea that the affirmative specification of limits on Congress was a danger that the Convention had wisely avoided also suffered from a serious problem: it was untrue. Worse, it was transparently untrue. After all, the Constitution did contain several affirmative limits on the powers of Congress, including limits that protected the sorts of liberties that might be declared in bills of rights. In specific terms, the Constitution prohibited bills of attainder, ex post facto laws, federal prosecutions without jury trials, and so on. As a result, Wilson's argument offered the Constitution's opponents a rich and easy target: one of the Constitution's foremost advocates had tried to sell the people a false understanding. And in short order, people who believed the omission of a bill of rights to be a deep flaw in the Constitution began drawing attention to Wilson's argument in order to paint the Constitution as dangerous and its supporters as untrustworthy.

Blowback

Wilson's version of the limited-powers argument was vulnerable to at least four kinds of objections. First, Wilson had argued that it would be dangerous to specify affirmative limits on Congress—but the Constitution did not seem to be written on that theory, because it clearly specified such affirmative limits. Second, Wilson insisted that none of Congress's powers under the Constitution would let Congress abridge important liberties, but many Americans easily read the powers of Congress to authorize legislation that would abridge those liberties. Third, several critics completely rejected Wilson's claim that the Constitution gave Congress only a subset of all possible legislative power, arguing instead that the powers given to Congress were broad enough to warrant Congress's enacting any legislation it might choose to pass. And fourth, even if the Constitution did not confer the equivalent of plenary power on Congress, many critics doubted the claim that Congress could exercise no power beyond what was enumerated.

The first objection was easy to make. In a letter to Samuel Adams, Lee wrote that the "futility" of Wilson's argument was obvious based on "the conduct of the Convention itself, for they have made several reservations. . . . But they have no reservation in favor of the Press, Rights of Conscience, Trial by Jury in Civil Cases, or Common Law securities."[34] A critic writing under the pseudonym "Brutus" made the same point. Obviously Wilson's theory could not have been the real reason why the Convention omitted a bill of rights, Brutus noted, because the Constitution did specifically protect habeas corpus and the rights against bills of attainder and ex post facto laws.[35] A writer calling himself Cincinnatus put the point a bit more sharply. In a published letter addressed directly to Wilson, Cincinnatus noted that Section 9 limited Congress affirmatively and then asked this rhetorical question: "Which are we to believe, sir,—you or the constitution?"[36]

It is tempting to try to defend Wilson's argument by limiting its scope. Perhaps, one might say, Wilson did not mean that it would be dangerous for the Constitution to include *any* affirmative prohibitions designed to protect people's rights. Perhaps he meant only that it would be dangerous for the Constitution to include such prohibitions in cases where nothing in Congress's powers could be understood to endanger those rights. For example, maybe the Constitution's affirmative protections for habeas corpus and jury trial were needed because Congress would obviously have the power to conduct criminal prosecutions. The affirmative prohibitions that would be dangerous, in this line of thinking, would be only those Congress had no power to violate anyway. In later generations, people defending the enumerationist story about why the Convention omitted a bill of rights have sometimes used this rationale.

But this attempted defense falls victim to the second major category of objection Wilson's critics pressed: that in fact the powers of Congress were sufficient for all sorts of liberty-violating regulation. Indeed, Wilson's core example of a liberty that should not be affirmatively specified—the liberty of the press—is a liberty Congress could easily have abridged using its enumerated powers. Wilson's critics understood that point well. For example, a writer calling himself "A Republican" wondered what he was to make of Wilson's claim that Congress would have no power sufficient to abridge the liberty of the press in light of the fact that the Constitution authorized Congress to issue copyrights. Quite obviously, the copyright power would entail the regulation of printing, up to and including the enactment and enforcement of laws prohibiting the printing of certain texts without permission. Could it really be said that a Congress wielding that power had no power that threatened the freedom of the press? Similarly, a writer using the pseudonym "Federal Farmer" cautioned that, though a right-acting Congress would do no such thing, nothing would prevent Congress "from laying duties particularly heavy on certain pieces printed"—that is, from impeding the circulation of disfavored communications by raising the cost of printing with heavy taxation.[37]

Wilson's critics also pointed out that Congress's powers were sufficient to violate people's rights in all sorts of other ways that the Constitution's small suite of prohibitions was inadequate to prevent. Brutus drove the point home with respect to the powers of law enforcement. Surely the new government would make and enforce laws, and Brutus reminded his readers that law enforcement affords many opportunities for rights violations. The government's police might search people and their property in unreasonable and invasive ways. The Constitution specified that criminal trials would be by jury, but it said nothing about whether defendants would have the right to the assistance of counsel, to cross-examine the prosecution's witnesses, to know the charges against them, or to be free from cruel and unusual punishments if convicted. Once the government was going to have a criminal apparatus, and it clearly was, it could make no sense to say that the government had no capacity to violate people's rights, nor even to say that it could only violate people's rights in ways accounted for by the Constitution's small set of affirmative prohibitions.[38]

The criticism that Wilson had implausibly understated Congress's capacity to violate important rights lay along a continuum with the third category of objections to his argument, which attacked the more general idea that Congress's powers would be limited in scope. According to several critics, the enumerated powers of Congress were sufficiently broad or ill-defined that Congress would be able to invoke them to support any legislation it might wish to enact. Brutus is again illustrative. In his first essay, he warned that Article I, Section 8, was "very general and comprehensive, and it may receive a construction to justify the passing [of] almost any law."[39] In his various writings, Brutus pointed to the Constitution's Preamble, the General Welfare Clause, the Treaty Clause, and the Necessary and Proper Clause (including the Sweeping Clause) to demonstrate that the Constitution would give the government the authority to legislate virtually at will. The Treaty Clause, he wrote, gave the new government authority to make treaties that would be supreme law just like statutes, and the Constitution in no way limited the scope of what the government might agree to in a treaty.[40] The General Welfare Clause— the language in Article I, Section 8, authorizing Congress to "provide for the common defence and general welfare of the United States"—was nearly a general legislative warrant all by itself, because Congress might deem almost anything to be a matter of the general welfare.[41] Brutus acknowledged that some people read the General Welfare Clause as merely a power of taxation— a reading of which Brutus was skeptical—but he maintained that in the end reading the clause in that narrower way would make no difference. After all, whatever power that clause conferred had to be read in conjunction with the clause granting Congress the power "to make all laws which shall be necessary and proper for carrying into execution the foregoing powers, and all other powers vested by this Constitution in the government of the United States, or in any department or officer thereof." "A case cannot be conceived of," Brutus warned, "which is not included in this power," even if it were deployed only in support of a power to raise revenue.[42] And if the power described in the Necessary and Proper Clause were combined with the power to provide for the general welfare, then "the legislature under this constitution may pass any law which they may think proper."[43]

Brutus acknowledged that interpreters determined to construe Congress's powers as limited might read the language of these authorizations more narrowly. But Brutus thought it naïve to expect things to play out that way. Legal instruments, Brutus noted, are interpreted in light of their purposes. The Constitution's purposes, as stated in its Preamble, included a more perfect union, justice, domestic tranquility, defense, the general welfare, and liberty.[44] That was pretty much everything that a government might do: "If the end of the government is to be learned from these words, which are clearly designed to declare it, it is obvious it has in view every object which is embraced by any government."[45] Assuming that officials would interpret the enumerated powers of Congress in light of these ends, Congress's powers would "extend to every case for which any government is instituted, whether external or internal."[46] Indeed, on the most straightforward reading, the combination of the Preamble and the Sweeping Clause established "that the legislature will have an authority to make all laws which they shall judge necessary for the common safety, and to promote the general welfare." In short, the entire premise that the enumeration of congressional powers would limit the new government was false, and its falsehood appeared on the face of the Constitution itself.

Brutus's reading of the Constitution was not universally shared, but neither was it idiosyncratic.[47] Madison regarded Brutus as a serious critic whose arguments had to be addressed.[48] Moreover, skepticism that the enumeration of powers would limit Congress was not limited to those who, with Brutus, read the Constitution as conferring plenary power on Congress. A more moderate concern was also prominent. And that more moderate concern animated the fourth and last category of objections to Wilson's argument.

Even if the expressly enumerated powers were not broad enough to let Congress legislate at will, the idea that the enumeration of powers would prevent Congress from abridging liberties depended on the premise that the powers enumerated were the only ones Congress could exercise. But why should that be? Even if Congress did not have general legislative jurisdiction, it might not be restricted to the specific powers the Constitution's text enumerated. Wilson insisted that Congress could only do what it was affirmatively authorized to do—but carefully parsed, his speech was cagey about whether Congress was affirmatively given more powers than were textually enumerated in the Constitution. And even if Wilson were clearly saying that Congress could exercise its textually enumerated powers only, why should people believe him, given his famous Bank of North America essay of 1785? Nothing in the Constitution specified that the enumerated powers of Congress were exclusive. As Lee had pointed out in Congress, the Articles of Confederation provided that Congress had only those powers "expressly delegated" to it, but the Constitution had no parallel restriction. Wasn't it reasonable to infer that the Constitution freed Congress from the limitation that the Articles had imposed? In the weeks after Wilson's speech, several writers hammered away at this point.[49]

One critic, writing as the Federal Farmer, shrewdly diagnosed the likely results of ratifying a Constitution whose text did not clearly close the door to nonenumerated powers. Some people, he noted, said the states would hold all power not expressly delegated to the national government, and some people said the opposite. His assessment: "The truth is, in either case, it is a mere matter of opinion, and men usually take either side of the argument, as will best answer their purposes." In practice, that ambiguity would favor national power. "[T]he general presumption," he wrote, is "that men who govern, will, in doubtful cases, construe laws and constitutions mostly favorably for increasing their own powers."[50] In other words, a constitution under which people could argue either side of the question as to whether the general government had powers beyond those enumerated would, in operation, be a constitution under which that government would exercise nonenumerated powers.

In sum, a gallery of critics rejected the claim that Congress would enjoy only its enumerated powers as unfounded or worse. Writing to Madison from Paris, Jefferson summed up his view of the matter as follows:

> [T]o say, as [M]r Wilson does, that a bill of rights was not necessary because all is reserved in the case of the general government which is not given, while in the particular ones all is given which is not reserved, might do for the Audience to which it was addressed; but it is surely a *gratis dictum*, the

reverse of which might just as well be said; and it is opposed by strong inferences from the body of the instrument, as well as from the omission of
the clause of our present confederation, which had made the reservation in
express terms.[51]

Jefferson's statement that Wilson's argument "might do for the audience to
which it was addressed" may have reflected something more than general
condescension toward a mass gathering of Philadelphians (though it may
have reflected that posture, too). Wilson had been speaking to a friendly
crowd. He was promoting the Constitution to a generally pro-ratification audience, and the crowd frequently burst into loud applause during his speech.[52]
In short, Wilson had made his argument about limited federal power and a
bill of rights in a setting much like a campaign rally. Such an environment is
a setting where it is especially easy, and perhaps tempting, for a speaker to
cut corners when making an argument, because the audience is not disposed
to push back critically. The reception among the broader public was not as
generous.

The Pennsylvania Convention

By the time Pennsylvania's ratifying convention opened on November 21,
some of the Constitution's opponents seem to have concluded that Wilson's
argument was so weak that they could score points by getting him to repeat
it, thus destroying his credibility and discrediting the cause he represented.
On the floor of the Convention, John Smilie—a leader of the anti-ratification
delegates—said he hoped that Wilson, as the sole member of the General
Convention in attendance, would explain why the Constitution had no bill
of rights.[53] Smilie was baiting Wilson. Every person following the public
conversation about the Constitution already knew both Wilson's argument
and the trenchant responses to it. The question was just whether Wilson
could be induced to offer the Pennsylvania Antifederalists a target.

Wilson took the bait. Perhaps aware by this point of the hazards of in-
vesting too heavily in the argument he was about to rehearse, Wilson said he
could not speak for all of the Constitution's drafters, many of whom had
probably not considered the question while the General Convention was sitting. After all, he said, the issue of a bill of rights had not been raised at that

Convention until the very final stage, and it had not been much discussed even then.[54] But rather than leaving things there, Wilson continued. To adopt a list of protected liberties, Wilson maintained, would have been not just unnecessary but dangerous, because it "would have supposed that we were throwing into the general government every power not expressly reserved by the people."[55]

If the reported version of Wilson's remarks captured him accurately here, then Wilson may again have been carefully calibrating his argument so as to avoid repudiating the idea that the federal government could exercise inherent or resulting powers. The key to this possibility is Wilson's use of the word "every." As reported, he warned that including a bill of rights would have implied that the general government enjoyed *every* power not expressly reserved. And it was no part of Wilson's thought that the general government had plenary power. His view, rather, was that the government of the United States—before the Confederation, under the Confederation, and under the Constitution, too—enjoyed *some* nonenumerated powers, not that it enjoyed all possible powers. Logically, Wilson could reject a bill of rights that would imply a general government possessing all powers not expressly reserved while still leaving himself free to embrace the idea that the United States possessed not just its enumerated powers but also whatever powers were implicit in the Union, given the purposes for which it existed. Indeed, Wilson reaffirmed his view that the general government would have nonenumerated as well as enumerated powers. The implication of the enumeration of powers, he explained, was "that nothing more is intended to be given than what is so enumerated, *unless it results from the nature of the government itself.*"[56]

But if Wilson intended his explanation to be elegant and subtle, his adversary's response was brutally simple. Wilson was arguing from the premise that the affirmative specification of rights in the Constitution would imply that the general government possessed all powers not expressly reserved. But as Smilie pointed out, the draft Constitution did specify certain rights. Congress could not arbitrarily suspend habeas corpus, for example, or abolish jury trial. So how exactly was the Pennsylvania convention supposed to understand Wilson's argument?[57] A couple of pro-ratification delegates tried to intervene: rather than letting the case for the Constitution depend on Wilson's argument, they conceded that Wilson's formula had problems and defended the absence of a bill of rights on other grounds.[58] Smilie duly tried to steer the conversation back to the ground where the Federalists were weak: he challenged Wilson to answer his objections, calling him out by name. But Wilson—perhaps having at last figured out when it was time to stop— refused to give satisfaction. "I intend to give answers when I hear any objection worthy of an answer," Wilson responded. "Until I hear much stronger reasons, I shall not trouble the Convention with any further observations."[59] Given the weakness of his position, this refusal to engage might have been the best he could do.

Perhaps Wilson's most telling move about the extent of federal powers at the Pennsylvania convention, however, came in the course of his defenses of the Necessary and Proper Clause. More or less as Brutus had charged in his essays, several Pennsylvania delegates argued that that clause would enable Congress to justify any legislation at all. More than once, Wilson replied that the critics were mistaken, because Congress's power under the Necessary and Proper Clause was limited by the enumeration of powers that preceded it. On December 1, Wilson pronounced himself unable to "conceive by what means [the opponents] will render the words [of the clause] susceptible of that expansion. Can the words, the Congress shall have power to make all laws, which shall be necessary and proper to carry into execution the forgoing powers, be capable of giving them general legislative power?"[60] Three days later, Wilson reprised the point. The language of the Necessary and Proper Clause, Wilson protested, did not

> in any degree go beyond the particular enumeration; for when it is said, that Congress shall have power to make all laws which shall be necessary and proper, those words are limited, and defined by the following, 'for carrying into execution the foregoing powers.' It is saying no more than that the powers we have already particularly given shall be effectually carried into execution.[61]

People might differ about how to assess Wilson's argument, taken at face value. A sympathetic audience might agree that the power to make laws necessary and proper for carrying into execution the other powers conferred in Section 8 was, albeit significant, still a limited power. A less sympathetic audience might think that a power to make all laws necessary and proper for carrying into execution seventeen clauses worth of legislative power— including the powers to tax, regulate commerce, and raise armies, and perhaps even the power to pursue the general welfare, broadly understood—would be so broad as to make any formal limitation substantively unimportant. But the most important thing to notice about Wilson's argument does not appear on its face. It is that Wilson on both occasions defended the Necessary and Proper Clause with a reading that relied on a truncated version of its text—one that erased the Sweeping Clause from the Constitution.[62]

The final clause of Section 8 does not merely say that Congress has the power to carry into execution the *foregoing* powers—that is, the powers listed in the first seventeen clauses of Section 8. It says that Congress has the power to make laws necessary and proper for carrying into execution "the foregoing powers, *and all other powers vested by this Constitution in the government of the United States*, or in any department or officer thereof." Nobody knew the Sweeping Clause language better than Wilson. He was likely its author. As described earlier, he had probably written the clause to leave open the possibility that the Constitution knew the government of the United States to be vested with "other powers" beyond those enumerated in the document. His decision to handle the charge that the Necessary and Proper Clause would confer unlimited power on Congress by pretending that the Sweeping Clause did not exist—and to do so repeatedly—suggests his awareness that it would be difficult to answer the charge if he acknowledged what the clause actually said.

Still, one wonders a bit at Wilson's willingness to defend the Constitution this way. Omitting the relevant language should have made his defense transparently weak and, perhaps, opened him to the charge of disingenuousness. It seems unlikely that Wilson assumed his adversaries would not notice what he was doing. It is more plausible that he simply was not invested in persuading the objectors. As the historian Pauline Maier described in depth, Pennsylvanians on both sides of the issue took a thoroughly hardball approach to ratification.[63] For example, Antifederalist members of the state legislature tried to prevent the scheduling of a ratification convention by absenting themselves from the state house, thus denying the legislature a quorum for doing business. The sergeant-at-arms and a posse of Federalists subsequently secured a quorum by bodily dragging Antifederalist members from their lodgings into the legislative chamber, whereupon the legislature by majority vote scheduled a convention.[64] In short, the Pennsylvania Federalists were going to ram the Constitution through if they could, with little regard for whether those on the other side might cry foul.

So at the state convention, where the Constitution's supporters had a majority on their side, Wilson's major objectives probably did not include persuading the doubters—or even making them feel that their concerns had been fairly addressed. The task at hand was to secure a vote in favor of ratification, and Wilson's side had the votes. So perhaps Wilson aimed to present confident if indefensible arguments in support of the Constitution as a way of keeping his base energized, rather than to wrestle in nuanced ways with the Constitution's weaknesses as well as its strengths. If so, it is hard to say that he failed: Pennsylvania ratified the Constitution. Whether anyone emerged from the convention more persuaded than before of the merits of Wilson's argument about limited federal power is hard to say, but it may not have been the main point.

South Carolina: A Tale of Two Pinckneys

By the time the Pennsylvania convention rose on December 12, the argument that the Constitution's enumeration of powers made a bill of rights unnecessary had well-ventilated weaknesses. But some prominent Federalists went on making it. Perhaps they failed to appreciate that the argument was weak. Or perhaps they understood that point but figured the argument was still worth making, either because snappy ideas sometimes have power in politics even when they are substantively weak or because the enumerated-powers argument, though flawed, still seemed better than any other excuse they could muster for the Convention's failure to include a bill of rights in the Constitution. One way or another, the idea that the Constitution's enumeration of federal powers would limit the federal government remained part of a ritualized script about the Constitution for some participants in the debate, despite its analytic weaknesses. And at least in southern states, the idea that the Constitution would limit the federal government to its textually enumerated powers also became part of a second ritualized script: one explaining that the Constitution would give Congress no power to interfere with slavery. Considered critically, that slavery script was as vulnerable as the one about a bill of rights. But in both cases, the arguments lived on anyway, more for their political utility than for their analytic strength. Two examples from debates in South Carolina illustrate the point.

Pinckney the Younger on a Bill of Rights

In a speech in the South Carolina House of Representatives on January 16, 1788, Charles Pinckney described the Constitution's failure to include a clause guaranteeing liberty of the press as unfortunate. He had recommended such a clause at the Convention, he explained, and he still thought it would be a good idea. Nonetheless, Pinckney said, he was satisfied by the argument that such guarantees were not essential, because in the federal government, "no powers could be executed, or assumed, but such as were expressly delegated."[65]

Unlike Wilson, Pinckney did not formulate the point in a way that left open the possibility of nonenumerated powers. The only federal powers, on Pinckney's view, would be those "*expressly* delegated." But even on this restrictive view of congressional power, one wonders whether Pinckney was really satisfied that the liberty of the press was sufficiently protected. He was aware that the enumerated powers of Congress included a power to issue copyrights. Did Pinckney think that copyright regulation would raise no issues about freedom of the press? Was he similarly unconcerned that Congress might deploy its powers to tax, to regulate commerce, or to suppress insurrections, either on their own or in conjunction with the Necessary and Proper Clause, in a way that might threaten the freedom of the press? Pinckney had been invested enough in a clause protecting freedom of the press to move for the inclusion of one at the Convention.[66] Why do so if such a guarantee would not matter?

Similarly, Pinckney's willingness to pronounce himself satisfied by an argument whose premise was that Congress could exercise only powers "expressly delegated" calls for further explanation. He knew as well as anyone that the Constitution contained no language limiting Congress to "expressly delegated" powers. In fact, Pinckney should have been especially sensitive to that point. At the Convention, Pinckney recommended that the Committee of Detail include "expressly delegated" language like that in the Articles of Confederation, and he was surely aware that his suggestion had been rejected.[67] Was there some reason for him to think that Congress would be as limited as if that language had been included in the Constitution? If so, he did not explain his reasoning.

Perhaps Pinckney could have answered all of these questions to his own satisfaction. But it is also possible that he put his concerns about press freedom aside in favor of helping get the Constitution ratified. Perhaps Pinckney in South Carolina, like Wilson in Pennsylvania, was repeating a talking point that could not be fully defended against criticism but still seemed like a tool worth using in the effort to secure ratification. Perhaps it could persuade audiences who were happy to be persuaded. Or perhaps Pinckney reasoned that this was the argument to make simply because no better argument justifying the absence of a bill of rights seemed available.

Pinckney the Elder on Enumerated Powers and Slavery

Pinckney's cousin Charles Cotesworth Pinckney also sought to persuade his South Carolina colleagues to support the Constitution, but his approach to the bill of rights issue added something important. Responding to a representative who opposed the Constitution on the grounds that it lacked a bill of rights, the elder Pinckney first repeated the argument that "[t]he general government has no powers but what are expressly granted to it."[68] But Pinckney also offered another reason why it made sense for the Constitution not to have a bill of rights. Bills of rights in the states that had them—South Carolina was not one—generally included declarations that all men are by nature free. "[W]e should make that declaration with a very bad grace," Pinckney told the South Carolina legislature, "when a large part of our property consists in men who are actually born slaves."[69]

Pinckney's offering these two explanations side by side helps highlight that *both* were calculated to reassure his audience on the same sensitive point: the future of slavery. Attributing the absence of a bill of rights to the conflict over slavery went directly to that point. It turned a potential weakness of the Constitution into a sign that the Convention had been attentive to South Carolina's slavery-related interests. And by bolstering the idea that the new government would have only the powers expressly delegated to it, Pinckney could reinforce the sense that South Carolina would retain the authority to maintain its slaveholding, free from congressional interference.

For proslavery Americans at the time of the Founding, the proposition that Congress had no power to abolish slavery was indispensable to the acceptability of the Constitution. As John Mikhail has explained, many of them were keenly aware that that proposition required rejecting the broad readings of congressional power about which Antifederalists like Brutus warned.[70] If Congress had the power to pass laws providing for the general welfare under the first clause of Article I, Section 8, then Congress could abolish slavery if abolition would promote the general welfare. If the Sweeping Clause's authorization of congressional lawmaking to execute "all other powers vested by the Constitution in the government of the United States" referred inter alia to powers *implicitly* vested in the government of the United States, then it would be easy to imagine an argument for abolition laws on the theory that the government was charged, in the Preamble, with not just promoting the general welfare but also establishing justice and securing the blessings of liberty.

Such concerns might seem far-fetched to twenty-first century Americans who know how entrenched slavery remained during the Constitution's first seventy-five years. But proslavery Americans in 1788 did not know the future. And they were concerned that Americans who considered slavery shameful and unjust would try to end the practice if they could. So they wanted assurances that the Constitution would not empower the government to interfere with slavery. As South Carolina's Pierce Butler (in Madison's rendering) put the point at the Convention, "The security the South[er]n States want is that their negroes may not be taken from them[,] which some gentlemen within or without doors [i.e., among the Convention delegates and in the public at large] have a very good mind to do."[71] During the ratification debates, proslavery southerners probably knew that some northern advocates of robust national power were advertising the Constitution as a vehicle for ending slavery. At the Pennsylvania convention, for example, Wilson had said not only that he saw the acknowledgment in Article I, Section 9, that Congress could prohibit the slave trade in 1808 as "laying the foundation for banishing slavery out of this country," but that under the Constitution, Congress would soon "have power to exterminate slavery."[72] Wilson did not further spell out the mechanism. But given the prospect of a more powerful general government, such a suggestion was enough to make slaveholders concerned. As the Federal Farmer noted, people in power tend to find ways to construe their power as adequate for the projects they wish to pursue.

The way to block abolitionist readings of the Constitution, the standard thinking ran, was to insist that Congress could only exercise powers expressly delegated to it. If that limitation were observed, then expansive readings of congressional power that would authorize legislation for the general welfare, legislation to accomplish the ends of the Preamble, or anything else of the sort would be inadmissible. So when South Carolina's convention voted to ratify the Constitution, it attached to its statement of ratification a declaration that "no Section or paragraph of the said Constitution warrants a Construction that the states do not retain every power not expressly relinquished by them and vested in the General Government of the Union."[73] The decision to adopt that statement indicates, of course, that the South Carolina convention recognized that the Constitution could be read otherwise. One does not generally bother to issue statements of clarification about matters that are already unmistakably clear. Perhaps people at the South Carolina convention believed that their declaration's interpretation of the Constitution was objectively correct and that the function of their declaration was to fend off any misunderstanding. But it is also possible that people at that convention recognized that a good-faith interpreter could read the Constitution as giving the federal government more than its enumerated powers and thought the declaration necessary as a way of saying that South Carolina rejected that view—and perhaps valuable as a bid to shape later interpretations.

The idea that limiting Congress to its enumerated powers would prevent abolition was more political creed than tightly reasoned analysis. As a logical matter, even a rule limiting Congress to its expressly delegated powers would not prevent a creative and properly motivated Congress from passing an abolition law. A Congress empowered to raise armies and to make laws necessary and proper for carrying the army-raising laws into execution might conscript slaves and, to motivate them, promise freedom to all who served honorably.[74] Congress could not ban the slave trade before 1808, but under its power to regulate commerce among the states it could provide that any sale of a person, or at least any interstate sale of a person, would be legal only if accompanied by the proviso that the person sold would become free no more than three years later. And so on. South Carolina's delegates at the Convention seem to have appreciated that their most reliable mechanisms for protecting slavery against the general government's interference would be process limits and external limits rather than the internal limits of Congress's enumerated powers. Still, southerners who wanted to preserve slavery reasonably preferred the idea of a Constitution under which Congress lacked the power to end slavery to the idea of a Constitution under which Congress could abolish slavery if only it could muster the votes. The principle that Congress could only exercise the powers expressly delegated to it represented that idea.

In the South Carolina debates, the elder Pinckney explicitly articulated the link between preserving slavery in South Carolina and limiting Congress to expressly delegated powers. One day before Pinckney justified the absence of a bill of rights to his fellow South Carolinians, he asserted that Congress could never extinguish slavery. The Constitution granted Congress no power to emancipate slaves, Pinckney pointed out, and "it is admitted, on all hands, that the general government has no powers but what are expressly granted by the Constitution."[75] There was no explanation of why the enumerated powers could not be deployed for emancipatory purposes, and there was no explanation of why people should read the Constitution as limiting Congress only to those powers "expressly granted." Indeed, the claim that that limitation was "admitted, on all hands" might have been necessary precisely because no constitutional text established the proposition. What later historians would call the "federal consensus" that the Constitution gave Congress no power to abolish slavery was just that: a generally prevailing opinion, not a textual limitation in the written Constitution.[76]

Seen this way, both Pinckneys' statements that the Constitution permitted Congress to exercise only the powers expressly delegated to it appear not as mistakes about what the Constitution authorized but as attempts to establish the understanding of the Constitution that South Carolina needed in order for the Constitution to be acceptable. In this light, there was in fact a relationship between the Constitution's lack of a bill of rights and the idea that Congress was strictly limited to its enumerated powers, but it was an uglier relationship than the one Wilson propounded. Rather than the enumeration's making a bill of rights unnecessary (or dangerous), the absence of a bill of rights and the idea of a limiting enumeration were both essential aspects of a system compatible with the southern imperative to protect slavery against a potentially hostile national government.

Madison's Approach

At the same time, Madison was articulating a different view of federal power. In a series of nine Publius essays published in January 1788, Madison endorsed the idea that the enumerated powers would limit the general government. But he did not repeat the argument that the enumerated powers made a bill of rights unnecessary. And unlike the Pinckneys, Madison rejected the idea that the Constitution would restrict Congress to the powers "expressly" granted. On the contrary, he argued that Congress was implicitly authorized to exercise whatever nonenumerated powers were reasonably necessary for exercising the enumerated powers. The power specified by the Necessary and Proper Clause, Madison contended, would have been implicitly vested in the general government even without that clause. And rather than presenting the Necessary and Proper Clause as an "express" grant of the relevant auxiliary powers, which might have enabled him to agree that the general government could only wield powers "expressly granted," Madison rejected the idea that the government should be limited to expressly delegated powers. The enumeration of powers would limit the general government, but the powers granted would include what the enumeration conveyed implicitly as well as what it conveyed expressly.

More fundamentally, however, Madison did not treat the enumeration of federal powers as primarily a mechanism for limiting the federal government. There were two reasons why not. First, Madison in these essays and elsewhere distrusted textual descriptions of legislative power as means for limiting that power. He argued instead that the important work of limitation would be done with process limits—by the checks and balances among the federal branches and by federal officials' dependence on voters and state governments. Second, Madison's focus in these essays was on the need to empower the general government, not to limit it. Rather than praising the Constitution for its capacity to prevent the general government from growing too strong, Madison argued that America needed a strong general government with every one of the powers the Constitution allocated to it. Properly structured, Madison argued, that strong general government would not overbear the states. But if it turned out that sufficiently empowering the general government meant creating a government that eventually would overbear the states, that was no reason to empower the general government any less. The important project was creating a sufficiently strong national government, whether or not doing so was consistent with preserving any particular role for the states.

The Need for Power

The first in the series of essays was *Federalist* 37. Opening with a statement of his major theme, Madison wrote that "the defects of the existing Confederation . . . cannot be supplied by a government of less energy than that before the public." In other words, readers should not be worried that the

Constitution empowered the general government too much. They should focus on making sure that the general government would be empowered *enough*. To be sure, Madison endorsed the idea that the general government would be limited by its enumerated powers. He wrote that Congress would have jurisdiction over "certain enumerated objects only"[77] and that "in the new government, as in the old, the general [government's] powers are limited," while "the states, in all nonenumerated cases, are left in the enjoyment of their sovereign and independent jurisdiction."[78] But he also urged his readers to accept that it was not possible to establish clear limits on what the general government would be able to do. The "task of marking the proper line of partition between the authority of the general and that of the State governments," he wrote, must be "arduous." Rather than presenting the enumeration of congressional powers as defining a clearly bounded zone of decisionmaking, Madison counseled that real-world phenomena often lack clear demarcations. "[N]o skill in the science of government," he wrote, "has yet been able to discriminate and define . . . its three great provinces—the legislative, executive, and judiciary." Similarly, "[t]he precise extent of the common law, and the statute law . . . remains still to be clearly and finally established in Great Britain, where accuracy in such subject has been more industriously pursued than in any other part of the world." If those traditional and well-known categories could not be clearly differentiated, Madison urged, it would not be reasonable to expect clarity "in delineating the boundary between the federal and State jurisdictions." Certainly no such clear distinction could be imposed by the text of the Constitution, because the inherent limitations of language would make textual specifications susceptible of varying interpretations. "When the Almighty himself condescends to address mankind in their own language," Madison wrote, "his meaning, luminous as it must be, is rendered dim and doubtful by the cloudy medium through which it is communicated."[79] In sum, the complexity of the subject and the inherent limitations of language made it impossible to specify, in the Constitution's text, where the boundary of national power would be. Given the imperative for a strong general government, that meant that Americans should ratify the Constitution even in the absence of guarantees about where the new government's power would end.

Madison warned that the likely consequence of a too-stingy grant of powers to the general government would be a general government that behaved lawlessly on a regular basis, because the imperatives of governance would push Congress to do what needed to be done even in the absence of formally granted power. To illustrate this tendency, Madison pointed to Congress's legislation for the Western Territories under the Articles of Confederation.[80] But he also generalized the point. "A list of the cases in which Congress [under the Articles] have been betrayed, or forced by the defects of the Confederation, into violations of their chartered authorities would not a little surprise those who have paid no attention to the subject," Madison wrote.[81] To be sure, "Congress is going to do this anyway, so you should authorize Congress to do it, so that Congress doesn't go around acting illegally" might not seem like a compelling argument to a skeptic of congressional action. But from Madison's perspective, the point was that a responsible Congress would need to do all sorts of things. Better to give it broad authority and let it govern responsibly than to empower it grudgingly and force it to choose between legality and the public welfare.

Near the end of these essays, in *Federalist* 44, Madison offered the fullest form of his argument against limiting the general government to powers expressly granted and in favor of the idea that whatever power Congress would have under the Necessary and Proper Clause would belong to Congress implicitly even without such a clause. "Without the *substance* of this power, the whole Constitution would be a dead letter," he wrote, because no government can exercise its powers reasonably if it is denied the necessary means for making those powers effective. In light of that reality, a prohibition on the exercise of powers not expressly delegated would be either destructive or self-defeating. If the prohibition were strictly construed, Madison wrote, it would "disarm the government of all real authority whatever." If it were less strictly construed, it would "destroy altogether the force of the restriction."[82]

The real question, Madison argued, was not whether the government could be restricted to expressly delegated powers but how best to signal the scope of its implied powers. In Madison's view, enumerating particulars would not work. To try to specify a closed set of means that the government could use to execute its powers would be a fool's errand, because it is impossible to predict and list all the things that a government might need to do in order to execute its appropriate functions, especially over a long period of time. The better solution was either to say nothing and trust reasonable interpreters to know that the Constitution's grant of certain powers implied a grant of the necessary powers for execution or, in a more realistic vein, to write the principle into the Constitution, with something like the Necessary and Proper Clause. If the Constitution included such a clause, unreasonable people (or improperly motivated ones) would have a harder time trying to deny Congress's authority to exercise those implicit powers.[83]

With this formulation, Madison found a way to try to defuse two sets of objections to the Constitution: one based on the document's lack of an "express powers" limitation and one based on the Sweeping Clause's potential to signal the existence of federal powers untethered to any specific constitutional text. There was no clause limiting the government to "expressly delegated" powers, and that was a virtue. But on Madison's account, it was still not the case that the government had powers beyond what the document contemplated. In contrast to Wilson's likely view, on which the Sweeping Clause pointed to nonenumerated powers inherent in the national government, Madison described the universe of permissible implicit powers as confined to the ones necessary for executing the expressly granted powers—and even the principle that Congress could exercise that set of implicit powers was, in the end, expressly stated in the document. The result was a conception of implied powers that skeptics of broad national power would find less threatening than the inherent-powers conception the Sweeping Clause had probably been written to invite. In other words, it was a conception of implied powers that might justify (or rationalize) the omission of an express-powers limitation without raising the major worries such an omission might otherwise provoke.

In the final essay of this series, Madison returned to the theme that people should not worry that Congress would have too much power. The problem to worry about, he explained in *Federalist* 45, was that Congress might have too *little* power. "The more I revolve the subject," he wrote, "the more fully I am persuaded that the balance is much more likely to be disturbed by the preponderacy of the [states] than of the [federal government]." So when evaluating the Constitution, Madison urged, the right question to ask was whether Congress would have all the power it needed, not whether it might have a bit too much. And if it turned out that granting the Union the powers it needed was adverse to the interests of the states, so much the worse for the states. An adequately empowered Union, Madison argued, was essential "to the happiness of the people of America." And "as far as the sovereignty of the States cannot be reconciled to the happiness of the people, the voice of every good citizen must be, Let the former be sacrificed to the latter."[84]

"Few and Defined" versus "Numerous, Extensive, and Important"

Late in that essay, Madison expressed his view that Americans should worry about an insufficiently powerful federal government partly by characterizing that government's powers as "few and defined."[85] In later centuries, constitutional interpreters have quoted that phrase as if it described a virtue of the constitutional order—that is, in support of the idea that it is a good thing that the federal government's powers are few and defined.[86] But in *Federalist* 45, that phrase was not simply a hosanna. It was, or also was, a warning. Madison was telling his readers to worry about an insufficiently powerful general government, not an overly powerful one. Describing that government's powers as few and defined was part of his statement of the problem.

It also may have been a subterfuge. The question "How many powers did the original Constitution allocate to the general government?" has no uniquely correct answer, both because it is not always clear when the Constitution is allocating a "power" (as opposed to, say, a responsibility) and because there is no standard for deciding how many powers a power-conferring text confers. (Is the power "to lay and collect taxes" one power or two?) But it is hard to read the original Constitution as conferring fewer than several dozen powers. (While drafting this chapter, I unscientifically asked 126 law students to count how many powers the original Constitution assigned to the federal government, working independently and making their own judgments about what counted as "a power of the federal government," but with the instruction that a power that merely affects something internal to the federal government, like the impeachment power, does not count. The median response: forty-one powers. Feel free to try it yourself.) So the claim that the general government's powers are "few" is hard to square with the text of the Constitution. And given texts like the General Welfare Clause and the Sweeping Clause, it is not clear what it means to say that all of those powers are "defined." In short, Madison's famous formula might have minimized the Constitution's complement of national powers in order to persuade readers that they should not be worried about a too-powerful national government.

One way to see that Madison's "few and defined" formula might have been a rhetorical understatement rather than either a dispassionate assessment or a normative commitment is to contrast it with the rather different way the other principal author of *The Federalist*—Hamilton—presented the same

RATIFICATION WITHOUT AGREEMENT

subject. "Every one knows," Hamilton told New York's convention, "that the objects of the general government are numerous, extensive, and important. Every one must acknowledge the necessity of giving powers, in all respects, and in every degree, equal to these objects."[87] "Numerous, extensive, and important" conjures an image considerably unlike "few and defined." But Hamilton knew the Constitution as well as Madison did, and he had no incentive to overstate the degree to which it would empower the general government. Nor is it clear that he was overstating, given the suite of powers enumerated in the Constitution's text.

Hamilton was alert to the need for constitutional mechanisms that would prevent the general government from exercising power abusively, as well as the need to give his audience assurance on that score. But for the most part, he did not point to the enumeration of congressional powers as such a mechanism. The Constitution's devices for preventing bad behavior by the new government, Hamilton usually contended, did not reside in the provisions specifying that government's powers. They resided in the Constitution's structural provisions—that is, in the composition of its institutions and the power of each to check the others.

Thus, in the same speech to the New York convention where he described the objects of the general government as "numerous, extensive, and important," Hamilton responded to worries about "the danger of giving powers" in part by saying that "[t]he true principle of government is this—Make the system compleat in its structure; give a perfect proportion and balance to its parts; and the powers you give it will never affect your security."[88] In expressing that view, he repeated his recommendation from *Federalist* 31 that "all observations founded upon the danger of usurpation ought to be referred to the composition and structure of the government, not to the nature or extent of its powers."[89] After all, any government, regardless of its formal powers, might behave abusively if staffed by unscrupulous persons with the ability to pursue their agendas unchecked.

Indeed, Hamilton continued, anyone who feared that the general government might overwhelm the states but who was basically content with the state governments should already realize that the key factor preventing governments from acting as tyrannies was structural rather than being rooted in a limited delegation of power. The state governments, Hamilton pointed out, were authorized to pass laws on any subject. How, then, could those governments not be monstrous? The answer lay in the way that the governments were structured, with internal checks, and also in the democratic mechanisms that kept officials dependent on the voting population.[90] By the same token, it would be structural limits on the new government rather than the specifics of its delegated powers that would prevent it from acting abusively.

Virginia

By the summer of 1788, the main arguments about enumerated power, express delegation, the Sweeping Clause, and so on were familiar from essays and conversations going back to the previous autumn. At the climactic Virginia convention, which opened on June 2, the rival camps would persist in their differing interpretations. No two conventions were exactly the same, and naturally the debates at Virginia's convention did a bit more than reiterate precisely the arguments people elsewhere had already made. But there was no sign that the previous eight months of argumentation had narrowed the range of disagreement about what the Constitution meant. Some people read the Constitution as limiting the general government to its enumerated powers, and others very much did not.

The Debates

The anti-ratification forces at Virginia's convention were led by Patrick Henry, who had preceded Randolph as governor, and George Mason, whose opposition to the Constitution had hardened over time. They denounced the Constitution's lack of a bill of rights, and they criticized the idea that the enumeration of congressional powers guaranteed a limited Congress as a dangerous fantasy.[91] The powers expressly given to the new government, they contended, were sufficient for making law on any topic.[92] And the Necessary and Proper Clause was maximally pliable—a warrant, Henry warned, for comprehensive legislative authority.[93]

But Henry was not content with the charge that the enumerated powers of Congress were tantamount to plenary power. He also disputed the claim that Congress would be limited to the powers enumerated. Proceeding just as Wilson had warned that constitutional interpreters might, Henry pointed out that Article I, Section 9, listed external limits on the powers of Congress and then suggested that the specification of prohibitions on what Congress could do implied that Congress could do anything not affirmatively prohibited.[94] Henry also pressed the point that the Constitution conspicuously failed to limit Congress to those powers "expressly delegated" to it. Given the contrast with the Articles of Confederation, which had reserved to the states all powers not "expressly delegated" to Congress, Henry reasoned that the enumerated powers of Congress under the Constitution would surely be construed as only a subset of the powers that Congress was entitled to exercise.[95] Other implicit powers would be recognized as well.

One might wonder what additional damage Congress could do with non-enumerated powers if, as Henry also charged, the enumerated powers by themselves added up to general jurisdiction. But from Henry's point of view, it may not have mattered whether he convinced his audience that the proposed Constitution was dangerous because its express grants to Congress amounted to plenary power or because it failed to limit Congress to a specified set of authorities. The point was that Congress would be dangerously and uncontrollably powerful. Indeed, Henry and Mason argued that Congress under the new Constitution would ultimately arrogate all legislative power in the United States, destroying the state governments and merging the whole Union into one undifferentiated polity.

According to Henry, the Constitution announced the coming consolidation in its first words, which stated that the agents of the agreement were "We the People" rather than the states.[96] Mason explained the practical dynamics of the consolidation. It flowed, he said, from Article I's grant to Congress of the power to lay taxes directly on the public, rather than requiring Congress to work through the state governments in order to raise money. Articulating a scenario that several opponents of ratification had described in the preceding months, Mason predicted that this power of taxation would annihilate the state governments. The people, he said, would not tolerate being subject to two different taxing authorities. Before long, either Congress would have to destroy the states or the states would have to destroy Congress— and Mason predicted that Congress, as the stronger body, would prevail.[97]

Henry also emphasized the danger that a Congress not confined to enumerated powers would pose for Virginia's vital interests—including crucially its interest in slavery. A Congress not limited to a set of specified powers, Henry warned, would sooner or later legislate emancipation. Henry's analysis on this point was complex: it took as a premise that slavery was an evil, indeed a deplorable practice, and that fair-minded people rightly hated it. Slavery persisted in Virginia, Henry maintained, not because white Virginians approved of slavery but because they understood the problems of emancipation. Emancipation would be catastrophically disruptive. Its costs would be so great that retaining slavery with all its evils was preferable. But did northerners understand that part of the problem, Henry asked? Surely not. They shared with Virginians the distaste for slavery, but they lacked sensitivity to the costs of emancipation. So the leaders of a northern-dominated Congress would seek to end slavery.[98]

When they did, Henry reasoned, they would confront the question of whether abolishing slavery was within Congress's power. Using the same logic that had animated Pinckney in South Carolina, Henry argued that it would then make a great deal of difference whether it were generally agreed that Congress could exercise only its expressly delegated powers. If Congress could exercise powers beyond those enumerated in the text of the Constitution, antislavery congressmen would find ways to argue that Congress implicitly had the power to emancipate. So to prevent the North from destroying Virginia through emancipation, Henry warned, Congress must be limited to the powers expressly delegated to it.[99] And given that the Constitution did not so limit Congress, Virginians needed to reject the Constitution.

Randolph pushed back in three ways against Henry's slavery argument. One was to shame Henry, or at least to try. In Randolph's view, it was "dishonorable to Virginia" to object to the Constitution on the ground that it contained a "spark of hope, that those unfortunate men now held in bondage, may, by the operation of the General Government, be made *free*."[100] Another was to appeal to the authority of the drafters, albeit while denying that he was doing so: "Were it right to mention here what passed in Convention on the occasion, I might tell you that the Southern States, even South-Carolina herself, conceived this property to be secure." The third was to deny that anything in the Constitution tended toward the abolition of slavery. "Point out the clause," he challenged, "where this formidable power of emancipation is inserted."[101]

Randolph's denial that any clause of the Constitution gave Congress the power to emancipate slaves did not really come to grips with Henry's argument. Henry had not asserted that any specific clause clearly contained a power to legislate emancipation as of 1788. He had warned that in a system where Congress could exercise powers beyond those expressly articulated in the text, the boundaries of congressional power would be uncertain and dynamic, such that a motivated Congress would be able to reason its way to an emancipation power, one way or another. Perhaps Henry simply had a good point, and Randolph's less-than-responsive response was the best he could offer. Indeed, as noted earlier, given a Congress sufficiently motivated to end slavery, it is not clear why even a limitation to powers "expressly" conferred would prevent federal abolition laws, or at least federal laws making emancipation considerably more likely. But like Pinckney in South Carolina, Henry in Virginia propounded the view that a limitation to express powers would put matters in a meaningfully different posture.

Randolph continued to insist that slavery in Virginia was secure because no clause authorized Congress to abolish it. But he did not pretend that there was nothing at all to Henry's concern. On the contrary, Randolph conceded that he could not foresee how broadly future interpreters would read Article I, Section 8. In his final remarks to the convention, Randolph acknowledged that the Sweeping Clause was ambiguous and that it might be construed more and more broadly over time. "My fear," Randolph said, "is that it will, by gradual accretions, gather to a dangerous length."[102] But with the full awareness of that possibility, Randolph explained, he favored ratification, because America needed a more powerful government than the one it had.[103]

The same realistic sense that told Randolph that the Sweeping Clause might be construed to give Congress extensive powers also told him that the most important force limiting Congress would not be a matter of the textual formulas in which congressional power was articulated. It would be built into the political process. Congress, Randolph hazarded, would not be a cabal of schemers and tyrants. The states would not elect wild adventurers to make decisions for the nation.[104] In other words, the important checks would be matters of structure and process rather than the abstract potential of the constitutional clauses specifying congressional power. The question was not what those texts could be made to mean but what the people with the power to make decisions would be willing to do with them. In essence, that was Henry's view as well. The difference between him and Randolph lay in their estimations of what future officials would be inclined to do and in their views about whether America in 1788 could afford to be without the stronger general government the Constitution offered—and perhaps also in their sense of how damaging emancipation would be, if things really came to that.

The common ground between Henry and Randolph—that one should think not just about the power-conferring texts but about the likely agendas of the people who would hold office—was also central to Madison's arguments at the Virginia convention. In part, Madison met Henry's and Mason's objections to the Constitution by asserting that Congress would be limited by the enumeration of its powers.[105] The principle that every power not granted to Congress was reserved, Madison insisted, was "obviously and self-evidently the case," even without constitutional language saying so.[106] (He did not explain in any detail why that proposition was "obviously and self-evidently" so.) And on the last day before the Convention voted, Madison returned to an argument he had not made since his exchange with Lee in Congress the previous September: that including a "declaration of our essential rights" would be "unnecessary and dangerous—Unnecessary, because it was evident that the General Government had no power but what was given to it, and . . . Dangerous because an enumeration which is not complete is not safe."[107]

That said, Madison does not seem to have wanted these claims to be the mainstay of his argument for the Constitution. On several occasions, he shifted the terrain of debate from the formal limits of Congress's powers to the process mechanisms that would control how those powers were exercised. For example, Madison made a two-step argument responding to the charge that the treaty power enabled the government to agree to virtually anything and give it the force of law. First, he denied that the treaty power was as broad as Mason and Henry alleged. That power was delegated to the general government to let it manage the nation's external affairs, and "[t]he exercise of the power must be consistent with the object of the delegation."[108] In other words, Madison was saying, the treaty power could only be used to make law in the realm of external affairs—whatever that might be. But having suggested that the power was limited in that way, Madison voiced his long-standing skepticism about enumerating powers with particularity. To try to enumerate the kinds of treaties the government could make, rather than giving the power generally, would be a mistake, because any such enumeration would be underinclusive and leave the government unable to do things it might need to do. The better course was to give a power to make treaties in general terms, as the Constitution in fact did.

At that point, Madison shifted to the second step of the argument. What would keep the government from abusing its treaty power? The president, he said, would likely act in the national interest. If he did not, the Senate provided additional security: those "representatives and guardians of the political interest of the States" would not go along.[109] Similarly, Madison responded to Mason's allegation that Congress would eventually destroy the state governments by pointing out that officials in Congress would be dependent on state officials for their offices—directly so in the Senate and indirectly so in the House, because nobody could get elected without the support of the local powerbrokers.[110] To imagine Congress plotting the destruction of state governments, Madison argued, was to forget these basic facts about the structure of the new system.

Madison's response to Henry's prophecy about forced emancipation again brought the two kinds of argumentation together, as Madison first responded to Henry's allegation on its own terms and then shifted ground to highlight the real reasons why, in his view, Henry's concerns were misplaced. Suppose, Madison said, that a future Congress tried to legislate the abolition of slavery, as Henry said would happen.[111] Such a measure would be invalid, Madison declared, because the Constitution contained no power to warrant it. What, though, of Henry's prediction that an antislavery Congress would find ways to read the grants of power broadly enough to authorize emancipation? Rather than resting on his argument that the Constitution's language could not be so construed, Madison suggested that decisionmakers in Congress would never attempt such a thing. Did Henry really think that a majority of the people elected to Congress would be bent on a measure that would eliminate a huge category of property and "alienate the affections of five thirteenths of the Union?"[112] The real security against the threat of emancipation, in other words, was the expectation that Congress was not going to force an issue that would bring North and South into all-out conflict.

The "Form of Ratification"

It is impossible to know how persuasive the Virginia ratifiers found the competing views. The majority of delegates voted to ratify the Constitution, but we do not know why. That said, Virginia's convention agreed on more than the mere fact of ratification. It also approved a statement laying out a series of understandings on which it ratified and a set of recommended amendments. The statement, called a Form of Ratification, provided in part

> that the powers granted under the Constitution being derived from the people of the United States may be resumed by them whensoever the same shall

be perverted to their injury or oppression and that every power not granted thereby remains with them and at their will: that therefore no right of any denomination can be cancelled abridged restrained or modified by the Congress by the Senate or House of Representatives acting in any Capacity by the president or any Department or Officer of the United States except in those instances in which power is given by the Constitution for those purposes.[113]

In some manner, this statement was surely intended to endorse the view that Madison had described to his fellow Virginians as self-evident: that under the Constitution, the general government would have only those powers the Constitution delegated to it. As if to make the point unmistakable, the first of the Virginia convention's proposed amendments provided, in language that mostly echoed the Articles of Confederation, "[t]hat each state in the Union shall respectively retain every power, jurisdiction, and right, which is not by this Constitution delegated to the Congress of the United States, or to the departments of the federal government."

Note what Virginia's Form of Ratification and its first proposed amendment did *not* say. After nearly a year of high-profile arguments about the significance of the fact that the Constitution did not repeat the Articles of Confederation's language about the states reserving all powers that were not "expressly delegated to the United States," the Virginia convention approved statements in which the word "expressly" did not appear. The Form of Ratification spoke of "every power not granted" and "those instances in which power is given by the Constitution," not "every power not *expressly* granted" and "those instances in which power is *expressly* given by the Constitution." Similarly, the first proposed amendment spoke of the states retaining all powers "not by this Constitution delegated" to the federal government, rather than "not by this Constitution *expressly* delegated" to that government.

The omission of the word "expressly" was surely deliberate. Debate both at the Virginia convention and through the previous year had highlighted the potential significance of that word's absence from the Constitution. The Virginia ratifiers were fully on notice that a text discussing the delegation of powers to the general government and failing to specify that such delegation must be express would have a contestable meaning on that crucial point. If the Virginia convention's intention had been to assert that it understood the Constitution to grant power to the general government only so far as it did so expressly, its Form of Ratification could have included the magic word, just as South Carolina's had. Given how salient this question had been since the previous September, it is hard to think that the omission was an oversight.

To be sure, Virginia's Form of Ratification did not say that Congress could exercise implicit powers as well as expressly delegated ones. Nor did it explain what sort of implicit powers (if any) might be valid. One could argue, for example, that Virginia meant to adopt Madison's view from *Federalist* 44: Congress had implied powers, but only those necessary and proper for carrying the expressly delegated powers into execution. But neither in its Form of Ratification nor in its proposed amendments did the Virginia convention limit the scope of implied powers in that way. Nor was there any conceptual reason why implicit powers, if admitted at all, would need to be read so narrowly. As public argument had demonstrated since the previous autumn, the Constitution could also be read to mean that the Preamble, the Sweeping Clause, or some other feature of the system implied national powers separate from any of the specific grants in the Constitution's text. There is no reason to think that most of the Virginia ratifiers meant to endorse that more expansive vision, but surely most were aware that the Constitution could be read that way. Rather than precluding that reading, Virginia's convention left the possibility open.

Federalist 84

According to the Constitution's own terms, the new system would go into force upon ratification by nine states. On June 21, while Virginia's convention was meeting, New Hampshire became the ninth state to ratify. One wonders what might have happened if Virginia had then voted against ratification: formally, the ratifications of nine states made the Constitution valid, but a viable general government without Virginia would have been hard to conceive. When Virginia voted to ratify on June 27, the die was pretty clearly cast. Yes, there were three remaining states—New York, North Carolina, and Rhode Island. But with ten states on board, including all three of the big states, the new system would go into effect with or without the last three. The ratification campaigns would continue but in the mode of denouement.

Because the process was not yet complete in New York, Hamilton continued to publish essays over the signature of Publius. (The Publius essays

initially aimed at a national audience, but their official target was the ratification process in New York. All of the essays were published in New York
newspapers and addressed "To the People of the State of New York.") In the
eighty-fourth installment in the series, Publius addressed the Constitution's
omission of a bill of rights. Hamilton's discussion in that essay would, for
later generations, be a canonical source for the idea that the Convention
omitted a bill of rights because it trusted the enumeration of Congress's powers to do the necessary limiting work, and, indeed, that the inclusion of a bill
of rights might jeopardize the principle that the federal government had no
powers except those the Constitution enumerated.

In considering *Federalist* 84, the first thing to notice is precisely that it
was *Federalist* 84. In the previous eighty-three essays, the sum total of Publius's attention to the bill of rights issue consisted of two glancing references
mentioning or at least alluding to the fact that some people objected to the
absence of a bill of rights in the Constitution.[114] No ink at all was spilled on
explaining or defending that absence until the eighty-fourth essay of an
eighty-five-essay series—an essay first published on May 28 at pages
344–357 of a volume containing forty-nine *Federalist* essays.[115] So it seems
reasonable to infer that the authors of *The Federalist* did not consider their
arguments about a bill of rights to be among those they most wished to
highlight. Good rhetoricians do not make their important arguments for the
first time more than three hundred pages into their books. And by the time
Federalist 84 appeared as a freestanding newspaper essay, on July 16, ten
states had already ratified the Constitution.

Moreover, *Federalist* 84 introduced itself as an exercise in mopping up
rather than as an argument addressing crucial concerns. When first published
as part of the book of *Federalist* essays, its title was "Concerning several
miscellaneous Objections."[116] In both its book and newspaper incarnations,
Hamilton opened the essay by proposing to address with "brevity" some
"miscellaneous points" he had not addressed earlier. There is some humor (or
bravado?) in classifying one of the central objections pressed by the Constitution's opponents as a miscellaneous point. But be that as it may, Hamilton in
Federalist 84 offered several arguments to justify the Constitution's omission
of a bill of rights. None was original; all had been offered by other defenders
of the Constitution in the preceding year. So perhaps Hamilton's project in
Federalist 84 is best understood not as an exercise in creative argument or
public persuasion but as cataloging the debate and giving the Publius essays
a sense of completeness. In any event, Hamilton marched through the argu-

ments. First, he pointed out that some states did fine without bills of rights, New York among them. Second, he noted that various important protections for individual liberty were guaranteed in the Constitution's text—jury trial, habeas corpus, and so on—albeit not in a part of the document officially styled a bill of rights. Third, Hamilton argued that bills of rights were out of place in a Constitution founded on the idea that all power flows from the people. Bills of rights, on this conception, dealt with concessions wrung from princes, as had been true of Magna Carta and the English Bill of Rights. Where the people were the source of power, there was no point in specifying particular retained liberties. The people were free generally, not only where express legal provisions said so.

One curious feature of this third argument was its implication that most of the American states misunderstood what bills of rights were for. New York did not have a bill or declaration of rights at the time, but most states did. The constitutions of those states were all officially grounded in the idea that power flows from the people. Their having bills or declarations of rights was accordingly in considerable tension with Hamilton's claim that such bills or declarations were out of place in popular governments. That Hamilton gave no attention to this reasonably obvious problem suggests that in this essay at least, he was not taking scrupulous care about the cogency of the arguments he offered.

And then, finally, Hamilton propounded something like the most aggressive form of Wilson's argument from the previous October. "I go further and affirm that bills of rights," he wrote,

> . . . are not only unnecessary in the proposed Constitution but would even be dangerous. They would contain various exceptions to powers which are not granted; and, on this very account, would afford a colorable pretext to claim more than were granted. For why declare that things shall not be done which there is no power to do?

There it was—the idea that specifying affirmative limits on the powers of the general government would imply that the government had powers beyond those the Constitution granted to it.

Perhaps Hamilton took this argument seriously. But perhaps not. Presumably, he knew all the criticisms to which that form of the argument had been subjected in the preceding ten months. He offered no defense against them. He said nothing to reconcile his argument with the fact that the Constitution already specified certain liberties. Indeed, in *Federalist* 84 itself Hamilton praised the Constitution for affirmatively protecting several specific rights like jury trial and habeas corpus, yet he made no effort to explain why the untoward implication that he said would arise from rights specified in a bill of rights would not arise from the specification of those protected rights. For whatever reason, he seems to have been content to make an apparently self-contradictory argument on this point, much as he was willing to argue that bills of rights were out of place in a Constitution founded on popular sovereignty even in an essay that recognized that several American states had bills of rights. Similarly, he praised the Constitution for specifying important liberties while also explaining that the specification of particular liberties was categorically inappropriate in a Constitution under which power flowed from the people. And perhaps most tellingly, Hamilton on the floor of New York's ratifying convention never made the enumerated-powers argument in defense of the Constitution's absence of a bill of rights. He was willing, it seems, to make the argument pseudonymously, tucked into a late essay on stray odds and ends. But apparently he preferred not to own the argument when standing before a well-informed audience in a forum where critics could respond to him directly.

These facts do not prove that Hamilton did not believe what he wrote, nor do they mean that nobody found the argument persuasive. But the weaknesses in the argument are sufficiently patent, and were already sufficiently well known from prior rounds of debate when *Federalist* 84 was written, to raise the question of whether Hamilton was trying to offer a considered argument that might convince a thoughtful audience. His declining to make the argument in person at New York's ratifying convention suggests the limits of his confidence in its persuasive power—and perhaps also his reluctance to be associated, in the light of day, with an argument known to be weak. So in keeping with Hamilton's characterization of the essay as concerning "miscellaneous points," perhaps *Federalist* 84 is better understood as an attempt to wrap things up by addressing a previously ignored subject of debate and throwing on paper all of the various arguments that might be made on the topic. But regardless of Hamilton's own subjective understanding of the essay, there is little reason to think that its argument about enumerated powers and a bill of rights would have persuaded anyone who had been following the ratification controversy and had not already bought into the idea. There had been serious doubts all along, and *Federalist* 84 offered nothing new to allay them.

North Carolina

As a final example of persistent skepticism toward the argument that the Constitution's enumeration of federal powers rendered a bill of rights obsolete or dangerous, consider the fate of that argument in North Carolina, at the last ratification convention of 1788. One of the leading Federalists at that convention was James Iredell, a staunch supporter of the Constitution who would later serve on the Supreme Court of the United States. In February 1788, Iredell published a pseudonymous essay responding to Mason's objections to the Constitution, prominent among which was the lack of a bill of rights. Iredell had answered in terms taken from Wilson's October 6 speech in Philadelphia, which he cited. The Constitution, Iredell argued, expressly defined the powers that Congress could exercise. That having been done, it would have been "both nugatory and ridiculous" to specify other powers that Congress could not exercise. Indeed, it would have been dangerous, because it might imply that without the reservation, Congress would have the authority to exercise the relevant power. And that would open the door to claims that Congress could exercise all sorts of powers the Constitution had not delegated to it.[117]

Nonetheless, North Carolinians were still pressing the bill of rights objection at their ratifying convention five months later. So Iredell made his argument again. A bill of rights would be of no use, he said, in a Constitution "where the people expressly declare how much power they do give, and consequently retain all they do not."[118] Moreover, "[a] bill of rights . . . would not only be incongruous, but dangerous," because people would read it to mean that the general government was not strictly limited to the powers it had been given.[119] He reprised the argument the next day, saying—perhaps exasperatedly?— that he "thought the objection against the want of a bill of rights had been obviated unanswerably" but that he still found it necessary to explain the point. "It would be the greatest absurdity," Iredell continued, to think that Congress "can have any authority but what is so expressly given to it . . . Congress can have no right to exercise any power but what is contained in that paper."[120] That being the case, "it would be not only useless, but dangerous, to enumerate a number of rights which are not intended to be given up, because it would be implying, in the strongest manner, that every right not included in the exception might be impaired by the government without usurpation."[121]

An older delegate named Samuel Spencer gave a thoughtful response. Iredell, he said, was expressing "admiration"—in twenty-first century terms, something like "wonderment"—that some of his colleagues were still stuck on the issue of a bill of rights. But perhaps Iredell was putting too much faith in the argument he was making. Not, Spencer said, that Iredell's idea was wrong: "I acknowledge," he said, "that the doctrine is right."[122] But where important matters were concerned, it might be worth erring on the side of caution. Making a point that could have come from Madison's *Federalist* 37, Spencer noted that the extent of Congress's power under the Constitution would be a case where "there is no rule but a vague doctrine."[123] And sometimes power has a way of expanding even in the face of a doctrine that is supposed to prevent it, especially if that doctrine is vague. Given that possibility, Spencer reasoned, and given that the Constitution contained "no express negative"—that is, no language explicitly limiting the general government to powers expressly delegated—might it not be prudent to add some language protecting specific rights, even if in principle such a thing should not be necessary?[124]

We cannot know the tone in which Spencer spoke. But it is easy to imagine Spencer, who was about fifty years old at the time, deploying a sort of avuncular realism as he tried to calm Iredell—still in his thirties—by reassuring the younger man that yes, his ideas were good, but maybe we should do something else anyway, because the world is not always as governed by good arguments as it ought to be. Indeed, Spencer continued, he was quite sure that Iredell would acknowledge the wisdom of that course of action after he had had time to think about it. "I have no doubt," Spencer said, "that when he coolly reflects, he will acknowledge the necessity of it."[125] Perhaps Spencer was suggesting that by that point in the process, everyone understood that the enumerated-powers argument against a bill of rights was lacking. Perhaps it was time to let it go.

The North Carolina convention seems to have sided with Spencer. Despite Iredell's best efforts, the delegates not only refused to ratify the Constitution but by well more than a two-thirds majority approved a long list of rights that they wished to see written into the Constitution before they would consider the question again.[126] Not until November 1789, after Congress had approved a set of rights-specifying amendments and sent them to the states for ratification, did North Carolina agree to the new Constitution.

◄◄‹‹·›·►◄‹‹·›·►►

At the end of 1788, fundamental questions about how the written Constitution should be read and how the system would operate remained unsettled.

The ratification process did not include a mechanism for resolving issues other than whether the Constitution—whatever it meant—would be adopted. And the debates did not suggest any convergence of opinions over time. There were rival readings at the start, and there were rival readings at the end.

But although the discourse of ratification cannot tell us what was persuasive, it can tell us what was arguable. It demonstrates that a class of well-informed people who wanted to persuade a larger public to support or reject the Constitution believed that a certain set of arguments was likely to be useful in that enterprise. If those people made their choices soundly, then the range of arguments offered would map a range of interpretations Americans could plausibly entertain about national power and the Constitution in 1787–1788. Some of these arguments seem sounder than others. Wilson's more aggressive arguments about a bill of rights might seem irredeemably flawed, along with Hamilton's reprise of those arguments in *Federalist* 84. But Madison's account of a government limited to expressly delegated powers plus those implied by the express delegations seems tenable. So does Brutus's argument about a government authorized by the Preamble and the Sweeping Clause to pursue the public welfare in ways not limited by the enumeration of federal powers. There is a lot of space between those conceptions, and the history of the ratification debates does not make either one of them authoritative. It makes little sense to say, "Go with Madison, because his side won," because a vote to ratify the Constitution is not necessarily a vote to endorse any particular argument made in favor of ratification.

Rather than understanding the ratification process to have settled issues about the powers of Congress, it makes more sense to see it as having ventilated possible positions that would then be argued in the actual practice of American governance. At least some of the more perceptive participants in the state conventions understood that whatever Americans might think about the scope of congressional power in 1788, the operative scope of that power would be a product of later people's decisions. As the Federal Farmer noted, a Constitution whose text is formally ambiguous about whether the government it creates is limited in any particular way is, in practice, a Constitution under which that government is probably not so limited.[127] At the Virginia convention, both Henry in his role as the Constitution's leading opponent and Randolph in his role as its equivocal defender faced this reality squarely. Henry deployed the point as a warning: we may say today that these powers will limit Congress and prevent it from legislating against slavery, but in antislavery hands these grants of power will be construed to authorize emancipation. In urging his fellow Virginians to ratify, Randolph did not deny the underlying point. It was true, he said, that this Constitution contained seeds that could foreseeably grow into broad authorizations for congressional power. He decided it was worth the risk. And with all of those possibilities in view, the voting public ratified the Constitution.

CHAPTER FIVE

INTERNALIZED
ARGUMENTS

A FTER THE CONSTITUTION WAS ratified and the new government began to function, Congress became the nation's leading forum for constitutional debate. The business of building the federal government raised
many questions about federal power. Perhaps not surprisingly, members of
Congress often disagreed about the answers. In some respects, they also disagreed about how to analyze the questions.

Formally, the First Congress's most consequential action on the subject of
federal power was its formulation of what became the Tenth Amendment,
which provides that "[t]he powers not delegated to the United States by the
Constitution, nor prohibited by it to the States, are reserved to the States
respectively, or to the people." Congress twice rejected proposals for the amendment to speak of powers "not *expressly* delegated" to the United States, thus
preserving the possibility of implicit as well as express delegation. But the
Tenth Amendment is important to enumerationism mostly because of its
text and the way it has been deployed over time, rather than because of the
way it was debated in the First Congress. The political debate in the First
Congress that has done the most to shape ideas about federal power is the
debate over creating the Bank of the United States. And the prevailing memory of that debate is distorted in ways that make the First Congress seem
considerably more enumerationist than it actually was.

The 1791 bank debate is usually remembered through the arguments of four famous Founders.[1] In the House of Representatives, Madison argued that incorporating a bank lay beyond the enumerated powers of Congress. After Congress passed the bank bill over Madison's objections, Secretary of State Jefferson and Attorney General Randolph urged President Washington to veto the bill on enumerated-powers grounds. On the other side, Treasury Secretary Hamilton argued that the bank bill was within Congress's authority under its enumerated powers. So it is no wonder that the bank controversy is remembered as reflecting the fact—as if it were a fact—that from the dawn of the Republic, everyone has taken the tenets of enumerationism as established premises in constitutional law.

But the standard presentation misleads in at least two ways. First, not everyone involved shared the view that Congress could legislate only on the basis of specifically enumerated powers. Some members of Congress believed that Congress inherently enjoyed certain powers as the nation's legislature. Some believed that Congress was implicitly empowered to act when the general interest called for governmental action the states could not take on their own. And some read the Constitution to vest the national government with all powers necessary for achieving the ends of government listed in the Preamble— the formation of a more perfect union, the establishment of justice, and so on.

For modern lawyers, this diversity of Founding-era opinion is perhaps masked most powerfully by the way we remember Hamilton's memorandum to Washington defending the constitutionality of the bank bill. Hamilton argued that the bank bill was a valid exercise of Congress's enumerated powers.[2] Modern readers whose expectations are shaped by enumerationism accordingly tend to see the debate between Madison and Hamilton as an argument about how to construe the enumerated powers rather than an argument in which nonenumerationist views are in bounds. But there were also broader conceptions of national power in play, both in Hamilton's own analysis and in those of his contemporaries. Although he did not present his conclusion as resting on this point, Hamilton's opinion followed Wilson in asserting the existence of "resulting powers"—that is, powers resulting more "from the nature of political society, than a consequence of . . . the powers specially enumerated."[3] And in Congress, several of the bank's leading supporters argued that Congress had the power to incorporate the bank on the basis of something other than its enumerated powers.

The standard presentation of the bank debate also misleads in a second important way. If we think of the debate as a set piece featuring Madison and Hamilton (and perhaps Jefferson and Randolph in supporting roles), then we are likely to imagine that the bill proposing the creation of the bank clearly raised an enumerated-powers issue and the central question to be decided was how that issue would be resolved. But in fact, the question of whether Congress had the power to charter a bank was not at issue during most of the time that the bank proposal lay before Congress. The idea that Congress might not have that power was a mostly unexpected argument that Madison brought forward late in the legislative process, as a way of articulating his objections to the bank in a constitutional register.

Madison's enumerated-powers argument against the bank was a paradigm case of a phenomenon I will call *internalization*. To internalize a constitutional objection to some piece of federal legislation is to take an objection that would be most straightforwardly articulated as an external limit on Congress (that is, as an affirmative prohibition) but is not stated in the Constitution's text, and articulate it in terms of internal limits (that is, as the absence of a relevant enumerated power). Internalized arguments often come about as a way of constitutionalizing objections to legislative proposals when those objections can otherwise find no footing in the written Constitution.

Perhaps the earliest important example of internalization is the argument that the federal government had no power to emancipate slaves. As described earlier, many Founding-era Americans understood that the Constitution could not be adopted unless proslavery southerners were reassured on this point. The constitutional rule that would have best served their purpose would have been an external limit, along the lines of "The federal government may not emancipate slaves" or, more broadly, "The federal government may neither emancipate slaves nor take measures having the purpose of producing emancipation." But no such prohibitions were written into the Constitution's text. In the absence of such external limits, many Americans who wanted to establish the same substantive point (whether to protect slavery or to give assurance to those who wanted slavery protected) argued that the *internal* limits on federal power would prevent the government from pursuing emancipation. That is, they argued that the federal government could act only on the basis of its enumerated powers and that none of the enumerated powers warranted interference with slavery. In so doing, they took a substantive proposition most naturally expressed as an external limit ("No emancipation") and tried to establish it as a matter of internal limits.

Internalized arguments against federal legislation often require forced readings of the Constitution's clauses enumerating congressional powers. Consider the slavery example. As several proslavery Antifederalists pointed out, it is not hard to draft an emancipation statute on the basis of Congress's enumerated powers. A favorite example was the possibility that Congress would use its enumerated power to raise armies to conscript slaves into the military and, with its power under the Necessary and Proper Clause, give the conscripts an incentive to be good soldiers by promising freedom to those who served well. Other alternatives are easy to identify. Under its commerce power, Congress could have declared that all persons sold as slaves would automatically become free five years after the date of sale. (If necessary to qualify as a regulation of commerce "among the several states," such a rule could have been limited to interstate sales.) Under its bankruptcy power, Congress might have declared any slave who was part of a bankrupt estate to be free rather than being part of the assets to be distributed. Under its naturalization power, Congress could have encouraged emancipation by declaring all slaves to be citizens.

The idea that Congress had no power to emancipate slaves would work only if the community of constitutional interpreters were willing to agree that possibilities like these were off the table. Such an agreement would in effect build a slavery-related limit into each of the enumerated powers, even though the text of the Constitution does not mention such a limit. What historians call the "federal consensus" on slavery in the early republic was just such an agreement.[4] And the real force preventing Congress from using its enumerated powers to interfere with slavery in the early republic was not anything about the inherent limits of commercial regulation, conscription, bankruptcy, naturalization, and so on. It was the strength of American officials' commitment to what was, in substance, an external limit: that Congress must not interfere with slavery.

Madison's argument against the bank was an internalized argument. What Madison wanted in 1791, for a variety of reasons, was a constitutional rule prohibiting the federal government from chartering a national bank (and, indeed, from chartering corporations more broadly). That rule is most naturally expressed as an external limit: "No federally chartered national bank." (Or "No federally chartered corporations.") But no such prohibition appeared in the text of the Constitution. The absence of such a prohibition was not a matter of happenstance: during and after the ratification process, several states proposed constitutional amendments prohibiting Congress from chartering corporations, or at least corporations with monopolistic privileges—like the Bank of the United States.[5] Congress voted those proposals down.[6] So Madison could not oppose the bank on the basis of external-limit rules written into the Constitution.

At some point in the process, however, Madison realized that he could try to establish the substance of a "No federal banks" rule as a matter of internal limits rather than external ones. The Constitution articulated no affirmative prohibition on federally chartered corporations, but it also did not expressly authorize Congress to create any, and that absence was not a matter of happenstance either. At the Convention, Madison had proposed giving Congress an express power to grant charters of incorporation in cases where state legislation would be inadequate for the task.[7] (Madison's opposition to federally chartered corporations in 1791 was a change in position since 1787; some of the reasons for the change are discussed later in this chapter.) The Convention rejected that proposal, with the delegates voting no apparently making up a coalition between some who did not want Congress to have such a power and others who did want Congress to have such a power but thought its express specification unnecessary—or feared that naming that power in the Constitution would provoke opposition in the ratification process.[8] The Convention's choice to leave out an affirmative authorization did not reflect a choice to withhold an incorporating power from Congress, but it left open the possibility that someone might argue that Congress had no such power. Four years after the Convention, Madison did just that. By "internalizing" his argument, Madison could oppose the bank not just as a matter of policy but on the ground that chartering the bank would be unconstitutional.

It didn't work. As Madison himself had cautioned Wallace six years earlier and repeated at the Convention, an enumeration of powers is in practice a poorly suited technology for limiting what a legislature will do. And Article I, Section 8, did not lend itself well to Madison's project. Without much trouble, Madison's colleagues rejected his enumerated-powers argument and approved the bank bill. What's more, many of them doubted that Madison really believed what he was arguing. It is not hard to see why. In an earlier congressional debate over where to locate the permanent seat of government—an issue with important if often forgotten connections to the bank issue—Madison had shown himself willing to manufacture tendentious constitutional arguments at the last minute when he was in danger of losing on an issue where he badly wanted to win. A short time later, during the bank debate, Madison at the last minute again came forward with a constitutional argument that nobody else was making but that would stave off defeat if accepted. That seemed suspicious. So in arguing that chartering the bank would be beyond Congress's constitutional authorities, some members of Congress thought, Madison was hoping to use a constitutional smokescreen to defeat a bill he did not like.

These critics may have been too dismissive. Madison had been critical of the idea of a limiting enumeration at the Convention, but he may have authentically changed his position by 1791. Indeed, his embrace of a restrictive view of enumerated powers in the bank debate might have been part of a general shift in his views about national power during the Constitution's first decade. But for present purposes, what matters is not whether Madison sincerely believed his argument. It is that his argument was less a straightforward application of an obviously relevant constitutional framework than an attempt to manufacture a constitutional basis for a prohibition the written Constitution did not establish. As such, it was an instance of the dynamic in constitutional argument that I am calling internalization. And recognizing this paradigmatic enumerated-powers argument as an exercise in internalization can alert us to the possibility that other enumerated-powers arguments have similar foundations.

This chapter describes two important pieces of context for the bank debate and then analyzes the debate itself. The first piece of context is the First Congress's debate over Congress's power to prescribe the language of the oath that state officials would take when swearing to uphold the Constitution. The second piece of context is the struggle over where to locate the permanent seat of government. Against those two background elements, I narrate the bank debate not as a set piece featuring Madison and Washington's cabinet secretaries but as a more sprawling debate in a Congress where both enumerationist and nonenumerationist arguments were in play.

The Oath: "Point to the Part"

During the First Congress, the Senate met in secret, and the proceedings of the House of Representatives were open to the public. Not that we are completely in the dark about the Senate: a few sources, including the opinionated journal of Pennsylvania Senator William Maclay, give us partial views. But we have much more documentation of what occurred in the House. Analysis of the ideas debated in the First Congress accordingly focuses on the House, not because what was argued there was more important, more representative, or more insightful than what was argued in the Senate but simply because we know more about it.[9] And as it happens, the very first bill proposed in the House of Representatives—House Resolution 1, First Congress, first session—provoked discussion and disagreement about the limits of congressional power.

The question was whether Congress could enact a statute requiring state officials to take the same oath to uphold the Constitution that was required of federal officials. Under Article VI, Section 3, of the Constitution, federal and state officials alike had to take such an oath. But the Constitution did not specify the language for such an oath, nor did it expressly authorize Congress to choose that language. Apparently reasoning that Congress should nonetheless compose the oath that federal officials would take, Virginia's Alexander White on April 14, 1789, presented a bill creating standard language for the federal officials' oath—"I, A.B., do solemnly swear or affirm (as the case may be) that I will support the Constitution of the United States"—as well as prescribing when the oath should be taken and by whom it should be administered.[10] Again, nothing in the Constitution expressly authorized Congress to prescribe or regulate the oath. But if anyone in the House had constitutional qualms about the proposal to that point, the surviving records do not reflect them.

On April 22, however, Richard Bland Lee (also of Virginia) moved to amend the proposal. Under Lee's amendment, the law would prescribe the wording of the oath and the circumstances under which the oath should be taken not just for federal officials but also for state officials.[11] That extension troubled Madison, and it is not hard to see why. Madison had excellent reasons, of two different kinds, to be cautious about Congress's imposing its authority directly on state officials. One set of reasons had to do with his commitment to having the new Constitution succeed. The other had to do with his own precarious position within the politics of Virginia.

As Madison was keenly aware, Virginia had ratified the Constitution only by a narrow margin, and much of its political elite remained skeptical.[12] That is why Madison was serving in the House, after all: his state legislature was

not inclined to send such a strong Federalist as Madison to the Senate, opt-
ing instead for the Antifederalists William Grayson and Richard Henry
Lee.[13] Even to secure his less-exalted seat in the second chamber, Madison
had to win a close election against the Antifederalist James Monroe, in a district that the Virginia legislature seems to have drawn for the purpose of
making it hard for Madison to get elected.[14] As a matter of political self-
preservation, Madison knew that his continued viability as a candidate for
office with a Virginia constituency required him to avoid being identified as
too strong a partisan of national power. And at a larger level, he knew that
the success of the new Constitution required securing greater buy-in from
the largest and most powerful state in the Union. As of 1789, Madison had
seen two regime changes in thirteen years. Nothing guaranteed that this
third regime would last. Virginia, more than any other state, could strengthen
the new Constitution by becoming fully invested or undermine it by acting
recalcitrantly. So Madison had reasons to seek opportunities to show Virginians that the Constitution was a good thing—and to avoid occasions where
the newly reconstituted general government might stoke the fears or resent-
ments of Virginia's political elite. A direct order from Congress that Virginia's legislators take a specific loyalty oath, legislated as the very first bill to
issue from the House of Representatives, might have seemed like just the
sort of thing that should be avoided.

According to the shorthand reporter's notes, Madison asked Lee to
"[p]oint to the part of [the] Constitution which gives authority" to Congress
to legislate the form and manner of the oath for state officials.[15] Madison may
have felt conflicted about raising this concern: he pronounced himself generally eager to see Congress exercise its powers.[16] But in the absence of a
clause empowering Congress to prescribe the text of the oath, Madison suggested that the Constitution's oath requirement might be one of those things
"that must execute themselves without invitation of [the] legislature."[17] In
other words, state officials might have to decide for themselves how to comply, whether individually or pursuant to state legislation.

Lee answered. In his view, the Necessary and Proper Clause authorized
his amendment, because it was "necessary to the existence of this government that the members of [state governments] should take the oath."[18] If we
assume that Lee meant to tether his argument to a precise reading of the
clause—and, given the loose-by-modern-professional-standards way that early
Americans invoked constitutional clauses, he may or may not have—then

he was implicitly skipping a step, but the missing reasoning is easy to supply. The Necessary and Proper Clause empowered Congress to make laws
necessary and proper for carrying into execution the powers vested in the
government of the United States. The law prescribing the oath was not a law
carrying any specific federal power into execution. But for any of the powers
vested in the government of the United States to be carried into execution,
the government of the United States would have to exist. The existence of
that government required the allegiance of the state legislatures. In an indirect but fundamental way, a law requiring state officials to take the oath was
therefore a necessary measure for ensuring that the powers vested in the
government of the United States could be carried into execution. Indeed,
Lee continued, he thought that prescribing rules for the oath was the very
least the Necessary and Proper Clause could be interpreted to do. "I don't
see why the clause [was] inserted," the shorthand reporter recorded him as
saying, "if [the] general government has not the power of requiring [this] oath
from them."[19]

Whether by this logic or otherwise, the other representatives who addressed the issue seem to have shared Lee's conclusion.[20] Nonetheless, the
House rejected Lee's amendment.[21] If the reasons for the rejection are those
visible in the discussion, the major impetus behind the House's decision was
a desire to avoid provoking the resentment of state legislatures by presum-
ing to impose congressional authority on them. (Madison's concern in this
vein was acute, but it was not limited to him, nor to Virginia.) So whether
Congress had the power to do so or not, several representatives argued that
it was wiser not to enact a rule binding on state officials, especially if the
states would probably comply on their own. For example, White, who had
introduced the initial measure prescribing the oath for federal officials, did
not "doubt [the] power of [the] house" to impose the requirement on state
officials, but he considered doing so "inexpedient."[22] In a similar vein, New
York's Peter Silvester thought it "clear [that] the exercise [of the power] ought
not to be insisted on at present."[23] Congress was in its infancy, and ratification had been a close question in several states; discretion probably called
for avoiding measures that state legislatures would experience as direct com-
mands. The House passed the bill as applied to federal officials only.[24]

But if the House had hesitated to take an action that might seem imperious toward the state legislatures, the Senate—composed of agents of those
very state legislatures—had fewer compunctions. Much as Lee had tried to

do, the Senate amended the proposal and included state as well as federal officials.[25] Perhaps the senators felt more connection with the state legislatures than the representatives and accordingly trusted themselves more to know what would and would not offend those bodies. Or perhaps a different group of men simply felt differently about the issue. Regardless of the explanation, though, the Senate extended the bill's strictures to state officials and sent the measure back to the House.

When the House confronted the issue a second time, Madison did not renew his constitutional objection. But Gerry pressed the point. The power of Congress to decide how state officials would comply with the oath requirement, Gerry argued, "is not expressly given by any clause of the constitution, and if it does exist, must arise from the sweeping clause."[26] Gerry had warned against the expansive scope of the Sweeping Clause since the Convention, and he now proffered a reading considerably narrower than Lee's. According to Gerry, the Sweeping Clause—indeed, the entire Necessary and Proper Clause—gave "no legislative authority to congress, to carry into effect any power not expressly vested by the constitution."[27] In other words, because there was no express constitutional language empowering Congress on the specific matter of oath-taking, the Necessary and Proper Clause was not relevant. A chain of reasoning whereby the law could be valid because it was necessary for the existence and therefore the functioning of the government as a whole, rather than for the execution of a specifically articulated power, was beyond the pale.

Most of Gerry's colleagues felt differently, and the House approved the measure as amended. Indeed, it did so without bothering to hold a roll-call vote, which suggests that the question was not close. Perhaps the Senate's endorsement of the measure mitigated the concerns of those representatives who had previously thought it inadvisable to impose upon the state legislatures. Perhaps it explains why Madison remained silent during the second debate: if he was by then persuaded that the measure was not toxic to the regime, he might have felt free to drop his opposition, even though he had presented that opposition as a matter of constitutional principle. But whether or not the Senate's stance was a factor changing Madison's view, or the House's view more broadly, the House overcame its previous qualms.

Some members explained their reasoning, as Lee had, by reference to the Necessary and Proper Clause. In an argument that might have been even broader than Lee's, New York's John Laurance argued that the Constitution required state officials to take the oath and that Congress had the "power to make all laws necessary, or proper to carry the declarations of the Constitution into effect."[28] In other words, Laurance seemed to read the Necessary and Proper Clause as empowering Congress not just to execute those portions of the Constitution that labeled themselves grants of power to the general government but as empowering Congress to carry out the "declarations" of the Constitution as a general matter. New Jersey's Elias Boudinot concurred. "[I]t was the duty of the house," he maintained, "to detail the general principles laid down in the constitution, and reduce them to practice."[29] That the Constitution enumerated no specific power to prescribe oaths for state officials to swear was not important. The law prescribing the oath fit within the Constitution's general scheme, and Congress had the power to make that scheme operate.

Other representatives defended the congressional power at issue without referring to any particular language in the Constitution. According to some representatives, Congress's power to make this rule for state officials arose from the fact that the matter called for national uniformity, which only Congress could supply. Virginia's Theodorick Bland, for example, pointed out that "if the state legislatures were to be left to arrange and direct this business, they would pass different laws, and the officers might be bound in different degrees to support the Constitution."[30] Roger Sherman similarly argued that it made sense to have "a general provision for taking the oath, [rather] than particular ones" and that "no other legislature is competent to all these purposes; but if they were, there is a propriety in the supreme legislature's doing it."[31] Perhaps these representatives meant their arguments to be explanations for why the Necessary and Proper Clause authorized Congress to act, and that portion of their thinking was simply implicit (or not recorded). But perhaps not. To judge from the arguments as recorded, it is also possible that their reasoning floated free of any particular clause and rested instead on the idea that Congress, as the national legislature, was empowered to vindicate the Constitution whenever national legislation alone would be adequate for the task.

The debate on the constitutionality of the expanded reach of the oath law was not a momentous episode, and it is not part of the shared memory of modern constitutional lawyers. But it illustrates some noteworthy dynamics of constitutional debate in the First Congress, including some that are useful context for assessing the debate over the bank that would come thereafter.

First, the debate for the most part did not proceed on the basis of close readings of the Constitution's text. Second, to the extent that the Constitution's text mattered, the key provision was the Necessary and Proper Clause. Third, a fair amount of the debate trafficked in arguments about what the general government was well suited to do, given its position as the general government, and many representatives took the view, in one way or another, that the general government was empowered on that basis to do certain things irrespective of whether specific constitutional texts granted particular powers. Fourth, Madison played a distinctive role by coming forward with an enumerated-powers argument that others might or might not have identified. And fifth, the argument Madison offered was not one many of his colleagues found persuasive. They had a more capacious understanding of federal power.

The Seat of Government: Desperately Fighting Susquehanna

We do not know just why Madison did not insist on his constitutional objection to the oath law. Perhaps he found his colleagues' views of the Sweeping Clause persuasive—though if so, he would have been abandoning the narrower view of that clause that he had endorsed during the ratification debates. So perhaps it is more likely that the Senate's approval of the proposal (and the support of several of his Virginian colleagues in the House) convinced Madison that a federal law prescribing the form of the oath for state officials would not offend the Virginia legislature and, with the stakes thus lowered, he was willing to put constitutional scruples aside. But a short time later, when a different measure threatened Virginia's attitude toward the new system in a more material way, Madison raised a constitutional objection and insisted on it tenaciously.

The issue was where to locate the nation's capital, described in the Constitution as "the seat of government." The First Congress met in New York City. Madison badly wanted to locate the permanent capital in or near Virginia, and more was at stake in that preference than a shorter commute.[32] As noted earlier, Madison knew that putting the system on a sound footing required the full buy-in of the Union's largest state. He also suspected, perhaps wisely, that a national capital in Virginia's orbit would help move marginal Virginians into the new system's camp.[33] A national government in New York or Philadelphia might be an alien entity, from a Virginian point of view. A national government in an essentially Virginian location would be easier to embrace.

A full appreciation of how much Virginia's attitude toward the national government might be affected by the location of the capital requires attention to something usually omitted from the story of the siting of Washington, DC: slavery.[34] Most Virginians who might aspire to federal office were slaveholders, and they were accustomed to bringing enslaved people with them when they traveled. If the seat of government were in a northern city like New York or Philadelphia, Virginians holding federal office would have to navigate hostility to slavery during their time of service. New York had enacted a statute in 1781 freeing slaves who had fought on the American side during the war against Britain, and by the end of the decade there was a considerable free Black population in New York City, as well as an established and growing manumission society.[35] Pennsylvania enacted a gradual abolition law in 1780, and in 1788 it enacted legislation designed to make it difficult for slaveholders from other states to keep slaves while in Pennsylvania temporarily.[36] The point was not merely theoretical: while Attorney General Randolph resided temporarily in Philadelphia during the Washington administration, the slaves he brought with him were emancipated by Pennsylvania law.[37] Needless to say, this sort of thing might deter slaveholding Virginians from serving in the federal government if the capital were someplace like Philadelphia. And even if it did not deter them from serving, the experience of having to work in a place where the surrounding mores looked askance at slavery—sometimes powerfully so—would make the seat of government of the United States a place where a Virginian slaveholder would feel distinctly not at home.

Madison saw that the location of the capital could be either an important asset or a significant liability for the cause of getting Virginia to become fully invested in the new system. Partly for that reason, he was determined to bring the seat of government to, or at least near, Virginia. He also liked the idea of a capital that was centrally located and far away from urban financial markets.[38] But Madison nearly lost his chance to secure the capital for Virginia when a group of northern representatives beat him to the issue. In September 1789, Representative Benjamin Goodhue of Massachusetts introduced a resolution calling for the permanent seat of government to be placed in Pennsylvania, somewhere along the Susquehanna River.[39] Madison was vexed. He seems to have suspected, perhaps correctly, that representatives from New England and New York had cut a deal to support a Pennsylvania location for the capital, figuring that Pennsylvania was as far north as a majority of Congress could conceivably agree to go.[40] Unexpectedly, Madison saw the possibility of a Potomac capital slipping away.

The day after Goodhue introduced his resolution, Madison rose in the House and made a battery of arguments against the proposed Pennsylvania location. It wasn't sufficiently central geographically.[41] It wasn't sufficiently central relative to the American population.[42] The rivers leading to the place were not sufficiently navigable.[43] Its proximity to stagnant water would risk high rates of disease.[44] It was as if Madison had left Congress the day before and gone straight to the library, seeking all possible data that could be marshaled to argue against the Pennsylvania site. But to no avail. The House approved the resolution, thus triggering the next step of the legislative process: the drafting of an actual bill to place the seat of government in Pennsylvania.[45]

Two weeks later, that bill was before the House, and Madison raised a different objection. This time, he did not argue about location or population or navigation or disease. He argued that the proposal was *unconstitutional*. To fix the permanent seat of government by law, Madison now contended, would violate the Constitution.[46]

Madison reasoned as follows: under Article I, Section 5, clause 4, "[n]either House, during the Session of Congress, shall, without the Consent of the other, adjourn . . . to any other Place than that in which the two Houses shall be sitting." By implication, the two houses of Congress acting concurrently could decide to adjourn to some other place. According to Madison, it followed that Congress's authority to change the location of its meetings was immune from interference by the president: where to meet was a decision for the legislature alone.[47] Indeed, Article I, Section 7, clause 3, expressly exempted questions of adjournment from the normal requirement that Congress's work product be presented for presidential approval. Any attempt to specify *by statute* where Congress would meet, Madison argued, would therefore be invalid.[48] Such a statute would bind Congress to meet in a certain location unless repealed, and repeal would require either the concurrence of the president or a two-thirds supermajority in each House. As a result, such a statute would deprive Congress of its Article I right to decide where to adjourn on the strength of the concurrence of majorities in the two houses alone, without any need for supermajorities or presidential approval.[49] Like it or not, Madison concluded, the bill to fix the permanent seat of government at a location in Pennsylvania (or anywhere else) could not be constitutionally enacted.

To say that this argument did not persuade Madison's colleagues would be to put the matter gently. The recorded reaction of Massachusetts representative Fisher Ames is suggestive:

> Mr. Ames . . . admired the abilities of the honorable gentleman [Madison], and doubted not but the Constitution was the better in consequence of those abilities having been employed in its formation; but he was not disposed to pay implicit deference to that gentleman's expositions of that instrument.[50]

In other words, Ames tipped his hat to Madison's ingenuity and did not think that Madison's argument made any sense at all. As a Massachusetts man happy to have the capital as far north as possible, Ames favored the bill Madison was opposing, so perhaps he was not the most sympathetic judge of Madison's argument. But even some southerners who shared Madison's opposition to putting the seat of government in Pennsylvania were dismissive of this reading of Article I. South Carolina's William Loughton Smith, for example, responded that of course the site of the seat of government could be fixed by law, with presidential participation; Georgia's James Jackson politely described Madison's constitutional contention as "not well founded."[51]

The narrative, then, seems to run as follows: Madison was deeply invested in securing a location in or near Virginia for the permanent seat of government. When confronted with legislation that threatened the outcome he sought, he marshaled as many arguments as time and effort permitted. In the first instance, none of those arguments rested on the text of the Constitution, probably because nothing in the text of the Constitution seemed to speak to the issue. But none of his arguments worked. So in due course, he came forth with a different kind of argument—an argument involving a reading of the Constitution's text. It was a clever argument. But it was also a tendentious argument, and Madison's fellow representatives didn't buy it. They understood that Madison's purported theory explaining why a bill he opposed on the merits was not just undesirable but unconstitutional had been cooked up ad hoc. They brushed him aside.

The bill for a Pennsylvania capital was approved on September 22, with Madison voting against it.[52] But Madison did not give up. He seems later on to have instigated a disagreement about exactly where along the Susquehanna the seat of government would be located, and the resulting impasse opened the door for the famous deal the following summer whereby Madison would get a capital on the Potomac River and Hamilton would win approval for his plan for the national government to assume state debts.[53] When that deal came before Congress, Madison gave pretty good proof of the ad hockery of his constitutional objection the year before. Not only did Madison now vote in favor of fixing the seat of government by statute, but he advised Washington in a written opinion that, as a matter of constitutional law, the seat of government *must* be fixed by statute.[54] Contemporary commentators skewered Madison for the self-contradiction. "What is become of [Madison]'s oath which stuck in his throat last session, and prevented his voting for the Susquehannah?" one critic asked. "[H]ave the waters of the *Patowmac* the virtue of the *Lethe*, that those who drink of them may lose their memory?"[55]

In short, by the time the bill to charter the Bank of the United States was drafted, Madison had shown himself willing to manufacture a tendentious constitutional argument and insist on it in the House of Representatives. Not, of course, that all of his arguments should have been dismissed as tendentious and ad hoc. But the possibility had been demonstrated. And when Madison made his famous enumerated-powers argument against the bank in February 1791, many of his colleagues believed that he had done it again.

The Bank Debate without the Enumeration Question

The possibility that incorporating the bank might be beyond Congress's powers was something Madison injected into the debate at a very late stage, when the bill had already passed the Senate and was on its third and final reading before the House of Representatives. Until that last stage of the legislative process, the bank bill was not the subject of any enumerated-powers controversy. It had critics and opponents, Madison among them. Some of the bases of their opposition are reasonably described as "constitutional" in the small-c sense of the word: that is, they pertained to fundamental issues about the organization and workings of the system of government. But nobody, Madison included, seems to have thought that Congress lacked the authority to create the bank by legislation. That idea—like the idea that Congress could not fix the location of the seat of government by statute—surfaced only when the bill stood on the brink of passage.

Hamilton

Hamilton delivered his bank proposal to Congress on December 14, 1790. His report was more than fourteen thousand words long, and it devoted a fair amount of space to anticipating and responding to arguments against the bank.[56] But at no point did Hamilton mention the possibility of an enumerated-powers issue—not even to say, "Some people might think that chartering a bank is beyond the power of Congress, but that's a bad view, and here's why." The report contains no indication whatsoever that Hamilton could foresee an enumerated-powers objection.

That Hamilton anticipated no enumerated-powers objection does not prove that there was no such objection to make. People often overlook the potential obstacles to projects they support. But as noted above, Hamilton's report paid a lot of attention to analyzing and overcoming potential arguments against the bank. Moreover, Hamilton was not just any advocate, and the objection Madison ultimately propounded was—in Madison's presentation, anyway—founded on a central feature of the Constitution. So the question is not just whether people sometimes overlook problems with their pet projects. It is whether the author of fifty-one *Federalist* essays was likely to overlook an issue going to the heart of the new Constitution on a topic to which he had devoted fourteen thousand words.

The point can be sharpened further, because Hamilton's report did take account of the Constitution in other ways. One of the topics Hamilton covered was the possibility of the government's creating paper money. In the course of explaining the system of which the bank would be a part, Hamilton noted that the states were prohibited from creating paper money under Article I, Section 10. He then argued that although the Constitution did not impose the same prohibition on the federal government, it would be wise for the federal government not to create paper money either.[57] So Hamilton had not put the Constitution out of mind while writing his report. Where he thought the Constitution relevant to an issue he was discussing, he said so. And in cataloguing and discussing many possible objections to the bank, he wrote not one word about the possibility that someone would claim that Congress lacked the power to grant a corporate charter.

Madison

The person who would ultimately make the enumerated-powers argument that Hamilton apparently did not foresee—Madison—had multiple reasons for opposing the bank bill. Some were prosaic. For example, the bank was structured as a shareholder corporation, and the proposed system for offering shares to the public was such that Madison's Virginian constituents were unlikely to come away with many shares.[58] But more fundamental matters were also at stake. The bank would be an institution controlled by a financial elite. Madison had no problem with elites holding power, but the elite he trusted was a landed-gentry elite, not a financial-markets elite.[59] In the tradition of a country-party ideology that had recently animated Antifederalists and that would soon be important to the Democratic-Republican Party, Madison worried that relationships of financial credit and debt could undermine the political and economic independence of citizens and thereby erode an important basis of republicanism.[60] A national bank could be particularly threatening, because it would be a vehicle through which a financial elite—much of it located in England—could hold the debt, and thereby compromise the independence, of the Republic itself.

More generally, Madison worried that recognizing a federal power to create corporations would have unwelcome repercussions in the national political process. Four years earlier, when defending the Constitution in *The Federalist*, Madison had argued that the large geographic scale of the United States would make congressional legislation less prone to capture by self-interested factions, and therefore more just and more public-regarding, than lawmaking in the states would be.[61] By 1791, however, Madison was coming to think that the "extended republic" he previously idealized gave a structural advantage to the financial class, which seemed better able to mobilize politically on a national scale than the more locally oriented planter-gentry.[62] If Congress had the power to grant charters of incorporation, then the financial class would be able to use its advantage in national politics to secure a great deal of what it wanted—that is, power-wielding corporations controlled by financial elites. By contrast, if the creation of corporations were exclusively within the power of the state governments, those financial elites would be forced to pursue their interests in state-level politics. And in state politics, the gentry could not be so easily overwhelmed.[63]

Madison was also concerned that the bank proposal might prompt Congress to back away from its decision to locate the national capital on the Potomac River.[64] According to the 1790 legislation, Congress was to leave New York, spend ten years in Philadelphia, and then move to a newly built location on the Potomac.[65] But as many Americans recognized at the time, getting Congress in 1790 to vote in favor of a Potomac capital was one thing, and actually moving the government there ten years later would be another.[66] Ten years is long enough for an operation to put down roots, and temporary arrangements sometimes have a way of making themselves permanent. Philadelphia was America's largest city. The Potomac alternative was an undeveloped swamp. Was Congress really going to pick up and move there, leaving behind the quarters and routines that it would have become accustomed to during ten years of residence in the metropolis? (Gerry charged that people might just as easily believe that Congress was serious about relocating to Mississippi or Detroit.[67]) And there was a widely understood practical connection between the creation of a national bank and the odds that the capital would one day move. Everyone knew that if Congress created a Bank of the United States, the institution would be located in Philadelphia, where the government was working and where there was a capital market with which to do business.[68] To create the bank was accordingly to deepen the government's ties to its existing Philadelphia location, and every increase in the government's footprint in Philadelphia during the 1790s would make it harder to move in 1800. Many members of Congress had this dynamic on their minds as Congress considered the bank bill: one Massachusetts representative wrote that some of his southern colleagues "look upon a national bank established at Philadelphia as throwing a monstrous sheet anchor in that Harbour, which no future Congress will ever be able to weigh."[69] And if the seat of government did not move to the Potomac, a major Madisonian strategy for securing Virginia's support for the new regime would come to nothing.

In an important sense, some of Madison's reasons for opposing the bank bill were constitutional concerns. Institutional arrangements that could enhance or undermine the independence of citizens or of the government in general, allocations of legislative power that would channel political competition in different ways, a (geographic) separation of powers between the capital markets and the seat of government, a location of that seat of government that could encourage or endanger the loyalty of the Union's largest state—all these things are matters of constitutional design. But they are constitutional matters in the small-c sense: they are about the structure and operation of government rather than about the text of the document called "the Constitution." And the text of the written Constitution did not vindicate Madison's concerns about the bank. No language in the Constitution expressly spoke to the possibility of a national bank, or to federally chartered corporations, or to the relationship among the government, the gentry, and the financial class, or to the merits of putting the seat of government in this or that location.

So perhaps it should not be surprising that Madison's writings in the seven weeks between Hamilton's proposal and the debate in the House of Representatives contain no indication that Madison saw the bank bill as in any way in conflict with the new written Constitution.[70] He spent considerable time during those weeks preparing arguments against the bill, and he compiled several pages of notes based on his preparations.[71] Nothing in those notes suggests that Madison was preparing to argue that issuing a charter of incorporation was beyond the powers of Congress. Nor does the possibility that the bank was beyond Congress's powers appear in Madison's correspondence during that time. To be sure, it is possible that Madison always believed incorporating the bank to be beyond Congress's powers and simply never wrote anything down on the topic. But it is also possible that he wrote nothing about an enumerated-powers problem with the bank because he did not see one, or at least not one worth taking seriously.

The Senate

The Senate took up consideration of the bank bill in January 1791, ahead of the House.[72] Because the *Senate Journal* recorded only a procedural account of the Senate's business, it does not disclose what arguments senators made about the bank bill. But the *Journal* does reveal that the bill passed with little controversy on the main question. On controversial questions, or on issues where senators on the losing side wanted to be on record, the practice then as now was for senators to ask that the "Yeas and Nays" be reported in the *Journal*. Under Article I, Section 5, of the Constitution, the yeas and nays must be printed if at least one-fifth of the members present so request. In the short Senate proceedings on the bank bill that preceded the final vote, in which the Senate hashed out specific aspects of the bank's charter, the yeas and nays appear repeatedly.[73] But at the end of the process, when the main question was put, the *Journal* simply records that the bill passed, without recorded yeas and nays.[74] That indicates that less than one-fifth of the senators thought the final question was even worth being on record about.

The most detailed surviving evidence of what transpired among the senators comes from the diary of Pennsylvania senator William Maclay.[75] According to Maclay's notes, the Senate discussed the terms on which private individuals could hold stock in the bank, the size of a subscription by the United States on behalf of the public, the time period for which the charter would be valid, and whether Congress could repeal the charter once it was enacted.[76] In short, Maclay's diary reflects the Senate's giving close attention to many aspects of the bank issue. But it contains no suggestion that anyone questioned Congress's constitutional authority to issue the charter of incorporation.

Maclay was a fastidious republican. He disliked banking systems, which he regarded as "[m]achines for promoting the profits of unproductive Men."[77] He feared that the Bank of the United States would serve the interests of a small financial elite and neglect the broader public.[78] He characterized Hamilton as a "damnable Villain."[79] And he suspected several of his more nationalistic Senate colleagues of aiming to annihilate the state governments.[80] On balance, and perhaps because he suspected the bill had the votes to pass, Maclay devoted himself to cutting the best deal he could rather than trying to block passage of the bill.[81] But given his ideological stance, Maclay would hardly have been one to underplay constitutional objections to Congress's power to incorporate the bank. He recorded none. So perhaps there were no such objections for him to record, or at least none worth taking seriously.

This is not to say that Maclay never considered that Congress might lack the power to incorporate the bank. On the contrary, his diary contains one reference to that possibility. In an entry dated December 24, 1790, Maclay wrote critically about the bank proposal, saying among other things that banks "may be regarded [a]s opposed to republicanism" because of their tendency to concentrate wealth in a few hands.[82] But Maclay did not doubt Congress's power to incorporate a bank if it chose to do so. "The power of incorporating may be inquired into," Maclay wrote. "But the old Congress enjoyed it. Bank Bills are promisary Notes and of Course not Money. I see no Objection on this Quarter."[83] In other words, Maclay—who viewed banks as unrepublican and who feared that his colleagues were seeking to extend congressional power so far as to annihilate the state governments—thought it clear that Congress had the power to incorporate a bank. As far as he could see, there was no serious constitutional issue to discuss. And there is no indication that any of Maclay's Senate colleagues thought differently. In all of the letters, diaries, and other documents collected in the *Documentary History of the First Federal Congress*, there is nothing—nothing at all—in any document written while the bank proposal was pending that indicates that any member of the Senate doubted Congress's power to incorporate a bank.[84]

Much as it seems unlikely that Hamilton would have failed to anticipate an objection to the bank based on a core tenet of the new Constitution, it seems odd that the entire United States Senate would overlook one. The Senate in 1791 included many men who had recently attended constitutional conventions. Every senator served as the agent of a state legislature, so it would be particularly strange for the whole Senate to miss a basic constitutional problem sounding in the general government's exceeding its proper authority and intruding on the prerogatives of state governments. This is all the more so because the Senate in 1791 included outspoken opponents of extensive congressional power. Maclay is a less famous example. A more famous one is Virginia's James Monroe. At Virginia's ratifying convention, Monroe had voted against the Constitution, and the Virginia legislature subsequently sent Monroe to the Senate in preference to Madison precisely because Madison was too solicitous of national power.[85] Not surprisingly, Maclay's diary indicates that Monroe opposed the bank when the proposal first came before the Senate.[86] But there is no indication—not in Maclay's notes, not in Monroe's own papers, and not anywhere else I have been able to discover—that Monroe doubted Congress's constitutional power to incorporate the bank at any time before Madison pressed that argument in the House.[87] It would be curious if a plausible objection to Congress's authority—indeed, an objection serious enough to be championed by the man Virginia considered too much of a nationalist to represent it in the Senate—had not occurred to the Antifederalist Virginia sent instead.[88]

Other Evidence

To further test the hypothesis that the enumerated-powers objection to the bank did not seem like a serious argument before Madison spoke in the House, I read the surviving letters not just of the senators but of all members of both houses of Congress for the seven-week period between December 14, 1790, when Hamilton submitted his report, and February 2, 1791, when Madison rose in opposition, as well as the surviving letters written to members of Congress by other persons during that period, as collected in the *Documentary History of the First Federal Congress*. That correspondence occupies 495 pages.[89] I discovered exactly one document mentioning the possibility that Congress might lack the power to incorporate the bank: a letter written by Theodore Sedgwick of Massachusetts on January 30, 1791, as the bank bill approached its third and final reading in the House. Like Maclay's diary entry, Sedgwick's letter mentions the possibility of an objection based on the limits of congressional power but does not regard such an objection as serious.

In his letter, written three days before Madison's first big speech against the bank bill, Sedgwick told a friend that he expected Madison to argue that Congress had no power to incorporate the bank. So in the last stages of the legislative process, Madison's intention to make some such argument was known to, or at least suspected by, another member of Congress. But Sedgwick also suspected that Madison's likely argument about congressional authority, if it materialized, would be pretextual. In Sedgwick's estimation, Madison opposed the bank bill because he was concerned "that it will tend to defeat the potowmack project" by deepening the government's ties to Philadelphia. But, Sedgwick continued, Madison's motive for his opposition "will not be avowed." Instead, "he will probably deny the constitutional authority of congress on the subject."[90] In other words, Sedgwick was saying, Madison regarded chartering the bank as a threat to moving the nation's capital, so he wanted to block the bill, and he needed a tool for doing so. For the purpose, he would make an argument about the limited authority of Congress.

Sedgwick might not be a reliable narrator as to Madison's motives. He supported the bank bill, and people often interpret their political opponents' motives uncharitably.[91] But regardless of how well Sedgwick diagnosed Madison's motives, his letter, like Maclay's diary entry, mentions a possible constitutional objection to the bank only to dismiss it. Neither of them took an enumerated-powers problem seriously on its merits. And apart from those two sources, nobody in the First Congress seems to have left any record of the view, at any time between Hamilton's proposal in December and the last stage of House proceedings in February, that the bank bill was unconstitutional because Congress had no power to charter corporations.

The picture, then, looks like this. In December, the secretary of the treasury, one of the Founding generation's leading expositors of the Constitution, wrote fourteen thousand words explaining why Congress should incorporate a bank, devoted considerable attention to overcoming possible objections, and apparently could not foresee a constitutional challenge to Congress's authority to pass the relevant legislation. Nor did any members of Congress seem to see such a problem. The United States Senate, with signers of the Constitution and prominent Antifederalists in the room, passed the bill with little dissent and no apparent discussion of an enumerated-powers issue. The bill was then sent to the House and progressed to the very last stage of consideration, whereupon Madison—a determined opponent of the bill, a creative thinker, and a man who had shown himself willing to make tendentious constitutional arguments when the interests he sought to advance were threatened—produced an argument explaining why Congress could not incorporate a bank even if it wanted to.

The Enumeration Issue Appears

Madison first made his enumerated-powers argument at the very last stage of the bank bill's legislative process. In 1791, as today, a bill pending before the House of Representatives was read three times before it could be the subject of a final vote.[92] It was standard practice in 1791 for members of the House to raise objections to bills, or otherwise enter into substantive discussion, at the time of any of the three readings.[93] But Madison raised no constitutional objection to the bank bill until its third reading.[94] Indeed, by the time he made his speech against the bank on February 2, the legislative process had officially moved from considering the bill in the Committee of the Whole to considering it before the House itself—the final stage before passage.[95] Only then, for the first time, did Madison argue that Congress lacked the authority to incorporate a bank, and even then, he did not lead with his constitutional argument. He instead began his speech by arguing at length against the bank on policy grounds.[96] Only after making his case about the dangers of national banking as a policy matter did Madison turn to the constitutional argument for which the debate is famous.[97] A law incorporating the bank, Madison urged, would be invalid because it was authorized by no congressional power enumerated in the Constitution. Six days later, Madison spoke again, repeating parts of his argument and in some respects developing his points further.[98]

Considered schematically, Madison's enumerated-powers argument went like this: it is a fundamental principle that the Constitution confers on Congress not general legislative power but only particular powers. Varying his formula slightly as he went—or perhaps the variations are merely the result of the era's nonstenographic reporting—Madison called that proposition "the very characteristic of the Government," "[t]he essential characteristic of the Government," and "the main characteristic of the Constitution."[99] Next, and now endorsing the *Federalist* 84 argument from which he had kept his distance during most of the ratification process, Madison argued that the justification for the Convention's having omitted a bill of rights rested on the understanding that the powers of Congress were specified and "not to be extended by remote implications."[100] Any construction of Congress's powers that would in effect give Congress plenary legislative jurisdiction was accordingly inadmissible.[101] A power to grant charters of incorporation was not among the enumerated powers of Congress. Indeed, offering his personal testimony on the matter, Madison told his fellow representatives— half a dozen of whom had also attended the Philadelphia Convention—that the Convention had rejected a proposal to enumerate a congressional power to grant charters of incorporation.[102] And no congressional power enumerated in the Constitution authorized Congress to incorporate the bank.[103]

At different times in his two speeches, Madison addressed specific constitutional clauses that might be thought to confer a power to incorporate the bank and explained why, in his view, none of them did. The first clause of Article I, Section 8, would not do the trick because its language describing the power to provide for the "general welfare of the United States" merely described the purposes for which Congress could exercise its power to tax, and the bank bill would impose no taxes.[104] The second clause of Section 8 could not authorize the bank bill as a bill to borrow money, because the bill would borrow no money.[105] The third clause—the Commerce Clause—would not suffice because the bill did not regulate trade.[106] Nor, in Madison's view, was the bank bill authorized as a rule "respecting . . . Property belonging to the United States" under Article IV, Section 3. That clause, Madison argued, referred only to the process of disposing of the property the government held at the end of the war for independence and did not reach issues of general government finance.[107]

The only other potentially relevant clause, Madison submitted, was the Necessary and Proper Clause.[108] Madison asserted three important principles for interpreting that clause. First, any argument that the Necessary and Proper Clause justified an exercise of congressional legislation would have to show why the legislation at issue was necessary and proper for the execution of some other enumerated congressional power. A more general claim that a law was necessary and proper for advancing the purposes of the government or the Union in general was inadmissible.[109] (In this respect, Madison aligned himself with the position that Gerry had taken, alone and unsuccessfully, in the oath debate.) Second, the Necessary and Proper Clause did not give Congress more power than Congress would have had in the absence of that clause. The clause merely confirmed the commonsense proposition that Congress had the authority to do those things that might be necessary for executing those other powers.[110] Last, the Necessary and Proper Clause must not be interpreted in a way that would in practice undermine the essential principle that Congress had only particular legislative powers.[111] A construction of the clause that would justify incorporating the bank as necessary and proper to the execution of Congress's enumerated powers, Madison warned, would be so permissive that Congress would be able to justify any legislation at all, because any legislation could be connected to one of the enumerated powers if one were willing to indulge connections as attenuated as the one between the bank and, say, collecting taxes or borrowing money. In short, Madison here asserted the proposition that I am calling the "internal-limits canon": that the powers of Congress, collectively, must leave Congress unable to do some things that it could do with a general police power.

Madison did not argue that Congress could do only what was expressly specified in the Constitution. In keeping with his view during the ratification debates, Madison asserted that Congress could also do things that were necessary for carrying out its enumerated powers.[112] But the undoubted good sense of reading Section 8 to give Congress the means needed for executing its enumerated powers should not be used as a pretext, Madison warned, for letting Congress wield powers that would have been affirmatively specified if Congress were supposed to have them.[113] A power to grant corporate charters, Madison argued, would be a big deal. The Constitution would not leave it to mere implication.[114]

The Responses

Several members of Congress believed that Madison's understanding of Congress's enumerated powers was unduly narrow. In their view, legislation incorporating the bank would exercise, or would be necessary and proper for executing, one or more enumerated powers of Congress—collecting taxes, borrowing money, regulating commerce, supporting armies, regulating and disposing of its own property, and others as well.[115] Several representatives also pushed back against Madison's narrow construction of the Necessary and Proper Clause. Yes, some of them acknowledged, one could elect to take a stingy view of that clause. But what was the point of replacing the Articles of Confederation with the Constitution, they asked, if not to take a more generous attitude toward national legislative power?[116] Moreover, several representatives argued, Congress had already established a clear practice of legislating as if the Necessary and Proper power were broader than Madison allowed, or more generally as if the enumerated powers should be read as giving substantial permission for the exercise of powers inferred by implication. As Elias Boudinot of New Jersey put the point, most of what Congress had actually done in its first two years of business involved the exercise of powers only implicitly connected to, rather than expressly stated in, constitutional clauses specifying congressional powers.[117] Or, in Sedgwick's somewhat sharper formulation: if the Necessary and Proper Clause were as miserly as Madison claimed, pretty much everything Congress had already done must be unconstitutional.[118]

But the responses that justified the bank bill on the basis of specific constitutional texts were only a subset of the arguments that members of the First Congress raised in reply to Madison. Several representatives who spoke in support of the bank rejected the premise that Congress could legislate only on the basis of particular grants of power in the text of the Constitution. In what follows, I canvass the ideas of representatives who did not share Madison's enumerationist framework for assessing the scope of Congress's legislative authority.

Two caveats are appropriate here. First, the representatives whose arguments I discuss below—Boudinot and Sedgwick, along with William Smith (South Carolina), John Vining (Delaware), John Laurance (New York), and Elbridge Gerry and Fisher Ames (both Massachusetts)—were not necessarily better guides to the Constitution than Madison was. Like Madison's, their views were contestable (and contested). Like Madison, these representatives had political and economic interests that informed their constitutional visions—and, like Madison's, their constitutional visions likely also reflected sincere intuitions about what was best for the American polity and how the Constitution should be read. So the point of noticing their various ways of rejecting Madison's enumerated-powers framework is not to suggest that their approaches reflected an objective meaning of the Constitution from which Madison had strayed. It is to show that at the time of the First Congress, the enumeration principle was a contested proposition among well-informed participants in the constitutional discourse. Their views do not demonstrate that Madison was mistaken about the Constitution. But Madison's views do not demonstrate that his opponents were mistaken about the Constitution, either.

Second, when I describe representatives as having rejected the premise that Congress could legislate only on the basis of enumerated powers, I am not saying that these representatives never made enumerated-powers arguments in favor of the bank. On the contrary, some took a both-and position. On that view, Congress had the authority to incorporate a bank irrespective of its enumerated powers, and Congress also had enumerated powers sufficient for incorporating a bank.[119] Several representatives who argued that Congress's enumerated powers authorized the chartering of the bank made clear that they also thought Congress could exercise powers on bases other than textual enumeration.

Inherent Authority Checked by External Limits

Some representatives rejected the enumerated-powers paradigm altogether and denied that exercises of congressional authority needed to be grounded in specific textual warrants within the new Constitution. John Vining of Delaware, for example, made the simple argument that the United States, on becoming an independent nation, assumed "all the powers appertaining to a nation thus circumstanced, and consequently the power under consideration."[120]

That was it—no fretting about powers enumerated in this or that bit of constitutional text. Congress was the legislature of an independent nation, and as such it could do the things that national legislatures can do, incorporating a national bank included.

Fisher Ames of Massachusetts also took the view that the government of the United States had inherent powers, independent of the Constitution's text, simply by virtue of its being the government of the United States. In support of this position, Ames noted that corporations have certain inherent powers simply by virtue of being corporations, and he then argued that "[g]overnment is itself the highest kind of corporation."[121] It followed, he said, that "from the instant of [the government's] formation, it has tacitly annexed to its being, various powers . . . essential to its effecting the purposes for which it was framed."[122] Congress could obviously lend money, for example, even though no such power was expressly given.[123] (And, he might have added, even though the Constitution expressly enumerated a congressional power to *borrow* money, which an enumerationist might think made the absence of an enumerated power to lend especially salient.) What's more, in Ames's view the inherent powers of Congress were not confined to minor matters. They could be powers of the highest importance. If the Constitution had not enumerated a congressional power to raise armies, Ames reasoned, Congress would still obviously have that power, because national governments raise armies, and because the purposes of the Constitution require armies to be raised.[124]

Ames did not take the view that Congress had the authority to do whatever it wanted. Like everyone else in the debate, he believed that Congress needed to operate within constitutional limits.[125] But he thought it fallacious to imagine that those limits would come from an enumeration of powers. "[T]o declare, in detail, every thing that government may do, could not be performed, and has never been attempted," he maintained.[126] The better way to think about limiting Congress was in terms of affirmative prohibitions: "[E]xceptions of what it may not do," Ames continued, "are shorter and safer."[127] If the power to make a law were expressly denied to Congress in the Constitution, Ames explained, then such a law would be invalid. The same would be true if a law were "repugnant to the natural rights of man" or if making a law required exercising a power that only the states could exercise.[128] But so long as it did not transgress those limits, "Congress may do what is necessary to the end for which the constitution was adopted."[129] In short, Ames thought that Congress should be understood to be limited by external constitutional limits, not internal ones.

Collective Action

Some representatives described Congress's power to create the bank in a way that echoed James Wilson's argument about the Bank of North America, back in 1785. On that conception, the government of the United States (even under the Articles, and certainly under the Constitution) had powers arising from the fact that it was created to act for the entire American Union. For example, Vining argued "that the power of Congress alone was equal to establishing a bank competent to creating currency which shall pervade all parts of the union; the paper of the State banks cannot circulate beyond the bounds of the particular States."[130] In other words, Vining saw Congress's creation of a national bank as appropriate in light of the fact that it was the only legislature that could act for the Union as a whole. Similarly, William Smith of South Carolina argued that "[t]he power to establish a national bank must reside in Congress—for no individual State can exercise any such power."[131] These representatives believed that the states' inability to establish a national bank established Congress's authority to act; no part of their arguments relied on any constitutional provision affirmatively specifying a congressional power.

No Difference in Defaults

One of the core enumerationist tenets of modern constitutional law is that the federal and state governments face different default positions for justifying legislation: state governments may act for any reason not prohibited, but the federal government may act only when some affirmative reason warrants federal action.[132] The arguments described so far for congressional authority beyond the enumerated powers in the bank debate could in principle be compatible with that idea. Consider the argument that the general government has the power to do things that no state could do alone. That view could justify congressional actions that would not be justified if Congress could only act on the basis of its enumerated powers. But it could still be the case that in order to legislate, Congress would have to make an affirmative showing of a sort that state legislatures were not required to make (here, that no other legislature could get the job done). Similarly, the idea that the federal government has inherent powers as the legislature of an independent nation or as a corporation could be compatible with the different-defaults approach. No, the thinking would run, Congress is not restricted to the list of enumerated powers. But it is still the case that for Congress to be able to do something, there must be an affirmative reason justifying congressional action. The inherent-powers approach might merely add a set of nonenumerated subject headings—the specific powers inherent in national legislatures or in the corporate form—to the list of acceptable affirmative reasons.

In the bank debate, however, some representatives not only rejected the idea that the federal government needed specific textual warrants in order to act but also showed no sense that federal legislation requires some special kind of justification that state legislation does not. On the contrary, they seem to have assumed that the principles determining what legislative powers the federal government could exercise were the same as those applicable to states. Consider Sedgwick, who strongly supported the bank bill and who told the House that "he never conceived the authority [to charter the bank] granted by the express words of the Constitution."[133] Instead, Sedgwick said, the power belonged to Congress "by necessary implication."[134] And in explaining his view that the Constitution delegated power to Congress implicitly as well as expressly, Sedgwick pointed out "[t]hat all the different legislatures in the United States [that is, all the state legislatures as well as Congress] had, and . . . must assume such auxiliary powers, as are necessarily implied in those which are expressly granted."[135] Sedgwick was not here arguing that Congress's power to charter the bank was implied by some completely nontextual source, like the nature of the Union or the purpose for which the Constitution had been created. The implicit power of which he spoke was implied by express grants of power. But his argument was that the power delegated to Congress extended beyond what those grants of power said expressly. It also included what those grants further implied. And to make that point, he argued that Congress must have implicit powers in this way *because the state legislatures had implicit powers in that way.* A lawyer whose thinking is shaped by later orthodoxy would know never to make such an argument: to the modern lawyer, it is fundamental that the powers of Congress must be justified in a way that the powers of state legislatures need not be. But in 1791, Sedgwick—a delegate at the Massachusetts ratifying convention, a member of the First Congress, and later both Speaker of the House and president pro tempore of the Senate—was willing to assert that if state legislatures could exercise implicitly as well as expressly granted powers, Congress could do so as well.

The analogous idea that federal legislation is supposed to be exceptional or disfavored—also familiar in modern constitutional law—was similarly rejected.[136] Ames, for example, argued against putting a thumb on the scale against federal legislation, contending that denying Congress a power it should have would be just as bad as letting Congress exercise a power it should not have.[137] Or consider even Gerry, who at the Convention had been famously skeptical of extensive national power and who had insisted during the oath debate on a narrow reading of the Necessary and Proper Clause. Responding to opponents of the bank who asked where the outer limit of congressional power could be drawn if the bank were deemed legitimate, Gerry asked where the line marking the *minimum* that Congress was clearly authorized to do could be drawn if the power to create the bank were denied.[138] Gerry's argument here, like that of Ames, seems at odds with the presumption that the Constitution regards federal legislation as generally disfavored. That presumption would seem to argue for erring on the side of less congressional power.

Consider also Boudinot, who took a view almost directly opposite the idea that the Constitution would not leave important congressional powers to mere implication. Some people, Boudinot said, seemed to think that incorporating a bank would involve the exercise of a particularly important authority—that it would be, in Boudinot's reported characterization, "a high act of power."[139] Boudinot disagreed: in his view, the power to grant charters of incorporation was, within the world of governmental powers, nothing special. But if he were wrong and the power at issue were in fact of great significance, Boudinot continued, that would only strengthen the case for letting Congress exercise it. "[A]llow the position" that issuing charters of incorporation was an especially important thing, Boudinot reasoned, "and who so proper as the legislature of the whole union, to exercise such a power for the general welfare[?]"[140]

The Preamble as a Grant of Powers

Finally, consider a possibility that in form is compatible with the idea that Congress has only those powers textually granted by the Constitution but in substance would yield general congressional power of the kind

enumerationism rejects. Modern constitutional doctrine denies that the Preamble has distinctive legal force. But as noted earlier, some Americans during the ratification period read the Preamble's recitation of the purposes for
which the Constitution was created as a grant of power to the national government to pursue those purposes. In the bank debate, Laurance adopted
that argument. The published version of his remarks, which is more a report
of one of Laurance's speeches than an attempt to transcribe it, reads in relevant part as follows:

> The great objects of this government are contained in the context of the
> constitution; he [i.e., Laurance] recapitulated those objects, and inferred
> that every power necessary to secure these must necessarily follow: For as
> to the great objects for which this government was instituted, it is as full
> and complete in all its parts as any system that could be devised.[141]

The word "context" here refers to the Constitution's opening sentence, which
modern Americans know as the Preamble. (The word "Preamble" did not
appear before the words "We the People" on the original copies of the Constitution, and in the first years after ratification the sentence beginning "We
the People" was sometimes referred to as the Constitution's "context" or "introduction."[142]) The "great objects of this government" contained in that
"context" are, of course, the purposes that the Preamble announces for the
adoption of the Constitution: to form a more perfect union, establish justice,
ensure domestic tranquility, and so forth. The statement that Laurance "recapitulated those objects" means that in his speech, Laurance read or spoke
the Preamble's list of purposes. And he then maintained that "every power
necessary to secure" those purposes "must necessarily" be vested in the general government.

   In making that argument, Laurance was in essence reiterating the position he had taken at the start of the First Congress, during the debate over
Congress's power to prescribe a loyalty oath for state officials. In the oath debate, Laurance had argued that the Sweeping Clause gave Congress the "power
to make all laws necessary, or proper to carry the declarations of the Constitution into effect."[143] That statement clearly meant more than that the Sweeping Clause gave Congress the power to make all laws necessary and proper
for carrying into execution those things that the text of the Constitution
explicitly labeled as federal "powers," because no constitutional clause

expressly gave Congress the power to prescribe oaths. Instead, Laurance's assertion that the Sweeping Clause empowered Congress to effectuate the "declarations" of the Constitution meant that Congress was authorized to legislate as needed to construct and operate the system of government the Constitution envisioned.[144] On that theory, Laurance believed that Congress had the power to prescribe the oath state officials would take. Similarly, the Preamble does not label anything in its text a power of the federal government, but its statement of purposes is without doubt a "declaration" of the Constitution. Laurance's view that Congress was empowered "to carry the declarations of the Constitution into effect" encompassed not just the minor matter of the oath but the larger matter of a congressional power to pursue the ends stated in the Preamble.

In a formal sense, Laurance's view of the Preamble as a grant of powers (or a declaration that Congress was empowered to carry into effect) might be reconciled with the proposition that the federal government has only those powers enumerated in the text of the Constitution. The Preamble is part of that text, after all. So if the Preamble's statement of purposes is read as list of powers given to the general government, Congress could do everything Laurance claimed without exercising any nonenumerated powers. It is easy to see, though, that on such a reading the enumeration of federal powers would not do much to limit the federal government. Indeed, on the day after Laurance's speech, Maryland's Michael Jenifer Stone—an opponent of the bank— asked rhetorically whether there was "any power under Heaven which could not be exercised within the extensive limits of this preamble?"[145] Surely Laurance understood that point. But there is no indication that he was bothered by it. The Constitution had been established for a certain set of purposes, and in Laurance's view, Congress could legislate accordingly.

≺≺⋯≻≻≺≺⋯≻≻

The debates in the First Congress featured two important and underappreciated dynamics of arguments about congressional power. The first is disagreement. As was true in the ratification debates, well-informed Americans took different positions on the question of whether Congress had nonenumerated powers as well as enumerated ones. The second is internalization. As Madison's argument against the bank illustrated, opponents of federal action whose opposition was more straightforwardly described in terms of external limits ("no federally chartered banks" or "no federally chartered corporations") found that they could articulate their opposition in terms of the internal limits of Congress's enumerated powers. Given that the external limits these opponents wanted to invoke did not appear in the Constitution's text, an argument about internal limits offered the best available way of grounding an objection to the bank in some aspect of the written Constitution.

Internalization is a normal occurrence in constitutional reasoning. People make arguments based on the materials they are given. If the system does not furnish materials for a straightforward argument, people will build arguments from less well-suited materials, because they are the best available. The ratification debates did not conclusively establish enumerationism's reading of the Constitution as correct, but they made that reading a prominent tool of argument. Once that tool was available, it could be used any time the federal government considered an action that was not expressly within its textually enumerated powers (and what is "expressly" within those powers is, of course, itself subject to interpretation).

Madison might not have made his enumerated-powers argument against the bank if he had been less committed to opposing that project. Given his substantive commitment, though, it made a certain amount of sense to attempt a constitutional objection based on whatever foundation the Constitution might give him. And it could have worked. The difference between the "federal consensus" about congressional power over slavery and the First Congress's willingness to charter the bank was not a function of the different results that a dispassionate reader of English would reach when asked to read Article I, Section 8. It was a function of Congress's greater willingness to accept a truncated understanding of its powers in one of those contexts than in the other. And neither the slavery issue nor the contest over the bank would be the last time that constitutional advocates "internalized" an objection to a potential federal law, presenting opposition that is best understood as a desire for external limits on congressional power in the form of the internal limits of Congress's enumerated powers.

Madison's enumerationist argument did not persuade the First Congress to reject the bank. But his argument set a paradigm. The bank was a defining issue for two generations, and Madison had shown what a constitutional argument against the bank could look like. As the 1790s wore on, his copartisans in what became the Democratic-Republican Party continued to invest in the enumerationist idea as a rubric for articulating their opposition to disfavored initiatives of the Washington and Adams administrations. And when the Democratic-Republicans triumphed in the early nineteenth century, enumerationism triumphed with them—at least officially.

But the idea of nonenumerated powers was never completely retired. As the judiciary gradually replaced Congress as the most salient locus of constitutional interpretation, the Supreme Court implemented enumerationism in a more modest way than constitutional lawyers generally believe. Through the nineteenth century and into the twentieth, the Court would often insist that Congress could act only on the basis of its enumerated powers. But at several critical junctures, ideas reminiscent of those that people like Ames, Vining, Laurance, Smith, and Boudinot endorsed during the bank debate, and that several other members of Congress endorsed during the oath debate, would animate the jurisprudence of the Supreme Court.

CHAPTER SIX

IMPLIED POWERS

THE ENUMERATIONIST APPROACH TO national power fit well with the ethos of the Democratic-Republicans who dominated the national government after Thomas Jefferson was elected president in 1800. For a variety of reasons, including their determination to prevent federal interference with slavery, the Jeffersonians rejected the view that the United States was a genuine national government and instead propounded the idea that the Constitution was a mere compact among the states. A genuine national government, after all, might be authorized to do all the things that national governments do, as people like John Vining and Fisher Ames had argued in the First Congress. In contrast, a compact among the states could be limited by the strict terms of whatever agreement the compacting parties had made. Indeed, the Jeffersonians promoted the idea of the federal government as a compact among the states largely because they agreed with the nationalists that a genuine national government could not be confined to the powers enumerated in the Constitution.[1] But much as enumerationism encourages interpreters to read the Constitution as if its text were a bit different from what it actually is, compact theory required the Jeffersonians to insist that the Constitution was something different from what it said it was. In 1798, when Jefferson asserted that the (written) Constitution was "a compact under the style and title of a Constitution for the United States," he was saying that if the Constitution were taken at face value—as a Constitution for the United States, which is what its Preamble says it is—it would be something more than a mere compact.[2] To establish the theory that was the predicate for enumerationism, the Jeffersonians had to discount the Constitution's self-presentation.

Ironically or revealingly, Jefferson as president could not bring himself to limit the federal government in the ways his theory demanded. Most famously, he approved the Louisiana Purchase despite believing that the treaty of acquisition committed the federal government to a course of action warranted by no power enumerated in the Constitution.[3] Madison too would have an equivocal relationship with enumerationism as president. In his last days in office, he vetoed major legislation favored by his own party—a gargantuan infrastructure outlay called the Bonus Bill—on the ground that it exceeded Congress's enumerated powers.[4] But he also signed the Second Bank of the United States into law, despite there being no better support in the enumerated powers for chartering the Second Bank in 1814 than there had been for the First Bank in 1791.

Jefferson's experience with Louisiana and Madison's with the Second Bank proved to be early illustrations of a recurring dynamic. Officially, enumerationism reigned. But as a practical matter, the federal government expanded its activities in ways consonant with its role as the national government of an independent country, and a large and growing country at that. Sometimes, people resisted that expansion in enumerationist terms. Like Madison before him, President James Monroe vetoed a major domestic infrastructure bill on enumerated-powers grounds, and the Democratic Party subsequently articulated an enumerated-powers ideology justifying Congress's refusal to support controversial banking and infrastructure projects.[5] Between 1870 and 1936, the Supreme Court struck down more than a dozen federal laws on the grounds that they exceeded Congress's enumerated powers. But that is only part of the picture. In several key domains in the nineteenth and early twentieth centuries—slavery, greenback currency, territorial expansion, federal elections, foreign affairs—the Supreme Court sidestepped the enumerated-powers framework and validated federal laws on the theory that the government of the United States had inherent powers or powers implicit in the reasons for which it was created.

In this chapter, I discuss the Supreme Court's jurisprudence of inherent and implied national powers from the time of Chief Justice John Marshall to the eve of the New Deal. Within that jurisprudence, "implied powers" names three different things. The first is the power to make laws for carrying the government's expressly enumerated powers into execution. That power is expressly warranted in the Constitution's Necessary and Proper Clause, so there is a sense in which it is awkward to describe it as "implied" rather than express or enumerated. But partly on the theory that Congress would have this implementing power whether or not the Necessary and Proper Clause appeared in the Constitution, some jurists (including Marshall) often described this implementing power as implied.

Second, the Court sometimes read constitutional clauses enumerating congressional power to imply authorization for the national government to do more than the texts of those clauses expressly specified. A core example is the power "to establish Post Offices and post Roads," which was understood as a mandate not just to establish offices and roads but to create and operate a system for carrying the mail. The power to create and operate a system for carrying the mail goes beyond the power to establish post offices and post roads. And it cannot be justified under the Necessary and Proper Clause as a power necessary and proper for carrying the power to establish post offices and post roads into execution, because carrying the mail is not a means toward the ends of establishing post offices and post roads. (On the contrary, establishing post offices and post roads is a means toward the end of carrying the mail.)

Third, the Court in several cases declared that certain powers were inherent in the government of the United States. Unlike the first two categories of implied powers, these implied powers are not implied by particular power-granting clauses in the Constitution. They are implicit in the sheer fact that the federal government is the national government of the United States or, in a slightly different formulation, implicit in the purposes for which the federal government was formed. Some of the powers that the Supreme Court has recognized as inherently vested in the federal government deal with foreign affairs, and some that do not involve relations with foreign governments still concern matters occurring outside the geographic boundaries of the states, such as territorial governance. But others have involved core issues of domestic policy, like currency and slavery.

The first of these categories of "implied powers"—the power to carry enumerated powers into execution—can be reconciled with enumerationism. The Necessary and Proper Clause exists, so Congress's exercising this power does not contradict the principle that Congress can act only on the basis of powers stated in the text of the Constitution. The second category poses a greater challenge. Implied powers in this second sense are tied to specific enumerated powers, but they contradict the idea that the text enumerating congressional powers articulates the limits of those powers. Finally, the third category of implied powers poses the largest problem for enumerationism. If Congress has powers either inherently as the national government or implicitly in light of the purposes for which the national government was created, then it is not true that Congress can legislate only on the basis of powers enumerated in the Constitution. During the century and a half of Supreme Court jurisprudence before the New Deal, the Court asserted the existence of implied national powers of all three kinds.

That the second and third categories of implied powers pose problems for enumerationism does not mean that it is impossible to reconcile such powers with the enumeration principle. On the contrary, it is possible to justify many or even all of the congressional powers that the Supreme Court historically described as "implied" powers in enumerationist terms—so long as one is willing to adopt expansive constructions of the enumerated powers. For example, the power to create and operate a system for carrying the mail might not be within the Necessary and Proper Clause as a means toward the end of establishing post offices or post roads, but perhaps it is a valid exercise of Congress's power to spend money for the general welfare. But as I will explain, a willingness to use workarounds of that kind to preserve the idea that all of Congress's powers are textually enumerated comes at a price: it validates interpretations of the enumerated powers broad enough to authorize Congress to do more or less anything that it could do with a grant of general legislative jurisdiction. In other words, it is possible to insist that all of the recognized powers of Congress are enumerated, but only at the risk of stripping the enumeration principle of its capacity to limit the scope of what Congress can do.

Expression, Implication, and Inference

Before proceeding to the specifics, it is worth making two points about the classification of powers as "implied" (or "implicit"—I regard those terms as interchangeable). The first is about the distinction between expressly granted powers and implied powers. The second is about the difference between thinking of nonexpressly granted powers as "implied" and thinking of them as "inferred."

First, the distinction between express and implied powers is liable to blur under close analysis. Article I, Section 8, clause ii, authorizes Congress "[t]o borrow money on the credit of the United States." I presume that under that clause Congress has the power to write a letter to a bank asking for a loan, to negotiate terms, to take possession of funds, to make principal and interest payments, and to designate officers to do all these things on Congress's behalf. I similarly presume that under that clause Congress has the power to decide the rate of interest government bonds will pay, to direct the printing of the bonds, to make rules for the sale of the bonds, to advertise the sale of the bonds, to sell the bonds, and to make the scheduled payments. I would find it difficult to say which of those things come "expressly" within the terms of clause ii and which are only "implicit." (If you think it would be easy to sort, try asking four friends to do the exercise separately, and then see whether you are all in agreement.) The more expansive a reader's sense of what a power-conferring clause says "expressly," the less need the reader will have to resort to ideas about "implied" powers when explaining why a given clause empowers Congress to do a given thing. So this chapter's discussion does not presume anything like clean lines of demarcation between what is express and what is implied. But it does presume that the distinction is not wholly empty, such that it is sometimes intelligible to say that a congressional action falls within the explicit terms of an enumerated power or, alternatively, that if the Constitution warrants a given action, it does so implicitly rather than expressly.

Second, an argument that some federal power is implicit in a constitutional text depends on a judgment about what inferences from the text are the most sensible ones to make. For that reason, the powers often said to be "implied by" the Constitution's text could alternatively be described as "inferred from" that text. The difference in labeling reflects a different orientation about how much work is done by the text of the Constitution and how much is done by an interpreter or community of interpreters. To say that a power is implicit in the text is to say that the text makes it the case that the correct answer to the question "Does Congress have this power?" is "Yes." To say that a power is inferred from the text does not contradict that possibility, but it foregrounds the reader's role in producing the conclusion. And the more a reader feels (correctly or not) that certain inferences from a text are the correct inferences to make, the more the reader is likely to feel that those inferences are implicit in—that is, properties of—the text itself. As a result, describing a power as "implied by" rather than "inferred from" the Constitution's text might reflect the speaker's confidence about which inferences to make. That confidence might reflect a subjective sense of the merits, a sense that a particular reading is widely accepted in the community of interpreters, or some combination of the two.

Implied Powers as Means to Ends:
The Necessary and Proper Clause

Any discussion of the judiciary's approach to the first kind of implied power—the power to implement textually enumerated powers—must give a prominent place to Chief Justice Marshall's opinion for a unanimous Court in *McCulloch v. Maryland*, which in 1819 upheld Congress's legislation chartering the Second Bank of the United States. The *McCulloch* opinion is a foundational text, regularly deployed in modern constitutional law as if it straightforwardly endorsed the enumeration principle. That use of *McCulloch* is somewhat problematic: taken on its own terms, Marshall's analysis concluded that the legislation creating the bank was valid not because it fell within Congress's enumerated powers but in spite of the fact that it did not. Marshall used the terms "enumerated" and "implied" in ways that might not be intuitive to modern readers, and as a result it is possible to reconcile at least some of his analysis with the substance of enumerationism. But in Marshall's view, Congress's power to charter the bank was implied and not enumerated.

The *McCulloch* passage customarily used to support the enumeration principle in modern constitutional law reads as follows:

> This government is acknowledged by all, to be one of enumerated powers.
> The principle, that it can exercise only the powers granted to it . . . is now
> universally admitted.[6]

Both Chief Justice Roberts in *National Federation of Independent Business v. Sebelius* and Chief Justice Rehnquist in *United States v. Lopez* quoted this passage as a statement of the enumeration principle, and it is easy to see why.[7] Modern readers generally understand the statement that the government is "one of enumerated powers" to mean that the government can exercise *only* enumerated powers. Similarly, modern readers commonly take the

phrase "the powers granted to it" in the second quoted sentence to be another way of saying "enumerated powers." On that understanding, Marshall
was repeating in the second sentence what he said in the first: that everyone
agrees that the federal government can exercise only its enumerated powers.
But this is a mistaken reading—one that comes about by reading the quoted
language through an enumerationist lens and ignoring the rest of Marshall's
analysis. On the very next page of the *McCulloch* opinion, Marshall clearly
rejected the idea that chartering the bank was an exercise of Congress's enumerated powers only. So when he wrote that the government was "one of
enumerated powers," he could not have meant that the government was entitled to exercise enumerated powers and no others. And when he wrote that
the government could exercise "only the powers granted to it," his conception of "the powers granted" to the government had to be broader than the
set of enumerated powers.

Marshall wrote as follows:

> Among the enumerated powers, we do not find that of establishing a bank
> or creating a corporation. But there is no phrase in the instrument which,
> like the articles of confederation, excludes incidental or implied powers.[8]

Marshall here pressed the point that Richard Henry Lee had raised in Congress in September 1787 and that any number of others had subsequently
repeated: the Constitution contained no text limiting Congress to its enumerated powers, and the contrast with the Articles of Confederation made
the omission salient. Marshall reasoned that Congress should be understood
to have not only enumerated powers but also "incidental or implied powers," and he located Congress's power to charter the bank in the latter domain. Congress had no enumerated power to charter a bank, Marshall noted,
but its enumerated powers included the powers "to lay and collect taxes; to
borrow money; to regulate commerce; to declare and conduct a war; and to
raise and support armies and navies."[9] In Marshall's view, the existence of
those powers indicated that the national government was expected to do the
things named. It then followed that the Constitution should be construed to
facilitate its ability to do those things. In Marshall's words, "a government,
intrusted with such ample powers, on the due execution of which the
happiness and prosperity of the nation so vitally depends, must also be intrusted with ample means for their execution."[10] Creating a bank would be a

reasonable means toward the execution of those powers. So it followed that creating a bank was within Congress's power—not because a bank-chartering power was enumerated, but implicitly.

That said, one can reconstruct Marshall's logic concluding that Congress had the power to create the bank without claiming that Congress has non-textual powers. As Marshall noted, the Constitution does not leave Congress's right "to employ the necessary means, for the execution of the powers conferred on the government, to general reasoning."[11] Instead, Article I, Section 8, ends with a clause stating expressly that Congress has the power to make laws necessary and proper for carrying the government's powers into execution. Congress's power to charter the bank can be described as an exercise of its power under the Necessary and Proper Clause, exercised in conjunction with one or more of the federal government's other powers—like the power to tax, borrow, regulate commerce, or raise armies. On that understanding, the power to create the bank would fall within powers the Constitution's text expressly gives to Congress.

Notice, though, that Marshall asserted both (a) that the Necessary and Proper Clause indicated that Congress had sufficient power to charter the bank and (b) that the power to charter the bank was not within the enumerated powers of Congress. To a modern reader, this combination of statements might be puzzling. Most modern lawyers use the phrase "enumerated powers" to mean "powers appearing in the text of the Constitution," and the Necessary and Proper Clause appears in the Constitution. So if chartering the bank was something Congress was entitled to do based on the Necessary and Proper Clause, it was within Congress's enumerated powers.

Marshall did not describe things that way. Like some of his contemporaries, Marshall at least sometimes used the term "enumerated powers" to refer to a *subset* of the congressional powers appearing in the Constitution's text. Three years after *McCulloch*, for example, President Monroe would write that neither Congress's power to admit new states nor its power to regulate federal territories was an "enumerated" power, despite the fact that those powers appear in the text of the Constitution, because those functions "are not among the ordinary duties of that body."[12] Other power-conferring clauses that have sometimes been considered sources of "nonenumerated" power include the Vesting Clause of Article II and the Treaty Clause.[13] In *McCulloch*, Marshall similarly regarded the Necessary and Proper Clause not as a clause that enumerates a power (or several powers) of Congress but as a clause that points to *nonenumerated* congressional powers.[14]

The sources that have regarded those clauses as pointing to nonenumerated powers have not offered a well-developed explanation of why the relevant powers do not count as "enumerated." But, and setting aside Monroe's somewhat unusual use of the category, the basic sense of the distinction seems to rest on the idea that "enumerated" powers are not just *textually articulated* but also *substantively particularized*. If one wanted a synonym for "enumerated" that conveys both of these meanings, a good choice would be "specified." "Specified" can mean "expressly stated," and it can also mean "particularized." (Think of "specified" as meaning "made specific.") "Specified powers" in the first sense are opposed to *implicit* powers; "specified powers" in the second sense are opposed to *general* powers. "Enumerated powers" has sometimes meant both things rather than just the first.

Like the distinction between express and implied powers, a distinction between "specific" and "general" powers might turn out to be fuzzy or unstable if subjected to careful scrutiny. But the fact that a distinction is fuzzy or unstable does not mean that it cannot do work in the mind of a jurist. And in a rough-and-ready way, each of the clauses that has sometimes been described as a source of "nonenumerated" power (again, setting Monroe's use aside) articulates a power that can be understood as substantively general rather than a power to act in a specific domain. The text of the Necessary and Proper Clause *specifies* (in the sense of "expressly states") a power, but the power so specified might seem rather *nonspecific* by comparison to powers like the power to coin money and the power to declare war. Congress can do all sorts of different things when exercising its power "to make all laws which shall be necessary and proper for carrying into execution [all] powers vested by this Constitution in the government of the United States."[15] Similarly, the president's textually articulated power to make treaties with the advice and consent of the Senate is a power to make law across many different substantive domains—economic, diplomatic, military, scientific—rather than a power to govern within a single specific domain. And at least according to one school of thought, Article II's opening statement that "[t]he executive power shall be vested in a president of the United States" grants the president a general category of power—the executive kind.[16] Probably on this basis, Marshall took the view that Congress's powers under the

Necessary and Proper Clause were not "enumerated" powers. Hence his ability to conclude, simultaneously, that the Necessary and Proper Clause attested to Congress's power to charter the bank and that the power to charter the bank could not be found among the enumerated powers.

Marshall believed that Congress would have had the power to charter the bank whether or not the Necessary and Proper Clause appeared in the Constitution. He described that clause as *confirming*, rather than *conferring*, Congress's implied power to execute the government's other powers.[17] But an interpreter committed to the view that congressional power can have no basis other than affirmative grants in the Constitution's text can easily reach the result in *McCulloch* while setting these parts of Marshall's thinking aside. The power to charter the bank, such an interpreter can say, is Congress's power under the Necessary and Proper Clause, which is a power expressly stated (or, if you like, enumerated) by the Constitution, exercised in conjunction with one or more of the federal government's other powers. As a result, such an interpreter can say, Congress's power to charter the bank does not demonstrate that Congress has any "implied" powers, if "implied" means "not falling within the terms of the powers articulated in the constitutional text."

Given Marshall's view that the "enumerated powers" were only a subset of the congressional powers expressly described in the text, it is clear that when he wrote that "This government is . . . one of enumerated powers," he did not mean to say "This government can exercise *only* enumerated powers." Nor did he understand himself to be saying that "this government can exercise only enumerated powers" when he wrote that the government "can exercise only the powers granted to it." In his view, the government had been granted various nonenumerated powers, too, including those attested to by the Necessary and Proper Clause. But these aspects of Marshall's analysis, one might conclude, are a problem for enumerationism only at the level of terminology. If we adopt the dominant tendency in modern constitutional law and regard the Necessary and Proper Clause as a source of "enumerated" power, then nothing about Marshall's claim that the federal government has power to carry its enumerated powers into execution need be in tension with the enumeration principle.[18] Marshall called that power "implied," but the rest of us can say it is enumerated, in the Necessary and Proper Clause. And whether or not we call it "enumerated," it is power ordained by the text of the Constitution, and that is what matters in substance.

Implied Powers as Larger Projects:
The Post-Office Point

That said, not every part of Marshall's exposition of implied powers—and not every implied congressional power broadly accepted in constitutional law—can be explained away in these terms. In *McCulloch*, Marshall made this point explicit in a discussion of the federal government's postal power.

The text of Article I, Section 8, clause vii—the Post Office Clause—states that Congress may "establish Post Offices and post Roads." The clause does not say that Congress may deploy agents to transport and deliver the mail. Nor can a power to transport and deliver mail be justified as a means for carrying the powers named in the Post Office Clause into execution, because transporting and delivering mail is not a means toward establishing post offices and post roads. On the contrary, establishing post offices and post roads is a means toward transporting and delivering mail. So if the Post Office Clause (with or without assistance from the Necessary and Proper Clause) authorizes Congress to create and operate the Postal Service as we know it, it does so only implicitly.

In *McCulloch*, Marshall used this point to illustrate what he took to be a commonsense attitude toward construing Congress's powers:

> Take, for example, the power "to establish post-offices and post-roads." This
> power is executed, by the single act of making the establishment. But, from
> this has been inferred the power and duty of carrying the mail along the post-
> road, from one post-office to another. And from this implied power, has again
> been inferred the right to punish those who steal letters from the post-office,
> or rob the mail.[19]

Marshall did not explain why a clause granting power to establish post offices and post roads implicitly also granted the power to cause the mail to be carried and the power to punish mail thieves. He just said that the inferences had been made. But it is not hard to supply the reasoning. By giving Congress the power to establish post offices and post roads, the Post Office Clause suggests that the national government is expected to maintain a system for getting mail from one place to another. If the national government is to maintain such a system, it will need to deploy and organize a corps of mail carriers. It will also need to secure the mail entrusted to those mail carriers against foul play. So Congress should be understood, implicitly, to have the power to do those things.

The words of the Constitution do not require that line of inference. Setting aside considerations not visible in the text itself, a competent reader of American English (whether today or in 1787) could read the Post Office Clause and conclude that it authorizes Congress to do just two things: establish post offices and establish post roads. If the Constitution had meant to give Congress the power to provide for the carrying and delivering of mail, such a reader might argue, it could have said so. Perhaps the fact that it does not say so indicates that Congress may establish offices and roads but should let private actors do the rest.

The point here is not that these two interpretations are equally strong. It is that a decision to regard the Post Office Clause (alone or in conjunction with the Necessary and Proper Clause) as implying the federal government's power to hire, organize, oversee, and protect mail carriers requires the judgment that clauses enumerating congressional power sometimes imply more power than their terms expressly specify. The validity of any given claim about the implications of expressly conferred powers can be a matter of disagreement. But at the level of method, *McCulloch* took the position that the congressional power associated with a power-granting clause of the Constitution is sometimes broader than what the text of the clause says expressly, and not only in the way covered by the Necessary and Proper Clause.

Schematically, one could map the idea that the Constitution's enumeration of federal powers authorizes Congress to pursue larger projects than the text denotes in either of two ways. On one conception, Congress has a set of enumerated powers and a set of implicit powers, the latter derived but distinct from the former. On another conception, there is no meaningful distinction between the two categories: what the first conception calls Congress's implied powers are merely aspects of Congress's enumerated powers, when the clauses enumerating congressional power are read reasonably. On the first conception, the power to organize the Postal Service is an nonenumerated power implied by the postal power. On the second conception, it is an aspect of the postal power itself (and the phenomenon of implied power is better described that way—as a matter of implied *power*, singular, rather than implied *powers*, plural). Someone who prefers not to describe Congress as having any nonenumerated powers might prefer the second framing, but nothing practical turns on the difference between the two conceptions.

Either way, Congress exercises power beyond the express terms of the Constitution's power-granting clauses. Either way, that fact might be reconcilable with the enumeration principle on the ground that every congressional action is ultimately associated with some enumerated power. But that move gives up, or at least significantly attenuates, the idea that the enumeration of powers is a device for saying "This far and no farther." Rather than marking the limits of what Congress may do, the enumerated powers are then bases for action beyond their specific terms.

Inherent National Powers

McCulloch recognized two kinds of implied power: one that is easily assimilated to the enumerationist view because it can be attributed to the Necessary and Proper Clause and another that is less easily assimilated but at least traces its source to constitutional clauses conferring power on the national government. Conventional thinking in constitutional law regards the first kind as unproblematic and tends to push the second kind to the edge of its consciousness.[20] But there is also a third kind of implicit power the Supreme Court has often recognized, and it poses a yet greater challenge to the enumeration principle. In several cases decided between the end of the Marshall Court and the triumph of the New Deal, the Supreme Court sustained federal legislation that was not even purportedly grounded, expressly or implicitly, in any particular power-granting clause of the Constitution. Like the post-office point, these cases tend to live on the edge of the constitutional lawyer's professional consciousness. But in the development of American constitutional law, they have been anything but marginal. On the contrary, they have helped structure crucial areas of the legal system.

In what follows, I discuss three leading examples, each of which addressed a major issue in American government. In 1842, the Supreme Court in *Prigg v. Pennsylvania* upheld the Fugitive Slave Act not because any enumerated power authorized that legislation but based on a structural theory and an account of the Constitution's purposes. In 1871, the Court in *Knox v. Lee* upheld Congress's creation of greenback currency not on the basis of any enumerated power but on the theory that the federal government had the power to do what was necessary to protect its own existence. In 1936, the Court in *United States v. Curtiss-Wright Export Corporation* held that in foreign affairs the federal government is entitled to all of the powers of sovereign nations, without regard to anything in the Constitution's enumeration of powers. And these three cases do not stand alone. They are but three prominent instances of what was once a broad phenomenon in the Supreme Court's constitutional jurisprudence.

Prigg v. Pennsylvania

In 1837, a man named Edward Prigg, acting as the agent of a Maryland slaveholder, traveled to Pennsylvania, seized a woman named Margaret Morgan, and forcibly brought Morgan and her children to Maryland, claiming that Morgan was an escaped slave. For that action, Prigg was later indicted in Pennsylvania for kidnapping. In his defense, Prigg argued that the federal Fugitive Slave Act, adopted in 1793, blocked Pennsylvania's power to prosecute him. Among other things, the Fugitive Slave Act authorized slaveholders and their agents to "seize or arrest" escaped slaves and return them to slavery.[21] As a federal law, the Fugitive Slave Act preempted any contrary state law. So if Prigg was acting within the authority given to him under the Fugitive Slave Act, Pennsylvania could not prosecute him for his conduct. (Immunizing slavecatchers against state-law prosecutions was a large part of the point of passing the Fugitive Slave Act.) In support of its decision to prosecute Prigg as a kidnapper, the State of Pennsylvania argued that Prigg could not claim the protection of the Fugitive Slave Act because that law was unconstitutional. In particular, Pennsylvania contended that Congress had no authority to pass the Fugitive Slave Act, "because it does not fall within the scope of any of the enumerated powers of legislation confided to that body."[22]

The Supreme Court upheld the Fugitive Slave Act and decided the case for Prigg. But it did not do so by identifying some enumerated power that authorized Congress to pass the act. Writing for the Court, Justice Joseph Story instead denied that federal legislation must always be justified by "the express powers of legislation enumerated in the constitution."[23] According to Story, Congress's power to pass the Fugitive Slave Act was implicit in the structure and purposes of the Constitution, even in the absence of a relevant enumerated power.

Story reasoned as follows: Article IV, Section 3, clause ii, of the Constitution provided that a "person held to service or labor" who escaped to another state "shall be delivered up on claim of the party to whom such service or labor may be due." That clause gave slaveholders a right to recover enslaved people who escaped. But in the absence of federal legislation, there would be no mechanism for enforcing that right. Slaveholders certainly could not count on the state authorities in states where slavery was illegal to do the job. The southern states, Story wrote, would never have agreed to the Constitution without some way of enforcing this provision, and only the national government could provide that enforcement. So he concluded that it made sense to recognize the national government as having the power to do so. "If . . . the constitution guaranties the [slaveowners'] right," Story declared, "the natural inference certainly is, that the national government is clothed with the appropriate authority and functions to enforce it."[24]

Story's analysis is reminiscent of arguments by the members of the First Congress who understood Congress to have the power to carry the Constitution's envisioned system of government into effect, whether or not the Constitution articulated specific federal powers for any particular piece of that project. Given a right protected by the Constitution and a set of institutional realities such that the national government was the entity best positioned to enforce that right, the power to enforce the right should be understood as implicitly vested in Congress. Story squarely recognized that this line of reasoning contradicted the claim that Congress had only those legislative powers the Constitution enumerated. If Congress lacked the power to secure constitutional rights unless some enumerated power authorized it to do so, he wrote, the Constitution must "fail to attain many of its avowed and positive objects. . . . Such a limited construction of the constitution has never yet been adopted as correct, either in theory or in practice."[25]

The fugitive slave law that *Prigg* upheld was painfully unjust. But regardless of the moral failings *Prigg* represents, the idea that the national government is implicitly vested with the power to protect constitutional rights has a plausible logic. (The moral problem in *Prigg* is not the proposition that Congress can protect constitutional rights. It is the existence of a constitutional right to treat people as slaves.) That said, the idea that the national government implicitly has the power to protect constitutional rights is not necessarily correct. A government might be structured on that premise, or it might not be: a federal system could vest the enforcement of some rights in the federal government and others in local governments. If the enumeration principle is a correct proposition of constitutional law, the United States should be a federal system of the latter kind. Quite straightforwardly, if Congress can only legislate on the basis of its enumerated powers, then the absence of an enumerated power to protect the rights announced in the Fugitive Slave Clause of Article IV ought to mean that Congress lacks that power. But writing for the Supreme Court, Story disagreed. In his view, Congress had the power to protect constitutional rights, or at least to do so when states could not be counted on to do the job, even without an enumerated federal power on point.

Story's view in *Prigg* was not some strange exception to his general understanding of constitutional law, manufactured for the malign purpose of upholding the Fugitive Slave Act. Long before *Prigg* was litigated, Story was on record in support of the view that Congress had powers beyond those enumerated in the Constitution. Story was perhaps the foremost academic constitutional theorist of his generation; his *Commentaries on the Constitution of the United States*, published nine years before *Prigg*, was the era's leading treatise on the subject. In the *Commentaries*, Story endorsed the view that the Constitution's enumeration of many particular congressional powers "excludes all pretension to a general legislative authority." But he also asserted that it would be wrong to think that Congress could exercise only the powers that the Constitution enumerated. The idea that "the expression of one thing is the exclusion of another," he wrote, though often a helpful guide, was "susceptible of being applied . . . to the subversion of the text, and the objects of the instrument."[26]

Indeed, Story asserted the existence of all three kinds of implied congressional power discussed in this chapter. First, like Madison in the ratification debates and Marshall in *McCulloch*, Story asserted that the constitutional clauses enumerating congressional powers implied the power to make laws for carrying those powers into execution, such that Congress would have that power even if the Necessary and Proper Clause did not exist.[27] Second, Story wrote that the Constitution's power-granting clauses often imply more power than a strict reading of their terms would indicate. The Post Office Clause implied the power to carry the mail, as *McCulloch* had explained, and the power to declare war implied the many powers that go into fighting wars rather than merely declaring them.[28] And crucially, Story cited Hamilton (and could also have cited Wilson) for the proposition that Congress also had "another sort of implied power, which has been called with great propriety a resulting power." Such a power might be "a result from the whole mass of the powers of the national government, and from the nature of political society, [rather] than a consequence or incident of the powers specifically enumerated."[29]

In short, this Supreme Court justice who was also his generation's leading constitutional theorist did not agree with the general proposition that Congress could legislate only on the basis of expressly enumerated powers. In his view, Congress implicitly had other powers as well—including some that did not owe their existence to any specific power-granting clauses in the Constitution. The power at issue in *Prigg* was of that kind. In Story's view, it arose not from some enumeration of congressional power—the Fugitive Slave Clause says nothing about who may enforce it—but from the logic of the role of the federal government and the purposes for which that government had been created.

Knox v. Lee

Consider next the Supreme Court's 1871 decision in *Knox v. Lee*, which upheld Congress's creation of greenback currency—that is, paper money—during the Civil War and the continued use of that paper as legal tender afterwards. (*Knox* and its companion case, *Parker v. Davis*, are often cited together as the *Legal Tender Cases*.)

As a general matter, the Framers were hostile to paper money, partly because of their experience with the quickly degrading value of paper money issued by both the states and Congress during the Revolutionary War period and partly for reasons predating that time. When arguing for the wisdom of empowering the national government in *Federalist* 10, Madison listed "a rage for paper money" as the sort of "improper or wicked project" that would be more likely to win favor in a given locality than in a larger republic, given the larger republic's greater tendency to let cool heads prevail. And indeed, Congress in the early republic did not create paper money. Congress's enumerated power "[t]o coin money" was generally understood as a power to create "hard money," or "specie," meaning metal coinage. During the War of 1812, the federal government also began to issue bills of credit, akin to modern Treasury Bills, which were essentially promissory notes pledging to pay holders certain sums at named future dates. Bills of credit sometimes circulated as a form of money: the initial holder of a bill of credit in the amount of, say, $100 might give the bill as payment to a subsequent party, who might use it to pay a third party, and so on. But no person was obliged to accept a bill of credit as payment, much less to accept it at face value. Instead, the choice of whether to treat the bill as having the value it promised (or any particular value) lay with the parties to each transaction. In other words, bills of credit were not *legal tender*. Only hard money had that status.[30]

Matters changed with the Civil War. Beginning in 1861, the federal government needed large sums of money to pay for military salaries and supplies. The government could only get that money by borrowing. Given the shaky status of the United States government at that moment, many banks worried about the reliability of the government's credit and refused to lend it gold specie. So beginning in 1862, Congress passed a series of laws called the Legal Tender Acts, authorizing the secretary of the treasury to issue a new kind of paper note. These new notes could not be redeemed for hard money but would nonetheless constitute legal tender. In other words, creditors were required by law to accept the new notes as having the same value as the amount of specie to which they corresponded. Because the new notes were issued on green paper, they became known as "greenbacks."[31]

In 1870, in a case called *Hepburn v. Griswold*, the Supreme Court struck down a portion of the Legal Tender Acts that made greenback currency legal tender for the payment of debts contracted before those acts were passed. In his opinion for the Court, Chief Justice Salmon Chase explained that no enumerated power authorized Congress to create paper money.[32] The enumerated power "to coin money" was certainly not such a power, he wrote.[33] Nor was the power to make paper money into legal tender properly understood as within the reach of the Necessary and Proper Clause, as an appropriate means of executing any of the enumerated powers.[34]

One year later, after the death of one of the justices from the *Hepburn* majority and the confirmation of two new justices appointed by President Grant, the Supreme Court in *Knox v. Lee* reversed course, repudiated *Hepburn*, and upheld the Legal Tender Acts in their entirety. Writing for the new majority, Justice William Strong expressly declined to dispute *Hepburn*'s assertion that the power to coin money did not include a power to make paper into legal tender.[35] But he also insisted that the express enumeration of a power to coin money (understood as a power to create specie) did not imply that other related powers, like the power to create paper money, were withheld.[36] If the Constitution had meant to deny the federal government the power to create legal tender as it wished—a power the Court described as "confessedly possessed by every independent sovereignty other than the United States"—it would have said so.[37] "Some powers that usually belong to sovereignties were extinguished," Strong wrote, "but their extinguishment was not left to inference."[38] In reasoning this way, Strong endorsed a picture of federal power that is the reverse of the enumerationist picture. Rather than assuming the federal government powerless in the absence of an enumerated power, he pointed to the fact that the Constitution did not deny the federal government a power usually associated with sovereign bodies as a reason to conclude that the federal government did have that power.

The Court's rejection of the enumeration principle in *Knox* was not merely implicit. Quite directly, Strong asserted the existence of congressional powers beyond those expressed in or implied by the enumerated powers. "[I]t is not indispensable to the existence of any power claimed for the Federal government," he wrote, "that it can be found specified in the words of the Constitution, or clearly and directly traceable to some one of the specified powers."[39] On the contrary, he wrote,

> in the judgment of those who adopted the Constitution, there were powers created by it, neither expressly specified nor deducible from any one specified power, or ancillary to it alone, but which grew out of the aggregate of powers conferred upon the government, or out of the sovereignty instituted.[40]

Citing Story's *Commentaries* for support, Justice Strong affirmed the existence of "resulting powers" that belonged to the national government implicitly.[41] The enumerated powers, he reasoned, should be understood not as the final touchstone of congressional power but as "instruments for the paramount object, which was to establish a government, sovereign within its sphere, with capability of self-preservation."[42] Legislation necessary to maintain that government was therefore broadly permissible: Congress was entitled to "a very wide discretion . . . in the selection of the necessary and proper means to carry into effect the great objects for which the government was framed."[43] And under the circumstances of the Civil War, creating greenback currency had been an appropriate means of preserving the government from destruction.[44]

As Strong's use of the phrase "necessary and proper" suggests, the Court in *Knox* asserted that the federal government's "right to employ freely every means, not prohibited, necessary for its preservation"[45] was part of the power described in the Necessary and Proper Clause. But the Court's view of the Necessary and Proper Clause was fundamentally nonenumerationist. The Court in *Knox* did not say that the Legal Tender Act was constitutional because it was necessary and proper as a means for executing some other specifically enumerated federal power. Instead, the Court regarded the Necessary and Proper Clause as authorizing Congress to do what was necessary and proper to preserve the government in general—"to carry into effect the great *objects* for which the government was framed."[46] In other words, the Court was recognizing a congressional power to pursue the Constitution's purposes, not merely to execute a specific set of enumerated powers. It was a conception of congressional power that might have come directly from any of several members of the First Congress in explaining Congress's power to prescribe a loyalty oath for state officials.

In a concurring opinion, Justice Joseph Bradley stated the case for nonenumerated congressional powers yet more boldly. In an argument reminiscent of John Vining's and Fisher Ames's 1791 arguments in favor of Congress's power to charter the Bank of the United States, Bradley declared that "[t]he Constitution of the United States established a government, and not a league, compact, or partnership. . . . [and a]s a government it was invested with all the attributes of sovereignty."[47] Moreover, he wrote, "The United States is not only a government, but a National government, and the only government in this country that has the character of nationality."[48] For Bradley, a great deal followed from that proposition:

> Such being the character of the General government, it seems to be a self-evident proposition that it is invested with all those inherent and implied powers which, at the time of adopting the Constitution, were generally considered to belong to every government as such, and as being essential to the exercise of its functions.[49]

The power to create legal tender, in Bradley's view, therefore belonged to the United States government, because "it is one of those vital and essential powers inhering in every national sovereignty and necessary to its self-preservation."[50] Like Story in *Prigg*, both the majority and the concurring opinions in *Knox* understood the power of the national government as something more than the sum of its enumerated parts.

United States v. Curtiss-Wright Export Corporation

In the history of Supreme Court doctrine, the high-water mark of enumerationism as a consequential idea occurred in 1936, as the Court fought against President Franklin Roosevelt's New Deal. In its decisions striking down New Deal legislation, the Court repeatedly asserted the enumeration principle as a basis for its actions. But even in that year, the Supreme Court in *United States v. Curtiss-Wright Export Corporation* treated the federal government as an entity with inherent rather than only enumerated powers.

The story of *Curtiss-Wright* begins in 1934, when Bolivia and Paraguay were at war. In a joint resolution, Congress authorized the president to prohibit the sale of arms to either country, if he found that such a prohibition would help restore peace. President Roosevelt made such a finding and duly issued a proclamation prohibiting arms sales to the two countries. Shortly thereafter, the Curtiss-Wright Export Corporation was indicted for conspiring to sell weapons to Bolivia. And in the course of an opinion rejecting a constitutional challenge to the prosecution, Justice George Sutherland—one of the Court's most uncompromising enumerationists in other contexts— explained that in foreign affairs, the federal government exercises both enumerated and nonenumerated powers. "The broad statement that the federal government can exercise no powers except those specifically enumerated in the Constitution, and such implied powers as are necessary and proper to carry into effect the enumerated powers," Sutherland wrote, "is categorically true only in respect of our internal affairs."[51] In foreign affairs, he explained, the federal government was empowered to exercise all powers of sovereign governments (whatever those might be) without regard to enumeration of particular powers in the text of the Constitution.

Sutherland's reasoning was largely historical. In his view, the Constitution could not be the source of the federal government's foreign-affairs powers, because the federal government had existed and exercised foreign-affairs powers before the Constitution was written. In an explanation that could have come from James Wilson, Sutherland wrote that "[t]he Union existed before the Constitution," and before the Articles of Confederation too. In the 1770s, the Continental Congress "exercised the powers of war and peace, raised an army, created a navy, and finally adopted the Declaration of Independence." Those things were done not by the colonies separately but "through a common agency." So when the United States became independent, it did so "acting as a unit, [and] the powers of external sovereignty passed from the Crown not to the colonies severally, but to the colonies in their collective and corporate capacity as the United States of America."[52] Using the ideas and the language of Wilson, Hamilton, and Story, Sutherland deduced this conclusion:

> It *results* [emphasis added] that the investment of the federal government with the powers of external sovereignty did not depend upon the affirmative grants of the Constitution. The powers to declare and wage war, to conclude peace, to make treaties, to maintain diplomatic relations with other sovereignties, if they had never been mentioned in the Constitution, would have vested in the federal government as necessary concomitants of nationality.[53]

Sutherland thought he could confine this way of thinking to foreign affairs, leaving domestic legislation subject to the enumeration principle. As noted above, he was one of the justices most insistent on enumerationism when the subject was Roosevelt's New Deal. But foreign affairs is not a small piece of what the federal government does, and it is hard to draw a clean line of separation between foreign and domestic matters. In *Curtiss-Wright* itself, the prohibited sale of weapons occurred in New York rather than outside the territorial limits of the United States.

Moreover, the idea that the Constitution contemplates a fundamental difference between the basis for the government's power when it acts internally and the basis for the government's power when it acts externally would fit awkwardly with the constitutional text enumerating congressional powers, because that text mixes those subject matters together freely. Article I, Section 8, describes several powers of domestic legislation, including the powers to tax, to regulate commerce among the states, to make bankruptcy law, to fix the standards of weights and measures, and to create tribunals inferior to the Supreme Court. It also describes many powers the national government exercises in its outward-facing capacity. These include the powers to collect duties, to regulate foreign commerce, to establish the rule of naturalization, to punish piracies and other felonies committed on the high seas, to punish offenses against the law of nations, to declare war, to grant letters of marque and reprisal, and to make rules for captures on land and on water. In several places, Section 8 mixes domestic and foreign-affairs powers within the very same clause. In short, the Constitution is not written as if it distinguished categorically between domestic and foreign matters when dealing with congressional powers. And finally, whatever view Sutherland might have had about a difference between foreign and domestic affairs, it is not only in the realm of foreign affairs that the Court has sometimes been willing to set the enumeration principle aside. Indeed, *Prigg*, *Knox*, and *Curtiss-Wright* show the Court recognizing nonenumerated congressional power not only for the entire realm of foreign affairs but also in connection with two of the most important and contentious domestic issues in American history.

Other Examples

Prigg, *Knox*, and *Curtiss-Wright* are three important cases in which the Supreme Court treated Congress as having nonenumerated powers. There are others, too. In *Burroughs v. United States* (1934), the Court wrote that Congress had inherent power to protect the integrity of presidential elections.[54] In *Mackenzie v. Hare* (1915), the Court upheld a federal statute divesting American women who married foreigners of their US citizenship despite "the absence of an express gift of power" for doing so because—in words that directly echoed Bradley's concurrence in the *Legal Tender Cases*—"as a government, the United States is invested with all the attributes of sovereignty," including "the powers of nationality."[55] In *Chae Chan Ping v. United States* (1889) and a number of other nineteenth-century decisions, the Supreme Court held that Congress could pass laws forbidding foreigners to enter the United States, or expelling aliens already resident in the United States, not on the basis of any specific power enumerated in the Constitution but because the powers to forbid entry and expel aliens are inherent incidents of national sovereignty.[56] In *Jones v. United States* (1890), the Court upheld Congress's right to legislate for newly discovered or occupied territories as an inherent sovereign power under the law of nations, without reference to any power enumerated in the Constitution.[57] Similarly, in *United States v. Kagama* (1886), the Court wrote that Congress's power to make law for United States territories acquired after 1788 comes not from the Property Clause of Article IV but "from the ownership of the country in which the territories are, and the right of exclusive sovereignty which must exist in the national government."[58] The *Kagama* Court also upheld a federal felony code applicable to Native Americans on reservations and specifically denied that the source of Congress's authority to enact the code lay in any particular enumerated power, concluding instead that the power arose from the history and logic of the national government's relationship with indigenous people.[59]

Some of these cases are almost completely forgotten, except by small circles of academics. It is entirely normal for a good lawyer never to have read the *Legal Tender Cases* at all. Others are better known but usually associated with niche areas of legal practice rather than imagined as part of the general fabric of constitutional law. Immigration lawyers know *Chae Chan Ping*, Indian-law specialists know *Kagama*, and so on. The best known of the cases is *Curtiss-Wright*, but it is known for a proposition about executive power within the federal government rather than for the idea that the federal government has nonenumerated powers.[60] None of these cases is part of the main storyline about federal power. The main storyline includes the cases that form the backbone of the study of federal power in most introductory constitutional-law courses: *McCulloch* on the Bank of the United States, *Gibbons v. Ogden* on the New York steamboat controversy, *Hammer v. Dagenhart* on child labor and *United States v. Darby* on labor conditions more generally, *Wickard v. Filburn* on small-scale activity, *Heart of Atlanta* on racial discrimination in public accommodations, *Lopez* on school safety, and *National Federation of Independent Business v. Sebelius* on the Affordable Care Act. In that story, the enumeration principle is front and center. But these other cases exist too, and the domains of law they have structured are not trivial. Foreign affairs is a large part of what the federal government does. Nothing was of greater concern to constitutional law in the Constitution's first hundred years than the intersectional conflict over slavery. And the *Legal Tender Cases* underlie about as fundamental a feature of American government and society—the paper money in your wallet—as has been at issue in any Supreme Court decision.

◄◄--►►◄◄--►►

Enumerationism draws strength from the premise that constitutional law has respected the enumeration principle ever since the Founding. And so it has, in the sense that official pronouncements have endorsed that principle throughout American history. But it does not follow that constitutional law has always conformed to those pronouncements. From Marshall's Court to the eve of the New Deal, the judiciary often recognized nonenumerated federal powers. Sometimes the logic of recognizing those powers was about what is inherent in a national government; sometimes it was about what is implicit in the decision to create this particular national government. And if the national government has the nonenumerated powers that the courts recognized in the nineteenth and early twentieth centuries, perhaps there are also other cases, not yet specified, in which Congress can legislate even without enumerated powers on point. Maybe the enumeration principle is an overgeneralization, or an overrated nostrum, or just a mistake.

In assessing that possibility, it is important to notice that the justices who in past cases wrote opinions sustaining congressional legislation on grounds other than that of enumerated power were sometimes aware that it was possible to make enumerated-power arguments for the same result. As noted above, the *Kagama* Court saw the possibility of predicating Congress's power of plenary legislation over federal territories on Article IV's language authorizing Congress to "make all needful rules and regulations respecting the territory or other property belonging to the United States." But the Court rejected that possibility in favor of a theory of inherent sovereign power. In the *Legal Tender Cases*, Justice Bradley entertained the possibility that the power to create greenback currency could be considered implicit in Congress's enumerated power to borrow money. When a government makes paper into legal tender, Bradley reasoned, it is in essence demanding that it be granted credit, which is a form of borrowing.[61] (A coercive form of borrowing, but still borrowing.) But rather than bringing his analysis within the safe harbor of an enumerated power on that basis, Bradley vigorously defended the government's inherent sovereign power to create a national currency and do all other such things, not specifically prohibited, that sovereign governments can do.

Similarly, Justice Story knew that some of the powers he described as "resulting" could be characterized as flowing from the enumerated powers. One of the examples he used to illustrate the national government's resulting powers was the power to govern conquered territory, and Story noted that that power might be considered implicit in "the power to make war."[62] (The power "to make war" does not appear in the text of the Constitution either, but Story thought it fairly implied by Congress's power to declare war in the same way that the power to establish post offices and post roads implies the power to operate the Postal Service.[63]) But despite recognizing that he could trace the power to govern conquered territory to a specific enumerated power, he asserted that the power should be understood as "a result from the whole mass of the powers of the national government, and from the nature of political society, [rather] than a consequence or incident of the powers specifically enumerated."[64] That justices like Story and Bradley advanced arguments for inherent or resulting powers even in cases where enumerated-powers arguments were available suggests that for them, departing from the enumeration principle was not particularly uncomfortable. Given the choice between an argument based on enumerated powers and an argument not based on enumerated powers, it was not necessary to prefer the enumerated-powers argument.

Reconciliation and Its Perils

Someone wishing to insist on a strong form of the enumeration principle could of course deny that the examples given above show that Congress sometimes legitimately exercises inherent or otherwise nonenumerated powers. Most straightforwardly, one could simply dismiss all the cases recognizing such powers as wrongly decided, on the grounds that they all violate a bedrock principle of constitutional law. But that solution would be hard to put into practice. After all, it would require throwing out many elements of our existing constitutional order, from plenary federal control of immigration policy to the paper money in our wallets.

   As a less radical alternative, one might argue that the powers the Court has described as inherent, or as implicit in the Constitution's purposes or its structure, are really justified as a matter of the Constitution's enumeration of federal powers, correctly understood. For example, one could justify the result in the *Legal Tender Cases* by adopting the money-borrowing rationale that Justice Bradley noted but held at arm's length. Alternatively, one could interpret Congress's enumerated power to "coin money" as a power to create any sort of currency, rather than, as the nineteenth-century Court did, as a power to make money out of precious metals. The power to safeguard presidential elections, treated as an inherent congressional power in *Burroughs*, could be reinterpreted as a power necessary and proper for carrying into execution the powers of the president as conferred in Article II and therefore as falling within the power enumerated in the Necessary and Proper

Clause. The power to govern the territories could be attributed to Article IV's Property Clause, the *Kagama* Court's rejection of that option notwithstanding. The power to forbid entry into the country to foreigners could be attributed to Congress's power "to regulate commerce with foreign nations": the movement of persons has long been understood as a form of "commerce" under the Commerce Clause, and anyone entering the United States from outside is presumably coming from some other country. And so on.

The possibility of articulating enumerationist rationales for the congressional powers at issue in these nineteenth- and early twentieth-century cases is not merely hypothetical. In 2023, Justice Neil Gorsuch pursued exactly this strategy in *Haaland v. Brackeen*, a case in which the Supreme Court upheld the Indian Child Welfare Act against a constitutional challenge. The act established an extensive system for deciding child-custody cases involving children who are or could be affiliated with Native American tribes. Normally, child custody is a question of state law, and several states and private parties challenged the act, arguing among other things that Congress had no power to enact it. In an opinion for the majority of the Court, Justice Amy Coney Barrett asserted Congress's broad power to legislate regarding Native American affairs but hedged on the question of the source of that power. It derives, she wrote, from multiple sources, including the Indian Commerce Clause and the Treaty Clause but also "principles inherent in the Constitution's structure"—and it also "might rest in part on 'the Constitution's adoption of preconstitutional powers necessarily inherent in any Federal Government.'"[65] (The internal quotation at the end is from a 2004 decision called *United States v. Lara*, which in turn relied on *Curtiss-Wright*.[66]) In writing this way, and in particular by saying only that Congress *might* have preconstitutional powers in this area, Barrett displayed the tension between a body of case law that forthrightly recognizes inherent congressional powers and the modern impulse to trace all congressional action to specific textual enumerations. In a concurring opinion, Gorsuch banished all such tension. Reasoning from the first principles of enumerationism, he argued at length that the nineteenth-century Court's recognition of inherent plenary power over Native American affairs was a fundamental error. Whatever federal power exists in that domain, Gorsuch maintained, must exist only as a function of a specific enumerated power like the Indian Commerce Clause.[67]

The Indian Child Welfare Act and probably the rest of federal Indian law would remain valid if the Court were to jettison the idea of inherent federal power and adopt Justice Gorsuch's expansive interpretation of the Indian Commerce Clause instead. Such an approach would eliminate one of the major examples of nonenumerated congressional power recognized by the pre–New Deal Supreme Court. And if a persuasive reinterpretation of this kind were available for each power the Court in the past sustained on some basis other than pointing to a relevant enumerated power—or at least for each one that the reinterpreter believes is a power the federal government legitimately possesses—then it would be possible to say that the only powers Congress has legitimately exercised are those warranted, expressly or implicitly, by the textual enumeration of powers, even though the courts of earlier times failed to make that point clear.

This strategy could not alter the fact that, as a historical matter, the Supreme Court in the nineteenth and early twentieth centuries often acted on the premise that Congress had powers beyond those enumerated in the Constitution (or implicit in the particular powers enumerated). But supporters of a strict enumerated-powers doctrine can always say that the Court has sometimes stumbled—or more charitably, and adapting the words of Emerson's poem, that the justices who purported to recognize powers on other grounds built better than they knew, deciding cases correctly even while not quite articulating the reasons why.[68] If so, we could go forward with more or less the constitutional law we have while still maintaining that the federal government may only exercise those powers enumerated in the Constitution's text—understood, of course, as including the powers reasonably implied by the power-conferring clauses as well as those granted in express terms.

But the prospect of such a reconciliation could mean more than one thing about the system of enumerated powers. One possibility is that the Constitution's enumeration of congressional powers reflects the deep logic of American federalism and that the judges, being well-socialized American lawyers, intuitively decided cases in line with that underlying logic even when they failed to use the enumerated-powers analysis. Another possibility, however, is that the enumerated powers do not really define a stable boundary of national governance. Instead, they are licenses for national power that, in the hands of skilled and properly motivated jurists, can justify pretty much anything the national legislature has the political will to do, except for things that would violate affirmative constitutional prohibitions. Fugitive slavecatching, paper money, territorial acquisition, immigration control, Indian child welfare, and so on can all be brought within the enumerated powers. And if the enumerated powers can be reasonably interpreted to reach those topics, they can also be reasonably interpreted to reach all the other subjects in the canon of controversies over the extent of congressional power—child labor, small-scale agriculture, school safety, domestic violence, homegrown marijuana, health insurance—and likely anything else that congressional majorities believe the national government should regulate.

To be clear, this second possibility need not mean that the jurists proffering expansive interpretations of congressional power are acting cynically. They might be construing the Constitution in perfectly good faith. The lens of enumerationism directs constitutional lawyers to justify congressional power in enumerated-powers terms. The text of the Constitution might bear interpretations on which pretty much anything Congress would want to legislate can plausibly be shown, retrospectively, to be within the enumerated congressional powers. The result would be a system that, unlike the pre–New Deal system, adhered rigorously to the principle that Congress can act only on the basis of enumerated powers—but those enumerated powers would not limit the scope of federal governance.

CHAPTER SEVEN

CUMULATIVE COVERAGE

A S NOTED AT THE start of this book, enumerationism asserts two basic propositions. The first—the enumeration principle—is that Congress can legislate only on the basis of enumerated powers. The second—the internal-limits canon—is that Congress's powers collectively leave Congress unable to do some things it could do with a police power. Ordinary thinking in constitutional law tends to conflate these two ideas, but they are not the same. And because they are distinct propositions, there is more than one way that congressional power could differ from enumerationism's model. In a world that respected the internal-limits canon but not the enumeration principle, Congress could have nonenumerated powers but still not have as much power as it would have with a police power. In a world that respected the enumeration principle but not the internal-limits canon, Congress would be limited to its enumerated powers but might be able to use those powers to do anything that a legislature with a police power could do.

Enumerationism insists that neither of possibilities is the case. In practice, however, the history of congressional power suggests that constitutional law has functioned on the basis of both of those alternatives. Chapter 6's discussion of implied powers showed that constitutional law has not always respected the enumeration principle. This chapter turns the focus to the internal-limits canon and shows that since the middle of the twentieth century, constitutional law's compliance with that proposition has been largely a matter of form without substance.

Since the 1940s, congressional power in practice has functioned on the basis of what I am calling the model of *cumulative coverage*. On that model, Congress can enact virtually any regulatory regime it could enact with a police power. That is not because the courts treat the Constitution as affirmatively committed to giving Congress a police power. It is because the enumerated powers, when added together, turn out to be functionally as broad as a police power would be. Put in terms of enumerationism's two basic propositions, the model of cumulative coverage is a model of enumerated powers but without, or potentially without, internal limits.

◅◄••►►◅◄••►►

As Chapter 6 showed, the Court in the nineteenth and early twentieth centuries often sustained federal legislation on the basis of implied powers, in all three senses of "implied powers." Since the New Deal, however, the judiciary's attitude toward implied powers has been more circumspect. From time to time, modern opinions have reaffirmed pre–New Deal analyses recognizing implicit congressional powers.[1] But although the modern Court sometimes tolerates long-established bits of implied power, it does not recognize new ones. On the contrary, twenty-first century justices have subjected older decisions recognizing nonenumerated powers to considerable enumerationist skepticism. Justice Gorsuch's attack on the cases recognizing nonenumerated congressional power with respect to Native American affairs, mentioned in Chapter 6, is one example.[2] In another case, Justice Thomas went so far as to question the validity of Chief Justice Marshall's account of the federal government's implied power to operate the postal service.[3] Most of the time, though, the idea that Congress has nonenumerated powers is neither affirmed nor criticized but simply pushed to the edge of the judicial consciousness: the modern Court regularly speaks as though the enumerated powers are the only powers Congress has. Thus, Chief Justice Rehnquist opened his analysis in *United States v. Morrison* with the sentence, "Every law enacted by Congress must be based on one or more of its powers enumerated in the Constitution."[4] And Chief Justice Roberts declared in *National Federation of Independent Business v. Sebelius* (*NFIB*) that "[i]f no enumerated power authorizes Congress to pass a certain law, that law may not be enacted."[5]

But the modern Court's insistence on the enumeration principle has not meant that Congress has less latitude for legislation than it had before the

New Deal, when the Court was more willing to say that Congress had none-numerated powers. On the contrary, Congress has more freedom to legislate now than it did then, and the scope of federal law is considerably broader. The Supreme Court has not been the cause of that growth in federal law: the first institutional movers are the lawmaking branches, and federal law would not have grown without the election of Congresses and presidents whose view of the national regulatory mandate was broader than that of their predecessors. But since the New Deal, the Court has played an enabling role by not standing in the way—and, more affirmatively, by assuring political decision-makers and the legal profession that extensive federal action is constitutional.

Notice, then, that the Supreme Court during and after the New Deal validated a dramatic expansion in national lawmaking while becoming *less* inclined to say that Congress has nonenumerated powers. Rather than licensing a broad federal regulatory footprint by recognizing a significant suite of nonenumerated powers, the New Deal Court licensed that footprint by taking a broad view of what the enumerated powers authorize. That broad construction of the enumerated powers bears an ironic relationship to the fiercely articulated principle that the enumerated powers are the only ones that Congress may exercise. If Congress can pass more or less any legislation on the basis of its enumerated powers, it has no need for nonenumerated powers. Put differently, the Court's ability to insist on the enumeration principle in the post–New Deal era was underwritten, whether intentionally or otherwise, by its willingness to let the enumerated powers authorize whatever legislation Congress enacted.

For more than fifty years after the New Deal, constitutional law operated on that basis—that is, on the model of cumulative coverage. Then, at the end of the twentieth century, the Court seemed to balk. In two landmark decisions, Chief Justice Rehnquist argued that a construction of Congress's enumerated powers broad enough to warrant any regulatory project that Congress might seek to pursue would necessarily be a mistaken construction. In so doing, he insisted not just on the enumeration principle but also on the internal-limits canon. If congressional power is not constrained by internal limits, the thinking goes, then the enumeration of powers is not doing the work it is supposed to do. On that theory, the Court in 1995 and 2000 struck down provisions of federal law on enumerated-powers grounds for the first time since the 1930s. It nearly did so again in 2012, in the first challenge to the Affordable Care Act.

But as I will explain, the Court's decisions purporting to vindicate enumerationism by enforcing the internal-limits canon have not managed to create judicial doctrine that limits the scope of federal regulation. The Court adheres to the enumeration principle, and at least at the level of appearances, it also adheres to the internal-limits canon. But it does so without producing the substantive legal regime that those principles are supposed to produce. In substance, cumulative coverage abides.

Since the 1940s, then, the United States has been a government *of* enumerated powers, but not a government *limited by* those enumerated powers. From an enumerationist perspective, the fact that the enumerated powers have not done limiting work in the modern regime is an important failure in constitutional law. But the diagnosis of failure is a mistake. The problem is not that the enumerated powers are failing to do limiting work. The problem is the idea that the enumerated powers must limit what Congress can do.

Enumeration and Limitation

In the enumerationist paradigm, the point of enumerating Congress's powers is to confine the federal government to a few particular functions, leaving the large residuum of other governance to the states. But as a logical matter, the enumeration of a government's powers need not limit the power of that government. Enumeration and limitation are two different things. A constitution could limit a government's powers without enumerating them, and a constitution could enumerate a government's powers without limiting them.

It is easy to see that a government can have limited powers even though its powers are not enumerated. Most state legislatures are legislatures of general jurisdiction rather than legislatures with enumerated powers, but their powers are limited by state constitutions and by federal law. States may not establish religions, declare wars, grant titles of nobility, or pay hourly employees less than the federal minimum wage, even though they are entitled to exercise general legislative authority. In the terms used throughout this book, state legislative power is subject to external limits even if it is not subject to internal limits. Similarly, the federal government's powers are limited by the Constitution, even without respect to any limiting force that the enumeration of federal powers might have. Even in the exercise of an enumerated power, Congress may not grant titles of nobility, abridge the freedom of speech, or impose cruel and unusual punishments.

Conversely, a government wielding only enumerated powers could be a government with unlimited power. Imagine a constitution with no external-limit provisions and with seven power-granting clauses, each one authorizing the government to legislate on a different day of the week. Even on the assumption that that government could exercise only its enumerated powers, it could make any law it wanted, because it would always have an enumerated power sufficient to justify proposed legislation. It would invoke the Monday power on Mondays, the Tuesday power on Tuesdays, and so on. Such a set of enumerated powers would not limit what the government could do, and it would surely not be intended to do so.

The days-of-the-week example is stylized. It makes a conceptual point, but it is hard to imagine writing a real constitution that way. So consider a less far-fetched illustration. Suppose that the list of goals in the Preamble to the United States Constitution were a list of governmental powers—as some early Americans took it to be.[6] If the federal government were authorized to (1) form a more perfect union, (2) establish justice, (3) ensure domestic tranquility, (4) provide for the common defense, (5) promote the general welfare, and (6) secure the blessings of liberty to ourselves and our posterity, then one or more of its enumerated powers would likely be sufficient to underwrite any legislation that Congress was inclined to enact. (That is why it has been important to enumerationists throughout American history to insist that the Preamble must not be read as an operative grant of powers.)

These examples demonstrate that an enumeration of powers need not be limiting. But so long as we do not read the Preamble as a grant of powers, the enumeration of powers in the United States Constitution differs from these examples in an important way. Giving a government the power to legislate on each day of the week is obviously tantamount to giving that government plenary legislative power. Giving the United States government the power to legislate for each purpose mentioned in the Preamble might or might not be tantamount to giving it plenary legislative power—the Preamble could be read to authorize legislation for all national or general purposes but not for purely local matters—but nobody would think that it confined the government to a substantively discrete subset of regulatory projects. In contrast, the set of congressional powers that the (non-Preamble parts of the) Constitution enumerates does not look like it was intended to give general legislative jurisdiction to the national government. It looks like an assortment of powers collectively constituting only a subset of all possible legislative power. The intuition that the Constitution's enumeration of powers gives the federal government only a limited legislative mandate thus arises not from the fact of enumeration per se but from facts about this enumeration in particular, as well as from the fact that constitutional lawyers are taught that the Framers intended the enumeration to limit the federal government.

But it is possible for an enumeration of powers not designed as the practical equivalent of a grant of general legislative jurisdiction, and that does not initially function as one, to become tantamount (or practically tantamount) to a grant of general power over time as facts about the world change. Suppose a national legislature with several enumerated powers, including the power to regulate affairs affecting Presbyterians. At the time of the adoption of the relevant constitution, we imagine, Presbyterians were a recently persecuted minority group, and this provision was intended to let the national government protect Presbyterians from local discriminatory legislation. If a hundred years later a Presbyterian revival swept the land and all residents became Presbyterians, the national legislature would turn out to enjoy general regulatory authority—at least until religious diversity reasserted itself, at which time the practical scope of the power might wane again.

This example may seem fanciful. But a prominent school of thought within American constitutional law regards Congress's power to regulate "commerce among the several states" as having expanded over time in a similar way. As the national economy became more integrated, the thinking goes, more and more aspects of American life affected or became part of interstate commerce, until the commerce power came close to becoming a general power to regulate. The dominant view, however, and the one that prevails as a matter of judicial doctrine, is that although the commerce power is extensive under modern conditions, it must stop short of being the functional equivalent of plenary legislative power. The conventional thinking insists, as a matter of principle, that the enumeration of congressional powers limits the range of what Congress can do.

In sum, it is both clear and fundamentally important that the national government's powers are limited. (Congress has the power to punish mail thieves, but the Eighth Amendment prohibits boiling them in oil.) But enumerationism insists on something more. It claims not merely that the powers of Congress are limited but that the enumeration of congressional powers itself works a limitation. That is a particular commitment of enumerationism in American constitutional law, not a logical entailment of every system of enumerated powers. To put the point precisely, enumerationism insists not just that the federal government is a government of *enumerated* powers, and not just that the federal government is a government of *limited and enumerated* powers, but that it is a government limited *by* the enumeration of its powers.

In the three-part typology of the kinds of limits to which governments can be subject—internal limits, external limits, and process limits—the idea that the government is limited by the enumeration of its powers means that the government is subject to internal limits. That is why it makes sense to call the idea that the enumeration of powers limits the scope of federal governance the *internal-limits canon*.

The Internal-Limits Canon, the MustBeSomething Rule, and the Unlimited Congress Fallacy

The internal-limits canon is a proposition about all of Congress's powers taken collectively, rather than a proposition about each congressional power considered on its own. Considered separately, most of Congress's enumerated powers have meaningful internal limits. Congress's enumerated power to govern the District of Columbia cannot be used to govern Michigan, and Congress's enumerated power to punish pirates cannot be used to fix the day on which the Electoral College votes. What the internal-limits canon requires, however, is that there be meaningful internal limits on congressional power taken as a whole. Some meaningful volume of potential legislation must lie beyond *any* of Congress's powers, even without considering external limits.

As its name indicates, the internal-limits canon is a canon of construction— that is, a principle guiding the interpretation of texts that might otherwise bear multiple readings. It is not formally recognized as such: courts and commentators do not list the internal-limits canon among the established canons of construction in American law, alongside canons like the rule of lenity in criminal cases and the principle that statutes in derogation of the common law are to be narrowly construed. But in substance, a canon of construction is exactly what it is, and courts consciously use it when interpreting the scope of the powers of Congress. The internal-limits canon directs that, among possible readings of the clauses granting power to Congress, no reading that would in effect give Congress plenary legislative power is acceptable.

Every law student knows the reductio question that courts and law professors use to enforce the internal-limits canon. Anyone who defends the constitutionality of a federal law must explain why that law comes within one or more of the Constitution's enumerated federal powers, and anyone who defends the constitutionality of a federal law by offering what the audience thinks is a too-generous reading of those enumerated powers must answer the question "If Congress can do *that*, what *can't* Congress do, other than the things the Constitution specifically forbids?"[7] This trope played a famously large role in the battle over the constitutionality of the Affordable Care Act, with the act's critics wanting to know what regulation would be beyond Congress's enumerated powers if those powers were sufficient to compel private individuals to buy health insurance. Could Congress pass a law requiring Americans to eat broccoli?[8] In a snappy coinage, David Schwartz has called the idea implicit in this question the "MustBeSomething Rule."[9] There must be something, the rule holds, that Congress cannot do, even without reference to external limits.

It is worth noting that when courts invoke the MustBeSomething Rule, they often do so with a simplifying and perhaps distorting shorthand. On many occasions, judges (and other people) fail to specify that the MustBeSomething Rule is about the reach of Congress's power *without reference to external limits*. In so doing, they write as if a Congress not checked by internal limits would be a Congress empowered to do anything at all. Thus, Chief Justice Rehnquist wrote in *United States v. Lopez* that accepting the theory that the commerce power authorized federal regulation of the possession of firearms would make it "difficult to perceive any limitation on federal power."[10] But of course it would not. Even if the commerce power were broad enough to authorize Congress to regulate the possession of firearms, Congress could not impose firearms regulations that violated the Second Amendment. Nor could Congress grant titles of nobility, establish a religion, institute a system of unreasonable searches and seizures, impose cruel and unusual punishments, and so forth. For ease of reference, I will call the problem in Rehnquist's statement the *Unlimited Congress Fallacy*, because it makes the mistake of thinking that an absence of internal limits would mean that Congress is not limited by anything.

Competent jurists are presumably always aware that the Constitution imposes external limits on congressional power. So perhaps judges who seem to be committing the Unlimited Congress Fallacy are actually just skipping a detail in the interests of smooth expression. "There must be something that Congress cannot do even without reference to affirmative prohibitions" is a more cumbersome thing to say than "There must be something that Congress cannot do." But there is also another possibility, or at least another aspect worth noticing about the use of the shorter expression. When the qualification about affirmative prohibitions is omitted, the possible absence of internal limits on Congress's powers seems considerably more ominous than when the qualification is acknowledged. "The federal government can do anything it wants" resonates with fears about tyrannical majorities, despotic bureaucracies, and other dystopian dangers. "The federal government can do anything that sufficient majorities of Congress agree to, as long as it doesn't violate any of your constitutional rights or do anything else the Constitution says it can't do" is a lot less scary. So whether intentionally or otherwise, the simplification rhetorically heightens the apparent importance of internal limits in the constitutional system, because it presents those limits as if they were the only barrier to overweening federal power. Seen that way, the Unlimited Congress Fallacy is not just a fallacy. It is a rhetorical trope.

Gibbons v. Ogden

With the content of the internal-limits canon now firmly in view, it is worth noting something about one of the most important sources of constitutional authority that, since the end of the twentieth century, has standardly been understood to support it. Much as constitutional lawyers associate the enumeration principle with Chief Justice Marshall's statement in *McCulloch v. Maryland* that "[t]his government is . . . one of enumerated powers,"[11] they associate the internal-limits canon with Marshall's statement in the famous case of *Gibbons v. Ogden* that "[t]he enumeration presupposes something not enumerated."[12] It is not hard to see why: Marshall's dictum is pithy, and it is easily understood to mean that there must be something that Congress cannot do with its enumerated powers. But much as Marshall's statement about a government of enumerated powers in *McCulloch* was not really an assertion of the enumeration principle as modern lawyers imagine it, Marshall's dictum in *Gibbons* was not an assertion of the internal-limits canon. That his formula is standardly quoted as support for that idea is a testament to enumerationism's power to distort modern understandings of the constitutional past.

Gibbons, decided in 1824, was the first case in which the Supreme Court construed the Constitution's Commerce Clause. One important question in the case was whether Congress's power under that clause could be applied to commercial behavior occurring entirely within the boundaries of a single state. Representing the petitioner, no less a lawyer than Daniel Webster argued a highly nationalist position. The Framers, Webster argued, went to Philadelphia to do away with the state-versus-state economic squabbling that existed under the Articles of Confederation. They sought to end destructive state protectionism by centralizing commercial regulation. The Constitution the Framers drafted accordingly regarded commerce as one integrated system to be regulated by Congress. And not just interstate commerce—*all* commerce.[13] On this vision, the Commerce Clause's language stating that "Congress shall have power to . . . regulate commerce with foreign nations, and among the several states" was a way of saying "Congress shall have power to regulate all commerce, both foreign and domestic." The clause's further language giving Congress the power to regulate commerce "with the Indian Tribes" was, on this view, intended to prevent the argument that there might be a category of commerce not covered by the clause because it was neither foreign nor domestic.[14]

In his opinion for the Court, Chief Justice Marshall agreed that a power to regulate commerce among the several states must be a power to regulate commerce occurring within particular states, if only because commerce among the states must occur within state borders.[15] But Marshall did not read the clause as expansively as Webster did. The Commerce Clause, Marshall wrote, did not authorize Congress to regulate commerce that was entirely contained within a single state.[16] To support that conclusion, he gave a limiting interpretation to the clause's text specifying that Congress could regulate commerce "with foreign Nations, and among the several States, and with the Indian Tribes." Marshall parsed that language as follows:

[T]he enumeration of the particular classes of commerce, to which the power was to be extended, would not have been made, had the intention been to

extend the power to every description. *The enumeration presupposes some-*
thing not enumerated; and that something, if we regard the language or the
subject of the sentence, must be the exclusively internal commerce of a State.[17]

In other words, the clause enumerates three "particular classes of commerce."
They are (1) commerce with foreign nations, (2) commerce among the several
states, and (3) commerce with the Indian tribes. By separately listing those
three, Marshall argued, the clause suggests the existence of some other kind
of commerce not included in any of the three classes listed. That is the thought
that Marshall elegantly captured with the italicized words above: "The enumeration presupposes something not enumerated."

So when Marshall wrote that phrase, he was not writing about the Constitution's overall enumeration of congressional powers. He was writing only
about the commerce power. His argument was that the Commerce Clause's
listing of three categories of commerce—with foreign nations, among the several states, and with Indian tribes—presupposed some commerce not falling
within those categories. He was not arguing that the fact that the Constitution lists many powers of Congress, in many different clauses, presupposes
subjects of regulation not reachable with any congressional power. In short,
the idea that Marshall's *Gibbons* dictum was a statement of the internal-limits
canon rests on a mistake about which enumeration Marshall was describing.

One might be tempted to argue that Marshall's dictum supports the internal-limits canon even though Marshall in context was making a more local
point, because his observation was generalizable. If enumerations generally
presuppose things not enumerated, then it does not matter which enumeration Marshall happened to be writing about. But it would be unfair to Marshall to read him as making the broader statement that enumerations in general presuppose things not enumerated, because the broader statement is
untrue. Some enumerations presuppose things not enumerated, and others
do not. (When a priest blesses his congregation in the name of the Father,
the Son, and the Holy Spirit, he does not imply the existence of some fourth
branch of the Deity whose blessings are withheld.) That is why the canon
expressio unius est exclusio alterius—that the expression (or specification) of
one thing is the exclusion of another—is, in the practice of legal interpretation, merely a rule of thumb to be treated as defeasible when the circumstances make it inapposite.[18] So even if the enumeration of three classes of
commerce in the Commerce Clause signals the existence of some other kind

of commerce not covered by that clause, it does not follow that the enumeration of congressional powers in eighteen different clauses of Article I, Section 8—or those clauses plus the twenty-five or so other constitutional clauses specifying congressional powers—signals that there are subjects of regulation beyond the reach of any congressional power.

One might also be tempted to think that Marshall's analysis in *Gibbons* supports the internal-limits canon because it identified a subject matter—purely intrastate commerce—that Congress cannot regulate. But that too would be a mistake. Marshall did not say, and *Gibbons* did not hold, that Congress may not regulate purely intrastate commerce. Marshall concluded that Congress could not regulate purely intrastate commerce *on the basis of its authority under the Commerce Clause*. But the fact that one congressional power cannot underwrite a particular federal law does not mean that no other congressional power could do so. Even if purely intrastate commerce is beyond the scope of the Commerce Clause, Congress can regulate many aspects of intrastate commerce with its powers to tax, make bankruptcy law, regulate the value of money, or grant patents and copyrights. Indeed, Marshall specifically indicated that commerce too local to be regulated under the Commerce Clause alone might be federally regulated "for the purpose of executing some of the general powers of the government"[19]—that is, under the Necessary and Proper Clause. Properly read, therefore, nothing about Marshall's analysis deemed any particular subject matter immune from federal regulation on internal-limit grounds. And it has been settled doctrine for more than a century that intrastate commerce is federally regulable whenever such regulation is a necessary and proper part of regulating interstate commerce.[20]

Marshall's statement that the enumeration of kinds of commerce in the Commerce Clause limited the reach of that clause was significant, but not because it marked a boundary between what Congress could regulate and what it could not. It was significant because it marked a boundary between what Congress could regulate with its commerce power alone and what it could regulate with other powers, including its power under the Necessary and Proper Clause to carry Commerce Clause regulations into execution. To most modern lawyers, it is not intuitive that that distinction would matter. But in 1824, the distinction mattered—not for any bearing it might have on the scope of federal power but for its potential implications about the permissible scope of regulation by the states.

As previously noted, the idea of concurrent legislative jurisdiction—that is, that Congress and the state legislatures can have the power to regulate in the same domains simultaneously—is more intuitive to modern Americans than it was in the Constitution's early years. At the Founding, many Americans thought of assigning power to the national government as tantamount to denying that power to the state governments. Over time, intuitions would shift, and concurrent jurisdiction in most domains would come to seem normal. By the 1820s, when *Gibbons* was decided, it was clear that the federal and state governments would exercise concurrent jurisdiction in at least some subject matters. But the prevailing thinking still favored exclusive jurisdiction on some subjects, and in other domains the question was contested. Three years after *Gibbons*, the Supreme Court's seven justices divided four to three on the question of whether Congress's power to make bankruptcy law precluded states from legislating on that topic, with Marshall and Story both arguing for exclusive federal jurisdiction.[21] Where the power to regulate commerce was concerned, many leading lawyers—Marshall probably among them—considered the federal government's jurisdiction exclusive.[22] On that view, if some subject matter came within the scope of the Commerce Clause, states were barred from regulating it, whether or not Congress had acted in that area. To use the preferred doctrinal terminology: state law would be "preempted" (that is, nullified) by the federal commerce power even if that power lay "dormant" (that is, unexercised). So in a world where the national government's limited capacity made it impossible for that government to provide most of the regulation that society needed to function, it was essential that the commerce power be interpreted as not reaching matters in need of local regulation.

Suppose, for example, that the town butcher or the local roads were regulated by state and local authorities—as they indeed were.[23] Even in 1824, Americans understood that the town butcher and the local roads had connections to interstate commerce. In *Gibbons* itself, the lawyers defending the position hostile to federal power noted that "a vast range of State legislation, such as turnpike roads [and] licenses to retailers," would "necessarily affect, to a great extent, the foreign trade, and . . . trade and commerce with other States."[24] But if Congress's power under the Commerce Clause were construed to reach such matters, and if Congress's commerce power were exclusive, the local authorities would be unable to regulate in those domains. The commerce power, though dormant, would preempt state law. That would leave the butcher, the roads, and many other aspects of social life completely unregulated. Congress could not fill the gap: the national government lacked the practical capacity to undertake all of that regulation, even if it had wanted to do so.[25] So if the Commerce Clause was a grant of exclusive power to Congress, it was essential that it be construed to cover only a relatively small slice of society's economic life.

But this rubric supplied no reason to prevent Congress from regulating local commerce with tools that would not preempt broad swaths of local regulation in areas for which Congress was not going to assume responsibility. As noted above, it was clear by 1824 that only some of Congress's regulatory powers excluded concurrent exercises of power by the state governments. Marshall worried that the commerce power was exclusive, but he did not think that every other congressional power was. And perhaps because it does not map any particular substantive area of regulation, nobody seems to have thought that Congress's power under the Necessary and Proper Clause was preemptive of state law even when it lay dormant. (That is, nobody seems to have thought that anything Congress could potentially regulate under the Necessary and Proper Clause was automatically exempt from state regulation.) So if Congress's power under the Necessary and Proper Clause could reach local commerce, or indeed if any congressional power that did not preempt state regulation even when dormant could do so, the problem of wrecking necessary regulation that the national government could not replace would not arise. Given that understanding, it made all the sense in the world for Marshall to articulate a limit on the commerce power, even if there were no similar limit on the powers of Congress taken as a whole, nor even on what Congress could do with its power to make laws necessary and proper for carrying its commerce-power laws into execution.[*]

---

[*]The idea that Marshall was articulating a limit on the power of Congress as a whole, rather than on the commerce power in particular, may arise in part from a misunderstanding of Marshall's statement, a few sentences after he wrote that the enumeration presupposes something not enumerated, that "[the] completely internal commerce of a State . . . may be considered as reserved for the State itself." *Gibbons*, 22 U.S. (9 Wheat.) at 195. In some other contexts, a "reserved" state power is one with which Congress may not interfere. But Marshall was not summarily rejecting the basic idea that Congress can routinely do under one power something it cannot do under another. He was simply saying that states had the authority to regulate local commerce in the first

In sum, Marshall's famous dictum that the enumeration presupposes something not enumerated was not intended to mean that the Constitution's enumeration of congressional powers indicates that there are things beyond the reach of any congressional power. Nor does anything in the substance of Marshall's analysis in *Gibbons* establish that proposition. Indeed, for nearly 170 years after *Gibbons* was decided, no court quoted that dictum as if it were a statement of the internal-limits canon.[26] Because it wasn't.

◄◄··►►◄◄··►►

Whether the internal-limits canon is a fundamental tenet of constitutional law does not depend on whether Marshall meant to assert it on any particular occasion. We should not overstate its prominence by finding it where it was not operating, but we should also not think it chimerical just because it was not operating in all the places where we thought it was. There is no doubt that there have been periods of constitutional history when the internal-limits canon was insistently articulated and consequentially deployed. But the force of the canon has waxed and waned. For a period of time between the Civil War and the New Deal, the Supreme Court's attitude toward the canon seemed deadly serious, and the Court struck down congressional legislation that threatened the idea of a federal government limited by its enumerated powers, even though it was sometimes prepared to sustain federal laws on implied-power grounds. Then, by the middle of the twentieth century, the Court shifted, relegating implied powers to a marginal status but also becoming comfortable with federal legislation that was hard to

---

instance, until and unless Congress enacted a conflicting law under some appropriate power. Modern lawyers take for granted that states can regulate in the absence of federal law, so it may not occur to them (us) that Marshall felt it necessary to make this point. But in 1824, many leading constitutional lawyers—like Webster in the *Gibbons* litigation—believed that the power specified in the Commerce Clause lay in Congress exclusively, such that state regulation in that domain was categorically invalid. *Gibbons*, 22 U.S. (9 Wheat.) at 14. Against that background assumption, characterizing intrastate commerce as "reserved" to the states was a way of saying that state laws regulating such commerce would not automatically be preempted. In other words, Marshall's statement that the regulation of purely intrastate commerce was "reserved for the State" meant "the state has not lost its power to regulate instrastate commerce," not "the power to regulate intrastate commerce belongs to the state exclusively."

square with the idea of the enumerated powers as limiting. To a first approximation, the former period was one of strong internal limits but a relaxed enumeration principle, and the second period—which extends into the present—is one of a strong enumeration principle but nearly inconsequential internal limits.

The Era of Internal Limits

The first Supreme Court decision holding federal action unconstitutional on the theory that it exceeded the enumerated powers of Congress came after Marshall's time, in the wake of the Civil War. Between 1870 and 1883, the Court in at least seven cases concluded that a federal statute, or at least some provision or application of a federal statute, was not warranted by any congressional power.[27] Not coincidentally, this first burst of court decisions striking down federal laws on internal-limit grounds came at a time when the national government's capacities and ambitions had dramatically expanded. The government grew substantially in order to fight the Civil War, and the war's successful conclusion proved that the national government could do big things. Given that the war had been fought against a group of states opposed to national governance, the Civil War also helped persuade many Americans (most white southerners excepted) of the wisdom of committing important governmental responsibilities to the national government rather than the states. During the war and also during Reconstruction, Congress accordingly undertook significant new legislative programs. Some, like the Legal Tender Acts and the major civil rights and enforcement acts of Reconstruction, related directly to the distinctive needs and issues of the Civil War. Others, like the Homestead Act of 1862, the Land-Grant College Act of 1862, and the Trademark Act of 1870 were not directly related to those issues but were facilitated by the general trend toward active national governance. Not surprisingly, all of the Supreme Court cases in this era that curtailed federal law on the grounds that it exceeded the enumerated powers of Congress featured legislation passed during or shortly after the Civil War—including, on three occasions, Reconstruction legislation intended to protect the rights of African Americans.[28]

These decisions bespoke an important shift in the judiciary's engagement with federal power. Marshall had been intent on avoiding a too-expansive construction of Congress's commerce power in part because he worried about preempting state regulation in a world where the federal government's capacity was small. In the Reconstruction-era cases striking down federal law on internal-limit grounds, however, the Court was not worried about limited federal capacity. It was worried about the power of a massively capable federal government—one that operated in a world with telegraphs and railroads, that had mobilized an army to subdue state governments, and that at least for a few years seemed keen to deploy its power to remake fundamental aspects of American society.

By the turn of the twentieth century, the Court was explaining the need to enforce internal limits on congressional power by invoking the specter of an all-powerful federal government as the alternative. In *United States v. E.C. Knight Company* (1895), for example, the Court limited the reach of the new Sherman Antitrust Act by holding that the commerce power could not authorize the regulation of manufacturing, even when the goods manufactured were obviously destined for interstate commerce. To decide otherwise, the Court warned, would mean that Congress could regulate "not only manufactures, but also agriculture, horticulture, stock-raising, domestic fisheries, mining; in short, every branch of human industry."[29] In the *Employers' Liability Cases* (1908), which struck down a statute making interstate railroad companies liable for employee injuries occurring during intrastate as well as interstate operations, the Court explained that upholding the statute "would extend the power of Congress to every conceivable subject."[30] And in *Keller v. United States* (1909), the Court reasoned that reading the commerce power to authorize a federal statute prohibiting the practice of corralling newly arrived immigrant women into prostitution would open the door to "the assumption by the national government of an almost unlimited body of legislation."[31]

Perhaps the Court's most aggressive deployment of the internal-limits canon came in *Hammer v. Dagenhart* (1918), which struck down a federal law aimed at eliminating child labor in physically dangerous settings like factories.[32] Aware of the Court's insistence in cases like *E.C. Knight* that the commerce power could not reach manufacturing, Congress prohibited not the employment of children in factories but the interstate shipment of goods produced in factories using child labor.[33] That prohibition was plainly within the text of the Commerce Clause, which authorizes Congress "to regulate . . . commerce among the several states." Given the economic reality of a national market for goods, a prohibition on the interstate shipment of goods produced with child labor would greatly reduce child labor: factory owners have much less incentive to produce what they can only sell within a single state than what they can sell nationwide. With the Child Labor Act, Congress sought to produce that effect with a law that regulated precisely what the Commerce Clause authorized Congress to regulate.

But by a vote of five to four, the Court struck down the Child Labor Act as exceeding the limits of the commerce power. In giving its reasons, the Court did not deny that the act was, formally, a regulation of interstate commerce. But the Court recognized that permitting Congress to use its commerce power this way would in practice let Congress govern all sorts of things that had previously been governed only by the states. "[I]f Congress can thus regulate matters entrusted to local authority by prohibition of the movement of commodities in interstate commerce," the majority opinion declared, "all freedom of commerce will be at an end, and the power of the states over local matters may be eliminated."[34] That could not possibly be constitutional. So it followed that the act was not warranted by the commerce power, even though formally it was a regulation of interstate commerce.

To a considerable extent, *Dagenhart* reproduced the reasoning of the earlier decisions invoking the internal-limits canon. But in one significant respect, *Dagenhart* differed from at least some of those earlier cases. In earlier cases, the Court's explanations of the unacceptability of construing the Commerce Clause as the practical equivalent of a police power often presented the power to regulate commerce as residing exclusively with Congress, such that anything regulable with the commerce power was immune from local regulation. In *E.C. Knight*, for example, the Court reasoned not just that a conception of the commerce power broad enough to let Congress regulate the manufacture of consumer goods would extend the federal reach to "every branch of human industry" but that "congress would be invested [with that power] *to the exclusion of the states*."[35] Similarly, in the *Employers' Liability Cases* the Court warned that a construction of the commerce power that "would extend the power of Congress to every conceivable subject" would also "destroy the authority of the states as to all conceivable matters."[36]

There are reasons to doubt whether the Court in these cases was actually concerned that a broad but dormant federal commerce power would actually nullify large bodies of necessary state law. Between the 1850s and the 1880s, the Court had held more than once that the authority to regulate commerce could sometimes be vested in Congress and the state legislatures concurrently. Where local conditions called for commerce to be regulated differently in different places, local authorities could regulate commerce until and unless Congress legislated to the contrary.[37] In a related set of cases, the Court had held that although states could not enforce laws regulating interstate commerce "directly," they were free to affect or regulate interstate commerce "indirectly."[38] Just how to distinguish direct from indirect regulations of commerce was of course a sticky question.[39] But for present purposes, the point is that the *E.C. Knight* Court could have held that Congress's commerce power authorized the regulation of manufacturing without holding that all state-level economic regulation was invalid, either by saying that manufacturing fell in a zone of concurrent jurisdiction or by describing such regulation as bearing only "indirectly" on the commerce that Congress alone could regulate. The same solutions were available for the regulation of intrastate transportation in the *Employers' Liability Cases*.[40] It is possible, of course, that the Court's choice to do neither of those things reflected, or partly reflected, a sincere jurisprudential view that such solutions were inappropriate on the facts of the cases presented. But it seems at least as likely that the Court declined those solutions because they would not have solved the real problem that the Court perceived with construing Congress's commerce power broadly. Simply put, a federal government that could regulate more or less comprehensively was not acceptable, regardless of whether the states could regulate in the absence of contradictory federal law. As the MustBeSomething Rule provides, a construction of Congress's enumerated powers on which Congress can regulate as broadly as it could with a police power must be incorrect.

Dagenhart featured no such ambiguity. Unlike the laws in *E.C. Knight* and the *Employers' Liability Cases*, which regulated things that were subject to pervasive state-level regulation—manufacturing in the former case, intrastate transportation in the latter—the Child Labor Act regulated something that no state could regulate: interstate shipments. So if the Court had sustained the Child Labor Act in *Dagenhart*, its ruling would not have threatened the constitutional erasure of any significant body of state law, even if the commerce power were exclusive. And indeed, the Court in *Dagenhart* did not raise the specter of preemption. The motivation for insisting on a limited scope for the commerce power was not, in whole or even in part, the need to preserve state regulation in areas where Congress could not be expected to do the job. It was an imperative to prevent Congress from making policy in domains where Congress had specifically and affirmatively determined to act.[41]

In that respect, *Dagenhart* perfectly exemplified the conventional enumerationist understanding of the need for internal limits on congressional power. According to the normal modern view, the enumeration of powers is supposed to limit Congress not because a too-expansive construction of congressional power might preempt necessary state law but because federal policymaking is to be treated with suspicion. The Court's language in *Dagenhart* made that orientation clear. In the passage quoted above, Justice William Day wrote for the majority that if Congress had the authority to regulate as it tried to in the Child Labor Act, "all freedom of commerce will be at an end."

It is not obvious, however, why recognizing federal power in a given domain would be tantamount to the end of freedom in that domain. The "freedom of commerce," however it might be conceived, is protected by process limits even when it is not protected by internal limits: it is hard to imagine Congress's deciding to deprive Americans of all choice-making in the commercial field. But in the *Dagenhart* Court's mind, the existence of federal regulatory power meant, or at least threatened, the end of freedom. It seems unlikely that the Court would have said something parallel about a state's regulatory authority: one doubts that the Court would have said that the states' power to regulate manufacturing made the field of manufacturing unfree. In short, the Court saw federal law as more problematic than state law, and it understood the limiting force of Congress's enumerated powers as a device for keeping federal law in check.

Dagenhart was a controversial decision; the Court divided five to four, with Justice Oliver Wendell Holmes Jr. writing the dissent. In Holmes's view, a law "within the powers specifically conferred upon Congress" should not be deemed "any less constitutional because of the indirect effects that it may have, however obvious it may be that it will have those effects."[42] In other words, the Child Labor Act was a regulation of commerce among the states, so it was within Congress's authority under the Commerce Clause, regardless of the implications for the potential breadth of federal regulation. Holmes did not expressly say that his analysis would hold even in the maximal case where upholding a federal law would signal that Congress could as a practical matter produce the same results it could produce with a police power. But neither did he shrink from the implication. And just two years later, he wrote a majority opinion illustrating about as clearly as possible that the federal government had the capacity to enact any legislation not prohibited by external limits, even while acting only on the basis of its textually enumerated powers.

Enumeration without Internal Limits

In 1913, Congress by statute authorized the Department of Agriculture to promulgate regulations prohibiting the killing of migratory birds.[43] Two federal district courts held the statute invalid on the ground that it was not within any enumerated power.[44] So in 1916, the federal government executed a workaround. First, the United States negotiated and ratified a treaty with Great Britain, acting for Canada, committing both countries to take certain steps to protect migratory birds. With that done, Congress enacted a statute, called the Migratory Bird Treaty Act, establishing a regime of protection for the relevant birds within the United States as contemplated by the treaty. The constitutional logic of this strategy was straightforward. Under Article II, Section 2, the president has the power to make treaties with the advice and consent of the Senate. Article VI provides that a treaty, once ratified, is part of the supreme law of the land. So as a matter of federal law, the ratification of the treaty committed the United States to protecting the relevant birds. Using its power under the Necessary and Proper Clause, Congress then passed the Migratory Bird Treaty Act as a means of carrying into execution the commitments the federal government made when ratifying the treaty.

In *Missouri v. Holland*, the Supreme Court upheld the Migratory Bird Treaty Act, rejecting the argument that the act was an unconstitutional invasion of state prerogatives in violation of the Tenth Amendment. Writing for a seven-justice majority, Justice Holmes presented a simple analysis. The Tenth Amendment was inapposite, because it reserves to the states only "powers not delegated to the United States, [and] the power to make treaties is delegated expressly."[45] The question was whether anything prevented the government from agreeing, by treaty, to protect migratory birds. In Holmes's view, that was a question about external limits, and the answer was no. "The treaty in question," he wrote, "does not contravene any prohibitory words to be found in the Constitution."[46] In the absence of such a prohibition, the treaty was valid. And "[i]f the treaty is valid," he reasoned, "there can be no dispute about the validity of the statute under Article 1, Section 8, as a necessary and proper means to execute the powers of the Government."[47] In sum, because the federal government has an enumerated power to make treaties and another enumerated power to make laws necessary and proper for carrying its powers into effect, the federal government could make any law not prohibited by external limits by first pledging in a treaty to make that law and then legislating as necessary to fulfill what the exercise of the treaty power promised.[48]

This approach flies in the face of the internal-limits canon and the Must-BeSomething Rule. Exercises of the treaty power are limited by external limits: the federal government could not pledge in a treaty to establish an official religion in the United States, because that would violate the First Amendment. Exercises of the treaty power are also constrained by a daunting process limit, because ratification of a treaty requires approval by a two-thirds vote in the Senate. But a treaty that can win the support of a president and two-thirds of the Senate and that violates no affirmative constitutional prohibitions is valid, no matter what content it has. So if Congress can pass any law not forbidden by external limits as long as it is doing so to fulfill a treaty obligation, then the federal government's enumerated powers do not prevent Congress from legislating as broadly as it could with a police power.

That said, *Holland* is fully consistent with the enumeration principle. It locates the federal government's authority to act in powers specified by the text of the Constitution, in the Treaty Clause of Article II and the Necessary and Proper Clause of Article I. Just as surely as if the Constitution had seven clauses authorizing Congress to legislate on the seven days of the week, or indeed a single clause saying "Congress shall have the power to make any and all laws that do not contravene affirmative prohibitions in this Constitution," *Holland* delivered a regime in which limiting the federal government to its textually enumerated powers does not limit the substantive scope of federal regulation.

But if Holmes's opinion in *Holland* formally complied with the enumeration principle, it also hinted broadly at a different approach to federal power—one that saw the government of the United States as vested with certain powers implicitly or inherently, rather than only by virtue of textually enumerated grants. Five years earlier, Holmes had joined the Court's eight-justice opinion in *Mackenzie v. Hare*, upholding a federal statute divesting American women who married foreigners of U.S. citizenship not because any enumerated power authorized it but because "as [the federal government] has the character of nationality it has the powers of nationality," and "we should hesitate long before limiting or embarassing such powers."[49] Now, in a similar vein—and in a statement of interpretive method that might have evoked James Wilson, Fisher Ames, or the *Legal Tender Cases*—Holmes wrote in *Holland* that "it is not lightly to be assumed that, in matters requiring national action, a power which must belong to and somewhere reside in every civilized government is not to be found."[50] National governments have and ought to have certain powers; the United States is a national government; so it would be odd to conclude that the United States lacked those powers. Moreover, Holmes asserted that the status of the United States as a national government was an accomplished fact as of his writing in 1920, even if it might have been reasonably doubted in 1788. He wrote as follows:

> When we are dealing with words that also are a constituent act, like the Constitution of the United States, we must realize that they have called into life a being the development of which could not have been foreseen completely by the most gifted of its begetters. It was enough for them to realize or to hope that they had created an organism; it has taken a century and has cost their successors much sweat and blood to prove that they created a nation. The case before us must be considered in the light of our whole experience and not merely in that of what was said a hundred years ago.[51]

Operating with that underlying theory, Holmes might have dispensed with the enumerated-powers framework and decided *Holland* in a manner reminiscent of *Mackenzie*, the *Legal Tender Cases*, *Kagama*, *Chae Chan Ping*, or any of the other cases asserting implicit or inherent national powers. He chose not to. Perhaps he reasoned that it was unnecessary to depend on a claim of inherent power. The Treaty Clause exists, and pointing to it as the source of federal authority was easy. One of things that enumerations of powers are good for, after all, is furnishing would-be exercisers and legitimators of power with specific textual warrants for their actions, thus avoiding the need for arguments of substance or principle.

Between his opinion for the Court in *Holland* and his dissent two years earlier in *Dagenhart*, Holmes had demonstrated that the federal government could exercise the practical equivalent of general legislative authority without ever needing to rest on claims of inherent and nonenumerated power.[52]

The enumerated powers, properly read, could supply everything Congress might need. It was a vision that would soon be realized.

The New Deal Court

The story of how the Supreme Court struck down a fair amount of federal legislation on enumerated-powers grounds early in the twentieth century but adopted a much broader construction of those powers by the 1940s is a staple narrative for constitutional lawyers.[53] In that story, cases like *Dagenhart* are followed by the Court's insistent but short-lived opposition to President Franklin Roosevelt's New Deal. When Roosevelt took office in 1933, in the depth of the Great Depression, he and his allies in Congress enacted sweeping legislation intended to foster economic recovery. Up through 1936, in cases like *ALA Schechter Poultry v. United States* and *Carter v. Carter Coal Company*, the Court invalidated important New Deal legislation on enumerated-powers grounds.[54] In 1937, freshly reinaugurated after a second landslide election victory, Roosevelt proposed to add several new justices to the Court. The proposal was couched in terms of the judiciary's workload but widely understood as aimed at changing the ideological composition of the Court. Congress declined to enact the "court-packing" plan, but common wisdom holds that the political pressure the proposal created helped persuade one justice—Owen Roberts—to stop voting to rule New Deal measures unconstitutional. In the same year, Justice Willis Van Devanter retired and was replaced by Justice Hugo Black. Van Devanter had been one of the Court's most determined opponents of the New Deal, and Black was a committed New Dealer. Between Roberts's switch and Black's appointment, the ideological complexion of the Court changed significantly. The Court stopped invalidating New Deal legislation. Indeed, for nearly sixty years, the Court did not invalidate any federal legislation on internal-limit grounds.

But when the Court reversed course in 1937, it did not repudiate either the enumeration principle or the internal-limits canon. In the first major case heralding the switch, *Jones & Laughlin Steel v. National Labor Relations Board*, the Court held that the National Labor Relations Act was a valid exercise of the commerce power, but its ruling highlighted the interstate nature of the case's facts rather than broadly declaring the commerce power to be much more expansive than previously acknowledged.[55] The Court took a larger step in 1941, when it overruled *Dagenhart* in *United States v. Darby.*[56] *Darby* did not contest the idea that Congress is limited to its enumerated powers. But it announced a conceptual shift that opened the way for a much broader understanding of the commerce power—one that would soon make it difficult, in practice, to identify meaningful internal limits.

Darby sustained the federal Fair Labor Standards Act of 1938 (FLSA) against the claim that it was not warranted by Congress's commerce power. The FLSA prohibited the shipment in interstate commerce of goods produced in workplaces that did not abide by certain minimum-wage and maximum-hour rules. Congress's strategy, of course, was the same with the FLSA as it had been with the Child Labor Act: force businesses to adopt different labor practices by threatening their access to the interstate market. Obviously, this strategy could only be sustained if the Court would overrule *Dagenhart*, so Congress's passage of the FLSA in 1938 reflected its confidence, or at least its suspicion, that the Court had changed sufficiently to be willing to take that step. That turned out to be the case. According to the Court in *Darby*, a federal statute regulating interstate commerce—here, by prohibiting certain goods from being shipped interstate—would not be invalid "merely because either its motive or its consequence is to restrict the use of articles of commerce within the states of destination."[57] *Dagenhart* was accordingly overruled.

The deeper move in *Darby*, however, came in the Court's sustaining a different part of the FLSA: one that directly imposed federal wage and hour standards on "employees engaged in production of goods for commerce."[58] In other words, unlike the Child Labor Act, the FLSA did not propose to achieve its ends only by policing interstate shipments. It also purported to regulate workplaces directly on the ground that the work performed there created products that would later be in interstate commerce. According to prior case law, such regulation was beyond the commerce power because it was a regulation of manufacturing rather than commerce. But in the *Darby* Court's view, that regulation was within Congress's authority, even though manufacture and commerce were different things. In his opinion for a unanimous Court, Chief Justice Harlan Fiske Stone wrote as follows:

> The power of Congress over interstate commerce is not confined to the regulation of commerce among the states. It extends to those activities intrastate

> which so affect interstate commerce or the exercise of the power of Congress over it as to make regulation of them appropriate means to the attainment of a legitimate end, the exercise of the granted power of Congress to regulate interstate commerce. See *McCulloch v. Maryland*.[59]

In other words, Congress had the authority to regulate manufacturing, and other activities that were not themselves interstate commerce, so long as it was doing so in aid of a regulatory scheme governing something within the commerce power.

Stone did not name the Necessary and Proper Clause as the source of that authority, though the citation of *McCulloch* may have done so implicitly: the cited page from *McCulloch* is where Chief Justice Marshall applied that clause. But regardless of whether the *Darby* Court conceived of the FLSA's wage and hour regulation as justified by the Necessary and Proper Clause or by the implications of the Commerce Clause itself, the proposition that the regulation was in *aid* of commerce regulation and not itself a regulation of commerce made it easy for the Court to dismiss the preemption problem decried in the *Employers' Liability Cases* and *E.C. Knight*. It was true, Stone acknowledged, that the Court had often "found state regulation of interstate commerce, when uniformity of its regulation is a national concern, to be incompatible with the Commerce Clause even though Congress has not legislated on the subject." But having maintained the distinction between commerce and manufacture, *Darby* could say that state laws regulating manufacture were not laws regulating interstate commerce. They were merely laws *affecting* interstate commerce. And as several prior decisions had established, "state laws which are not regulations of the commerce itself or its instrumentalities are not forbidden even though they affect interstate commerce."[60] In short, the world of subjects that Congress might regulate in aid of its power to regulate commerce—manufacture, mining, agriculture, even intrastate transportation—would in practice be subjects of concurrent federal and state jurisdiction.

It was less clear, however, that *Darby* had a compelling answer to the other warning issued in cases from *E.C. Knight* to *Carter Coal*: that such a construction of congressional authority would permit Congress to regulate more or less anything it chose, subject only to the Constitution's external limits. The ruling respected the enumeration principle: *Darby* located the broad power it validated in the Constitution's Commerce Clause. (Or perhaps in the

Commerce Clause and the Necessary and Proper Clause, taken in combination.) But the breadth of the authority recognized might reasonably make one wonder about the status of the internal-limits canon. *Darby* sustained congressional regulation of wages and hours on the ground that it helped enforce the prohibition on interstate shipments, even though that view of the FLSA was an obvious fiction. Congress's objective was to regulate wages and hours, and the prohibition on interstate shipments was a means to that end.[61] But *Darby* announced that the courts would not second-guess commerce regulations on the grounds of congressional motive. If Congress said a regulation was necessary in aid of an exercise of the commerce power, the courts would be inclined to accept that characterization.[62] Given that permissive approach, the commerce power might not be meaningfully narrower than a police power would be.

One year later, the Court's decision in *Wickard v. Filburn*[63] made the potential elimination of internal limits yet harder to ignore. In an effort to stabilize the price of wheat, the New Deal's Agricultural Adjustment Act imposed limits on how much wheat individual farmers could grow. An Ohio dairy farmer named Roscoe Filburn grew several hundred bushels of wheat on his farm, and he used some of that wheat to feed either his livestock or his family.[64] The rest, he sold. But in 1941, Filburn harvested more wheat than he was allotted under the act, and he was fined accordingly. In a lawsuit challenging the fine, Filburn's lawyer argued that the wheat consumed on Filburn's farm was neither "commerce among the several states" nor even production *intended* for commerce. The Supreme Court unanimously rejected this challenge. And if *Darby* had taken a scalpel to the pre–New Deal doctrines constraining congressional power, *Wickard* was a wrecking ball.

Darby had carefully assured its readers that it was not collapsing the distinction between commerce and other categories like manufacturing. It merely allowed Congress to regulate noncommercial matters like manufacturing when doing so was an appropriate means of regulating commerce. In contrast, *Wickard* dispensed with the formal distinctions among categories. "Whether the subject of the regulation in question was 'production' [is] not material," the Court wrote. What mattered were the "actual effects of the activity in question upon interstate commerce."[65] Assuming no violations of affirmative constitutional prohibitions, *Wickard* held, Congress could regulate any activity that substantially affected interstate commerce, "even if [that] activity be local and though it may not be regarded as commerce."[66] And the production and consumption of home-grown wheat, the Court explained, had an effect on the interstate wheat market, because it reduced demand.[67]

Filburn's wheat crop was more than just what a man might want to feed his family and a few dairy cows. It covered twenty-three acres and produced around four hundred fifty bushels—enough to produce roughly forty thousand loaves of whole wheat bread.[68] Still, in a vast national market, Filburn's crop probably had no measurable impact on prices. As the Court made clear, however, the question to ask when assessing Congress's warrant for regulation was not whether any particular person's conduct substantially affected commerce. It was whether making congressional regulation of the wheat market effective required regulating the conduct at issue in the aggregate. Filburn's wheat might not affect market prices, but a hundred thousand farmers each growing four hundred bushels of wheat certainly could. So to be effective, nationwide regulation of something like the wheat market would have to be binding on enormous numbers of people, even if each of them affected that market only imperceptibly. Hence the "aggregation principle" for which *Wickard* is famous:

> That appellee's own contribution to the demand for wheat may be trivial by itself is not enough to remove him from the scope of federal regulation where, as here, his contribution, taken together with that of many others similarly situated, is far from trivial.[69]

Given the aggregation principle, it was not hard to see how *Wickard* threatened to do the very thing that the Court denounced in cases like *Dagenhart* and *Carter Coal*: permit Congress to use its enumerated power over commerce to produce regulatory effects comparably broad to those it could produce with a police power. In a nation of more than a hundred million people, virtually any behavior would have substantial economic effects when considered in the aggregate. To be sure, the Court never openly repudiated the internal-limits canon. In commerce-power cases following *Wickard*, even the most committed New Deal justices sometimes felt the need to assert, or at least hold out the possibility, that they had not licensed the practical equivalent of plenary congressional power.[70] But asserting something and explaining why it is true are two different things. After *Wickard*, it was not easy to explain what Congress could not regulate, except where its action was blocked by external constitutional limits. And so matters stood for half a century. As a practical matter, Congress could use its commerce power (or its commerce power together with its power under the Necessary and Proper Clause—the Court was not punctilious about the difference) to legislate more or less as it wished, so long as it did not contravene affirmative constitutional prohibitions like those in the First Amendment. The enumerated powers were no longer limiting.

Five Possible Regimes

Constitutional lawyers commonly think in terms of just two possible models for congressional power. Either we have a Congress limited by its enumerated powers, or we have a Congress with a police power. But there are other possibilities. When we see that the enumeration principle and the internal-limits canon are distinct concepts, we can recognize five possible regimes for congressional power, each one characterized by two features: the powers that Congress has and the substantive reach of those powers.

The first variable has three possible values. First, Congress might have enumerated powers only, as the enumeration principle claims. Second, Congress might have a set of enumerated powers and also a set of nonenumerated powers, as the Court often held prior to the New Deal. Third, Congress might have general legislative jurisdiction, like the police power that state legislatures wield. Along the dimension of substantive reach, there are two possibilities. Either Congress's reach is necessarily partial, as the internal-limits canon claims, or it is potentially comprehensive. If the reach of Congress's powers is partial, there are aspects of social life that Congress cannot regulate, even without accounting for external limits. If the reach of Congress's powers is potentially comprehensive, Congress might be able to pursue any regulatory project, except as affirmatively prohibited.

Given three possibilities along the first dimension and two along the second, there are in principle six ways to mix and match, as shown in Figure 7.1.

Only five of these combinations describe actually possible regimes. Box 5 is not a possible arrangement, because a government with general jurisdiction can by definition regulate anything unless blocked by external limits. But all of the other combinations are possible.

Box 1 is the orthodox enumerationist view, according to which Congress has only enumerated powers and with those powers can reach only a subset of the world's possible subjects of regulation.

| | | Congress's Powers Reach . . . | |
		Less than Everything	Potentially Everything
	Enumerated powers only	(1) Enumerationism (orthodox view)	(2) Cumulative Coverage (de facto since the 1940s)
Congress Has . . .	Enumerated powers and some non-enumerated powers	(3) Implied Powers, version 1: Pre–New Deal Constructions	(4) Implied Powers, version 2: Road Not Taken (at least mostly)
	A general police power	(5) [unpopulated]	(6) Common straw position

FIGURE 7.1

Box 2 is the model of cumulative coverage, which respects the enumeration principle but not the internal-limits canon. Congress acts only on the basis of enumerated powers, but that fact does not limit what Congress can regulate. That is the model whose possibility Holmes demonstrated in *Holland* and that prevailed in practice after the New Deal.

Box 3 houses the model of implied powers that prevailed in the nineteenth and early twentieth centuries, when the Court decided *Prigg*, the *Legal Tender Cases*, *Kagama*, *Chae Chan Ping*, *Burroughs*, and *Curtiss-Wright*. On this model, Congress exercises nonenumerated powers implicit in its status as the national legislature as well as whatever powers are enumerated in the Constitution. But even when combined, Congress's enumerated and nonenumerated powers do not have comprehensive reach. Until sometime in the early twentieth century, the prevailing constructions of the enumerated powers meant that Congress's legislative mandate reached only a subset of the social world, and the practical reality of the federal government's limited capacity meant that those constructions would not be seriously challenged.

Box 4 houses the version of the implied powers model that would have come about if the Court had continued to treat nonenumerated powers as a normal part of Congress's authorities after the New Deal, as the federal government acquired the ability to regulate the social world pervasively. It can also be understood as the regime that prevails in those moments when the modern Court relaxes its strict enumerationist stance and acknowledges the validity of nonenumerated powers on the basis of earlier decisions like *Curtiss-Wright*.

Box 5 is a conceptual impossibility, as noted above. And Box 6 is the regime that constitutional lawyers usually imagine as the alternative to enumerationism. Indeed, the normal thinking is that Box 1 and Box 6 are the only possibilities: either the federal government is limited to and by its enumerated powers, or the federal government has a police power. But in fact, there are three other possibilities, depicted here in Boxes 2, 3, and 4.

Constitutional lawyers generally think in terms of only Box 1 and Box 6 in part because they do not usually differentiate between the two dimensions of the chart above—or, put differently, between the enumeration principle (which is about where the system falls on the chart's vertical dimension) and the internal-limits canon (which is about the horizontal dimension). Without that differentiation, a system of enumerated powers seems inherently limiting, and a legislature with comprehensive reach in practice is a legislature with a police power. And because constitutional lawyers generally think of Box 1 and Box 6 as the only alternatives, the New Deal Court's doctrinal shift seems like a shift—or at least the serious threat of a shift—from Box 1 to Box 6. But in fact, the New Deal transition was not a shift from Box 1 to Box 6. It is better understood as a shift from Box 3 to Box 2. And the enumerationist aspiration to stay in (or go back to) Box 1 is an aspiration to preserve (or restore) something that never really existed.

The Persistence of Cumulative Coverage

As a matter of practice, the model of cumulative coverage was stable for more than fifty years after *Darby* and *Wickard*. Naturally enough, observers during that period sometimes wondered aloud whether the internal-limits canon had any remaining force.[71] But the canon never disappeared. It lingered, both as a statement that jurists would assert as necessarily true and as a piece of pedagogy that teachers of constitutional law conveyed to new members of the profession. (In the class where I first studied constitutional law, in 1989, the MustBeSomething Rule was considered axiomatic.) Many people recognized that Congress had something close to plenary power in practice. But at the level of principle, the internal-limits canon remained.

When the Supreme Court underwent another ideological shift, the canon began to exert some force. Between 1969 and 1991, ten new justices joined the Court. All ten were appointed by Republican presidents. The legal elites associated with the major political parties were less ideologically homogenous then than they are at this writing, and some Republican-appointed justices of this era had, or often had, views about the scope of congressional power as broad as any New Deal justice. Still, Republicans in those decades were on average more skeptical of federal power than Democrats, and on balance these ten appointments shifted the Court's outlook considerably. After 1991, when Justice Clarence Thomas joined the Court, there was a majority willing to take the internal-limits canon more seriously than any Court had since the 1930s. Before the century ended, the Supreme Court was again in the business of striking down federal legislation on the grounds that it exceeded the enumerated powers of Congress.

It might seem, therefore, that the model of cumulative coverage prevailed for roughly half a century, after which a more enumerationist regime took its place. But that assessment, though probably conventional, is mistaken in an important respect. There is no doubt that the twenty-first century judiciary takes the internal-limits canon seriously. But as of this writing, and subject to a qualification about process limits, cumulative coverage may still be the operative regime. To see why, it is necessary to examine the modern cases asserting internal limits—and to notice their limited capacity to constrain federal policymaking.

United States v. Lopez

The case in which the turn-of-the-millennium Supreme Court made its commitment to the internal-limits canon clear was *United States v. Lopez*, decided in 1995.[72] In that case, the Court struck down the Gun-Free School Zones Act of 1990, which, subject to a series of exceptions, prohibited the possession of firearms in or near schools. The legislation was bipartisan, passed with just one dissenting vote in the House of Representatives and by voice vote in the Senate and then signed into law by President George H. W. Bush.[73] The law did not implicate any of the Constitution's affirmative prohibitions—the possibility that the Second Amendment might be a problem lay two decades in the future—and the judiciary had not struck down a federal statute on internal-limit grounds in more than fifty years. And it was not difficult to articulate a rationale on which the governing case law made the act valid legislation under the Commerce Clause. In the aggregate, the possession of firearms in or near schools had substantial economic effects. Guns are used to commit crimes, and crime causes economic damage: lost property, hospitalizations, and so forth. Those costs in the aggregate affect the market for insurance. Guns in schools cause schools to spend money on security, which affects the markets for security equipment and personnel as well as the budgets of the schools—and therefore every other market in which schools spend money. If gun violence at schools causes some students to stay away, learning suffers, and the future workforce is adversely affected. And so on. Under the then-prevailing view of *Wickard*, that should have been enough.

The Supreme Court of 1995 thought differently. The de facto reality that the enumerated powers of Congress did not seem to be doing limiting work was, in the majority's view, a problem—a sign that the constitutional system was not working the way it was supposed to. From that perspective, the fact that existing doctrine was generally understood to be sufficient to justify the Gun-Free School Zones Act did not make the act an appropriate exercise of constitutional power. It meant that existing doctrine had to be corrected. Indeed, the fact that the act had gone through Congress so easily might have seemed like a signal that matters had gotten out of control.

At oral argument in *Lopez*, the solicitor general of the United States defended the constitutionality of the statute. His case was surely lost when, less than five minutes into the argument, Justice Sandra Day O'Connor and Chief Justice Rehnquist asked a question that the solicitor general was unable to answer. O'Connor's version of the question went like this: "If this is covered, what's left of enumerated powers?"[74] Rehnquist pushed the point. Suppose that Congress using its commerce power could regulate the possession of guns in schools, he asked. What then would be an example of something Congress could *not* regulate with its commerce power?[75] The solicitor general could not provide an example. And reasonably not. In a country of hundreds of millions of people, any behavior, considered in the aggregate, has substantial effects on interstate commerce.

O'Connor and Rehnquist had invoked the MustBeSomething Rule: given the premise that the enumerated powers are limiting, there must be something that Congress cannot use them to regulate. The solicitor general's inability to say what that something might be demonstrated, in constitutional law's most prominent forum, that the idea of a national government limited by the enumeration of its powers either was, or was dangerously close to becoming, a sham. To uphold the Gun-Free School Zones Act at that point would have been for the Court to admit openly that the enumerationist paradigm was not how constitutional law really worked. The Court had no desire to do that. Most of its members regarded the idea of a limiting enumeration as a core premise of constitutional law. So once it was clear that upholding the Gun-Free School Zones Act would announce that congressional power was not subject to internal limits, the law was doomed.

Chief Justice Rehnquist's opinion for the majority did not dispute the government's empirical point that the possession of guns in schools, in the aggregate, had substantial economic effects. But if those economic effects brought gun possession within the commerce power, Rehnquist noted, then everything is within the commerce power. "[I]f we were to accept the Government's arguments," Rehnquist wrote, "we are hard pressed to posit any activity by an individual that Congress is without power to regulate."[76] In short, the Gun-Free School Zones Act had to be unconstitutional, because the Court could not otherwise maintain the internal-limits canon. And without the internal-limits canon, the whole idea of a government of enumerated powers seemed pointless.

The Court's opinion in *Lopez* was both a paradigmatic statement of enumerationism and a tour of several of the leading ways that the lens of enumerationism distorts the understandings of constitutional lawyers. Consider: the Court described the proposition that "[t]he Constitution creates a Federal Government of enumerated powers" as a matter of "first principles." As authority for that point, the opinion cited Article I, Section 8—which neither states nor illustrates the proposition that the federal government can exercise only its enumerated powers (as explained in the introduction).[77] A separate part of the opinion cited Article I, Section 8, as authority for the proposition that the Constitution withholds a police power from Congress—which, again, is an inference for which one could argue on the basis of Section 8 but not a proposition stated there.[78] The Court quoted Madison's statement in *Federalist* 45 that "[t]he powers delegated by the proposed Constitution to the federal government are few and defined" as if it accurately described the Constitution's suite of federal powers, even though it does not (as described in Chapter 4).[79] In an opinion covering only seventeen pages in the *United States Reports*, the Court three different times invoked Marshall's *Gibbons* dictum that "the enumeration presupposes something not enumerated" as if it meant that the Constitution's enumeration of congressional powers means that there must be things beyond the reach of the internal limits of those powers.[80] (Even though it does not, as explained earlier in this chapter.) Finally, the Court propounded the Unlimited Congress Fallacy: it wrote as if an absence of internal limits on congressional power would be tantamount to there being no limits at all on Congress, even though Congress would still be constrained by a robust set of external limits.[81]

United States v. Morrison

Lopez made clear that the Court regarded internal limits as fundamental. But it was not obvious from *Lopez* how courts and lawyers should describe the internal limit of the commerce power. (Insisting that there is a limit is not the same thing as explaining where that limit is.) Five years later, the Court in *United States v. Morrison* took a step toward articulating that boundary by suggesting that activities "economic in nature" are eligible for commerce regulation on the *Wickard*-aggregation model and noneconomic activities are not.[82] But the Court did not fully commit to that distinction. The real doctrine seemed still to be simply that there must be an internal limit, so any statute that could not be justified without violating the MustBeSomething rule would be struck down.

Morrison invalidated § 13981(c) of the 1994 Violence Against Women Act, which entitled victims of crimes of gender-motivated violence to sue their attackers for damages in federal court.[83] Writing for the same five-justice majority that decided *Lopez*, Chief Justice Rehnquist reprised the reasoning of that earlier case. Once again, Rehnquist did not dispute the government's argument that the regulated activity substantially affected interstate commerce. On the contrary, he acknowledged that Congress had compiled a thick record showing the substantial economic effects of gender-motivated violence, amounting to billions of dollars each year: hospital bills, lost days of work, countless potential business and recreational transactions forgone because women hesitated to travel at night, and so on. But those empirical realities could not be enough to bring gender-motivated violence within the commerce power, or else that power would have no internal limits, because virtually any activity has substantial effects on interstate commerce when considered in the aggregate. In Rehnquist's formulation, the government's defense of the statute relied "on a method of reasoning that we have already rejected as unworkable if we are to maintain the Constitution's enumeration of powers."[84] Rehnquist was here conflating the enumeration of powers with the internal-limits canon: strictly speaking, the Constitution's enumeration of powers would be maintained even if it turned out that those powers did not limit what Congress can do. But the idea that maintaining the enumeration of powers requires those powers to do limiting work made perfect sense on the enumerationist presumption that the point of the enumeration is to limit Congress.

Somehow, it had to be the case that only a subset of all possible subjects of regulation could come within the commerce power, even when their effects on interstate commerce were considered in the aggregate. By way of distinguishing those activities eligible for commerce regulation on the substantial-effects theory from those that are not, Rehnquist interpreted prior case law as upholding "Commerce Clause regulation of intrastate activity only where that activity is economic in nature."[85] Aware that the line between economic and noneconomic behavior might be hard to draw, Rehnquist made clear that the Court was not endorsing "a categorical rule against aggregating the effects of any noneconomic activity."[86] But some limit had to be articulated. The economic/noneconomic distinction seemed serviceable, and the judiciary has since treated that distinction as its doctrinal guide.

NFIB

As of this writing, *Lopez* and *Morrison* remain the only post–New Deal cases in which the Supreme Court has struck down Article I legislation on internal-limit grounds. But it nearly happened again in 2012, in *NFIB*, when the Court adjudicated the constitutionality of the Patient Protection and Affordable Care Act.[87] That law, often called "the ACA" or "Obamacare," was the most ambitious federal domestic policy legislation since the 1960s. It comprehensively reformed the nation's health insurance market and many other aspects of the health care system as well. Among its principal aims was to make health insurance available to tens of millions of otherwise uninsured Americans. Opponents of the act argued, among other things, that the act constituted a large and costly expansion of the federal government's role at the expense of the private market and of the decisions of individuals. Passage of the act was bitterly divisive along party lines.[88]

Among its provisions intended to make health insurance more broadly available, the ACA required health insurance companies to offer coverage to high-risk customers on the same terms as low-risk customers. Standing alone, that requirement would have created what economists call an adverse-selection problem, one serious enough to wreck the market for health insurance.[89] To pay for their increased costs, insurance companies would raise premiums. That would make health insurance a bad bet for low-risk customers. Rather than paying high premiums to insure themselves against costs they were unlikely to incur, low-risk customers could wait until they had significant medical needs before enrolling in insurance plans, knowing that the insurance companies would be required then to cover them. And without premium income from low-risk customers, insurers could not afford to cover high-risk customers.

To prevent the insurance market from unraveling, the ACA contained a provision intended to increase the number of low-risk customers paying insurance premiums. That provision, generally called the "individual mandate," required all Americans not specifically exempted to carry an amount of health insurance that the act called "minimum essential coverage." (The statute exempted several categories of people, including those with religious objections and those for whom compliance would cause financial hardship.) If the mandate sufficiently increased the size of the premium-paying population, and in particular if it did so by bringing in large numbers of young and healthy customers who were relatively cheap to insure, the insurance companies would be able to offer insurance at affordable rates to higher-risk customers, as the ACA required them to do. A similar system had succeeded at the state level in Massachusetts. With the ACA, the federal government proposed to take that solution national.[90]

But as the ACA progressed through Congress, some of its opponents began to argue that no enumerated power authorized Congress to impose the individual mandate. That objection came as a surprise to the ACA's supporters. Their general thinking had been that the mandate was obviously within the commerce power, because the ACA was legislation regulating a massive nationwide industry. At the very least, the individual mandate was legislation necessary and proper for carrying other parts of the ACA into execution: it was designed to make the ACA's rules regarding coverage for high-risk customers viable despite the adverse-selection problem. Moreover, the idea of using a mandate had circulated for years in the think-tank community without anyone's raising this objection. Indeed, the idea originated at the Heritage Foundation, a conservative institution whose general skepticism toward federal governance should not have disposed it to take a recklessly broad view of Congress's enumerated powers. Everyone knew, of course, that the ACA would be deeply controversial as a policy matter. But this enumerated-powers objection was a late entry onto the scene, and an unexpected one.[91]

Once the argument was made, however, it turned out to have considerable appeal. Five justices in *NFIB* concluded that Congress's commerce power, whether standing alone or in conjunction with the Necessary and Proper Clause, did not authorize Congress to enact the individual mandate. According to those five justices, the commerce power permits Congress to regulate economic *activity*, but it does not permit Congress to regulate people who are not active in the relevant market. Setting the prices at which insurance could be sold to high-risk customers was permissible. But requiring people who were not carrying health insurance at all to take the affirmative step of buying a product was not—not even as a means for carrying the rest of the law into execution under the Necessary and Proper Clause.[92]

As several authors have explained, the activity/inactivity distinction that five justices accepted in *NFIB* was a doctrinal innovation rather than a previously established limit on the commerce power.[93] And if one evaluates constructions of Congress's enumerated powers on the basis of their utility for distinguishing between what should be regulable nationally and what should only be regulable locally, the distinction between action and inaction has no obvious merit. There is no reason to think that Congress is better at policy-making for people who are active in a given domain than for people who are inactive in that domain, and not only because whether any given person is active or inactive might turn on characterization rather than on ontological fact. (One could say, as Chief Justice Roberts did, that a person who is not actively engaged in commerce should not be regulated with a power to regulate commerce, but that does not explain why such a person may not be regulated with a power to make all laws necessary and proper for carrying commerce regulation into execution.[94] That the Necessary and Proper Clause authorizes Congress to do things that it could not do without the power described in that clause should not be a controversial proposition.) To be sure, reasonable people might object to Congress's imposing burdens on them for the purpose of addressing some regulatory problem that they think has nothing to do with them. But reasonable people might have similar objections to such regulatory burdens imposed by state authority, too.

That said, it is not hard to understand why the ACA's opponents made the argument they made, and it is not hard to understand why many judges and justices deemed it persuasive. The ACA's opponents objected intensely to the individual mandate and to the law's regulatory scheme overall. Some of their objections were the stuff of ordinary politics. They might have thought the ACA too costly, or they might have wanted to prevent a president of the opposing party from scoring a major legislative success. But some of the objections were reasonably understood as constitutional, in the small-c sense of the term: they concerned fundamental aspects of the American system of government. For starters, being forced to buy a product one does not want is in conflict with libertarian ideals about the free market—ideals that many people regard as constitutional in the small-c sense. Moreover, the ACA's agenda of universal health insurance could easily be understood as a proposal to transform the basic American social contract. No longer would people be expected to make their livings in the capitalist market, subject to specific exceptions for those unable to do so for reasons like disability and old age. Instead, the government would provide significant support to everyone, as a matter of the ordinary course. And if the government could do that with respect to health insurance, it could also do it in other domains, or even generally, with something like a guaranteed income for every American. Many people found that prospect deeply objectionable—an offense to fundamental and traditional American values about government and society.

A written constitution might protect these interests expressly, with clauses saying things like "No universal subsidies" or "No compelled purchases." "The government cannot force me to become active in a commercial market" is, most straightforwardly, an external limit: it is a proposition about what the government is prohibited from doing. As it happens, though, the text of the United States Constitution does not specify prohibitions like these. Like Madison in his struggle against the Bank of the United States, the opponents of the ACA had objections that seemed constitutional in substance but had no footing in the written Constitution. In principle, they still could have argued their case in terms of external limits: to protect individual rights, the judiciary has sometimes invoked the general idea of due process of law to block governmental action even when the rights in question are not specified in the Constitution's text.[95] That might have been a difficult argument to win, though, because the twenty-first-century judiciary is reluctant to recognize new constitutional rights without textual support. So, like Madison, the opponents of the ACA internalized their argument. Rather than presenting their objections to the individual mandate in terms of desired external limits on governmental power, they articulated those objections in terms of internal limits.

In explaining why they found the internalized argument persuasive, five justices of the Supreme Court pointed to the MustBeSomething Rule. If the commerce power were broad enough to justify the individual mandate, Chief Justice Roberts wrote, then Congress would be capable of "drawing all power into its impetuous vortex."[96] In a separate opinion, Justices Scalia, Kennedy, Thomas, and Alito made the same point. "If Congress can reach out and command even those furthest removed from an interstate market to participate in the market," they wrote, "then the Commerce Clause becomes a font of unlimited power."[97] Narrating an episode that recapitulated a similar moment when *Lopez* was before the Court seventeen years before, they also wrote this:

> The Government was invited, at oral argument, to suggest what federal controls over private conduct (other than those explicitly prohibited by the Bill of Rights or other constitutional controls) could *not* be justified as necessary and proper for the carrying out of a general regulatory scheme. . . . It was unable to name any. . . . [But] the proposition that the Federal Government cannot do everything is a fundamental precept.[98]

In short, the individual mandate could not be within the commerce power because the internal-limits canon provides, as a fundamental principle, that the enumerated powers limit what Congress can do. So a law that cannot be defended without violating the MustBeSomething Rule cannot be constitutional. In *NFIB*, the challengers' proffered distinction between activity and inactivity gave the Court a way to assert that there is, in fact, some internal limit on what the commerce power authorizes Congress to do. Confident that there must be such an internal limit, five justices accepted the solution they were offered.

Workarounds

The cases in which the modern Court has insistently stood up for the internal-limits canon might seem to indicate that the scope of federal governance really is limited by Congress's enumerated powers, just as enumerationism teaches it must be. Even if that proposition was questionable in the decades between *Wickard* and *Lopez*, the thought would run, the limiting force of the enumeration has since been reasserted. But that thought would misunderstand the reality of constitutional law since *Lopez*, *Morrison*, and *NFIB*. Despite their strongly articulated adherence to the internal-limits canon, those decisions have not confined the scope of Congress's regulatory ability. In short, the Court has talked the talk of the internal-limits canon but, at least so far, has not found a way to walk the walk by making the Constitution's enumeration of congressional powers actually do the limiting work on which enumerationism insists.

The Court held in *Lopez* that the commerce power did not authorize Congress to regulate the mere possession of firearms in school zones. But the commerce power uncontroversially authorizes Congress to regulate commercial products that move from state to state. So after *Lopez* struck down the original version of the Gun-Free School Zones Act, Congress reenacted the substance of that act as a regulation of firearms that have moved in interstate commerce.[99] That is, rather than regulating the possession of firearms in school zones, the second version of the act imposed the same regulatory regime on the possession in school zones of all firearms that had crossed state lines. The lower courts uniformly upheld the reenacted version, and the Supreme Court declined to disturb their rulings.[100] Because a very large portion of all firearms moves in interstate commerce, there is little practical difference between a law regulating the possession of firearms that have moved in interstate commerce and a law regulating the possession of firearms in general.

What's more, Congress's inability to use its commerce power to regulate the possession of the small subset of firearms that have never moved in interstate commerce does not make even those firearms immune from federal regulation. So long as it did not transgress external limits, Congress could use its taxing power to tax the possession of firearms, regardless of any considerations about those firearms' connection to interstate commerce. The federal government could also regulate those firearms pursuant to a relevant exercise of its treaty power. (Imagine a duly ratified treaty between the United States and Canada whereby all civilian-owned firearms must be registered in a joint US-Canadian database.) So even after *Lopez*, the power to regulate the possession of most or even all firearms falls within the federal government's powers. To the extent that Congress's power over this subject matter is limited, it is limited by external limits, like those associated with the Second Amendment, and by the political process.

The activity/inactivity limit announced in *NFIB* is subject to similar workarounds. In *NFIB*, the agreement by five justices that the commerce power did not authorize the individual mandate did not result in the invalidation of the statute, because the Court upheld the individual mandate as an exercise of a different enumerated power—specifically, the power to lay and collect taxes. As a different group of five justices noted, the mandate offered covered individuals the choice between carrying insurance and paying a financial assessment. Viewed that way, this majority explained, the ACA was reasonably understood as a tax on the uninsured. Congress had not made it a crime to fail to carry insurance. It had simply made going without insurance more expensive. To permit a course of conduct but say that anyone engaging in it will pay money to the government, the Court reasoned, is tantamount to imposing a tax on that conduct. As such, the mandate was valid law as an exercise of Congress's power to levy taxes.[101]

Given that four justices denied that the individual mandate was justified as an exercise of the taxing power, one might think that the Court in *NFIB* actually came extremely close to imposing a consequential set of internal limits. But on the question of whether Congress had the *authority* to impose the individual mandate as an exercise of the taxing power, all nine justices agreed: the answer was yes. The four justices who would have declared the ACA unconstitutional—Scalia, Kennedy, Thomas, and Alito—denied only that Congress *had* proceeded under the taxing power rather than under the Commerce Clause.[102] In their view, it would be entirely constitutional for Congress to pass a statute clearly saying something like "All Americans who do not have health insurance shall pay a tax." Accordingly, even if the dissenters had prevailed and the ACA had been declared unconstitutional, *NFIB* would stand for the proposition that the enumerated powers of Congress are sufficient for the enactment of legislation like the individual mandate, so long as Congress characterizes its action the right way.

Given the realities of the social world and the text of the Constitution, Congress will usually have multiple ways to work around internal limits. Consider: throughout the public debate over the ACA, opponents of the act likened the requirement that people carry health insurance to a government mandate requiring people to eat broccoli.[103] A broccoli mandate, the thought ran, would be an obviously intolerable piece of paternalism. So if the courts could be persuaded that the ACA's mandate was not meaningfully different from a broccoli mandate, the ACA's mandate would have to fall. But the action/inaction distinction that five justices endorsed in *NFIB* would not even prevent Congress from establishing, in substance, the legal regime of the hypothetical broccoli mandate. Yes, the rule that Congress's commerce power (alone or in conjunction with the Necessary and Proper Clause) cannot be used to compel action would prevent Congress from using that power to pass a law formally compelling Americans to eat broccoli. But as Justice Ginsburg suggested in her *NFIB* opinion, Congress could create the same substantive regime by using its power to regulate commerce to prohibit the purchase or consumption of any food other than broccoli, except by persons who had recently eaten broccoli.[104] Setting conditions on the purchase or consumption of goods is uncontroversially within Congress's commerce power. And if eating broccoli were made a condition for the purchase or consumption of food, the legal regime would in practice compel people to eat broccoli just as surely as if it did so directly.

One might think that Justice Ginsburg's suggested workaround is too quick, because it neglects the interaction between internal limits and process limits. The alternative legislation Justice Ginsburg described is within the commerce power, but it is hard to imagine that Congress would ever pass a law setting draconian restrictions on the purchase or consumption of food. Elected officials do all sorts of crazy things, but they aren't going to do *that*. In other words, process limits would prevent Congress from enacting Justice Ginsburg's workaround. And if the workaround is not really an option, then the internal limit on the commerce power that keeps Congress from enacting the narrower broccoli mandate might indeed have the effect of preventing Congress from making people eat broccoli—not all by itself, but in combination with a different set of constitutional limits.

There is something to this response. Sometimes workarounds are costly, whether politically or financially or otherwise, such that forcing Congress to proceed by workaround will have the effect of preventing congressional action. But on careful consideration, internal limits are doing less work than the foregoing response suggests, even in the extreme case of the broccoli mandate. For internal limits to force Congress to choose between a work-around and declining to legislate, the legislation that internal limits prevent Congress from enacting must be legislation that Congress has the political will to enact. If Congress would never choose to enact a statute directly requiring people to eat broccoli, then it makes no sense to say that an internal limit blocking the enactment of that statute plays an important role in preventing a mandatory-broccoli regime. The mandatory-broccoli regime is off the table even without the internal limit. So yes, it is hard to imagine Congress enacting Justice Ginsburg's workaround. But it is also hard to imagine Congress enacting a law directly compelling people to eat broccoli. Process limits are doing the work in both cases, and the internal limit is superfluous.

One might think that these examples of how Congress can find ways to enact its preferred regulatory regimes rather than being confined by the internal limits of its enumerated powers are simply a small collection of flukes. But there is also another possibility. Perhaps these workarounds illustrate a general feature of the constitutional system. Given the substance of Congress's enumerated powers, the rule that Congress can exercise only those powers (including the powers described by the Necessary and Proper Clause) is not a good technology for constraining the federal government's regulatory footprint. As explained in Chapter 2, the Constitutional Convention's enumeration of congressional powers made more sense as a strategy for empowering Congress, both against the states and against the president, than as a strategy for limiting the federal government. To be sure, it makes the most sense to say that the enumeration was written for a mix of purposes, both to empower Congress and to limit it. But experience suggests that it works better as empowerment than as limitation. Yes, the Court can strike down federal laws on internal-limit grounds, as it did in *Lopez* and *Morrison*. But if Congress knows in advance what internal-limit rules it faces, it can probably find a way to legislate around them.

◄◄--►►◄◄--►►

The judiciary's approach to congressional power has not in practice been as enumerationist as the conventional wisdom believes. The courts have regularly professed the principles of enumerationism, and probably in good faith. On several occasions—mostly between 1870 and 1936—the Supreme Court has struck down federal laws on enumerated-powers grounds. But the Court's jurisprudence never consistently embodied both principles of enumerationism at the same time. Prior to the New Deal, the Court often violated the enumeration principle: it recognized nonenumerated congressional powers in many areas of important governmental action. Since the New Deal, the Court has in practice not adhered to the internal-limits canon: Congress can use its enumerated powers to pursue more or less any regulatory project for which it has the political will, so long as it does not violate external limits. Given that reality, the Court's post–New Deal reluctance to acknowledge nonenumerated powers has made little practical difference. The modern Court's insistence that the principles of enumerationism have always been fundamental to constitutional law is thus in significant part an exercise in revisionism—one that has, among other things, presented Chief Justice Marshall's canonical opinions in *McCulloch* and *Gibbons* as standing for propositions that Marshall did not in fact assert.

In light of the Founding-era history described in Chapters 2 through 5, it is hard to criticize the Supreme Court's nonenumerationist jurisprudence as the betrayal of a Founding vision. The Constitution's enumeration of congressional powers was designed first and foremost as a technology of empowerment. As the national government acquired the practical capacity to govern more comprehensively, and as the American electorate called for more robust national governance, the enumeration of powers enabled national governance to grow. In that light, the shift over time to a system of enumeration without meaningful internal limits—a system in which the national government could regulate generally, within the confines of process limits and external limits—should be seen as a success.

That said, there are two other potential bases for seeing the judicial treatment of congressional power over time as insufficiently enumerationist—that is, for thinking that if in fact the history of the doctrine has been as described here, the Court has failed to limit congressional power in the ways that it should. The first is a matter of federalism. Even if the enumeration of congressional powers was designed *mostly* as a technology of empowerment, it might also have a role to play in limiting national governance. If so, a system without internal limits might be a system in which American federalism is badly compromised. Second, there is the matter of the text of the Constitution, which is normally understood to require that the federal government be limited to and by its enumerated powers. If that understanding of the text is right, then it would be highly problematic to regard a regime without meaningful internal limits as successful.

In the next two chapters, I turn to addressing those concerns. First, in Chapter 8, I explain that the absence of internal limits is not a significant problem for American federalism. Then, in Chapter 9, I explain that if the text of the Constitution is read without the presumptions of enumerationism, it requires neither the enumeration principle nor the internal-limits canon.

CHAPTER EIGHT

FEDERALISM WITHOUT INTERNAL LIMITS

FEDERALISM HAS TWO ASPECTS: national decisionmaking for decisions that should be made nationally and local decisionmaking for decisions that should be made locally. According to the normal thinking, the fact that Congress is limited by its enumerated powers is of critical importance in protecting the localist half of federalism. The intuition animating that way of thinking is straightforward: internal limits mean less federal law, and less federal law means more space for state autonomy. But this is a mistake. Carefully considered, the imperative of protecting local decisionmaking does not call for an enumerationist approach to federal power.

The problem with the conventional wisdom does not lie in its belief that protecting local decisionmaking is important. On the contrary, local decisionmaking is enormously valuable, and a rich literature canvasses many reasons why. Local decisionmaking is often (not always, but often) better informed about local problems than national decisionmaking is.[1] Local decisionmaking may also be more democratic—though whether it is in fact more democratic in any given instance depends on local circumstances as well as on one's conception of democracy. (For most African Americans in the Jim Crow South, local politics were not democratic.) Decisionmaking in smaller polities can mean more opportunity for individual citizens to experience civic engagement, leadership, and political responsibility.[2] Differentiated decisionmaking in different states and different localities can create regulatory diversity, and regulatory diversity can satisfy the preferences of more citizens than uniform regulation can, assuming that the subject matter does not require wide coordination and assuming also at least some correlation between the aggregate preferences of different state populations and the regulatory schemes those states adopt.[3] Regulatory diversity may also let each jurisdiction operate as what Justice Louis Brandeis called a "laboratory" of democracy, increasing the store of knowledge available to future policymakers by demonstrating the operation of different legal rules.[4] Giving investigatory and enforcement powers to local officials who are not within the national government's chain of command can mitigate the risk that a corrupt national administration will insulate its corruption (while also creating the risk that local officials will abuse their powers by harassing national officials for political gain). For these reasons and others, federalism—or more particularly, the local decisionmaking that is one side of federalism—is deeply valuable.

But the conventional wisdom errs in thinking that preserving local decisionmaking requires an enumerationist approach to federal power. In practice, the enumeration of congressional powers is neither necessary nor particularly helpful in preserving local decisionmaking autonomy. It is not well designed for that function, and it does not in fact perform it. Indeed, the enumeration of powers has done virtually nothing to constrain federal lawmaking since the 1930s, and yet most governance in the United States today occurs at the state and local levels. If local decisionmaking in the American system depended on the limiting force of enumerated powers, that fact would be hard to explain.

In practice, American federalism sustains local decisionmaking with a variety of other mechanisms. Some are matters of process or practicality. Some are matters of constitutional culture. Some are canons of construction, by which federal statutes are read narrowly to preserve state law. Some are external limits on congressional power, like anticommandeering rules and limits on conditional federal spending. And crucially, the American system does not preserve local decisionmaking only—or even mostly—by limiting the scope of potential federal lawmaking. Rather than preserving a sphere of local decisionmaking beyond the legal limit of federal policymaking, the system fosters that decisionmaking within domains where federal and state policymaking interact. In an arrangement often called "cooperative federalism," which pervades the regulation of health care, education, transportation, policing, the environment, and many other fields, the allocation of decisionmaking between federal and state authorities turns out not to be a zero-sum game. Sometimes federal regulation displaces local regulation, but sometimes federal law empowers local policymakers more than it constrains them.

These mechanisms do not deliver *optimal* federalism. Probably no set of institutional arrangements could do that, even if people could agree about what optimal federalism would look like. Nor do these mechanisms deliver the exact form of federalism that the drafters and ratifiers of the Constitution expected, and not merely because those drafters and ratifiers did not all agree about how American federalism should function. Constitutional amendments have altered the relationship between the state and federal governments. Changes in society over two and a half centuries make it impractical and unwise to operate the government as if eighteenth-century conditions still prevailed. Without question, there is continuity as well as change. Indeed, the basic fact that the enumeration of congressional powers is not a significant means of limiting federal legislation is at least as consistent as it is inconsistent with the Framers' constitutional design (albeit inconsistent with the way many of them described the enumeration of powers during the ratification debates). But in this chapter, the important question about the modern system's mechanisms for fostering local decisionmaking is not whether they implement a Founding vision. It is whether they deliver what federalism ought to and can reasonably be expected to deliver. They do. Even after many decades during which the enumeration of congressional powers has done vanishingly little to limit federal lawmaking, the United States has a federal system in which local decisionmaking plays an enormous role. And whatever the merits and shortcomings of the existing scope of local decisionmaking in American law, that local decisionmaking is protected by these other mechanisms, not by the Constitution's enumeration of congressional powers.

In sum, the idea that the enumeration of powers is a critical mechanism for protecting the localist half of federalism is illusory. Local decisionmaking is critically important, but the need to protect it does not argue for an enumerationist approach to federal power.

Three Functions

Constitutional lawyers think of the enumeration of powers as a device for limiting the scope of federal law. But limiting the scope of federal law is, at best, a tertiary function of the Constitution's enumeration of congressional powers. The enumeration's first two functions, both in terms of its original design and in terms of the work it actually does, are to empower the federal government and, within the federal government, to empower Congress relative to the president. The common intuition that the enumeration would not be doing its work if it did not limit the scope of federal law arises partly from a failure to appreciate these other two functions of the enumeration.

Consider the enumeration's separation-of-powers function first. As described in Chapter 2, most of the congressional powers enumerated in Article I, Section 8, were probably included not to allocate power between the federal government and the states but to empower Congress against the president. Given background assumptions from sources like Blackstone about what powers were properly exercised by the executive, the Framers needed to specify expressly that many of the national government's powers would be vested not in the president but in Congress. And the Constitution's assignment of enumerated powers to the different federal branches has done practical work in a range of constitutional controversies.[5] Indeed, given how little the enumeration has done to limit the federal government in the modern era, it seems clear that it has done at least as much work during that period on separation-of-powers issues as it has done to limit federal power.

Constitutional lawyers consistently slight this separation-of-powers function and think instead of the enumeration of powers predominantly or even wholly as a matter of federalism. The typical formulations of the enumeration principle obscure the work that the enumeration does for the separation of powers by presenting the enumeration of powers as something that pertains to the federal government as a whole. For example, Chief Justice Rehnquist wrote in *United States v. Lopez* that "[t]he Constitution creates *a Federal Government* of enumerated powers."[6] In *National Federation of Independent Business v. Sebelius* (NFIB), Chief Justice Roberts similarly wrote that "*[t]he Federal Government* 'is acknowledged by all to be one of enumerated powers.'"[7] According to these formulations, the entity whose powers the Constitution enumerates is *the federal government*. But when the Constitution enumerates powers, it rarely if ever assigns those powers to the federal government as such. It enumerates powers belonging to the specific institutions that make up that government. Enumerated powers are assigned to Congress, and in a few cases to the houses of Congress separately, and to the president, and in a way also to the courts, in the form of an enumeration of the kinds of cases in which the courts can exercise jurisdiction. Virtually every power reposed in the federal government is assigned not to the federal government as an undifferentiated entity but to some specific actor within it. This fact about the Constitution's scheme for assigning powers does not make the normal formulations false: it is reasonable to describe a power held by Congress or the president as a power of the federal government. But by describing the entity whose powers the Constitution enumerates as *the federal government*, this way of speaking suggests that the importance of the enumerated-powers framework is its capacity to answer questions of the form, "Is that something that the federal government, as such, can do?" That question is a matter of federalism. But the system of enumerated powers is not only about federalism. It is also fundamental to the separation of powers, because the enumeration assigns powers not to the federal government in general but to Congress, the president, and the courts, separately.

The enumeration of powers does also play an important role in federalism. But most of the work it does in federalism is not a matter of limiting national power and thereby preserving meaningful decisionmaking by the states. It is a matter of the other half of federalism: empowering the national government where it ought to be empowered. In principle, of course, the enumeration could be a device for both empowering and limiting the national government, and both conceptions of its function have been present from the beginning. But it probably always made more sense as a device of empowerment than as a device of limitation. At least some of the leading Framers understood it that way, and over time it has turned out to be a much more effective device for empowering the national government than for limiting it.

Noticing the enumeration's separation-of-powers function of empowering Congress against the president can be a helpful step toward recognizing what is problematic about expecting the enumeration to limit Congress in its relationship with the states. Nobody, upon learning that many clauses of Article I, Section 8, were included in order to allocate power between Congress and the president, has the intuition that those clauses are there to protect the president's autonomous decisionmaking by limiting what Congress can do. Instead, one quickly grasps that the affirmative specification of one party's powers is a mechanism to empower that party: to give Congress a clear warrant, in writing, to exercise powers that might otherwise be contested. The situations are not entirely analogous: given differences between Congress's relationship to the president and its relationship to the states, it is possible to think of the same enumeration of powers as primarily empowering in the first context and primarily limiting in the second. But perhaps it is only the assumptions of enumerationism that would push one to that interpretation. At the very least, the reasonable intuition that it would be odd to regard the enumeration of congressional powers as primarily a device for protecting the president's autonomy from Congress might cause one to question the ease with which we assume that the same enumeration is primarily a device for protecting the autonomy of the states from the federal government.

Enumerated Powers and Reserved State Spheres; or, the Trouble with Dual Federalism

To understand the problems with expecting the enumeration of congressional powers to protect autonomous local decisionmaking, it is useful to begin by asking what vision of American federalism would make the most sense of the conventional view. The simplest way to think of the enumeration as preserving space for autonomous decisionmaking by state governments is by imagining that all possible policymaking space is divided into two domains. One domain, which the enumerated powers define affirmatively, consists of the subjects that Congress is authorized to superintend: taxation for the general welfare of the United States, borrowing on federal credit, regulating commerce (except, on the prevailing reading, for wholly intrastate commerce), and so on. The other domain, which the enumerated powers and the Tenth Amendment define negatively and implicitly, consists of all other matters that a government would need to address. Those matters are beyond the federal government's enumerated powers and accordingly reserved exclusively for the state governments. Because the second domain is defined negatively and implicitly, there is no comprehensive list of its subdomains. But by convention and tradition, constitutional lawyers know what some of the included topics are: education, family law, and so on. Prior to the New Deal, prevailing judicial opinion held that it included productive activities like agriculture and manufacturing. In the academic literature, the model on which the federal and state governments are responsible for regulating separate domains of the social world along the lines described above is usually called "dual federalism."[8]

If American federalism worked as the dual-federalism model imagines, then limiting the federal government to a set of enumerated powers really would preserve many domains of regulation for state decisionmakers alone. But as perceptive students of American federalism have long understood, the dual-federalism model relies on an unrealistic picture of social life as occurring in discrete domains that can be parceled out to different regulators, rather than recognizing how pervasively these spheres in fact overlap. In real life, "taxation," "commerce," "education," and "the family" do not define mutually exclusive regulatory realms. Instead, human behavior falling into one such category often also falls into other such categories. By the same token, the regulation of one such category is often tantamount to the regulation of other such categories. The terms of employment for schoolteachers could be regulated either as a matter of education policy or as a matter of interstate commerce. An international adoption is both family law and foreign affairs. The siting and maintenance of highways involves both local land use and national transportation policy. It follows that enumerating federal powers is a highly imperfect method of guaranteeing that particular domains of decisionmaking will be reserved exclusively for the states. If the social world were in fact composed of twenty discrete realms of potential regulation, then it would be possible to make realms seven through twenty into domains of exclusive state decisionmaking by saying that the federal government could regulate only realms one through six. But if realms seven through twenty overlap with realms one through six, then giving the federal government power over realms one through six means that states will not have exclusive control over realms seven through twenty.

Early in the Constitution's history, when federal regulation was sparse, it was perhaps possible to deny this reality, or at least to keep consciousness of it small. Through the nineteenth century and into the twentieth, courts often analyzed constitutional questions on the dual-federalism model. But as federal regulation became more common, the mental gymnastics required to classify state and federal law as occupying conceptually different regulatory spheres grew increasingly awkward.[9] By the time of *Wickard v. Filburn*, when the Supreme Court gave up the project of distinguishing the regulation of "commerce" from the regulation of "manufacture," judges and scholars seemed comfortable (or at least reconciled to) acknowledging that the separate-spheres idea was no longer tenable.[10] On a realistic understanding of the American system, the federal and state governments do not have wholly separate regulatory domains. There are considerable areas of overlap. So even if Congress can exercise only its enumerated powers, and even if those powers limit what Congress can do, it is clear that those powers permit Congress to regulate at least some of the same subjects as the states. And if the areas of concurrent jurisdiction turn out to be large, Congress will be able to displace a great deal of state regulation.

A constitutional system concerned with preserving state decisionmaking on particular subjects might rationally address this reality by affirmatively prohibiting Congress from regulating in certain domains, rather than trusting that the powers given to the national government would not reach into those domains and overlap with (or overtake) state decisionmaking. After all, if the goal is to reserve domains like agriculture, education, and family law for state decisionmaking, the most straightforward course of action would be to write constitutional clauses saying "The power to make policy on matters of agriculture (or education, or family law) shall reside exclusively with the states." Or "Congress shall make no law respecting agriculture (or education, or family law)." This is a solution based on external limits, not internal ones.

With a small number of notable exceptions, most of which long ago ceased to be operative, the Constitution has not used the strategy of affirmatively allocating specified policymaking domains to the states.[11] Instead, the Tenth Amendment provides as a general matter that powers not delegated to the United States are reserved to the states. But the Tenth Amendment gives no guidance about what substantive areas of policymaking are supposed to belong to state officials, other than to say that they are the ones not delegated to the federal government. Nothing in the Tenth Amendment indicates that state decisionmaking is especially to be protected in the realm of agriculture, or manufacture, or education, or family law. When constitutional doctrine tries to use the Constitution's text to identify policymaking domains allocated exclusively or predominantly to state decisionmakers, it must do so by making negative inferences from the enumeration of congressional powers rather than by reference to affirmative specifications.

So to the extent that enumerating the powers of Congress is deployed as a mechanism for preserving meaningful policymaking authority at the state and local levels, it is being used to accomplish something that a different kind of mechanism—external limits—would accomplish more directly. To be sure, the most direct way is not always the best way. Indirection is sometimes clever, and it is an orthodox principle in constitutional law that this particular indirection is a central aspect of the Constitution's wisdom. But sometimes an apparent mismatch between a stated end and a chosen means really is a mismatch. And sometimes the difference between a brilliant indirection and a simple mismatch is visible in the results. After all, things often go wrong when a tool is pressed into service for the wrong job.

The Limits of Internal Limits

From time to time, courts and commentators continue to write as if the Constitution implicitly (but authoritatively) recognizes some set of substantive regulatory concerns as the exclusive domain of state governments.[12] But a more moderate position is more common. Most jurists recognize that federal regulation touches a great many "spheres" of social life, even if they think it validly does so only as the incidental byproduct of the exercise of enumerated powers aimed at other concerns. So rather than insisting on mutually exclusive spheres of governance, judges standardly say that certain domains (including education, family relationships, and even criminal law) are *mostly* or *presumptively* for the states. In Justice Sandra Day O'Connor's formulation, courts limit the scope of Congress's enumerated powers "to protect historic spheres of state sovereignty from *excessive* federal encroachment."[13] Exercising the tools of soft judicial review, courts read federal statutes reaching those areas narrowly. That practice seeks to maintain the enumeration as a limiting force, but it generally accepts the idea that Congress's enumerated powers enable Congress to impose itself even within presumptively state domains if it chooses to. So for the most part, the crux of modern enumerationism's claim about the internal limits of Congress's powers is not that those limits keep Congress categorically out of certain regulatory domains. It is that the enumeration keeps the overall federal regulatory footprint relatively small. Yes, Congress's enumerated powers allow it to engage in policymaking with respect to education, family law, crime control, and other matters traditionally thought to be of local concern, because the domain of the enumerated powers sometimes overlaps with those subject matters. But a considerable amount of what happens in these domains is still beyond the reach of federal power.

Figure 8.1 illustrates this conception of federalism. The powers of Congress, represented by the two concentric circles, occupy an important but small space within the universe of potential legislative power. The gray

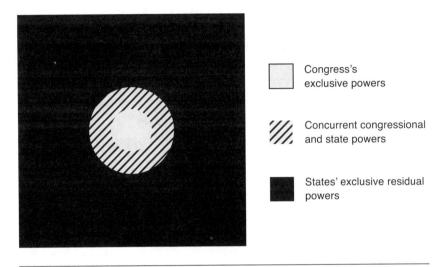

Congress's
exclusive powers

Concurrent congressional
and state powers

States' exclusive residual
powers

FIGURE 8.1 Reformatted from Richard Primus and Roderick M. Hills, Jr.,
"Suspect Spheres, Not Enumerated Powers: A Guide for Leaving the
Lamppost," *Michigan Law Review* 199, no. 7 (2021): 1431–1502, Figure 1.

circle in the center represents domains that are exclusively federal, like the
power to declare war. The striped wheel around that exclusively federal zone
represents areas of concurrent federal and state power, where states can legislate unless Congress legislates to the contrary. The recognition of this concurrent zone is an important advance over the simplest models of dual federalism. But on this conception, Congress's zones of exclusive and concurrent
jurisdiction, even when combined, form only a moderately sized island in a
considerably larger sea, shown in black. That black sea represents all other
policymaking domains, and decisionmaking in those domains belongs to the
states. Figure 8.1 thus reflects the canonical (and problematic) Madisonian
dictum with which the Supreme Court opened its analysis in *Lopez*: that federal powers are "few and defined," while those of the state governments are
"numerous and indefinite."[14]

    As it happens, though, Figure 8.1 depicts an imaginary legal system rather
than the one that actually operates in the United States. Federal law is not a
small or even moderately sized island in the sea of overall governmental regulation, nor has it been at any point in our lifetimes. Federal law is as normal
a part of the regulatory landscape as state law. Your house, your car, your
workplace, your internet connection, your medical care, your retirement

savings, the food you eat, and the air you breathe—all these things are subjects of federal law. State law is immensely important, but not because federal law is rare, and not because state law operates in a domain that Congress cannot reach.

The actual relationship between Congress's legislative powers and those of the states looks more like (but not quite like) Figure 8.2.

The sphere of exclusive federal power (gray) still appears as a small subset of all possible legislative power. But the zone of concurrent federal and state authority occupies the vast majority of the space. In that concurrent zone, states can regulate unless their regulations are preempted by federal law. Because Congress has fully preempted state law in only a limited set of areas, most subjects of federal regulation are also subjects of state regulation.[15] There is a lot of important state law out there, reflecting the regulatory choices of local policymakers.

But the zone of *exclusive* state jurisdiction is nothing like an encompassing sea. The vast body of state law lies in the zone of concurrent jurisdiction rather than in domains that Congress cannot enter because its enumerated powers have run out. What falls exclusively to the states because it lies beyond Congress's enumerated powers is at most a few disconnected ponds,

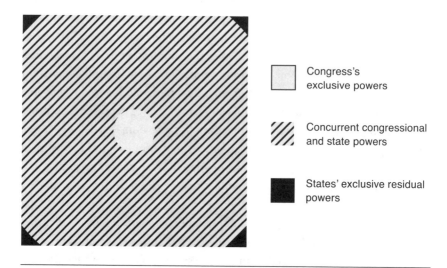

FIGURE 8.2 Reformatted from Richard Primus and Roderick M. Hills, Jr., "Suspect Spheres, Not Enumerated Powers: A Guide for Leaving the Lamppost," *Michigan Law Review* 199, no. 7 (2021): 1431–1502, Figure 2.

represented by Figure 8.2's corner patches of black. Indeed, the space that those black patches occupy in Figure 8.2 overrepresents the proportion of the social world that lies beyond the outer reaches of Congress's enumerated powers. The actual proportion is so small that it would be hard to depict graphically, except by using a substantially larger figure. As illustrated by Congress's successful workaround to *Lopez*, described in Chapter 7, a properly motivated Congress can usually find a way to regulate almost any subject matter not protected by an external limit. As a result, whatever zones of exclusive state jurisdiction internal limits might create are rather small and hard to describe as meaningful policy spaces. (The zone of exclusive power created by *Lopez* might be something like "The exclusive power to make laws regarding items that have never crossed state lines, and no component of which has ever crossed state lines, except for the power to make laws exempting such items from (a) federal taxation, (b) requirements imposed pursuant to treaties, or (c) such other regulation as may be within the powers of Congress.")

To the extent that Figure 8.2 captures the true extent of Congress's legislative powers, prohibiting the federal government from enacting any particular law does not give state decisionmakers meaningfully more regulatory autonomy than they would otherwise have enjoyed. Instead, the elimination of a given federal law often leaves a subject regulated by some other federal law rather than freeing that subject matter from federal regulation entirely. And if no other federal law already regulates the relevant policy space, it is likely that Congress could enact one, either with the same enumerated power that putatively underwrote its previous regulation or with a different enumerated power. As a result, limiting Congress to its enumerated powers is not an effective mechanism for preserving meaningful policy domains for local decisionmaking—or, more accurately, for local decisionmaking that is entirely free of federal law.

Internal Limits as (Surprise) Process Limits?

This is not to say that internal limits are completely incapable of preventing federal regulation. Workarounds are usually available, but some will be costly, whether financially or politically or otherwise, and in some cases that additional cost might dissuade Congress from enacting workaround legislation.

Suppose, for example, that the Court in *NFIB* had held that the ACA's individual mandate was valid neither under the commerce power nor under the taxing power. Congress could still have established a system of universal health insurance by creating a single-payer system, using its spending power to pay the costs of Americans' health care and its commerce power to ban (or sharply limit) the sale of private insurance. But given the financial and political costs, perhaps Congress would have decided to give up on the idea of near-universal coverage, and whatever legislation emerged instead would have been less ambitious.

Note too that the decision about whether to pursue a workaround will usually lie with a different Congress from the one that enacted the original legislation, because Congress cannot always predict that workarounds will be required. The Congresses that passed the statutes at issue in *Lopez* and *Morrison* were unaware of the internal-limit rules that would later be invoked to invalidate those statutes. In each case, the rule was announced for the first time only after the legislation was passed. If an enacting Congress does not foresee that its statute might be invalidated on the basis of an internal limit, the choice of whether to enact a workaround might be made by a different Congress that is less invested in the substance of the legislation. Consider, for example, why Congress did not use a workaround to reinstate the civil remedy provision of the Violence Against Women Act (VAWA) after *Morrison*. Congress could have reproduced VAWA's civil remedy by making the same instrumentalities-of-commerce move that Congress made to reinstate the Gun-Free School Zones Act after *Lopez*. Imagine a federal statute creating a civil remedy for crimes of gender-motivated violence committed with any product that had moved in interstate commerce. (Think about the role, in domestic violence, of baseball bats, or belts, or cars, or any of a hundred other common commercial items.) Such a workaround would not have covered every act for which the original civil remedy sought to create a cause of action, but it would cover a large portion. Nonetheless, Congress did not pursue that workaround, or any other, after *Morrison*. The reason it did not is not that no such workaround was available, nor that nobody could think of it: Justice Breyer's dissenting opinion in *Morrison* explained that Congress could work around that decision just as it had worked around *Lopez*.[16] That Congress did not enact any of the possible workarounds mostly reflects the differing preferences of Congress and the president in 1994, when VAWA was passed, and 2001, after *Morrison* was decided.

This dynamic might transform internal limits into a species of process limit—one that permitted Congress to pursue its chosen program so long as it made the heightened effort required to do so. As a general matter, the idea that sometimes the courts police federalism (or other constitutional interests) by requiring Congress to jump through extra hoops when legislating in ways that raise constitutional concerns is well known. So it is worth considering whether a properly tailored set of internal limits could have value as process limits. Requiring Congress to legislate twice, with the second time presumably coming after at least one election has intervened, could be a way to prevent Congress from legislating cavalierly at the outer margins of its jurisdiction while still permitting it to regulate at those outer margins if it evinced a sustained commitment to do so.

This model is familiar to federalism scholars from discussions of "soft judicial review" devices like clear-statement rules. According to one way of thinking, it makes sense for courts to require Congress to legislate with an especially high degree of clarity when regulating in ways that impinge on important state interests, such as by abrogating states' immunity from civil suits or restricting states' ability to choose their own officials. One classic example comes from the Supreme Court's decision in *Gregory v. Ashcroft*, which held that a federal age-discrimination statute would not be read to prevent the State of Missouri from setting a maximum age for state-court judges unless Congress made unmistakably clear that the statute was meant to cover those state officials.[17] By construing statutes not to interfere with important state interests unless Congress has made its intention to interfere unmistakable, the official reasoning runs, courts can put a thumb on the scale in favor of local control. But it is only a thumb on the scale and not a hard limit. Congress retains the ability to exercise its power as it sees fit if it musters the political will to legislate clearly.

It is worth noticing, however, that constitutional lawyers do not think of internal limits as soft-judicial-review tools like clear-statement rules. On the contrary, the idea that clear-statement rules are a form of soft judicial review is meant to contrast with the hard form of judicial review that prevailing doctrine associates with internal limits. When a court holds that some federal law exceeds Congress's enumerated powers, the thought runs, that court is saying "Congress cannot use its powers this way," not "Congress can use its powers this way if it clearly wants to and makes some extra effort." But given the availability of workarounds, it is likely that any given federal regulatory regime struck down on internal-limit grounds could be mostly restored if Congress were willing to use its enumerated powers creatively.* So the possibility that internal limits have some federalism-protective value as process limits is worth considering, but on the understanding that it would make internal limits something rather different from what constitutional lawyers have traditionally taken internal limits to be.

That said, the idea of internal-limit invalidations of federal statutes as a kind of process limit is problematic, and not merely because it requires rejecting the prevailing enumerationist account of internal limits as hard rather than soft. A second problem is that in many cases the judiciary can use an internal-limits ruling to force Congress to incur heightened process costs only if the internal-limit rule that the reviewing court enforces is one that Congress did not know about when passing the legislation at issue. After all, if Congress can design a workaround for a given internal limit, then a Congress with a reliable map of the internal limits of its powers can draft an acceptable statute the first time it legislates, rather than coming up with a workaround only after going to the trouble of legislating once and having that legislation struck down. Consider: if the Congress that passed the first Gun-Free School Zones Act in 1990 had known that Clarence Thomas would replace Thurgood Marshall on the Supreme Court a year later, and that by 1995 the Court would be inclined to say that the act's commerce rationale was not acceptable, it could have passed the 1996 version of the Gun Free School Zones Act in 1990 and saved itself the trouble of legislating again six years later.

The point can be generalized. For internal limits to function as process limits by requiring Congress to legislate twice, the specific doctrinal rules that courts invoke when striking down legislation on enumerated-powers grounds cannot be known to Congress while that legislation is under consideration, because a Congress that knows how internal-limit rules apply can figure out how to work around those obstacles. Only when Congress is unaware of an internal-limit rule can that rule exact a process toll by forcing Congress to legislate twice. The heightened process requirements that come

---

*Early in the twentieth century, the Court sometimes struck down workaround statutes on the grounds that they were mere pretexts for reaching unconstitutional ends. But as I explain later in this chapter, such judicial decisions should be understood as resting in substance on external limits, not internal ones.

with internal-limit invalidations of federal statutes arise largely by surprise. It follows that having internal limits function as process limits would require the courts, over time, to invent more and more new doctrinal rules with which to surprise Congress.

Moreover, there is little reason to think that the actual limiting effects of internal-limit rulings conceived as a species of process limit would map any consistent logic about what policies should be made locally rather than centrally. Instead, which laws Congress bestirred itself to reenact after internal-limit invalidations would mostly track accidents of timing and the vicissitudes of politics. Recall the contrast between the Gun-Free School Zones Act, which Congress reinstated, and the civil remedy of VAWA, which it did not. The difference between the two cases is not that the civil remedy was a greater incursion on important local interests. Over time, a series of decisions to which Congress did not respond could leave behind a hodgepodge of disallowed federal statutes, or applications of federal statutes, and perhaps the regulatory space opened thereby would add a bit to the regulatory space available for state policymaking. But it seems doubtful that that additional space would be large or well targeted enough to add meaningfully to the robust, extensive practice of state and local decisionmaking that exists today under a regime in which internal limits play almost no role.

But Didn't Internal Limits Work for a Long Time?

The preceding account of internal limits' unsuitability for establishing a sensible boundary between national and local policymaking might seem in tension with the way the system operated before the New Deal. The pre–New Deal Court sometimes recognized nonenumerated congressional powers, but it also struck down a nontrivial number of federal laws on internal-limit grounds, and federal regulation in that era occupied much less space than it does in the modern regime. It was only after *Holland*, *Darby*, and *Wickard* that the system became one of enumerated powers without internal limits. It might seem, therefore, that internal limits on congressional power worked pretty well as a framework for preserving large zones of exclusive state decisionmaking for the Constitution's first 150 years. If internal limits on federal law could preserve space for state policymaking at that earlier time, why could they not succeed now or in the future?

The question is worth asking. But it substantially overstates the work that internal limits did to constrain federal regulation in the generations before the New Deal. To see why, it is helpful to divide the pre–New Deal era into two periods, one before the Civil War and one after.

Before the Civil War, Congress did not regulate much. But the small size of the federal footprint might not have been due mostly to the restraining force of Congress's enumerated powers. Several other factors kept congressional regulatory ambitions modest. Most simply, a larger regulatory agenda might not have been feasible, given the practical-capacity limitations of the antebellum period. Congress might also have been constrained by its sense of what the electorate would support or its sense that some things should be exclusive domains of state regulation. Those constraints are process limits and external limits, respectively, rather than internal limits. This is not to say that the idea that Congress was limited by its enumerated powers played no role at all. Between the Jackson administration and the 1850s, the idea of a Congress limited by its enumerated powers was an important piece of the ideology holding the Democratic Party together, so it is plausible that that idea had some influence on Congress's behavior.[18] It is hard to know, however, whether that idea actually prevented Congress from enacting legislation that it otherwise would have. The enumeration principle was marshaled within Congress as an argument against legislation, but generally by people who were also opposed to the legislation on substantive grounds, such that it is hard to know whether the enumerated-powers argument did independent work.

To be sure, the number of occasions on which it is reasonable to say that internal limits did important constraining work is not zero. President Madison vetoed a major infrastructure bill supported by most of his political party in 1817, and President Monroe vetoed another in 1822. But the judiciary did not strike down a federal law on internal-limit grounds until the 1870s, and it is hard to identify occasions on which a majority of the antebellum Congress wanted to engage in some regulatory project, if only it had the power to do so, and held itself back because it believed itself to lack that power. (Again, members of Congress often asserted that as a constitutional matter Congress lacked the power to do something, but rarely was it something that the person making the assertion wished Congress could do.) So it is hard to disprove the null hypothesis that prior to the Civil War, internal limits on Congress's enumerated powers were not a major cause of the relative sparseness of federal law. To assert that internal limits actually did that work, outside of important instances like the 1817 and 1822 vetoes, might be to credit internal limits with a result determined on other grounds.

Matters changed with the Civil War. Congress became more ambitious. And between the 1870s and the 1930s, the judiciary did invalidate a variety of laws on internal-limit grounds. But for two reasons, the example of that era does not demonstrate that a jurisprudence of internal limits could preserve significant policymaking domains as exclusive state domains in the twenty-first century. The first reason is about a difference in background conditions between the two eras. The second is that even at the earlier time, judicial decisions ostensibly enforcing internal limits were often external-limit decisions in disguise.

Consider first the changed background conditions. When the nineteenth-century Congress began to enact more legislation, it did so against a background of relatively little federal law. In a world where federal regulation was sparse, the invalidation of a single law might leave the relevant subject matter unregulated by the federal government and therefore an open field for local policymaking. Over time, however, the landscape has grown more heavily populated with (uncontroversially constitutional) federal law. In to-day's densely regulated world, more than one federal law likely applies to any given subject matter, such that local policymaking must still share the environment with federal regulation even after any particular federal law is invalidated. (Think of the difference between erasing a line drawn on a mostly blank sheet of paper and erasing a line drawn on a piece of paper on which scores or hundreds of lines are already drawn.)

Second, even during the heyday of internal limits—that is, between 1870 and 1936—a fair amount of what presented itself as the enforcement of internal limits was in fact the enforcement of external limits, in the form of judicial declarations that certain domains of substantive regulation were reserved to the states. Consider *Hammer v. Dagenhart*'s invalidation of the Child Labor Act, which prohibited the interstate shipment of goods produced with child labor. The Court in *Dagenhart* did not deny that a prohibition on the interstate shipment of goods was a regulation of inter-state commerce. Instead, the Court held that Congress could not use its commerce power in a way that would impinge on the inherently local matter of manufacturing.[19] The Court's conclusion was thus driven by an external limit—a prohibition on federal interference with local control over manufacturing—rather than a conception of what constituted "commerce among the several states."[20]

Consider also the Supreme Court's 1936 decision in *United States v. Butler*, which struck down a federal program intended to stabilize the prices of farm products during the Great Depression. Under the Agricultural Adjustment Act, Congress authorized the secretary of agriculture to subsidize farmers who agreed to limit their production of agricultural commodities.[21] The Court deemed that program beyond the commerce power on the ground that agricultural production, like manufacture, was a category separate from commerce.[22] But the government also argued that the program was a valid exercise of Congress's spending power under Article I, Section 8, clause i—that is, its power to spend money to "provide for the . . . general welfare of the United States."[23] The Court acknowledged that under that power, Congress could spend for any purpose that qualified as spending for the general welfare, whether or not the spending fell within the subject matter of Congress's other enumerated powers.[24] But even if the spending were for the general welfare, the Court concluded, the program was unconstitutional, because Congress had no authority to regulate agricultural production.[25] Ostensibly, the Court's rationale for treating the regulation of agricultural production as beyond federal power was a matter of internal limits. "[P]owers not granted are prohibited," Justice Owen Roberts wrote. "None to regulate agricultural production is given, and therefore legislation by Congress for that purpose is forbidden."[26] But in substance, the Court's rationale was a matter of external limits. After all, the Court conceded that there was an enumerated power—the spending power—whose terms might cover the program. The rationale for holding the program unconstitutional was that even if the subsidies *were* spending for the general welfare, "another principle embedded in our Constitution prohibits [the program]. The act invades the reserved rights of the states. It is a statutory plan to regulate and control agricultural production, a matter beyond the powers delegated to the federal government."[27] In other words, the Court envisioned the regulation of agriculture as an exclusively state preserve, such that Congress could not regulate agriculture even if it did so with one of its enumerated powers. That is an external-limit rationale.[28]

The commerce power and the spending power are two of Congress's most far-reaching authorities. The pervasive federal footprint in modern

American law is mostly a function of those two powers, the taxing power, and Congress's power under the Necessary and Proper Clause. A system of internal limits able to keep the federal footprint small would urgently need to confine those powers. But in cases like *Dagenhart* and *Butler*, which ostensibly invalidated federal laws on internal-limit grounds, the considerations that the Court actually invoked to hold the laws unconstitutional were not accounts of commerce and spending. They were propositions about the Constitution's allocating the regulation of certain subject matters (manufacture and agriculture) exclusively to the states.

If the question is what sort of judicial doctrine would help protect local decisionmaking, reserving the regulation of certain subjects exclusively to the states makes a good deal of sense. A robust doctrine of exclusively reserved subject matters can limit congressional authority in ways that preserve meaningful and independent policymaking spaces for state governments. But that solution cannot vindicate the idea that there must be internal limits on Congress's enumerated powers, because it is a solution based on external limits rather than internal ones. Just like the Free Exercise Clause or the ban on titles of nobility, a rule that Congress may not regulate manufacture or agriculture crosscuts the enumerated powers, blocking congressional action on the basis of a constitutional concept arising somewhere outside the delegation of powers to Congress. And what the laws at issue in *Dagenhart* and *Butler* illustrate is that the enumerated powers of Congress are sufficient to allow pervasive federal regulation, except as blocked by external limits.

An interpreter committed to the enumerationist view of constitutional law could try to present reserved-sphere rules as internal limits by reading them into the interpretation of particular congressional powers. One could say, as the Court did in *Butler*, that the commerce power does not authorize Congress to regulate agriculture by defining commerce in a way that excludes agriculture. But unless one also ensured that Congress's other powers could not be used to regulate agriculture, this limitation on the commerce power would not prevent Congress from regulating in that area with some other tool. And if one purported to read the same internal limit into every one of the enumerated powers—if one maintained, in other words, that the proper interpretation of every power granted to Congress anywhere in the Constitution excluded any power to regulate agriculture—then observers might wonder whether the real operating force was an external limit prohibiting Congress from regulating agriculture, rather than a remarkable confluence of several different internal limits.

The Case of Commandeering

As in *Dagenhart* and *Butler* a hundred years ago, the modern Supreme Court sometimes presents decisions striking down federal law as internal-limit decisions even when external limits are doing the real work. Consider the anticommandeering cases. In *New York v. United States*, the Court held that Congress may not order state legislatures to pass particular laws.[29] In *Printz v. United States*, the Court held that Congress may not require state executive officials to carry out federal regulatory programs.[30] These rules against "commandeering" state officials help protect discretionary policymaking at the state level by limiting the federal government's ability to force the hands of state decisionmakers. They also help maintain meaningful state policymaking in a more diffuse way by ensuring that state officials do not come to think of themselves as agents of the national government.

The anticommandeering rules are external limits on congressional power. In substance, they are affirmative prohibitions, as the prefix "anti" aptly suggests. They reflect a judgment (correct or otherwise) that, for a combination of historical and structural reasons, Congress may not demand that state legislatures and state executives implement federal law. That judgment is not a conclusion reached by asking what might be a reasonable way of implementing each of Congress's enumerated powers, considered one by one, and discovering that for none of them does commandeering state officials make sense. It is a wholesale judgment about what is inappropriate for the federal government to do.

Not coincidentally, the Court has sometimes described anticommandeering doctrine as an external limit on congressional power. For example, in his 2000 opinion for a unanimous Court in *Reno v. Condon*, Chief Justice Rehnquist explained that a law regulating interstate commerce would be unconstitutional, even though Congress can regulate interstate commerce, if it violated the anticommandeering rules.[31] To say that a law falling within one of the enumerated powers would be unconstitutional if it violated a given rule is, of course, to treat that other rule as an external limit. More subtly, Justice Antonin Scalia's opinion for the Court in *Printz* treated the anticommandeering rules as external limits even though Scalia analyzed the constitutional question partly through the lens of a power-conferring clause of the Constitution: the Necessary and Proper Clause. The Court in *Printz* struck down a federal statute that imposed a waiting period on certain purchases of firearms and required local law enforcement officials to participate in a background-check process during the waiting periods. The portion of the law that imposed the waiting period was uncontroversially within the commerce power as a regulation of the purchase and sale of goods. According to the federal government, the portion of the law directing local officials to participate in the background checks was justified under the Necessary and Proper Clause as a means of making the regulation of commerce effective. But the Court rejected that argument. With its requirement that laws be "proper," Scalia wrote, the Necessary and Proper Clause houses constitutional rules about what federal laws may *not* do, even when enacting legislation that is "necessary" for carrying other powers into execution. Those rules include a prohibition on actions that violate "the principle of state sovereignty."[32] And in the Court's judgment, commandeering local law enforcement officials violated state sovereignty. It was therefore improper and unconstitutional.

Scalia's analysis is interesting because it located an affirmative prohibition on federal lawmaking within a clause usually regarded as power-conferring. In most cases, the question of whether some constitutional rule is an internal limit or an external one tracks the clause of the Constitution under which the question is decided. Commerce Clause questions are generally about internal limits, because the Commerce Clause is a source of congressional power; First Amendment questions are about external limits, because the First Amendment imposes affirmative prohibitions. To the extent that the Necessary and Proper Clause is a clause conferring power on Congress, questions about whether some piece of federal legislation comes within its scope are questions about internal limits, just like questions about the scope of the commerce power. And if the Necessary and Proper Clause were *only* a clause conferring power on Congress, an analysis concluding that a law was invalid because it could not be justified on the basis of the Necessary and Proper Clause would be an analysis about internal limits. But by reading the word "proper" to embody rules of state sovereignty that block federal legislation, the Court in *Printz* treated the Necessary and Proper Clause as a text that houses both grants of power and affirmative prohibitions—and therefore a potential source of external limits as well as internal ones. If the law in *Printz* had failed to come within the Necessary and Proper Clause because it was not sufficiently a mechanism for carrying some other power into execution, it would have failed for internal-limit reasons. But the actual reason it failed, in the Court's analysis, was that it violated an affirmative prohibition stemming from the principle of state sovereignty. That is an external-limit reason.*

But in 2018, in his opinion for the Court in *Murphy v. NCAA*, Justice Samuel Alito redescribed the anticommandeering doctrine as if it were a matter of internal limits. According to Justice Alito, the reason why Congress cannot commandeer state officials is that Congress may do only those things described in its enumerated powers, and nothing in the enumerated powers authorizes Congress to commandeer.[33] That cannot be a complete explanation. It is true that the Constitution enumerates no congressional power to commandeer state decisionmakers, but it also enumerates no power to charter corporations or ration the cultivation of wheat. Congress can do those things as means necessary and proper for carrying out powers that it clearly has. Why, then, is the power to direct state officials not a similarly permissible means for carrying out congressional power?[34] The best answer is the one Scalia gave in *Printz*: even if a law is a useful means for carrying a federal power into execution and would therefore be valid in the absence of some affirmative prohibition, it is not valid if some affirmative prohibition blocks Congress from using that particular means. That prohibition does not rest on the content of the particular powers Congress is given—to tax, to borrow, to regulate commerce, and so forth. It rests on a categorical judgment that it is affirmatively impermissible, for structural and historical reasons, for Congress to proceed in a certain way.

Justice Alito's attempt to characterize anticommandeering as an internal-limits doctrine is, in the language used in Chapter 5, an example of internalized argument. Like the federal-consensus view of slavery, Madison's argument against the Bank of the United States, and the action/inaction argument against the ACA, it seeks to establish a constitutional rule that is in substance an affirmative prohibition. But because no such prohibition appears

---

*When *Printz* was decided, the Court had not yet held that the Second Amendment protected an individual right to own firearms. If you have the intuition that the Second Amendment should have blocked the law in *Printz*, what is important to notice for present purposes is that a Second Amendment bar would have been an external limit—just as the anticommandeering bar was.

in the text of the Constitution, its advocates must either acknowledge the nontextual nature of the rule they seek to establish or else find some way to read the text as implying that rule. Given that choice, an advocate (including a judge) usually prefers to ground an argument in the Constitution's text, and for good reason. So when constitutional lawyers want to argue in support of a prohibition on federal lawmaking that does not appear in the text, the framework of enumerationism invites them to make their argument in terms of what can be inferred, negatively, from the enumerated powers.

But if we wish to understand the mechanisms that limit federal power, it is important to recognize that rules like the anticommandeering doctrine are, in substance, external limits rather than internal ones. Doing so helps the analysis in two ways. First, the merits of the anticommandeering doctrine are better analyzed if one has a clear view of the sort of rule that it really is. Second, misperceiving external limits as internal limits artificially inflates the apparent capacity of internal limits to constrain federal regulation and thereby protect autonomous zones of state decisionmaking. If in reality internal limits are not good tools for that purpose, we would make better decisions by recognizing that fact than by obscuring it.

The Reconstruction Powers

Anticommandeering doctrine rests less on an analysis of what is missing from Congress's enumerated powers than on a set of ideas about the distinctive status of state governments within the federal system. States are special. They are entitled to a level of protection that other entities do not enjoy, and constitutional law shields them from federal law in various ways. As in other contexts where constitutional law creates a shield to protect something special—like speech or religion—the relevant protection is best understood in terms of external limits. A shield, after all, is an affirmative prohibition.

The external limits on congressional power that arise from the special status of states play a crucial role in cases arising under Congress's enumerated powers to enforce the Reconstruction Amendments. Each of those amendments—that is, the Thirteenth, Fourteenth, and Fifteenth—ends with a clause giving Congress the power to enforce that amendment's provisions.[35] And in a set of decisions originating just two years after *Lopez*, the Supreme Court has held provisions of federal law invalid on the grounds that they exceed Congress's power to enforce the Reconstruction Amendments. Leading decisions in this category include *City of Boerne v. Flores* (1997), which curtailed the Religious Freedom Restoration Act, and *Shelby County v. Holder* (2013), which invalidated a critical portion of the Voting Rights Act.[36] The laws at issue in those cases were major federal legislation, and the Court's rulings had serious practical consequences. And in an important sense, *Boerne* and *Shelby County* are internal-limit decisions: the Court in both cases held federal legislation unconstitutional on the ground that it was justified by no enumerated power. These cases might therefore seem to demonstrate that internal limits really can impose significant limits on congressional power. But in fact, what blocks federal regulation in cases like *Boerne* and *Shelby County* is not the force of internal limits alone. It is the interaction between the internal limits of Congress's Reconstruction powers and a set of external limits—in essence, the same state-protective external limits that animate the commandeering cases.

Like the commandeering cases, *Boerne* and *Shelby County* are about Congress's authority to regulate state governments. The law at issue in *Boerne*—the Religious Freedom Restoration Act (RFRA)—forbade state governments to "substantially burden a person's exercise of religion" except as necessary for furthering compelling governmental interests.[37] According to the federal government, RFRA was legislation enforcing the Fourteenth Amendment's guarantee of religious freedom. The law at issue in *Shelby County*—section 4(b) of the Voting Rights Act—created a formula for prohibiting many state and local governments from altering their election practices without permission from federal authorities. According to the federal government, section 4(b) was legislation enforcing the Fourteenth Amendment's guarantee of equal protection and the Fifteenth Amendment's prohibition on racial discrimination in voting. The Supreme Court disagreed in both cases, concluding that the burdens Congress had imposed on state governments went beyond what could be justified in the name of enforcing the Reconstruction Amendments. So on the ground that no enumerated power justified the laws, the Court declared them unconstitutional.

Cases like *Boerne* and *Shelby County* accordingly do impose internal limits on enumerated congressional powers, and they do so in a way that has invalidated meaningful federal legislation. But to assess the significance of internal limits in these cases, it is important to understand why Congress needed to justify the relevant laws as legislation enforcing the Reconstruction Amendments in the first place. The reason, in essence, is that an affirmative constitutional prohibition protecting state governments against federal regulation—an external limit—prevented Congress from enacting RFRA and the Voting Rights Act as exercises of its Article I powers. Without that external limit, the internal limits of the Reconstruction powers would not have mattered.

For reasons of federalism, the Supreme Court has held that Congress cannot use its commerce power to single out state governments for regulation. If Congress regulates private entities under its commerce power, it can also apply the same regulation to state governments. Thus, every state government is an employer, and commerce clause legislation regulating employers can be applied to state government employers on the same terms as private ones. But Congress cannot use its commerce power to regulate state governments except with laws of general applicability.[38] Presumably, then, Congress could have enacted a law like RFRA that prohibited any entity substantially affecting interstate commerce, including state governments, from substantially burdening the free exercise of religion. (Federal employment law uncontroversially requires covered employers to make reasonable accommodations for employees' religious practices.) Similarly, one could imagine a federal law, applicable to all entities substantially affecting interstate commerce, providing that any election organized by a covered entity must conform to specified conditions. But RFRA and the Voting Rights Act were laws aimed specifically at state governments, and such laws, the Court has held, cannot be enacted with the commerce power. For reasons of federalism, the activities of state governments are partially shielded from federal law.

The Reconstruction Amendments allow Congress to overcome that shield. Those amendments were adopted as the result of a civil war that asserted the primacy of the national government over the states. The Fourteenth and Fifteenth Amendments protect fundamental constitutional rights against violation by state governments, and the power to enforce those amendments is, appropriately, a power to make law that binds state governments. The extent to which Congress can use the Reconstruction Amendments to regulate the behavior of state governments is limited, of course, by the internal limits of Congress's Reconstruction powers. Congress can override state-government immunity when it is acting within its Reconstruction powers but not when it exceeds those powers.

But the internal limits of the Reconstruction powers are internal limits *on a power to override an external limit*. The reason why Congress resorts to its Reconstruction powers to enact laws like RFRA and the Voting Rights Act is not that its other powers are inherently inadequate to justify such legislation. It is that the special status of state governments generates affirmative prohibitions—external limits—that block certain uses of other congressional powers. Absent the prohibition on Congress's using its commerce power to legislate specifically for state governments, Congress would not need the Reconstruction Amendments to impose regulation like that at issue in *Boerne* and *Shelby County*, and the internal limits on the Reconstruction powers would not prevent Congress from enacting that regulation.

If the Reconstruction Amendments did not exist, and Congress had no power to override the states' partial shields against federal legislation, it would be more clear that what blocked Congress from imposing laws like RFRA and section 4(b) of the Voting Rights Act on state governments was a set of external limits. Because Congress does have a set of powers capable of overriding the relevant prohibitions on regulating state governments, the internal limits of those powers matter: they define the cases in which Congress can overcome the shield. So it is true that *Boerne* and *Shelby County* are examples of cases in which the internal limits of congressional powers— specifically, the Reconstruction powers—prevented the federal government from imposing consequential systems of regulation. But to attribute that limit on federal lawmaking to those internal limits is a bit like saying that a person cannot walk through a wall because there is no available doorway. The point is correct as stated. But it should not divert our attention from the work that the wall is doing.

Federalism without Internal Limits

The limited capacity of internal limits to constrain federal power in no way suggests the demise of local decisionmaking. State governments exercise considerable sway over a broad swath of important policymaking domains. The list above of everyday domains that are subjects of federal law—your house, your job, your car, the food you eat, and the air you breathe—is also a list of subjects of state law. So the inability of internal limits to protect enough autonomous state policymaking to make federalism worthwhile has not nullified the important role that state and local decisionmakers play in the federal system. Local decisionmaking is simply perpetuated by other mechanisms—and more or less always has been.

A few of these mechanisms are external limits on Congress's powers. State immunity doctrines—including but not limited to the ones that figure in cases arising under the Reconstruction Amendments—are external limits. So are the anticommandeering rules. Congress may not tax a state's own tax revenue, and that prohibition plays an important role in guaranteeing a meaningful decisionmaking role for state governments because the ability to raise money independently is a crucial tool in policymaking.[39] Congress may not dictate the location of a state capital.[40] Perhaps most fundamentally, Congress may not unilaterally terminate or reconfigure existing states.[41]

The Supreme Court's decision in *NFIB* offers a good illustration of the different capacities of internal and external limits to preserve space for state decisionmaking. As discussed earlier, the conclusion of five justices that the Commerce Clause (alone or in combination with the Necessary and Proper Clause) did not authorize the individual-mandate provision of the ACA did not actually invalidate the individual mandate. A majority upheld the mandate as an exercise of the taxing power, and even the dissenters agreed that Congress had the authority to impose such a regulation with its taxing power; they just disagreed about whether Congress had actually done that when drafting the ACA. In short, *NFIB* does not showcase much in the way of internal limits' capacity for limiting what Congress can do. But in a different part of that case, the Supreme Court did impose a meaningful limit on Congress, and it was an external limit rather than an internal one. The ACA substantially expanded the coverage of Medicaid, and it made the federal government's continued disbursement of Medicaid funds to state governments conditional on the states' agreeing to that expansion. That condition would have all but guaranteed that every state would accept the expanded version of Medicaid, because no state could easily sustain the loss of the Medicaid funds it was already getting before the ACA. In other words, the ACA used conditional funding to take the decision of whether to expand Medicaid out of the hands of the individual states. And to protect the states' abilities to make their own decisions, the Court disallowed that use of conditional funding.

According to a seven-justice majority, the conditional-spending provision of the ACA's Medicaid expansion was invalid because it was tantamount to Congress's compelling the states to participate in that expansion, and

Congress is forbidden to compel states to enact or administer particular regulatory programs.[42] That prohibition is the same one animating the anticommandeering rules of *New York* and *Printz*, and the rationales given in *NFIB* echoed and cited those cases.[43] Like the anticommandeering rules, it is an external limit. After all, the principle that Congress may not compel the states to regulate is not particular to the spending power. It rests on a principle of federalism that transcends any specific enumerated power and blocks otherwise valid uses of any of the powers listed in Article I, Section 8. And unlike the internal limit on the Commerce Clause that five justices endorsed, the enforcement of this external limit materially affected the amount of policymaking discretion that state decisionmakers enjoyed. It meant that the choice of whether to expand Medicaid could be made differently by decisionmakers in different states.

Figure 8.3 represents the zones of federal and state legislative jurisdiction when external limits are made part of the picture. As in Figures 8.1 and 8.2, there is a zone of exclusive federal power—the gray circle—which includes things like the power to declare war. But now there is also a zone of exclusive state power—the black circle. Unlike the large black field in Figure 8.1, this zone of exclusive state jurisdiction is not defined negatively, as the residuum left behind after Congress's enumerated powers have run out. It is defined affirmatively by external limits. The space that belongs to states residually because Congress cannot reach it with its enumerated powers is still a few marginal and disconnected patches, as it was in Figure 8.2. And again as in Figure 8.2, most of the space is a zone of concurrent federal and state jurisdiction, where states can regulate unless preempted by contrary federal action.

The space that the black circle in Figure 8.3 represents is important. It matters that Congress cannot commandeer state officials, tax a state's own tax revenue, and so forth. But most of the meaningful authority that states wield does not lie within the black circle. It lies in the much larger zone of concurrent jurisdiction. Because authority in that zone is concurrent, state decisionmaking could be eliminated by preemptive federal law. But the fact that Congress has the authority to eliminate state decisionmaking from this zone does not mean that state decisionmaking in that zone is illusory as a matter of the actual functioning of American federalism. After all, there are many things that Congress has the authority to do but that we can be reasonably sure will not happen anytime in the foreseeable future (like enacting

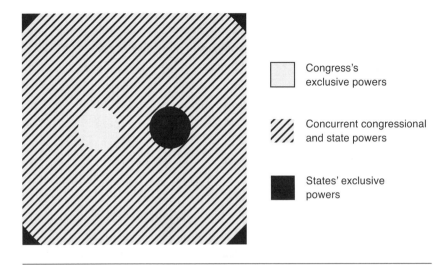

FIGURE 8.3 Reformatted from Richard Primus and Roderick M. Hills, Jr., "Suspect Spheres, Not Enumerated Powers: A Guide for Leaving the Lamppost," *Michigan Law Review* 199, no. 7 (2021): 1431–1502, Figure 3.

a 99 percent income tax, or replacing the current design of the American flag with a smiley face).

Some of the mechanisms that preserve meaningful spaces for autonomous state decisionmaking in the zone of concurrent jurisdiction are process limits (as is true for the 99 percent income tax and the smiley-face flag). As discussed earlier in this book, the Framers invested more heavily in process limits than in either internal or external limits when thinking about how their envisioned system would keep the national government from encroaching too far on what should be state and local policymaking domains. To be sure, the process limits that shape American federalism today are not coextensive with the process limits that the Framers imagined. Some of those limits never worked the way the Framers imagined they would, and others have been repudiated by constitutional amendment or undermined by changing practices and attitudes over time.[44] Nonetheless, process limits remain important aspects of American governance, in ways that include both formal and informal interactions between federal decisionmakers and their state counterparts. For a variety of reasons that prior scholarship has canvassed, state and local officials have substantial influence in the shaping of federal law, and they regularly deploy that influence to prevent federal authority from unduly contravening local interests or sidelining state deci-sionmakers.[45] One should not romanticize or overstate these mechanisms. The idea that political-process mechanisms will always maximize the bene-fits of local decisionmaking would be a just-so story, as would the idea that the political process always does right by any other kind of interest. But one need not subscribe to the idea that process federalism cures all ills to recog-nize that it has important effects.

A second set of mechanisms—perhaps overlapping with the first—falls within the rubric known as "cooperative federalism."[46] It is a normal feature of modern American governance that Congress works *with* states, rather than around them, when engaging in regulatory projects. The details vary from context to context, but the general picture is one in which federal law (itself partly shaped by the input of local officials) sets goals and parameters, and the federal government supplies money, expertise, and other resources, and state and local officials participate in the implementation of regulatory schemes in ways that make them real decisionmakers and not just ministerial functionaries carrying out someone else's programs. Federal statutory schemes addressing health care, social security, the environment, education, policing, transportation, and many other topics rely on the states as powerful players in deciding what will actually happen and who will get what.[47]

The Affordable Care Act provides obvious examples. One important piece of the ACA's regulatory regime was the creation of electronic marketplaces, officially called the American Health Benefit Exchanges, where consumers could buy health insurance on terms governed by the act. Congress made the exchanges state-based institutions, thus enabling state officials to decide how to implement the certification criteria that determined what plans were offered to the public in their states.[48] Some members of Congress believed that the policy of the ACA would be better carried out by a national health insurance exchange, but others took it as a matter of critical importance that the exchanges be put in state hands, and the latter view prevailed.[49] As noted above, the ACA also dramatically expanded Medicaid, which is a mas-sive cooperative federalism program: the federal government creates a frame-work and provides money, but the states provide the local knowledge and the boots on the ground that are needed to make the system actually func-tion. The workings of the program—who is covered, for what, for how much, and under what conditions—vary considerably from state to state, reflect-ing the different priorities and situations of policymakers in different states.

In short, normal federal governance involves a high degree of state involvement as a matter of routine, from law enforcement to the environment to highway management to social security. This way of operating is not a matter of congressional grace. It is a structural aspect of modern American government, shaped by the capabilities of the state governments and the limitations—practical rather than legal—of the federal government.[50] As of this writing, more than a trillion dollars in "federal" expenditures in every fiscal year since 2020 has been spent not directly by the federal government but by state and local governments administering cooperative federalism programs.[51] Even if Congress wanted to, the federal government could not tomorrow (or next year, or in five years) displace the states from their roles in governance under this system, in part because it could not simply summon into existence the personnel and institutional capacity that would be necessary for doing so.

Given that reality, state governments have considerable latitude to make decisions about the public policies that federal statutory schemes represent. Cooperative federalism is cooperative (or uncooperative) rather than dictatorial: the states are not passive conveyor belts for the implementation of federal programs.[52] State and local officials negotiate and bargain with federal officials, often modifying and sometimes obstructing or even undermining federal policy. Their opportunity to do all those things yields (among other things) the range of benefits that the literature on federalism standardly identifies as virtues of local decisionmaking: local knowledge brought to bear on local questions, local responsibility for those decisions, regulatory diversity, broadened opportunities for civic engagement and political leadership, and so on.[53] State officials' choices within these schemes are constrained by boundaries set at the national level, but that is true of any system of state autonomy that respects the principle of federal supremacy—or even just constitutional supremacy.

Again, process mechanisms and cooperative federalism do not magically produce the best possible governance. Sometimes the dynamics described above are wasteful. Sometimes they blunt salutary federal policies. But for present purposes, the question is not whether these features of modern federalism are optimal. It is whether they create space for meaningful state and local policymaking in a world where Congress is not practically constrained by internal limits. The answer to that question is yes. The example of the exchanges under the ACA is again instructive. In making the exchanges state-based institutions, Congress was not simply burdening state bureaucracies with an unwanted responsibility. Many state officials *wanted* responsibility for the health-care exchanges, because they understood the enormous power that would come with that responsibility. And in the years after the ACA became law, states that wanted to impede federal policies embodied in that act had ample opportunity to do so, and many issues about how health insurance and health care were actually delivered were fought out state by state.

Despite the thick reality and enormous importance of cooperative federalism, some constitutional lawyers have the intuition that the federalism involved in these schemes is, in the words of one Supreme Court opinion, "faux-federalism."[54] *Real* federalism, the intuition runs, does not reside in complex regulatory systems that are, at bottom, creations of Congress. On this view, the federalism that the Constitution ordains requires a more thorough separation between that which is national and that which is local—a separation more consistent with the values of early Americans who distrusted (or are imagined to have distrusted) central authority.[55] And that separation, the Supreme Court has explained, depends on the federal government's being limited by the scope of its enumerated powers.[56] But as the federalism scholar Abbe Gluck has cogently explained, the idea that that kind of separation can deliver the benefits of federalism depends on the existence of significant regulatory domains where state governments are the only policymakers—and there are no such domains.[57] In a world where dual federalism is gone and federal regulation is pervasive, disallowing this or that law as beyond Congress's powers will never yield the kind of separation that once made it sensible to think of state policymaking as independent of, rather than as constantly interacting with, federal governance.

The older vision of separate-sphere federalism has a strong hold on American imaginations. Its simplicity and historical resonance make it appealing, especially when contrasted with the bureaucratic technicality that cooperative federalism embodies. Fundamental constitutional intuitions are usually conceptions that well-socialized Americans appreciate without specialized professional training. We learn them as part of our civic education long before we arrive at law school. Because cooperative federalism is complex and bureaucratic, it does not lend itself well to the civics lessons of early life. Depicting its mechanisms can require multipage interlocking organizational charts, and the romantic national-identity aspects of federalism tend not to resonate in discussions about, say, the criteria for federal funding of state-initiated roadside lighting projects. But if the question is how American governance actually works—a question that should concern practical people, and a question that courts should keep in mind when exercising their considerable disruptive power—then cooperative federalism is a central part of the answer. It is what the bulk of federalism looks like in the United States in the twenty-first century, and it provides many of the benefits that make local decisionmaking valuable.

None of the mechanisms discussed here will provide the benefits of local decisionmaking perfectly. No system could do that, even if everyone agreed on what federalism was supposed to achieve. But process federalism and cooperative federalism yield the benefits that make federalism valuable more robustly than any system of internal limits has in a long time. Perhaps, during a particular phase of American constitutional development—after Congress acquired the capacity to legislate robustly but before it created a large volume of federal law—internal limits could sometimes do what enumerationism expects them to do. Even in that phase of the system's development, however, it is not clear that internal limits executed that function without the support of an underlying theory of separate spheres that courts were willing to enforce through external limits on federal power. In sum, internal limits are not doing the work, and yet federalism abides.

Official Stories and the Attitude of Federalism

If the account I have presented is correct, then limiting Congress to its textually enumerated powers is neither necessary nor particularly helpful in the maintenance of American federalism. But my analysis has assumed that most American officials, whether state or federal, believe that decisionmaking should in some way be allocated between national and local policymakers rather than being entirely centralized. So before concluding this chapter, it is worth considering another kind of concern about the damage that discarding enumerationism's commitment to internal limits might do to federalism. In particular, one might worry that it would undermine the attitude of commitment to federalist governance that sustains the current system.

Part of what maintains the dynamics of interaction between state and federal officials is a set of ideas about what each government is supposed to do. Process federalism and cooperative federalism are shaped partly by practical conditions and partly by a set of attitudes, and the two are mutually reinforcing. The mechanisms persist in part because the players who deliberate and negotiate and decide are inclined to consider local decisionmaking valuable. People's ideas about which government should do what are far from uniform, of course. But a certain amount of shared sense among officials and the public to which they respond is an important element of the system, and a wholesale shift in attitudes might cause existing dynamics to unravel. Not quickly: the limits on federal power are rooted in practical considerations as well as attitudinal ones, so it would take a fair amount of institutional reconfiguration to overcome those limits even if federal officials wanted to do so. Indeed, the practical difficulty of shifting more and more responsibility for governance to the center is one important force deterring any such ambition. But in principle, and over time, a broad and deep shift in attitudes could facilitate large changes in the dynamics of federalism.

That being the case, it is worth considering whether the official story embodied in enumerationism plays a role in preventing such a development. It is surely the case that official stories shape the way Americans think their system of government is supposed to operate. An articulated principle under which the powers of Congress are inherently limiting might teach Americans—including both officeholders and at least some of the civically literate citizens to whom they respond—to think twice about whether a given project is appropriate for the exercise of central power. If the internal-limits canon were repudiated, one of the influences supporting that consciousness would disappear. And that, one might worry, could gradually contribute to the disintegration of what has been a relatively healthy federal system.

One can only speculate as to the gravity of this concern. Different people will have different intuitions, just as people through the centuries have had different intuitions about whether preserving decency and social order requires public affirmation of orthodox religious beliefs. The internal-limits canon is salient within official ideas about federalism, but that does not tell us how much weight it bears in the attitudinal architecture. Maybe it is important.

But maybe it is less essential, for this purpose, than people who have learned it as a fundamental principle might assume. Many other influences also contribute to the attitudes necessary for maintaining a limited national government, some conceptual and some practical. The external limits that protect state decisionmaking are one set of examples. Others include the many canons of statutory interpretation that embody and reinforce the idea that national governance should not impinge too much on state governance. Absent clear statements to the contrary, federal statutes are not read to intrude on traditional state criminal jurisdiction, or to abrogate state sovereign immunity, or to preempt state law, or, speaking more generally, to alter an existing balance between federal and state power.[58] Perhaps moving away from enumerationism as an official account would provoke the loss of those canons of interpretation as well. But if those canons are actually doing work to help preserve what is valuable about federalism, then perhaps they and a host of other forces would go on teaching the basic lesson even without being supplemented by the particular practice of speaking, emptily, about the internal limits of enumerated powers.

Moreover, if we were to try to figure out how removing enumerationist ideas from constitutional discourse might shift attitudes, we should consider the possibility that enumerationism *undermines* as well as enhances the idea that the national government has a limited regulatory role. Everyone who knows the internal-limits canon also knows that in practice the national government has long enjoyed the equivalent of general legislative power, or very nearly so. Might the takeaway message for at least some audiences be that core tenets of federalism are quaint fables that practical people should not take seriously? Or more broadly, that constitutional law is an enterprise in which we say one thing and do another? Those attitudes might be at least as damaging as letting go of enumerationism would be.

There is no way to measure the net discursive effect of the internal-limits canon on the self-limiting tendencies of national officials. But in the absence of knowledge, there are reasons for skepticism about how much attitudinal damage would result if the canon were abandoned. Maybe the formula's very familiarity leads us to overestimate not just its cogency but also its importance as an attitudinal prompt. Given that uncertainty, it seems prudent to avoid making this concern into too strong a reason for holding on to the canon, especially at a time when taking the canon seriously might cause important distortions in constitutional decisionmaking. Other things being equal, describing a system accurately seems like a better idea than describing it misleadingly.

◄◄--►►◄◄--►►

According to the official theory, the enumeration of federal powers limits federal governance in a way that fosters the benefits of federalism. But it is not actually a useful means to that end. On careful consideration, the internal limits of Congress's enumerated powers do little to constrain federal governance and even less to enhance meaningful state decisionmaking. To use a good pragmatist image: for the project of limiting the national government and opening space for meaningful local decisionmaking, the Constitution's enumeration of congressional powers is a wheel that turns no part of the mechanism.

A committed enumerationist might think that this chapter's argument is an invitation to give up too easily. Maybe it is true, the thinking would run, that internal limits do not currently limit federal governance in the way that the official theory requires. But it does not follow that the enumerated powers could not possibly play that limiting role. Maybe the fact that they do not currently play that role is the result of an erroneously broad construction of those powers since the New Deal. If the judiciary would instead adopt a properly narrow construction of those powers, the share of the regulatory landscape that Congress could reach would contract substantially. The domains where states could regulate free from (or mostly free from) federal interference would grow, and the system would work as enumerationism envisions. Perhaps that would require repudiating a tremendous amount of modern doctrine, rejecting arrangements that have underpinned American government for nearly a century. Or perhaps it could be done in some more moderate and less destabilizing way. But one way or another, one might think, the inconsequentiality of internal limits described in this chapter might not mean that the enumerated powers are inherently unable to perform the role that enumerationism wants them to play. It might just mean that we are doing it wrong, and we should start doing it better.

But there is another possibility. Maybe enumerationism expects the enumerated powers to do something that they are not well suited to do. Setting aside the official story that enumeration tells, it is not clear why one should expect a system of internal limits, based on the powers enumerated in the Constitution, to protect significant domains of policymaking as exclusive state preserves. Under any circumstances, an enumeration of national powers is at best a roundabout mechanism for preserving local power. Because the social world does not come in neatly divided categories of regulable activities, the topics that Congress is authorized to regulate will overlap with many different domains of social life. Empowering Congress to regulate a certain set of topics, or with a certain set of tools, is thus not a reliable way of preventing it from regulating particular but unspecified domains thought to be better suited for local control. The better tool for that project is a system of external limits that affirmatively protects the domains of local governance from national interference. Some, and perhaps many, of the Constitution's drafters knew that. For the most part, they enumerated congressional powers to empower Congress—both against the states and against the president—rather than to limit it. To limit the federal government, they looked mostly to the structure of the political process. When they wanted to be certain to prevent federal regulation of a certain kind—like the taxation of exports or the discontinuance of the slave trade—they wrote external limits into the Constitution. Yes, many of them may have thought that the enumeration of powers would also have a limiting function, but it was not the primary mechanism of limitation. And perhaps not coincidentally, it has not in fact done much limiting work. Early in the Republic's history, the federal footprint was small, but not necessarily because internal limits were keeping things that way. Later, during the first decades after Congress became a more ambitious legislature, internal limits put up a certain amount of resistance—but even then, external limits were doing a good deal of the work. Once Congress developed the will and practical capacity to regulate pervasively, the awkward fit between the technology of enumerated congressional powers and the aim of preventing federal regulation in specific domains made the project unsustainable. Given the record of empirical experience and the conceptual awkwardness of trying to achieve this goal with that tool in the first place, what would motivate a reasonable constitutional lawyer to try to force the enumerated powers to do the work of limitation? Aside, of course, from the demands of an orthodox but misconceived way of thinking, which teaches that things must work that way?

There's an old joke in which a police officer on night patrol comes across a drunk man crouching under a lamppost. The officer asks the drunk man what he is doing, and the drunk man explains that he is searching for his lost wallet. So the officer crouches alongside the drunk man and joins in the search. After a minute or two of looking without success, the officer asks the drunk man, "Where were you when you lost your wallet?" The drunk man points to the other side of the street. The officer, perplexed, asks the obvious next question: "So why are you looking here?" "Well," the drunk man says, "this is where the light is."

Searching for sensible limits to national lawmaking by looking at the Constitution's enumeration of congressional powers is a bit like looking for the drunk man's wallet under the lamppost. Something about the environment— the light, or the textual list of powers—makes it seem like an auspicious place to look. But the thing being sought is not there to be found.

CHAPTER NINE

WHAT THE
CONSTITUTION SAYS

T HE TIME HAS NOW come to confront, directly and systematically, the relationship between enumerationism and the text of the written Constitution. Conventionally, constitutional lawyers understand the text to establish both the enumeration principle (that is, the idea that Congress can legislate only based on enumerated powers) and the internal-limits canon (that is, the idea that Congress's powers collectively add up to less than general legislative jurisdiction). As long as those understandings prevail, the enumeration principle and the internal-limits canon will be authoritative propositions of constitutional law. One can argue about a lot of things in constitutional law, but a rule established by the text of the Constitution itself is solid—until constitutional lawyers can be persuaded that it is not, in fact, a rule established by the text of the Constitution.

The enumerationist reading of the written Constitution rests principally on three aspects of the text. First, Article I, Section 1, states that "[a]ll legislative powers herein granted shall be vested in a Congress of the United States." On the enumerationist view, the words "herein granted" indicate that Congress can exercise only the subsequently enumerated powers. Second, Article I, Section 8, contains a long list of specific congressional powers. According to the standard thinking, the fact that the Constitution enumerates particular constitutional powers rather than straightforwardly giving

Congress general legislative power indicates that Congress is limited to powers enumerated. Third, the Tenth Amendment provides that "[t]he powers
not delegated to the United States by the Constitution, nor prohibited by it
to the States, are reserved to the States respectively, or to the people." On
the standard view, that text confines the federal government to its enumerated powers. These readings of the text are conventional and even orthodox.

But considered critically, each of those readings has weaknesses. Some of
them disregard the plain meaning of the Constitution's language. Some entail
dubious assumptions about the written Constitution, the system of American
government, or both. And in all cases, less problematic readings are available.

What makes these readings of the Constitution's text seem natural is not
the words of the Constitution. It is the lens of enumerationism, which conditions readers to approach the text with a certain set of ideas about the history of the Founding and the workings of federalism. And those ideas are
flawed, as the previous chapters have explained. If one sets them aside, it is
easier to see that the Constitution's text establishes neither the enumeration
principle nor the internal-limits canon. In other words, it is consistent with
the text of the Constitution for Congress to exercise nonenumerated powers.
It is also consistent with the text of the Constitution for Congress's powers,
collectively, to enable Congress to enact any regulatory regime that it could
enact with a general police power.

The Vesting Clause

Article I of the Constitution begins as follows: "All legislative Powers herein
granted shall be vested in a Congress of the United States." That text is commonly called the Vesting Clause, or, more precisely, the Article I Vesting
Clause, because Articles II and III also begin with Vesting Clauses. And
twenty-first-century interpreters commonly attribute significance to a difference in the way the three Vesting Clauses are worded. The Vesting Clauses
of Articles II and III say, respectively, "The executive Power shall be vested
in a president of the United States of America" and "The judicial Power of
the United States, shall be vested in one supreme Court, and in such inferior
Courts as the Congress may from time to time ordain and establish." They do
not say that the president and the courts exercise the executive and judicial
powers "herein granted."

The enumerationist reading of Article I's Vesting Clause takes that difference in phrasing to indicate that the legislative powers vested in Congress are limited to those enumerated in the Constitution's text. Rather than exercising general legislative power, Congress is entitled to exercise only those legislative powers *herein granted*—that is, those powers affirmatively specified in the text of the Constitution.[1]

A formulation of the point by the leading constitutional theorist Lawrence Lessig is illustrative:

> [T]he federal government, unlike state governments, has only the powers that are delegated to it by the Constitution. The Framers made this idea explicitly clear in Article I, where they wrote, "Congress has the powers herein granted." *"Herein granted"*—not any power you might imagine a government to have; just those powers specified in the Constitution.[2]

Note that in Lessig's presentation, the principle that Congress may exercise only the specific powers mentioned in the Constitution is not an inference from the text of the Vesting Clause. It is the plain meaning of the text: the Vesting Clause makes the enumeration principle "explicitly clear."

But it doesn't. And not coincidentally, almost nobody read the Vesting Clause that way for the first two hundred years after the Constitution was ratified. Because that isn't what the clause says.

All and Only

The enumerationist reading proceeds as if the Vesting Clause said "*Only* the powers herein granted shall be vested in a Congress of the United States." If the clause were worded that way, then it would indeed say, at least as a matter of ordinary language, that Congress can exercise no legislative powers except those granted "herein." But the word "only" does not appear in the Vesting Clause. Article I, Section 1, says "*All* legislative Powers herein granted shall be vested in a Congress of the United States." Not "only."[3]

If "all" and "only" are given their normal meanings, granting an institution all powers of a certain kind is not the same as granting it only those powers. The point should not be obscure. "All men are mortal" does not mean that only men are mortal. More prosaically, if only my green socks are in the laundry, then my blue socks are not in the laundry. But if all my green socks are in the laundry, some of my blue socks might be there too. In the Constitution's discussion of Congress, the statement in Article I, Section 7, that "[a]ll Bills for raising Revenue shall originate in the House of Representatives" does not mean that the House is powerless to originate other kinds of bills. By the same token, Congress can have all legislative powers of a given kind—those "herein granted"—and also have other legislative powers. (For example, the powers that Wilson, Hamilton, and Story described as resulting from Congress's status as the national legislature. Or those that the pre–New Deal Supreme Court recognized as inherent, as described in Chapter 6.)

One should not overstate this point. The fact that "all" and "only" have distinct meanings in ordinary language does not mean that no text could use the word "all" to convey the restrictive meaning that "only" usually conveys. Language is more complicated than that. So perhaps a text using the word "all" could be properly read to mean the same thing that it would mean if the word "only" were used instead, if circumstances of context and audience understanding conspired to that end. For many supporters of the enumerationist reading, the contrasting wording of the Constitution's Vesting Clauses is just such a circumstance.

But an argument that a constitutional clause should be given a non-ordinary-language meaning should acknowledge the gap between the proffered meaning and the one that ordinary language would produce. The audience for the argument can then decide whether the reasons given in favor of the proffered meaning are strong enough to overcome whatever presumption exists in favor of ordinary language. And proponents of the enumerationist reading of Article I's Vesting Clause do not usually argue that the Vesting Clause establishes the enumeration principle even though the most straightforward reading of its text says something else. On the contrary, they seem not to notice that the clause has an ordinary-language meaning different from the one they favor.

To be sure, the Vesting Clause does not establish that Congress has powers beyond those specifically enumerated. Taken in isolation, an ordinary-language understanding of the text is consistent with Congress's having "all legislative powers herein granted" as well as some other powers, and it is also consistent with Congress's having "all legislative powers herein granted" but no others. That the text is consistent with either possibility is precisely the point. Despite the widespread acceptance of the enumerationist reading, the text of Section 1 does not say that Congress is limited to powers "herein granted." The possibility of limitation is not addressed at all.

Original Usage: The Inference from Silence

Because the ordinary-language meaning of the clause does not support the enumerationist reading, the case for that reading depends on the idea that some set of contextual circumstances warrants reading the clause to mean something other than what it most straightforwardly says. If so, it would make sense that the people who wrote it, or the people who approved it, would have understood the Clause in the light of those contextual circumstances. But as far as can be determined, almost nobody at the Founding read the Vesting Clause in the enumerationist way.

That is not to say that the enumerationist reading was completely unavailable. In the sprawling discourse of ratification, a great many people made a great many arguments—some more tenable than others. But as far as I can tell, the surviving records reveal only two instances in 1787–1788 when anyone read Article I, Section 1, to mean that Congress could exercise only powers specifically enumerated in the Constitution's text.[4] A delegate named Stephen Chambers read the clause that way at the Pennsylvania ratifying convention, and so did the pseudonymous writer Cassius in the *Massachusetts Gazette*.[5] Perhaps the argument was also made on other occasions—the documentary record is imperfect. But regardless of whether the idea was articulated on just two occasions or also on half a dozen others, it was marginal in the conversation. Apparently, the enumerationist reading was neither natural enough to be common nor persuasive enough on the few occasions when it was articulated for others to pick it up and make use of it.

The near-total absence of the enumerationist reading of the Vesting Clause from the ratification process is particularly noteworthy because issues about the extent of congressional power were central to the debate. As described in Chapter 4, the Constitution's opponents repeatedly charged that Congress in the new system would be able to wield whatever power it wanted. The Constitution's defenders denied the charge many times. If the first words of Article I stated that Congress had less than general legislative authority, why did the Constitution's defenders not say so, loudly and often? Why, for example, did Madison and Gorham not point to the Vesting Clause when

Richard Henry Lee, in Congress, demanded to know why the Constitution, unlike the Articles of Confederation, did not confine Congress to the powers expressly delegated to it?[6] Even if the first words of Article I were just a plausible suggestion that Congress was limited to its enumerated powers rather than a clear statement of the point, the Constitution's defenders would surely have used it in these arguments. They did not. In all of the *Federalist* essays, for example, thirty or so of which specifically addressed questions about the extent of congressional power, Publius invoked the Vesting Clause exactly zero times.

Evidence from the First Congress points in the same direction. In the debate over the Bank of the United States, Madison spoke repeatedly and at length, arguing that Congress could exercise only its enumerated powers and that the principle of a limiting enumeration was fundamental to the system. He needed to argue these points, because not everyone agreed. If any members of the First Congress had thought that Article I, Section 1, decided this issue in Madison's favor, someone—likely Madison—would probably have said so. But so far as the records reflect, at no point in the entire debate did Madison or anyone else arguing for the limitation of congressional power point to the language of the Vesting Clause. Nor did anyone in the oath debate offer that reading.[7]

As far as I have been able to determine, the first prominent endorsement of the enumerationist reading of the Vesting Clause came two years after the bank debate. In 1793, Hamilton wrote a series of essays contending that President Washington had unilateral authority to proclaim American neutrality in the war between Britain and France. Writing under the pseudonym "Pacificus," Hamilton argued that issuing a neutrality proclamation was an "executive act" and that the Constitution vested the president with "the executive power"—meaning, on Hamilton's account, not just a set of specified powers (to command the army and navy, to receive ambassadors, and so on) but executive power in general.[8] To support that claim, Hamilton contrasted the language of Article I's Vesting Clause with that of Article II. The difference between "All legislative Powers herein granted shall be vested" and "The executive Power shall be vested," Hamilton contended, reflected the difference between conferring a specific set of enumerated powers and conferring a type of power categorically.[9] (That argument contradicted a position Hamilton had taken in his opinion on the constitutionality of the bank bill two years earlier, when he asserted that Congress had resulting powers in addition to its enumerated ones. But when presented with the need to defend Washington's proclamation, Hamilton—writing under a pseudonym—made what arguments he could.)

Hamilton's Vesting Clause argument is well known to modern lawyers.[10] And it likely masks the fact that the argument was all but unheard of before 1793. When a lawyer knows that a constitutional interpretation that is common today is an interpretation that Hamilton gave, it is easy to jump to the conclusion that it was a standard view at the Founding—or at least a view known and taken seriously. But as described above, the enumerationist reading of the Vesting Clause was all but unknown during the ratification debates and in the First Congress, despite the prominence during those times of debates about the extent of congressional power. Against that background, Hamilton's articulation of the view in 1793 seems like innovative lawyering by an attorney for the executive branch.

What's more, Hamilton's interpretation of the Vesting Clause did not catch on after he offered it. The cause for which Hamilton was lawyering—neutrality in the French Revolutionary Wars—was enormously consequential for the new republic, and the Pacificus essay was well known. But its argument about the phrasing of the Vesting Clauses did not become a normal part of constitutional interpretation. Consider that Justice Joseph Story's 1833 *Commentaries on the Constitution of the United States* devoted more than five thousand words to a discussion of Article I's Vesting Clause and at no point even hinted at the possibility that its text might bear on the scope of the powers vested in Congress.[11] (In Story's view, the significance of the Vesting Clause's text was its creation of a bicameral Congress.) Story's discussions of the other Vesting Clauses include no mention of their being differently phrased.[12] Indeed, I am aware of only one case in the Constitution's first two centuries in which a federal court read Article I's Vesting Clause to support the idea that Congress could exercise only a set of textually enumerated powers.[13] And in academic commentary, it is hard to locate arguments from the nonparallel phrasing of the Vesting Clauses before the 1990s.[14]

None of this proves that Hamilton's interpretation was wrong. Perhaps there can be such a thing as a good interpretation of a centuries-old text that almost nobody endorsed for most of its existence, and reading creatively is part of what good lawyers do. But when Hamilton argued for an enumerationist interpretation of the Vesting Clause, it is not clear that he thought the matter all the way through. For example, Hamilton did not explain why a text that says, "All legislative powers herein granted shall be vested in a Congress of the United States" should be read as if it said, "*Only* the legislative powers herein granted shall be vested in a Congress of the United States."

Confirmation Bias

Hamilton's failure to explain why he was reading "all" to mean "only" might not have been a deliberate evasion. It is ordinary, in the process of creative lawyering, for an advocate to find a text that looks supportive at first glance and run with it, attending insufficiently to the weaknesses of his interpretation. When we want a text to mean something, we sometimes read it to mean that thing in perfectly good faith, even if a less motivated or more critical reader could give good reasons why the text should not be read that way.

The popularity of the enumerationist view of Article I's Vesting Clause among modern constitutional lawyers can be explained in similar terms. Just as we tend to misread texts to say what we want them to mean, we tend to misread texts to say what we *expect* them to mean. Most constitutional lawyers expect the Constitution to say that Congress can exercise only its enumerated powers. Every law student learns that principle. So there is a tendency to read the Constitution as if it confirmed the point. And sure enough, two features of the Vesting Clause do correspond to features of the idea that Congress can exercise only specifically enumerated powers. First, the enumerated-powers idea indicates that Congress exercises specific *powers*, plural, rather than legislative power in general—and the Article I Vesting Clause, unlike its Article II and III counterparts, speaks of "powers" rather than "power." Second, the enumerated-powers idea insists that Congress can do only things that are affirmatively specified in the Constitution, and the language of "herein granted" might reflect the idea of affirmative specification in the constitutional text. For a reader who is primed to think that the Constitution promulgates the enumeration principle, these features of the Vesting Clause might be enough to confirm the presupposition. This is probably all the more so for readers who take the enumeration principle to be, conceptually, the most fundamental thing about the powers of Congress. After all, the Vesting Clause is not some stray clause in Article I. It is the first thing the Constitution says about Congress. What more appropriate way could there be for the Constitution to begin its discussion of Congress than with a statement of the essential and distinctive characteristic of congressional power—that is, that it is confined to the powers specifically enumerated?

The trouble is that that thought process gives in to confirmation bias rather than looking to see what the text actually says. The reader already believes that the Constitution permits Congress to exercise enumerated powers only. So the reader does not notice that the text says something else. And because the meaning the reader has attributed to the text is satisfying, the question of whether Americans in 1787–1788 understood the text this way probably does not arise. It is assumed—much as most modern lawyers assume that the Founders understood "thirty-five years" in the presidential qualifications clause to mean what we mean by the same phrase. Except that the assumption in the latter case is warranted.

The Importance of Alternatives

One other factor may help support the enumerationist reading of the Article I Vesting Clause: the absence of an alternative. The difference in syntax between the Vesting Clause of Article I and the Vesting Clauses of Articles II and III presents the conscientious interpreter with a question. Why is this Vesting Clause different from those other Vesting Clauses? The enumerationist reading offers an answer. If that answer is the only one available, then it is, by definition, the best available answer.

But the enumerationist answer is not the only way to explain the distinctive syntax of Article I's Vesting Clause. It is merely the most familiar. There are at least two other possible explanations, and each of them is better than the enumerationist answer.

The Ordinary-Language Reading

Consider an ordinary-language reading of Article I's Vesting Clause. On such an approach, "All legislative Powers herein granted shall be vested in a Congress of the United States" means that when the Constitution grants a legislative power, the body in which that power is vested is Congress. Not the president, not the courts, not the states, not the people directly. Just Congress.[15]

This ordinary-language reading supplies a straightforward answer to the question of why Article I's Vesting Clause differs in syntax from the other two Vesting Clauses. If the Constitution vests all legislative power in a single branch of the government, then it treats legislative power differently from executive and judicial power. As the Founding generation well understood, the Constitution does not vest the national executive power entirely in the president, nor does it vest the national judicial power entirely in the courts.[16] (The House of Representatives's power to impeach officers and the Senate's power to confirm appointments are executive powers not vested in the president. The Senate's power to try impeachments is a judicial power not vested in the courts.) Madison accordingly characterized the Vesting Clause of Article II, which says that "[t]he executive Power shall be vested in a president," as a default rule that is sometimes overcome by specific constitutional provisions varying the general pattern.[17] In other words, "The executive Power shall be vested in a president" did not mean that *all* executive power would be vested in the president. It could not mean that, because some executive power was *not* vested in the president.[18] On this understanding, the distinctive syntax of Article I's Vesting Clause simply reflects the fact that legislative power, unlike executive and judicial power, was vested exclusively in a single branch of the national government.

Given this understanding of the clause, one might wonder about the function of the words "herein granted." If the point of the clause were to say that only Congress was vested with legislative powers, Article I could have opened with the words "All legislative powers shall be vested in a Congress of the United States" rather than "All legislative powers *herein granted* shall be vested in a Congress of the United States." But it is easy to identify nonenumerationist rationales for the "herein granted" language that make sense within an ordinary-language reading of the clause. One is that the statement "All legislative powers shall be vested in a Congress of the United States" could have been read (or misread) to mean that the new Constitution would strip the state governments of their legislative powers. The drafters surely wanted neither to convey that idea nor to invite that misreading. Perhaps the Framers could have solved that problem by writing not "All legislative powers shall be vested in a Congress of the United States" but "The legislative power[s] of the United States shall be vested in a Congress." But that formulation might have created a different problem, as the Supreme Court noted in 1792. According to the Court, "the whole legislative power of the United States" included the power of establishing (or disestablishing) the Constitution, and that power belonged to the people rather than to Congress.[19] Understood in either of these ways, the "herein granted" language of the Vesting Clause does reflect a gap between the legislative powers vested in Congress and the complete universe of legislative power within the United States. But neither explanation suggests that the particular legislative powers enumerated in the Constitution must be the sum total of congressional power.

The ordinary-language reading of the Vesting Clause makes more sense than the enumerationist reading. But it too can be questioned. After all, two presidential powers might be classified as legislative. They are the power to sign bills into law and the power to make treaties. If those powers are legislative powers vested in the president, then it is not true that the Constitution vests legislative powers only in Congress.

A defender of the ordinary-language interpretation could push back in several ways. For example, one might argue that "vesting" a power means authorizing a party to exercise that power unilaterally rather than authorizing that party to participate in the process in which the power is exercised. We do not say, this argument might run, that the power to lay taxes is vested in the House of Representatives, nor in the Senate. It is vested in *Congress*. On this view, the power to sign bills into law "vests" no legislative power in the president, because the president cannot make law alone. In contrast, Congress—in which legislative powers are vested—can legislate without the president if he declines to act or, with two-thirds majorities, in spite of his veto. And there are several ways to parry the treaty-power objection. First, one could argue that treaty-making does not really fall within the definition of either "legislative" or "executive" power. (That was Hamilton's view in *Federalist* 75.) Second, one could argue that "herein granted" means "granted in Article I," not "granted in the Constitution"—in which case the Vesting Clause's statement about "legislative powers herein granted" says nothing about the treaty power, which appears in Article II. Third, and in line with the theory of cases like *Curtiss-Wright*, one could deny that the treaty-making power is "granted" by the Constitution at all, because it was a power that the United States already enjoyed under the Articles of Confederation.

Reasonable people will disagree about the strength of these responses. My own sense is that the attractiveness of the ordinary-language interpretation is partly a function of how committed one is to the idea that the difference in syntax between Article I's Vesting Clause and the other Vesting Clauses must reflect something substantive. If the difference in syntax must mean something, then the ordinary-language interpretation is defensible enough. It certainly seems more defensible than the enumerationist reading. After all, it reflects the normal meaning of the words in the clause.

The Drafting-Process Reading

But there is also a third and better possibility. Perhaps the difference in syntax between the Vesting Clause of Article I and the Vesting Clauses of Articles II and III should not be read to reflect any substantive feature of constitutional law. The argument for this view begins with the recognition that not every tic of language is significant, even in the Constitution. The Constitution is a complex document, drafted by committees and worked over in an even larger group. Anyone who has had the experience of drafting documents under analogous conditions should know that the product, even when good, is unlikely to be tight and elegant in every respect. Close reading is, of course, an important part of textual interpretation: where something seems irregular about enacted language, it makes sense to ask whether the irregularity signals something substantive. But sometimes the wisest conclusion, after due investigation, is that a linguistic irregularity is an accident with no particular meaning.

Notice that constitutional lawyers' impulse to treat differences in phrasing as significant is selective. There are textual anomalies in the Constitution that we glide past, including one that appears in the Vesting Clauses. Twenty-first-century constitutional lawyers make much of the fact that the Article I Vesting Clause is phrased differently from the Article II and Article III Vesting Clauses—but the Vesting Clauses of Articles II and III are not fully parallel to each other either, and nobody seems to care. Article II begins, "The executive Power shall be vested in a president of the United States." In contrast, Article III begins, "The judicial Power *of the United States*, shall be vested in one supreme Court." Why is the judicial power but not the executive power described as a power "of the United States"? This is not a question that constitutional lawyers worry about, and reasonably not. The difference between the first clauses of Articles II and III and the first clause of Article I might be no more significant.

Attention to the Constitution's drafting history suggests that the nonparallel phrasing of the three Vesting Clauses came about for reasons having nothing to do with limiting congressional power.[20] When the Committee of Detail presented the first full draft of a proposed Constitution to the General

Convention, Article I read, in its entirety, "The stile of the Government shall be, 'The United States of America.'"[21] Article II, also in its entirety, declared that "The Government shall consist of supreme legislative, executive, and judicial powers."[22] Article III then turned to the discussion of specific institutional arrangements, beginning with the words "The legislative power shall be vested in a Congress."[23] There was no mention of powers "herein granted." Congress's Vesting Clause was, in that respect, parallel to the subsequent vesting clauses for the president ("The Executive Power of the United States shall be vested in a single person") and the courts ("The Judicial Power of the United States shall be vested in one Supreme Court, and in such inferior Courts as shall . . . be constituted by the Legislature of the United States").[24]

This draft lay before the Convention from August 6 to September 12. Most of the Convention's discussions of specific congressional powers took place during that time. So far as appears from the surviving records, no one objected to the parallel formulations. No one suggested that the legislative Vesting Clause needed to be changed to say that Congress had only the powers "herein granted," nor that it should be changed in any other way that would reflect a choice to limit Congress to the subsequently specified powers only.

Later, the Committee of Style turned the earlier draft (as amended by subsequent proceedings) into something close to the constitutional text that was ultimately adopted. Among other changes, it eliminated the prior draft's first two Articles, such that Article III became Article I by default.[25] But Article III had not been written to be the document's opening article. It had been written to follow the two introductory articles that were now gone—the ones declaring that "[t]he stile of the Government shall be, 'The United States of America'" and that "[t]he Government shall consist of the supreme legislative, executive, and judicial powers." Without those two articles, the first words of what would now be Article I—"The legislative power"—would have no antecedent reference. The Committee of Detail's draft flowed: Article I introduced the government, Article II said that the government would have a legislative power, and Article III explained where that legislative power would be vested. To instead jump right in with a sentence about some heretofore unmentioned thing called "the legislative power" may have seemed awkward. Changing the language to read "All legislative Powers herein granted shall be vested . . ." might have been nothing more than the draftsman's solution to that problem: it let the new Article I begin with a more introductory flavor. If so, and given that virtually nobody in the ratification debates or the First Congress treated the Vesting Clause's distinctive wording as significant, it seems reasonable to think that the clause's syntax is better explained as an artifact of the drafting process than as the reflection of some substantive commitment about the limited power of Congress.

If that origin story is roughly accurate—and I do not claim to have done more than make it plausible—then it would be reasonable to understand the Constitution's three Vesting Clauses in either of two ways. First, they might be read not as operative provisions whose texts are finely crafted to allocate power in distinctive ways but as topic sentences for the first three articles. On this reading, Article I, Section 1, just means "Now we're going to talk about Congress, which is generally in the legislation business," and the first sections of Articles II and III mean the same thing, mutatis mutandis, for the president and the courts. Alternatively, the Vesting Clauses might do a bit more than introduce the branches: they might introduce the branches and say, substantively, that each branch is the normal or default exerciser of a certain kind of power. But on either reading, it is a mistake to think that the difference in syntax between Article I and the other articles means that Article I's Vesting Clause says something distinctively restrictive.

◄◄‒►►◄◄‒►►

Within the practice of American constitutional law, clauses are often read to mean things different from what the drafters and ratifiers would have expected. But the recognition that the Convention probably did not mean to signal anything substantive by writing, "All legislative Powers herein granted shall be vested . . ." rather than "The legislative power shall be vested . . ." might make it easier for constitutional lawyers to question the claim that the wording directs a particular attitude toward the limits of congressional power. When one also recognizes that the words of the clause do not say that Congress is vested *only* with the legislative powers herein granted, and that virtually nobody at the Founding read the clause as having a restrictive meaning, the case for the enumerationist reading becomes quite thin. At most, it is an idea hung on a clause, rather than an idea that fidelity to the text requires.

Article I, Section 8: The Nonlimiting List

Article I, Section 8, of the Constitution contains a long list of congressional powers. This fact is commonly taken to establish, or at least to reflect, both the enumeration principle and the internal-limits canon. The intuition behind this thinking is easy to grasp. On the logic of the interpretive principle *expressio unius est exclusio alterius*—that the specification of one thing excludes other things not specified—the standard reasoning holds that the affirmative enumeration of many particular powers signals that powers *not* enumerated are beyond Congress's purview. If there are powers Congress does not have, the standard thinking continues, then the sum total of what Congress can do must be less than what it could do with a grant of general legislative jurisdiction. But this familiar way of thinking is mistaken.

Why the Enumeration Does Not Imply the Enumeration Principle

The basic intuition behind the idea that the Constitution's enumeration of congressional powers signals that Congress has only the powers enumerated is that a list of specifics is something people write when they want to distinguish those things that are on the list from other things that are not on the list. As Chief Justice Roberts put the point, "The Constitution's express conferral of some powers makes clear that it does not grant others."[26] On this way of thinking, the enumeration of powers is the output of a thought process in which some things were deliberately included and everything else deliberately excluded.

Sometimes, enumerated particulars do reflect that sort of thought process. If the syllabus says that class will meet on Mondays, Wednesdays, and Fridays, students will reasonably assume that class will not meet on Tuesdays and Thursdays (to say nothing of Saturdays and Sundays). Or imagine a set of instructions for defusing a bomb. The bomb has four wires: one blue, one green, one yellow, and one red. If the instructions for defusing the bomb say "Cut the blue and green wires," they implicitly include the thought "and *only* the blue and green wires."

But not every list—nor even every list of instructions—should be read in a limiting way. Imagine instructions not for defusing a bomb but for maintaining a clock. Like the bomb, the clock has four wires, in the same colors. The instructions say that after five years, you should replace the blue and green wires. But if you open the clock and notice that the yellow wire is frayed, it might be a good idea to replace that one, too. Or imagine that I send my son to the grocery store with a shopping list that says "Buy milk, eggs, sugar, and baking soda." Is my son authorized to buy yogurt? By itself, the shopping list cannot answer that question, even if we assume that my son is spending my money and has no grocery-buying authority except as my agent. Maybe my family has a background understanding that whoever goes to the store should always get yogurt. Maybe my son and I have previously agreed that in addition to the items appearing on a given shopping list, he is authorized to buy such other items as are necessary and proper, given the family's needs or reasonable desires. In any of those cases, the list would not reflect an intention to preclude the purchase of yogurt.

Unless a list is explicitly labeled as exclusive or nonexclusive, determining which way it should be read requires looking outside the list itself. Here are some of the relevant considerations. For what purpose was the list written? Is the enterprise for which the list is used one in which what is *not* done is as important as what *is* done? (Yes for bomb defusing, but less so for most grocery shopping.) Did the compiler (or, if this is different, the adopter) of the list intend for it to be exclusive? Are there instructions given somewhere outside the list that say how the list should be read?

In the case of the Constitution's enumeration of congressional powers, constitutional lawyers know a standard set of answers to these questions. The purpose of the list was to prevent the federal government from exercising too much power. It is important that Congress be confined to the powers on the list, because permitting Congress to exercise powers not on the list would damage federalism and endanger individual rights. The Framers intended the list to be exclusive, and the public ratified the Constitution on that understanding. Throughout history, it has been clear that Congress can legislate only using powers on the list. And indeed, there are instructions given outside the list for how to read the list: the Vesting Clause and the Tenth Amendment say that the list is exclusive. That set of answers is cohesive: each proposition reinforces the others. And the enumeration will of course appear exclusive if it is read in the light of these ideas.

But imagine a different set of premises. Suppose that the drafters of the Constitution worried less about a too-powerful Congress than about an insufficiently powerful one. Suppose that they specified particular powers of Congress not (or not primarily) as a roundabout way of denying authority to Congress but as a straightforward way of making sure that Congress would be able to exercise the powers that it absolutely had to possess—both as against the states and as against the president. Suppose, therefore, that in compiling the list of textually specified powers, it was not the case that what was left off the list was as important as what was put on the list. Suppose that reading the list as exclusive is not a necessary mechanism, or even a particularly helpful one, for protecting either federalism or individual rights. Suppose that at least some of the Framers intended the list to be nonexclusive and that the public understood that it could be read that way. Suppose that the Supreme Court prior to the New Deal often validated congressional action on the basis of powers not enumerated in the Constitution's text but deemed inherent in national sovereignty. Suppose that Article I's Vesting Clause, properly read, does not mean that Congress can exercise only the powers affirmatively specified in the constitutional text and that the Tenth Amendment does not, either (as I will explain in this chapter's next section). Indeed, suppose that the list culminates in a Sweeping Clause giving Congress the power to carry into execution "all *other* powers vested by this Constitution in the government of the United States" and that at least some of the leading Framers understood that formula to refer to nonenumerated powers that the government would have, either inherently as a national government or in light of the particular purposes for which it was created. If constitutional lawyers approached the text with those understandings, they would not take the fact that the Constitution enumerates congressional powers to mean that Congress is limited to the powers enumerated.

And lest it be forgotten, there is a basic feature of the Constitution's specification of congressional powers that makes it distinctly odd to think of Article I, Section 8, as the kind of list of particulars that is meant to be exclusive. As mentioned in the introduction, the powers of Congress enumerated in Article I, Section 8, are only a subset of the congressional powers enumerated in the text of the Constitution. Other powers are scattered throughout the document. So Article I, Section 8, cannot possibly be the kind of list that should be presumed exclusive. It is unambiguously the kind of list that is only partial. It does not follow, of course, that Congress has more powers than the (whole) Constitution enumerates. But surely it tells against any tendency to think that Section 8 is implicitly headed "These powers, and no others."

Why the Enumeration Does Not Imply
the Internal-Limits Canon

According to the conventional view, the fact that the Constitution enumerates many particular powers of Congress establishes that the Constitution
does not give Congress what modern constitutional lawyers call a "police
power"—that is, general authority to legislate on any topic, subject only to
external limits. If the Constitution gave Congress a police power, the thinking runs, it would be unnecessary for it to enumerate all these specific powers. But the conventional wisdom goes wrong by thinking that if Congress
has no general police power, the sum total of what Congress can enact must
be less than what Congress could enact with a general police power. That
thought confuses the powers of Congress with the substantive regulatory
regimes that Congress can establish with those powers. (That is, it confuses
the two variables on the table shown in Figure 7.1.) Indeed, it is flawed for
that reason whether or not Congress is limited to the powers that the Constitution enumerates.

If the world of possible regulatory projects were divided into discrete
categories, and for each such category there were only one governmental
power authorizing regulation, then a legislature with only a discrete set of
enumerated powers would indeed lack the ability to regulate in some of the
ways that a legislature with a general police power could. For example, if the
social world included a domain called "education," and the only way to regulate education was with "the education power," and Congress had a bunch
of powers not including "the education power," then Congress would lack
the ability to regulate something that it could regulate with a police power.
But as explained in Chapter 8, the social world is not organized into mutually exclusive regulatory domains, each of which can be reached only with a
specific power to regulate that domain. As a result, the enumerated powers give
Congress the ability to regulate society in ways that overlap with the various
domains that courts have sometimes described as reserved to the states.

Because Congress has no police power, it cannot justify a regulatory project simply by invoking the authority to regulate in general. It must adduce a
more particular justification. But it does not follow that there must be regulatory projects that Congress cannot justify (except, of course, where external
limits apply). Sometimes, in light of the way that a collection of powers inter-
acts with the social world, it turns out that the set of particular authorizations

is just as empowering as a general authorization would be. Put differently, the fact that the Constitution does not give Congress a general police power means that the Constitution is not *affirmatively committed* to enabling Congress to regulate in all of the ways that it could with a police power. If it turned out that the powers of Congress were less capacious than a police power would be, the Constitution would not be violated. But neither does the text of the Constitution preclude the possibility that the powers of Congress, as applied to the social world, might turn out to let Congress enact whatever regulatory projects it could pursue if it had a police power. In other words, the text of the Constitution is compatible with the alternative to enumeration that I have called the model of cumulative coverage.

Consider the following analogy. You own a business, and you employ a general manager. Several years ago, you gave the general manager a standing set of instructions about awarding salary bonuses at the end of each fiscal year. According to your instructions, the general manager should award a bonus each year to each employee who meets any of five criteria, as follows:

(a) Employees finishing their first full year of employment with your company
(b) Employees who served, satisfactorily, as official mentors to new employees
(c) Employees who have been with the company for twenty years or more
(d) Employees who have had or adopted new children during the fiscal year (on the grounds that they will now have higher expenses)
(e) Employees who outperformed their previous year's performance metrics by at least 20 percent

It seems reasonable to assume that you did not want to establish, as a general matter, that every employee would get a bonus in every year. If you had wanted that outcome, you probably would have issued a single short instruction to that effect. Instead, you identified specific reasons that would justify giving bonuses to specific employees. You might expect the result in any given year to be that some employees would get bonuses and others would not. But it could easily happen that in a given year, every employee would get a bonus, because every employee would qualify on the basis of one or more of the given criteria. If that happened, your general manager should not think, "Well, the boss clearly did not want me to give everyone bonuses, because my instructions are a list of particulars rather than an instruction to give bonuses generally. So there must be someone here who should not get a bonus, and I need to figure out how to read these instructions narrowly enough to exclude someone." Instead, the manager should give every employee a bonus—not because the instructions contain the principle "Give everyone a bonus" but because the instructions state a set of reasons for giving bonuses, and for each employee such a reason is in point. Under those circumstances, giving everyone a bonus would be consistent with the text of the instructions. It would also fulfill the policy behind the instructions, and failing to do so would subvert it. (Whether you might decide to tighten the requirements for bonuses if you discovered that year after year pretty much everybody was getting one is a separate question.)

Clause and Effect

The (flawed) intuition that a list of particular powers must leave Congress unable to do something that it could do with a police power is not the only intuition prompting constitutional lawyers to think that a construction of Congress's powers that makes them tantamount to general legislative authority cannot be right. There is also the intuition that if the Constitution lists many powers of Congress, the full list must be necessary. If the Constitution could accomplish in a clause or two what it devotes eighteen clauses to accomplishing, the thought runs, its drafters would not have bothered to write eighteen separate clauses. This intuition matters because the process by which the enumerated powers of Congress have come in practice to be something close to general legislative power has been dominated by the expansive use of a small number of powers—the commerce power, the taxing power, and the spending power, in conjunction with Congress's powers under the Necessary and Proper Clause. The growth of the commerce power has been the most consequential. And according to a prominent strain of thought, articulated by Justice Clarence Thomas among others, the broad modern construction of the commerce power cannot be right because it makes much of Article I, Section 8, superfluous.[27] If the commerce power is as broad as modern doctrine takes it to be, the argument runs, then there is no need for the Constitution separately to give Congress the power to make bankruptcy law, coin money, grant patents and copyrights, and probably several other things as well. In the absence of those specific grants, Congress could do all those things under the Commerce Clause. That indicates, the argument concludes, that the commerce power has been construed much too broadly, because a proper reading of the text would not permit so many of its clauses to be redundant. It is not hard to understand the surface-level plausibility of this argument: as Chief Justice Marshall wrote, "It cannot be presumed that any clause in the Constitution is intended to be without effect."[28]

Marshall's statement is sensible, because as a general matter it is reasonable to think that people writing lists of rules intend those rules to do actual work. But the proposition that it cannot be *presumed* that any constitutional clause is *intended* to be without effect is not the same as the proposition that no constitutional clause can *be* without effect. Enacted texts—even enacted constitutional texts—sometimes contain superfluous words or clauses. Within Article I, Section 8, itself, consider clause vi, which states that Congress has the power "to provide for the punishment of counterfeiting the securities and current coin of the United States." That clause gives Congress no power that it would not have by virtue of the clauses granting Congress the power to issue securities and coin in the first place, considered in conjunction with the Necessary and Proper Clause. It cannot be that in the absence of clause vi Congress could coin money but would be powerless against counterfeiters. No constitutional clause expressly grants Congress the power to punish people who fail to pay their taxes or people who violate copyrights, but nobody doubts that Congress has those punishment powers, whether as inherent incidents of the underlying powers to tax and grant copyrights or as means necessary and proper for carrying those powers into execution. If the Constitution did not expressly specify a congressional power to punish counterfeiting, the power would be there just the same.[29] And the conclusion that here and there the Constitution has superfluous text should not be shocking: it was written by multiple authors, sometimes working at cross-purposes, with quill pens and limited time. Perfectly elegant composition is not to be expected.

Moreover, the amount of Section 8 that is in practice superfluous can vary over time. When the Constitution was written, it contained a certain amount of redundant text, as complex documents usually do. But Marshall was right to think that enacted clauses are generally intended to have effects, so it would be odd for the Framers to have written an eighteen-clause section in which they could have recognized *most* of the clauses as extraneous. But the amount of a text that is redundant can vary as circumstances change.

Imagine, for example, a treaty between Britain and France, signed in 1820, providing that neither country would maintain a naval presence "off the coast of the United States, or that of Texas." When written, the two provisions had separate consequences. After 1845, when Texas became part of the United States, the second provision would be completely redundant. But it would be a mistake at that point to read the treaty as if the second provision carried some meaning not entirely contained within the first. Similarly, the scope of the power "to regulate commerce with foreign nations, and among the several states" expanded over time, as local economies became increasingly indistinguishable from larger ones—and as the experience of that change made it more intuitive for people to think of their daily lives as bound up with that of a geographically larger system, and as jurists adjusted to the idea that federal and state power could exist concurrently.

The idea that every piece of a text must be construed to affect the text's meaning may arise from a well-intentioned effort to have the text make sense as a whole. But there is no iron law of clause and effect.[30] If a reading produces redundancies, it is worth thinking twice about whether one is reading correctly. But if one can give a reasonable account of the redundancy in question, and if the reading otherwise makes sense, there is no good reason to rule out readings simply because they make pieces of text extraneous. On the contrary, it is sometimes the very fact that the Constitution has been successful enough to persist over time that makes portions of its text redundant.

⊰⊱⊰⊱

Like Article I's Vesting Clause, the fact that the Constitution's text enumerates specific congressional powers is often adduced as textual proof for the enumeration principle and the internal-limits canon. And as with the Vesting Clause, the fact of enumeration in Article I, Section 8, does not prove either thing. Article I, Section 8, neither says nor demonstrates that Congress is limited to or by the powers it enumerates. Indeed, Article I, Section 8, could not possibly make that demonstration, because it is only a partial list of Congress's powers, even counting only those powers specified in the text of the Constitution. Section 8 could not be introduced with language stating that "The Congress shall have only the following powers," but it could be introduced with language stating that "The Congress shall have these powers, among others." That constitutional lawyers nonetheless think of Article I, Section 8, as proof of the enumeration principle and the internal-limits canon is a testament to the power of the lens that enumerationism brings to bear.

The Tenth Amendment

The Tenth Amendment comes closer than any other part of the written Constitution to addressing the issues of enumerationism directly. It reads as follows: "The powers not delegated to the United States by the Constitution, nor prohibited by it to the States, are reserved to the States respectively, or to the people." That text is conventionally understood to establish both the enumeration principle and the internal-limits canon, and it can be read that way. But as with the Vesting Clause and Article I, Section 8, the lens of enumerationism does a fair amount of work in making that reading seem natural. Without that lens, the Tenth Amendment does not restrict Congress to the exercise of enumerated powers. Depending on the circumstances, the Tenth Amendment can also be consistent with Congress's exercising the practical equivalent of general regulatory authority.

The Tenth Amendment and Implied National Powers

Jurists conventionally read the Tenth Amendment as if it said that the federal government may exercise only its enumerated powers. For example, in *Murphy v. NCAA*—the 2018 anticommandeering case discussed in Chapter 8—the Supreme Court wrote that "[t]he Constitution confers on Congress not plenary legislative power but only certain enumerated powers. Therefore, all other legislative power is reserved for the States, as the Tenth Amendment confirms."[31] That statement accurately captures the way the Tenth Amendment is usually understood. But it alters a key term, and it does so without acknowledgment. The Tenth Amendment does not speak of *enumerated* powers. It says that the "powers not *delegated* to the United States by the Constitution" are reserved to the states or the people. To people accustomed to the enumerationist view of constitutional law, that substitution might go unnoticed: the assumption is that the Constitution delegates powers to Congress by enumerating them. But without the assumptions of enumerationism, there is no reason why that must be the case. As a general matter, powers can be delegated textually or nontextually, expressly or implicitly. So with the enumerationist lens removed, the text of the Tenth Amendment is compatible with the national government's exercising nonenumerated powers, as long as those powers are delegated in some other way.

Some readers may have the intuition that although powers can as a general matter be delegated implicitly as well as explicitly, powers delegated "by the Constitution" are powers delegated in writing. But that need not be so, and for two reasons. First, at the time of the Founding, Americans regularly used the word "Constitution" (with or without a capital C) to refer not just to a certain kind of document but also to a larger system of rules, practices, and institutional arrangements. If "Constitution" in the Tenth Amendment is understood in that sense, then the powers delegated by the Constitution would not be limited to the powers delegated by the force of words in the document. They would also include whatever powers are reposed in the government of the United States by virtue of the logic of the system of government and the purposes for which it was created. The Founding-era theory of resulting powers is probably best understood on this model, as are the powers that the pre–New Deal Supreme Court recognized in cases like *Curtiss-Wright*. Second, even if "Constitution" in the Tenth Amendment refers only to the document, it does not follow that powers delegated by the Constitution must be delegated expressly, because written instruments often imply more than they expressly say.

That the Tenth Amendment speaks of delegation rather than express delegation is not an accident. When the text that became the Tenth Amendment was under consideration in the First Congress, the House of Representatives twice rejected proposals to insert the word "expressly" before the word "delegated."[32] As described in Chapter 4, the question of whether the Constitution did or should restrict the federal government to powers "expressly" delegated was hotly contested during the ratification process. The First Congress was well aware of that debate, and it chose not to include the word "expressly."[33] To be sure, the rejection of the word "expressly" did not affirmatively establish that the national government could exercise powers *not* expressly delegated to it. But the possibility of reading the Tenth Amendment as contemplating implicit delegations remained open, and deliberately so.

What's more, the text of the Tenth Amendment would invite the inference that the federal government can exercise some nonenumerated powers even if "delegated" were read to mean "enumerated." This point is rarely recognized, but it follows straightforwardly from the text. According to its language, the Tenth Amendment is not a rule about all of "[t]he powers not delegated to the United States by the Constitution." It is a rule about "[t]he powers not delegated to the United States by the Constitution, *nor prohibited by it to the states.*" A power prohibited to the states is therefore not within the category of powers that the Tenth Amendment withholds from the federal government. It follows that powers prohibited to the states (and not affirmatively prohibited to the federal government) are powers that the federal government could exercise without running afoul of the Tenth Amendment, regardless of whether the Constitution delegates those powers to the United States.

Consider the power to create paper money. Whether any of Congress's enumerated powers authorizes the creation of paper money was once a subject of serious dispute, as described in Chapter 6. In most cases, a power not delegated to the national government would, under the Tenth Amendment, be a power that the national government could not exercise. Where the power to create paper money is concerned, however, that consequence does not follow, because the Constitution prohibits the states from exercising that power: Article I, Section 10, provides that "[n]o state shall . . . make any thing but gold or silver coin a tender in payment of debts." As a power prohibited to the states, the power to create paper money is untouched by the Tenth Amendment. And if the Tenth Amendment is not in play, no rule written in the Constitution's text demands that there be an enumerated power—or even a delegated power—warranting congressional action.

Neither the Tenth Amendment nor anything else in the Constitution explicitly entrusts the federal government with all powers that are prohibited to the states and not also affirmatively prohibited to the federal government. But as the nineteenth-century legal theorist Christopher Tiedeman explained, there is a logic to thinking that the federal government is implicitly authorized to exercise some such powers. Some powers are prohibited to the states because no government should exercise them. But if a power that needs to be exercised by someone in government has been prohibited to the states, Tiedeman reasoned, it follows that the power belongs to the United States, regardless of whether the Constitution delegates it to the United States in any affirmative way.[34] Justice Holmes articulated the same logic when he wrote in *Missouri v. Holland* that "it is not lightly to be assumed that, in matters requiring national action, a power which must belong to and somewhere reside in every civilized government is not to be found."[35]

A committed enumerationist might think that this reading of the Tenth Amendment takes inappropriate advantage of an accident in the way the text is written. "Yes, I see the point," the thought would run, "but it misunderstands the function of the Tenth Amendment. The proviso about powers prohibited to the states is not intended to open a door to the exercise, by the federal government, of powers not delegated to it by the Constitution. It is merely intended to limit the portion of the amendment that reserves powers to the states. That is, the amendment is supposed to be read as if the language about powers prohibited to the states came later in the amendment's text: the thought would be better expressed if the Tenth Amendment read 'The powers not delegated to the United States by the Constitution are reserved to the states respectively, or to the people. Nothing in this provision shall be understood as reserving to the states any power that is otherwise prohibited to the states by the Constitution.'"

But the Tenth Amendment says what it says. The intuition that it should say something else is a function of a nontextual idea about how constitutional law is supposed to work.

That doesn't settle the issue. Intuitions about how constitutional law is supposed to work routinely shape constitutional interpretation, and sometimes they warrant reading the text in a way that no untutored reader would derive from the text alone. We read the First Amendment to protect the freedoms of speech and religion against the federal executive, even though the text of that Amendment is addressed only to Congress. And sometimes—as might be the case with the different phrasing of the Vesting Clauses—the Constitution's wording might be a matter of happenstance, such that it is a mistake to attribute substantive legal significance to it. But a decision to read the Tenth Amendment as if it were written differently cannot claim the simple authority of textualism. It must rest on other grounds, and those grounds must be strong enough to warrant overcoming the straightforward meaning of the text.

So if enumerationism were based on compelling understandings of history and federalism, it might make sense to read the Tenth Amendment to confirm the enumeration principle, even though the words of the text do not state that principle. But the structural and historical underpinnings of enumerationism are problematic. It is therefore hard to identify a powerful justification for declaring the text badly worded and reading it as if it required the enumeration principle, rather than reading it to mean the sensible thing that it straightforwardly says. As Holmes and Tiedeman understood, there is a clear logic to the proposition that a power necessary for government overall resides in the national government if it is denied to the states. And as between a straightforward reading of the text that yields a sensible proposition and a nonstraightforward reading of the text that produces a flawed one, choosing the former option should be easy.

The Tenth Amendment and Cumulative Coverage

Conventionally, the Tenth Amendment is understood to establish not just the enumeration principle but also the internal-limits canon. The logic of that interpretation is simple. The Tenth Amendment speaks of "powers not delegated to the United States by the Constitution." That implies the existence of such powers. Next—and ignoring the proviso about powers prohibited to the states—the amendment directs that such powers are "reserved to the States respectively, or to the people," meaning that they cannot be exercised by the federal government.[36] Most of the time, constitutional lawyers reason that if there are powers the federal government cannot exercise, then the powers of Congress do not enable Congress to do everything that it could do with general regulatory authority. But for reasons explained in this chapter's discussion of Article I, Section 8, that thought is a mistake. There is a difference between the powers that Congress has and the substantive regulatory regimes that Congress can create with those powers, and it is possible in principle for Congress to be able to create, with a discrete set of powers, all of the regulatory regimes that it could create with a police power.

The Tenth Amendment might seem to imply that the powers of Congress must not add up to the practical equivalent of a police power, because such a result would mean that the Tenth Amendment had no applications. It would make no sense, the thought runs, for an entire constitutional amendment to do no actual work. But as already explained, that line of reasoning confuses a proposition about the motivations of constitution-makers with a proposition about the functioning of constitutions. One can reasonably presume that people do not normally write rules that they *know* will never have applications. But it does not follow that every rule people write *has*, or in the future *will have*, applications. Sometimes people write rules providing for situations that *might* arise, just in case. Sometimes the world turns out to be different from what the writers of a rule expected, such that an anticipated set of applications fails to materialize or dissolves over time. This last possibility is especially plausible for rules that remain in place for centuries, because the circumstances for which a rule was written might be characteristic of the world the authors knew but not of the world at all later times. So even if we assume that the authors of rules expect those rules to have applications, it would be a mistake to assume that every rule people write will turn out to have applications forever.

For a long time after its adoption in 1791, the text of the Tenth Amendment addressed a situation that arose in practice. In the antebellum world, where the national government had sharply limited capacities and dual federalism encouraged circumscribed constructions of the enumerated powers, there were regulatory projects that lay beyond the federal government's authority, even without respect to external limits. But time passed, and the world changed. Governmental capacity increased; the electorate increased its appetite for national regulation; courts adjusted to concurrent jurisdiction; and an integrated national market made it possible for Congress to regulate comprehensively, or close to comprehensively, on the basis of its enumerated powers. At that point, the Tenth Amendment no longer constrained Congress. But that does not mean that the Tenth Amendment is being violated. It simply does not come into play. And it poses no problem for this understanding to say that the Founders must have expected the amendment to have some function. Of course they did—and indeed, the amendment's stated rule had applications when they wrote it. But it does not follow that it must have applications until the end of time. A provision of law can be worth adopting even if it only has consequences for a hundred years.

I am not arguing that the Tenth Amendment cannot be read to support the internal-limits canon. As noted before, it sometimes happens that constitutional provisions are understood to mean something different from what is stated in their text, given considerations about things like history and structure. If the internal-limits canon were a valid constitutional principle—because federalism required it, or because original meanings required it, or for any other reason or combination of reasons—then it might be consistent with the way American constitutional interpretation works to read the Tenth Amendment to represent that idea. But if the best understandings of history and structure do not require the powers of Congress to have meaningful internal limits, there is no good reason to (mis)read the text as making such limits mandatory. On its own, the text of the Tenth Amendment contains no such rule.

The Tenth Amendment and External Limits

The preceding explanation of why the Tenth Amendment does not require the internal-limits canon accepts that the rule stated in the Tenth Amendment's text currently has no (or almost no) applications. But to have a clear view of the Tenth Amendment's significance in current constitutional law, it is important to notice something about the subtle but crucial distinction between the text of a constitutional provision and its operative content.

Even if the rule stated in the *text* of the Tenth Amendment has no contemporary applications, it need not follow that *the Tenth Amendment* has no contemporary applications, because a constitutional provision as applied sometimes has force different from what an untutored reader of the text might expect. (Recall again that the First Amendment is applied against the executive branch, even though the rule stated in its text is addressed only to Congress.) As a matter of the way that courts and lawyers classify cases, the Tenth Amendment does have applications in modern constitutional law. Under existing judicial doctrine, the anticommandeering rule first announced in *New York v. United States* and the state sovereign immunity rule first announced in *Alden v. Maine* are applications of the Tenth Amendment, at least in part.[37] The Court in those cases did not apply the rule stated in the *text* of the Tenth Amendment, as the Court in both cases acknowledged.[38] It applied related but not identical propositions about the value of state sovereignty, propositions best understood as arising from some combination of a theory of federalism and a view of Founding-era history. Constitutional lawyers associate those propositions with the Tenth Amendment not because the text of the Tenth Amendment states them but because constitutional practice standardly associates doctrines with clauses, even when the clauses do not actually state the doctrines, and, given that practice, the text of the Tenth Amendment is sufficiently related to the content of those doctrines so as to make the Tenth Amendment a sensible choice of constitutional text with which to associate the doctrines.[39]

The Tenth Amendment rule that today may have no present applications is the rule prescribed by the text of the Tenth Amendment, not the more robust state-protective rules invoked in *Alden* and *New York*. Given that the Court has construed the Tenth Amendment to embody the more robust rules, it remains true even today that the amendment does work. It just might not do the work of directing results in cases where Congress has enacted legislation exceeding the internal limits of its delegated powers, because that situation might not arise.

The difference between construing the Tenth Amendment according to what the words of its text say and construing it to embody affirmative prohibitions on Congress for the sake of protecting state decisionmaking is the difference between internal and external limits. The text of the Tenth Amendment is about internal limits: it states a rule applicable in cases that lie beyond the scope of the federal government's delegated powers, whatever those might be. The more robust federalism rules that animate *New York* and *Alden* are external limits. Those rules limit what Congress can do with its delegated powers, and they do so on the basis of something outside the terms of any clause conferring power on Congress.

Prevailing doctrine on commandeering and sovereign immunity is controversial, and I do not mean to take a position here on whether *New York*, *Alden*, or any similar cases were rightly decided. But as a general matter, the Court's use of the Tenth Amendment as a source of external limits on congressional power is entirely consistent with this book's arguments about sensible approaches to federalism. I have argued throughout that a jurisprudence of internal limits is neither necessary nor particularly useful for constitutional federalism in the United States. But external limits have an important role to play. Much as it makes sense to protect individual liberty by specifying actions that no governmental institution may take, it makes sense to protect the localist half of American federalism by specifying actions that are prohibited to the national government. Whether any particular external limit is a good one is, of course, a separate question. But where the project is the preservation of state governments as consequential decisionmakers, it makes more sense to preserve space for that decisionmaking by specifying what Congress may not do than by trying to construct zones of state autonomy by negative inferences from the Constitution's enumeration of congressional powers. This basic point about how to limit legislatures was clear already to Madison when he wrote to Wallace in 1785. Two and half centuries of experience have vindicated his advice.

‹‹‹·›·›‹‹·›·›

The Constitution can be read in an enumerationist way. The question is whether it should be, and why. The answer cannot be that it should be read that way because the text compels it. On the contrary, to read the Constitution in an enumerationist way is, in several small but telling ways, to read the Constitution as if its text were different from what it actually is. People do that all the time. But what, if anything, justifies their doing so?

Within the practice of American constitutional law, it is normal for non-textual considerations to inform the way that the text is read. Indeed, if enough constitutional lawyers believe strongly enough in a rule of constitutional law, they can usually find ways to read the text as consistent with that rule—and in perfectly good faith. Sometimes that process involves choosing among different ways that a competent reader of English would find it plausible to read the text. Sometimes it involves giving the text a meaning that a competent reader of English unfamiliar with the practices of constitutional law would probably not have imagined. In either case, the practice might be sensible: we might say that in choosing what meaning to attribute to a bit of constitutional language, it makes sense to choose a reading that supports a rule that is rational, or just, or sound as a matter of constitutional structure, or consistent with the system's history, or some combination of all of these things, even if it is not a reading that the hypothetical untutored reader of English would settle on.

Most of the time, constitutional lawyers believe that the text of the Constitution straightforwardly establishes the principles of enumerationism. The fact that sophisticated interpreters usually have that view, even to the point of thinking the proposition "explicitly clear," testifies to the power of the enumerationist lens to shape the reading of the Constitution.[40] But if shown that the Constitution's text does not actually declare the enumerationist principles that are orthodox in constitutional law, most constitutional lawyers would quickly respond that the text must be read in light of principles of federalism and of the Constitution's original meaning or original design. In saying that a good reading of the text should make sense of those other aspects of constitutional law, they would be saying something sensible. Their mistake would be thinking that those other considerations direct an enumerationist reading of the text. They do not. And part of the point of seeing what is wrong with the stories that enumerationism tells about federalism and about Founding-era history is to open the way for constitutional lawyers to recognize, and perhaps not to fight against, the fact that the text of the Constitution does not require an enumerationist approach to constitutional law. In all likelihood, that text was written to invite both enumerationist and nonenumerationist readings. It does not decide the question.

CONCLUSION

THE UNITED STATES CONSTITUTION specifies many things about American government. It provides for a two-house Congress, a president, and a Supreme Court. It declares that Congress has the power to tax, the power to borrow, the power to regulate commerce, and many other powers. But the Constitution never specifies whether the enumerated congressional powers are the only powers Congress has.

Why does the Constitution enumerate congressional powers but not say whether the enumerated powers are exclusive? The most likely explanation is straightforward: because the Framers did not agree about the answer. They agreed that the fundamental point of writing the Constitution was to create a more powerful government. They wanted to make unmistakably clear that Congress would have the power to tax, the power to borrow, the power to regulate commerce, and many other powers, including the power to make all laws necessary and proper for carrying the government's powers into execution. So they specified those powers in writing. But the Framers did not agree about whether Congress would also have more powers, beyond those enumerated in the text. That question was controversial. So they drafted a Constitution that did not decide.

Because the Constitution did not decide that question, early Americans argued about it. During the ratification debates, and in the First Congress, some people contended that Congress was limited to its enumerated powers. Other people argued that the enumeration was not limiting. Who argued which position at any given time was partly a function of politics. Early in the nineteenth century, when the political party that preferred a more constrained federal government became the dominant force in American politics, enumerationism became the lens through which Americans read the Constitution. And so it has remained. Indeed, enumerationism shapes the reading of the Constitution to the point where most properly educated constitutional lawyers would bristle at the statement that the Constitution's text does not specify that Congress is limited to its enumerated powers. As an official theory, enumerationism has taught constitutional lawyers not just to read the Constitution in one particular way but also to believe that there is no other reasonable way to read it.

But consensus at the level of official theory has never succeeded in making constitutional law wholly enumerationist. Before the New Deal, the Supreme Court on many occasions acted on a theory of implied powers, sustaining federal lawmaking on the basis of powers inherent in national sovereignty or implicit in the purposes for which the federal government was created. Since the New Deal, on the model of cumulative coverage, the Court has read the enumerated powers broadly enough to let Congress pursue almost any regulatory project for which it has the political will, subject to external limits. So both before and after the New Deal, the constitutional system in practice has not conformed to enumerationism's picture. In short, the dominance of enumerationism in theory has obscured, rather than eliminated, constitutional law's fundamental ambiguity on the question of enumerated powers. Rather than arguing openly about whether Congress is limited to and by its textually enumerated powers, as Americans did in the eighteenth century, modern constitutional lawyers inhabit a system that gives one answer at the level of official theory and the other answer at the level of established practice.

The twenty-first-century judiciary seems inclined to resolve the longstanding dissonance between enumerationist theory and nonenumerationist practice by forcing practice to conform to theory. But there are only two reasons to think that the principles of enumerationism must be enforced in practice, and neither rationale is sound. First, one might think that the rule of law simply requires enumerationism—that the Constitution, rightly understood, limits Congress to its enumerated powers and requires that those powers constrain what Congress can do. For all the reasons given in this book, that view would misunderstand the Constitution's text and history— indeed, even its Founding-era history. Text and history can be read to support an enumerationist approach to constitutional law, but they do not require one. To justify altering long-standing practice and striking down the decisions of a democratically elected legislature, there must be a reason, and indeed a very good reason, for choosing to read those sources of authority that way. Second, one might think that strict enumerationist practice is necessary for protecting the localist half of federalism. If that were true, then the imperative to protect local decisionmaking could supply the reason for reading the Constitution's text and history to support enumerationism. But in reality, what is valuable in local decisionmaking does not depend on the internal limits of federal law. The case for disallowing laws adopted by the democratically enacted national legislature on internal-limit grounds therefore relies on a misunderstanding—either the misunderstanding that that step is legally required, or the misunderstanding that the system would work better if we chose to do things that way.

There are better alternatives. In the best case, constitutional law would openly embrace the model of implied powers. Congress would have enumerated powers, and Congress would have nonenumerated powers. More particularly, Congress would be understood to wield all three kinds of implied power described in Chapter 6: power to carry enumerated powers into execution (as described in the Necessary and Proper Clause), power to achieve the ends of the enumerated powers in ways that go beyond what is specified in the clauses describing those powers (as in the example of the power to organize and operate the Postal Service), and, crucially, power to do whatever other things the national legislature of the United States ought to be able to do. That last category of implied power, which aligns with what Wilson, Hamilton, and Story called "resulting powers," might be understood as vested in the government of the United States as a consequence of the decision to create that government or in light of the purposes that government is best understood to serve. It could also be understood as justified by the text of the Constitution, given the "all other powers" language of the Necessary and Proper Clause.

This last category of implied national power could be conceived either as one general power to legislate in the national interests of the United States or as several specific powers inherently or implicitly held by the national government—like the power to create paper money, the power to conduct foreign policy, and the power to superintend Native American affairs. In practice, the distinction between those two ways of thinking would not make much difference. Either way, the question asked about any exercise of federal power that did not come comfortably within an enumerated power would be "Is there a reasonable justification for thinking that this is a topic on which the national government should be able to make policy?" To the extent that such questions were asked in court, prior decisions would form the basis for common-law-style analogical reasoning, so exercises of power that were similar to previously approved exercises of power would be easily approved. That might make the system look like one of several different implied national powers. But crucially, the fact that an exercise of power did not fall squarely into some category of previously recognized implied power would not mean that that exercise of power was invalid. The question would still be whether there was a good reason why the national government should be able to do the thing in question. If so, the action would be valid, provided it did not violate external limits.

When presented with the question of whether some reason for national action justified a federal law, judges in an implied-powers regime would not limit the set of valid reasons for national action to what can be inferred from Congress's textually enumerated powers. Instead, the set of valid reasons might also include the purposes stated in the Preamble. It should certainly include considerations about the special responsibilities or competencies of the national government. Identifying those responsibilities and competencies would require the exercise of informed judgment rather than simply the application of a formal list. As a result, asking judges to adjudicate those questions might seem to give them a fair amount of unguided power. But that worry should not be overstated. Courts would adjudicate such questions only in cases where federal laws did not come within any of the textually enumerated powers, and such cases are few. Moreover, the judges who answered these questions should presume that legislation that can navigate the process limits of the national government is legislation supported by some reason for national action. Such a presumption could be overcome, but judges should not feel pressure to overcome it often. And there would be no principle stating that there must be things that Congress could not do, apart from those covered by external limits. In other words, this model of congressional power would do without both the enumeration principle and the internal-limits canon.

The model of implied national powers is not without shortcomings, but its virtues are considerable. The government of the United States, as it actually exists, is a real national government. Absent a compelling legal or democratic mandate to the contrary, it seems reasonable to regard it as vested not merely with a series of specific authorizations in the manner of a limited-purpose venture but with the responsibility for governing a nation in general, within the limits set out in the Constitution. On that understanding, it makes more sense to think of the enumeration of powers as ruling powers *in*, thereby making it unnecessary to argue about whether Congress can do essential things like tax and borrow and regulate commerce, than to think of it as an indirect mechanism for ruling *out* whatever might not be mentioned. So if something that is neither affirmatively prohibited nor expressly authorized is something that it makes sense for the national government of the United States to do, the national government of the United States should be able to do it, pursuant to the appropriate processes of democratic decisionmaking.

In the second-best case, constitutional law could openly embrace the model of cumulative coverage, which has been the de facto regime for most of the last century. Embracing that model openly would mean retaining the enumeration principle but eschewing the internal-limits canon. Every congressional enactment would need to be traced to an enumerated power, but it might turn out that any law Congress could enact with a police power could be traced and justified in that manner. If things did turn out that way, it would not be because the Constitution was designed to give Congress a police power. It would be because the enumerated powers, as they intersect with the actual social world, turn out to enable Congress to regulate pervasively if it has ambitions to do so. The coverage would be cumulatively comprehensive, or nearly so, but as a matter of contingency rather than affirmative commitment.

In practice, this is the regime that prevailed between *Darby* in 1941 and *Lopez* in 1995. Subject to the qualification that Congress may sometimes need to legislate twice to get its way, it is the regime that still operates as of this writing, as explained in Chapter 8. One advantage of this system, relative to the implied-national-power approach, is accordingly that it would require less change to the way courts have operated in recent generations. But it would still require a significant psychological change: constitutional lawyers would need to give up the MustBeSomething Rule and accept that no sensible principle requires the enumerated powers of Congress to be collectively limiting.

For people who worry about judges deciding what the federal government can do without being guided by specific constitutional texts, this second-best approach might seem preferable to the model of implied national power. On the model of cumulative coverage, every question about congressional power would arise under some specific constitutional text. One might wonder, of course, whether the requirement that judges justify their decisions by reference to the Constitution's text would change the outcomes of many cases, as opposed to being mostly a matter of form and appearances. Commentators have long suspected that courts adjudicating questions of national power are animated at least as much by implicit theories of federalism as by the words of the Constitution's text.[1] But perhaps form and appearance matter, and perhaps the distinction sometimes matters in more substantive ways as well.

The second-best approach also has disadvantages (which is why it is only second-best). So long as the enumeration principle persists, opponents of federal action will have incentives to argue that the particular actions they oppose are beyond the enumerated powers. That means, among other things, that they will have incentives to internalize their objections to federal regulation, presenting (often in good faith) what are in substance arguments for affirmative prohibitions as if they were arguments about enumerated powers. That distortion does not help decisionmakers determine what should and should not be within the ambit of national policymaking. If there are potential reasons for recognizing an affirmative prohibition on Congress, as in the case of commandeering doctrine, then those reasons can be adjudicated on their merits. But if a federal law is supported by a decent rationale for congressional action based on the responsibilities or capacities of the national government, the fact that it is not covered by the enumerated powers should not make it invalid. After all, the list of enumerated powers is not a good guide to what the federal government should *not* do, in part because it was written more to rule things in than to rule things out. Or, to make the point slightly differently: the best-case alternative is better than the second-best alternative partly because it encourages decisionmakers to ask the federalism questions that actually matter.

◄◄‥►►◄◄‥►►

Getting federalism right is of enormous practical importance. But this book's critique of enumerationism is not only aimed at improving the law of federalism. It also aims to alter conventional aspects of the way that constitutional history is remembered—and not just for the purpose of destabilizing enumerationism. After all, constitutional interpretation is not only an enterprise in which sources of authority like history and text are mobilized to produce law. It is an enterprise in which the real stakes of arguments about law often include the power to have one's preferred version of history become one of constitutional law's official stories.

Constitutional law's official stories matter for reasons that go beyond the way courts decide cases. For a set of contingent but deeply rooted reasons, the story of the Constitution plays a powerful role in shaping American national identity. So when we fight about history in constitutional law, we are usually fighting not just about whatever point of law is officially at issue but about who we Americans are as a people.

Enumerationism tells a particular story about the Constitution. It is a story of skepticism about national government. One can tell the story that way, and indeed that way of telling the story has a place in the complex history of American thought. But it is a stylized story, and an incomplete one. A more complete story would communicate that the Constitution was written first and foremost to empower the general government; that it represented an expression of confidence in the possibility of doing great things at the national level; and that over the generations, as organic American nationhood matured, the American people entrusted the government of the United States with the resources and the legitimacy necessary for justifying that initial expression of confidence. We are, without doubt, a people that values limits on government for the protection of liberty, and the Constitution represents and embodies that aspect of our national identity. It does so primarily through the many crucial provisions that affirmatively protect people's rights, and in more subtle ways it also does so through the process limits of lawmaking. But we are also a people that can, and must, do great things through collective political effort. We should be able to draw on the story of the Constitution to affirm that part of our national character.

◄◄··►►◄◄··►►

I have no illusions that the Supreme Court that sits as this book is written can be persuaded to abandon enumerationism. The change in perspective that I seek goes to fundamental propositions of constitutional law, and a professional community does not change its basic understandings quickly or easily. But even if the dominant view among American jurists remains enumerationist, there is something to be gained by showing that enumerationism is a contestable framework for thinking about constitutional law rather than a necessary truth. A better understanding is a better understanding, even if no change in the law follows.

That said, appreciation of the ideas of this book could improve the practice of constitutional law even if decisionmakers were not persuaded to reject enumerationism completely. A judiciary that applies enumerationism in the knowledge that the enumerationist lens is just one way of looking at the Constitution, and an imperfect way, is likely to apply enumerationism more cautiously than a judiciary that regards the tenets of enumerationism as fundamental and unshakably correct. A judiciary with the former perspective will be more inclined to balance the directives of enumerationism with other important considerations, like stability in the law and respect for the decisions of the democratically elected branches. A judiciary with the latter perspective will be more inclined to think that enumerationism must be vindicated even if the heavens fall—or, only a little less dramatically, that holding enumerationism at arm's length from time to time is tantamount to subverting the Constitution. The latter attitude is more imperious; it encourages judges to flex their power and strike down laws that Congress has adopted. The former attitude is more moderate or, dare one say, more judicious. It counsels judges to avoid striking down democratically adopted laws on internal-limit grounds if it is possible to do so. Given the stakes of federal governance, the difference between those two attitudes can matter a great deal.

In the longer run, perhaps a more thorough change in thinking is possible. Marshall wrote that the question of the extent of the federal government's powers "is perpetually arising, and will probably continue to arise, so long as our system shall exist."[2] Nobody knows, of course, how long the constitutional system as we know it will continue to operate; all systems of government eventually pass away. But if the Constitution continues to operate into the indefinite future, there will surely be major changes in the way it is understood, just as there have been significant changes from time to time so far. So perhaps, in time, the common sense of one era can give way to the common sense of another.

My hope is that the present critique of enumerationism, and others it may encourage, can help persuade a future generation of constitutional lawyers to adopt a different common sense about national power. Changes in circumstances and developments in politics would help. The more the American public appreciates the need for vigorous national action in order to address pressing problems, the more constitutional lawyers will be open to seeing that the lens of enumerationism does not provide the only way, nor the best way, of understanding the Constitution. But changed circumstances and changed politics are not the entirety of what constitutional change requires. There is also a need to articulate arguments—to explain why an existing way of thinking about the Constitution is flawed and what other ways are available instead. That explanation has been the work of this book.

FREQUENTLY ASKED QUESTIONS

This final section of the book provides quick summary answers to questions that I was often asked as I worked on the book, including questions about the meaning of terms used in the book.

❮❮‣❯‣❮❮‣❯‣❯

Are you saying that all law in the United States should be made at the federal level?

> Definitely not. That would be a terrible idea. Some things should be decided nationally, but many things should be decided locally. Indeed, I am tempted to say that *most* things should be decided locally, but it's hard to know what "most" means, because it's hard to establish a denominator. In any event, what I'm saying is that the enumeration of powers does not help us decide which things should be decided locally. For a more complete discussion, see Chapter 8.

OK, you don't think Congress should do everything. But are you saying that Congress has the authority to do whatever it wants?

> No. The Constitution prohibits Congress from doing lots of things. Congress cannot establish a religion, abridge free speech, deprive people of liberty without due process of law, and on and on. Under prevailing judicial doctrine, Congress cannot order a state legislature to pass a law, tax a

state's own tax revenue, attach coercive conditions to federal spending programs, and so on. All that is important. What I am saying is that the enumerated powers of Congress might not limit Congress, not that Congress is unlimited.

To think that Congress could do anything if it were not limited by the enumeration of powers is to commit the *Unlimited Congress Fallacy*. (I thank Jessica Ullom-Minnich for coining this term.)

What's the point of enumerating congressional powers, if not to limit what Congress can do?

Originally, the most important point of enumerating congressional powers was to empower Congress, not to limit Congress. Enumerating powers was a way of trying to make sure that Congress would be able to do the things on the list—more a way of ruling the specified powers *in* than a way of ruling other things *out*. Some of the enumerated powers were enumerated to make clear that the federal government could exercise them, and others were enumerated to make clear that within the federal government, the institution that could exercise them was *Congress*, rather than the president or the courts. For a more complete discussion, see especially Chapter 2.

That sounds like an originalist argument. Are you saying that the correct understanding of the original meaning of the Constitution establishes your views about congressional power?

No. I think the prevailing understanding of the Founding generation's ideas about congressional power is misleading, but I do not think a better understanding would compel my preferred position. The book's historical analyses are intended to show problems with an existing way of thinking and to reveal plausible alternatives, not to prove what the law must be.

Doesn't the Tenth Amendment say that Congress can only act on the basis of its enumerated powers?

No. The Tenth Amendment speaks of "delegated" powers, not "enumerated" powers. That difference is important, and it's also only the beginning of the reasons why the Tenth Amendment does not say what constitutional lawyers often take it to say. For a more complete discussion, see Chapter 9. Better yet, read the introduction, and then skip to Chapter 9 if you feel the need.

Didn't John Marshall say that the enumeration presupposes something not enumerated?

He did. But he didn't mean what people today think he meant. See Chapter 7.

What are internal limits, external limits, and process limits?

"Internal limits" are the limits inherent in grants of power. "External limits" are affirmative prohibitions—thou-shalt-not rules—that block the use of powers. "Process limits" are features of decisionmaking processes that make it difficult for certain sorts of laws to be adopted. For a more complete discussion, see Chapter 1.

What is internalization?

"Internalization" is my name for the phenomenon whereby people take arguments against federal law that in substance are really external-limit (thou-shalt-not) arguments and articulate them as if they were arguments about internal limits—that is, arguments about enumerated powers. There are lots of examples, from James Madison's arguments against the Bank of the United States in 1791 to the major opposition to the Affordable Care Act in the 2010s. For a more complete discussion, see Chapter 5.

And what is the internal-limits canon?

It's my name for the idea that the powers of Congress, collectively, authorize less than a power to legislate in general would authorize. For a more complete discussion, including an explanation of why the internal-limits canon is not the same thing as the idea that Congress can legislate only on the basis of its enumerated powers, see Chapter 7.

What are the differences between implied powers, implicit powers, and inherent powers?

I use the terms "implied" and "implicit" interchangeably. My sense is that a power is "implied" (or "implicit") when some particular source of positive authority like a text or a decision gives rise to that power but without stating the grant of power explicitly (or "expressly"—I regard "explicit" and "express" as synonymous). The boundary between what is express and what is implied can be fuzzy; for more complete discussion, see Chapter 6.

In contrast, it is my sense that a power is "inherent" when it derives not from a particular positive grant but from the nature of the power-wielding entity. In keeping with that understanding, one could argue that the government of the United States has certain powers *implicitly* in light of the particular purposes for which it was formed or *inherently* because it is a national government, and national governments as such have certain powers. (Whether the United States is in fact a national government, and whether national governments as such do have inherent powers, are contestable questions; I am just explaining the terms.) Again, for a more complete discussion, see Chapter 6.

I do not contend that there is any uniquely correct or universally observed way of distinguishing "inherent" from "implicit" and "implied." I am simply reporting my intuitions about language and explaining the way I use the terms in this book.

The book doesn't say much about Reconstruction. Isn't Reconstruction an important part of the story?

Reconstruction is extremely important in American constitutional history, and its impact is often neglected. In a way, this book participates in that neglect, but it does so for a reason. My aim is to unsettle the conventional story supporting enumerationism, and enumerationism's historical claims are overwhelmingly about the Founding era. So this book's historical analysis is predominantly about the Founding.

A somewhat different book might offer a history of ideas about enumerated powers throughout the constitutional past, rather than focusing on an argument about the merits of enumerationism. Such a history would need to give considerable attention to the Civil War and Reconstruction, which profoundly altered the relationship between the federal government and the states, and also to the Jacksonian era, when the Democratic Party used the idea of enumerated powers as part of its (selective) opposition to energetic federal governance. One plausible way of filling in the story would be to say that the dominant powers between 1800 and 1860 adopted an enumerationist reading of an originally ambiguous Constitution, after which the Civil War and Reconstruction moved the system toward a regime of implied national power, which prevailed until the New Deal's broad construction of the enumerated powers made resort to implied powers unnecessary. Such a periodization would have more than a grain of truth to it: the lion's share of leading implied-national-power cases discussed in Chapter 6 were decided between 1870 and 1940. But that periodization might also be too clean. As *McCulloch* and *Prigg* attest, there was a jurisprudence of implied powers even before the Civil War.

The book does contain a short but important discussion of the cases in which the Supreme Court since 1997 has limited Congress's power to enforce the Reconstruction Amendments. You will find it in Chapter 8.

If the Supreme Court could be persuaded to give up the enumerated-powers model, what would you think it should do instead?

The best alternative is something I'm calling the model of *implied powers*. The second-best alternative is something I'm calling the model of *cumulative coverage*. I describe these alternatives in the introduction, in the conclusion, and at several points in between, chiefly including Chapters 6 and 7.

Do you think that you can convince the Supreme Court?

No. But maybe I can convince you.

And even if you are not persuaded by all of the ideas in this book, maybe I can persuade you that enumerationism is just one way of looking at the Constitution, rather than the only correct way. That would be an excellent start.

ABBREVIATIONS

DHFFC   *The Documentary History of the First Federal Congress of the United States of America, 4 March 1789–3 March 1791*, ed. Linda Grant De Pauw, Charlene Bangs Bickford, Kenneth R. Bowling, and Helen E. Veit, 22 vols. (Baltimore: Johns Hopkins University Press, 1972–).

DHRC   *The Documentary History of the Ratification of the Constitution*, ed. John Kaminski, Gaspare J. Saldino, Richard Leffler, Charles H. Schoenleber, and Margaret A. Hogan, 29 vols. (Madison: State Historical Society of Wisconsin, 1976–).

Records   *The Records of the Federal Convention*, ed. Max Farrand, 4 vols. (New Haven, CT: Yale University Press, 1911–1937).

NOTES

INTRODUCTION

1. See, e.g., National Federation of Independent Business v. Sebelius (NFIB), 567 U.S. 519, 534 (2012) (opinion of Roberts, C.J.) ("The Constitution's express conferral of some powers makes clear that it does not grant others").

2. *DHFFC*, 14:371.

3. United States v. Lopez, 514 U.S. 549, 552 (1995).

4. To my knowledge, the first writer to use the term "enumerationism" this way was David Schwartz. See David S. Schwartz, "A Question Perpetually Arising: Implied Powers, Capable Federalism, and the Limits of Enumerationism," *Arizona Law Review* 59, no. 3 (Fall 2017): 575.

5. Compare *Lopez*, 514 U.S. at 552 ("The Constitution creates *a Federal Government* of enumerated powers") (emphasis added) with Youngstown Sheet & Tube Co. v. Sawyer, 343 U.S. 579, 610 (1952) (Frankfurter, J., concurring) (referring to presidential powers as "nonenumerated" after noting that "[t]he powers of the President are not as particularized as are those of Congress"); Myers v. United States, 272 U.S. 52, 128 (1926) ("The difference between the grant of legislative power under Article 1 to Congress, which is limited to powers therein enumerated, and the more general grant of the executive power to the President under Article 2 is significant").

6. See, e.g., *NFIB*, 567 U.S. at 535 (opinion of Roberts, C.J.) ("Indeed, the Constitution did not initially include a Bill of Rights at least partly because the Framers felt the enumeration of powers sufficed to restrain the Government"); Philip Bobbitt, *Constitutional Fate: Theory of the Constitution* (New York: Oxford University Press, 1982), 144–145 (setting forth this account).

7. *The Federalist*, ed. Jacob E. Cooke (Middletown, CT: Wesleyan University Press, 1982), no. 84 (Alexander Hamilton).

8. By and large, Americans at the Founding did not think of the first ten amendments as a bill of rights, and the adoption of that term for those amendments is a later phenomenon. See, e.g., Akhil Reed Amar, *The Bill of Rights: Creation and Reconstruction* (New Haven, CT: Yale University Press, 1998), 284–286; Gerard N. Magliocca, *The Heart of the Constitution: How the Bill of Rights Became the Bill of Rights* (New York: Oxford University Press, 2018).

9. Thomas Jefferson to James Madison, December 20, 1787, in *DHRC*, 14:482–483.

10. *Lopez* and *Morrison* are the only post–New Deal cases in which the Supreme Court has used the principles of enumerationism to strike down laws that Congress passed using its Article I legislative powers. A complete list of modern decisions striking laws down on enumerationist grounds would also include decisions about the scope of Congress's legislative powers under the enforcement clauses of the Reconstruction Amendments. Leading examples of such cases include City of Boerne v. Flores, 521 U.S. 507, 511–512 (1997), in which the Court held that the Religious Freedom Restoration Act was not valid Fourteenth Amendment legislation, and Shelby County v. Holder, 570 U.S. 529, 557 (2013), in which the Court invalidated the preclearance regime of the Voting Rights Act. For the purposes of laying out the general shape of this book's argument, I focus in this introduction on enumerationism as it applies to Article I powers. I discuss special issues connected to Congress's powers under the Reconstruction Amendments in Chapter 8.

11. As Abbe Gluck has explained, "cooperative federalism" is better understood as an umbrella term naming several varying arrangements rather than a single precise model of federal-state cooperation. See Abbe R. Gluck, "Intrastatutory Federalism and Statutory Interpretation: State Implementation of Federal Law in Health Reform and Beyond," *Yale Law Journal* 121, no. 3 (2011): 584–588. Good examples of literature on cooperative federalism include Abbe R. Gluck, "Federalism from Federal Statutes: Health Reform, Medicaid, and the Old-Fashioned Federalists' Gamble," *Fordham Law Review* 81, no. 4 (2013): 1749; Catherine M. Sharkey, "Inside Agency Preemption," *Michigan Law Review* 110, no. 4 (2012): 521; Jessica Bulman-Pozen and Heather K. Gerken, "Uncooperative Federalism," *Yale Law Journal* 118, no. 7 (2009): 1256; Roderick M. Hills Jr., "The Political Economy of Cooperative Federalism: Why State Autonomy Makes Sense and 'Dual Sovereignty' Doesn't," *Michigan Law Review* 96, no. 4 (1998): 813.

12. See, e.g., Jonathan Gienapp, *Against Constitutional Originalism: A Historical Critique* (New Haven, CT: Yale University Press, 2024); Jonathan Gienapp, "Written Constitutionalism, Past and Present," *Law and History Review* 39, no. 2 (May 2021): 321.

13. See, e.g., Chiafalo v. Washington, 591 U.S. 578, 606 (2020) (Thomas, J., joined by Gorsuch, J., concurring in the judgment); Lawrence Lessig, *Fidelity and Constraint: How the Supreme Court Has Read the American Constitution* (New York: Oxford University Press, 2019), 75; Laurence H. Tribe, *American Constitutional Law*, 3rd ed. (New York: Foundation, 2000), 789 ("Article I, § 1 endows Congress not with 'all legislative power,' but only with the 'legislative Powers herein granted'").

14. See John Mikhail, "The Constitution and the Philosophy of Language: Entailment, Implicature, and Implied Powers," *Virginia Law Review* 101, no. 4 (2015): 1063, 1080–1081.

15. The argument for reading the Vesting Clause as if it meant "only" rather than "all" rests on a difference between Article I's Vesting Clause and those of Articles II and III. Those clauses vest the president and the courts, respectively, with "[t]he executive power" and "[t]he judicial power," rather than with executive and judicial powers "herein granted." The enumerationist reading takes this difference to indicate that Congress is given not "legislative power" in general but only the specific powers subsequently enumerated—the powers "herein granted," rather than "the legislative power." For a full discussion of why neither the different phrasing of the three Vesting Clauses nor anything else about Article I's Vesting Clause justifies giving it an enumerationist reading in spite of its ordinary-language meaning, see Chapter 9.

16. *NFIB*, 567 U.S. at 534 (opinion of Roberts, C.J.).

17. See, e.g., Bond v. United States, 572 U.S. 844, 877 (2014) (Scalia, J., joined by Thomas, J., concurring) (quoting Gibbons); United States v. Kebodeaux, 570 U.S. 387, 402 (2013) (Roberts, C.J., concurring) (quoting Gibbons); United States v. Morrison, 529 U.S. 598, 616n7 (2000) (quoting Gibbons); *Lopez*, 514 U.S. at 553 (quoting Gibbons).

18. See Chapter 7. For a full treatment, see Richard A. Primus, "The Gibbons Fallacy," *University of Pennsylvania Journal of Constitutional Law* 19, no. 3 (2017): 567.

19. See Arnold Lobel, "A List," in *Frog and Toad Together* (New York: HarperCollins, 1972).

20. *Lopez*, 514 U.S. at 552.

21. This idea comes in different varieties. See, e.g., William Baude, "Constitutional Liquidation," *Stanford Law Review* 71, no. 1 (January 2019): 1; David Strauss, "Common Law Constitutional Interpretation," *University of Chicago Law Review* 63, no. 3 (Summer 1996): 877.

22. For examples of approaches foregrounding the need to respect the democratic constitution-making of the Founding generation, see Keith E. Whittington, *Constitutional Interpretation: Textual Meaning, Original Intent, and Judicial Review* (Lawrence: University Press of Kansas, 1999); Antonin Scalia, "Common-Law Courts in a Civil-Law System: The Role of United States Federal Courts in Interpreting the Constitution and Laws," in *A Matter of Interpretation: Federal Courts and the Law*, ed. Amy Gutmann (Princeton, NJ: Princeton University Press, 1997): 3. For examples focusing on the value of wise decisionmaking by the Framers, see Harry V. Jaffa, *Original Intent and the Framers of the Constitution: A Disputed Question* (Washington, DC: Regnery Gateway, 1994), and, in a different vein, Whitney v. California, 274 U.S. 357, 375 (Brandeis, J., concurring). For an example of treating the creation of the Constitution as the making of promises that it is the responsibility of later Americans to redeem, see Jack M. Balkin, *Constitutional Redemption: Political Faith in an Unjust World* (Cambridge, MA: Harvard University Press, 2011).

23. See generally Paul Connerton, *How Societies Remember* (Cambridge: Cambridge University Press, 1989).

24. For an expanded discussion of these themes, see Richard Primus, "Why Enumeration Matters," *Michigan Law Review* 115, no. 1 (2016): 1; Richard Primus, "The Functions of Ethical Originalism," *Texas Law Review See Also* 88 (2010): 79.

25. See, e.g., Richard A. Primus, "When Should Original Meanings Matter?," *Michigan Law Review* 107, no. 2 (December 2008): 165; Richard Primus, "Is Theocracy Our Politics? A

Response to William Baude's *Is Originalism Our Law?*," *Columbia Law Review Sidebar* 116, no. 1 (2016): 44; Richard Primus, "Lin-Manuel Miranda and the Future of Originalism," in *Hamilton and the Law*, ed. Lisa A. Tucker (Ithaca, NY: Cornell University Press, 2020): 3. For overlapping views, see Gienapp, *Against Constitutional Originalism*; Thomas B. Colby, "The Sacrifice of the New Originalism," *Georgetown Law Journal* 99, no. 3 (2011): 713; David Strauss, *The Living Constitution* (New York: Oxford University Press, 2010); Mitchell N. Berman, "Originalism Is Bunk," *New York University Law Review* 84, no. 1 (April 2009): 1.

26. See generally Connerton, *How Societies Remember*; Reva B. Siegel, "The Politics of Constitutional Memory," *Georgetown Journal of Law and Public Policy* 20, no. 1 (2022): 19; Jack M. Balkin, *Memory and Authority: The Uses of History in Constitutional Interpretation* (New Haven, CT: Yale University Press, 2024).

1. MADISON'S ADVICE

1. Caleb Wallace to James Madison, July 12, 1785, in *The Papers of James Madison*, ed. William T. Hutchinson et al. (Chicago: University of Chicago Press, 1973), 8:323.

2. On the growing concern during the 1780s that democratically responsive unicameral legislatures would behave irresponsibly, see Gordon Wood, *The Creation of the American Republic, 1776–1787* (Chapel Hill: University of North Carolina Press, 1969), 403–413. On the rise of the idea that a bicameral legislature could be a salutary check on legislative misbehavior even if the two houses did not represent separate social classes, as they had in the older model of mixed government, see Wood, *Creation of the American Republic*, 553–562.

3. James Madison to Caleb Wallace, August 23, 1785, in Hutchinson et al., *Papers*, 8:351–352.

4. Madison to Wallace, August 23, 1785, 8:351.

5. See, e.g., Laurence H. Tribe, *American Constitutional Law*, 2nd ed. (Mineola, NY: Foundation, 1988), 297.

6. A large literature explores continuity and change in Madison's views about national power over the course of his career. See, e.g., Noah Feldman, *The Three Lives of James Madison* (New York: Random House, 2017), 286–371; Jonathan Gienapp, "How to Maintain a Constitution: The Virginia and Kentucky Resolutions and James Madison's Struggle with the Problem of Constitutional Maintenance," in *Nullification and Secession in Modern Constitutional Thought*, ed. Sanford Levinson (Lawrence: University Press of Kansas, 2016), 53–90; Gordon S. Wood, "Is There a James Madison Problem?," in *Revolutionary Characters: What Made the Founders Different* (New York: Penguin Books, 2006), 141–172; Stanley Elkins and Eric McKitrick, *The Age of Federalism* (Oxford: Oxford University Press, 1993), 133–161; Jack N. Rakove, "The Madisonian Moment," *University of Chicago Law Review* 55, no. 2 (1988): 504.

7. "Is there any thing in the nature of the two cases that will justify this discrimination [between state governments and the general government]? Do they not both depend on compact, and receive their sanction from the people . . . ? . . . [I]n both cases the

powers conferred will be considered as efficient, as far as the nature of the compact extends. . . . In forming our present confederation, it was declared, 'that each state shall retain its sovereignty, freedom, and independence, and every power, jurisdiction, and right, which is not by that confederation expressly delegated to the United States in Congress assembled.' This declaration would have been idle and useless, if the [distinction between the state governments and the general government] was founded in fact." A Republican, in the *New York Journal*, October 25, 1787, in *DHRC*, 13:477, 478.

8. See Chapter 4.

9. Hutchinson et al., *Papers*, 4:21n7.

10. Hutchinson et al., *Papers*, 3:175n16.

11. James Madison to Edmund Pendleton, January 8, 1782, in Hutchinson et al., *Papers*, 4:22.

12. Madison to Pendleton, January 8, 1782, 4:22–23. On May 26, 1781, on a preliminary issue leading to Congress's approval of the Bank of North America, Madison had been one of four members of Congress voting no, with an overwhelming majority of twenty in favor. Hutchinson et al., *Papers*, 4:20n7. It is not clear how Madison voted in the vote held on final passage on December 31, because no roll-call vote was recorded. For the assessment that he was probably among those casting "acquiescing" votes, see Hutchinson et al., *Papers*, 4:21n7.

13. Ordinance of 1784, April 23, 1784, in *The Papers of Thomas Jefferson*, ed. Julian P. Boyd (Princeton, NJ: Princeton University Press, 1974), 6:613; Ordinance for the Sale of Western Lands, May 20, 1785, in *DHRC*, 1:156; Ordinance for the Government of the Territory of the United States Northwest of the River Ohio, July 13, 1787, in *DHRC*, 1:168; The Confederation Congress and the Constitution, September 26-28, 1787, in *DHRC* 13:229, 236.

14. Jonathan Gienapp, *The Second Creation: Fixing the American Constitution in the Founding Era* (Cambridge, MA: Harvard University Press, 2018), 51 and generally; Mary Sarah Bilder, "The Emerging Genre of the Constitution: Kent Newmeyer and the Heroic Age," *Connecticut Law Review* 52, no. 4 (2021): 1263; Mary Sarah Bilder, "Colonial Constitutionalism and Constitutional Law," in *Transformations in American Legal History: Essays in Honor of Professor Morton J. Horowitz*, ed. Alfred L. Brophy and Daniel W. Hamilton (Cambridge, MA: Harvard Law School, 2009), 28; Daniel J. Hulsebosch, *Constituting Empire: New York and the Transformation of Constitutionalism in the Atlantic World, 1664–1830* (Chapel Hill: University of North Carolina Press, 2008), 7–11; David M. Golove and Daniel J. Hulsebosch, "A Civilized Nation: The Early American Constitution, the Law of Nations, and the Pursuit of International Recognition," *New York University Law Review* 85, no. 4 (2010): 932, 934–935.

15. James Wilson, *Considerations on the Bank of North America* (Philadelphia: Hall and Sellers, 1785), 8–9.

16. See Wilson, *Considerations*, 10–11 (emphases in original).

17. See Chapter 3.

18. See Chapter 5.

2. WHY ENUMERATE?

1. See Pauline Maier, *Ratification: The People Debate the Constitution, 1787–1788* (New York: Simon and Schuster, 2010), 11.
2. Maier, *Ratification*, 12–13.
3. James Madison, "Vices of the Political System of the United States," in *The Papers of James Madison*, ed. William T. Hutchinson et al. (Chicago: University of Chicago Press, 1973), 9:345.
4. See Maier, *Ratification*, 12–13, 396.
5. See Maier, *Ratification*, 14–17; see generally Martin Kaufman, ed., *Shays' Rebellion: Selected Essays* (Westfield: Institute for Massachusetts Studies, 1987).
6. See Maier, *Ratification*, 15–16.
7. See Gregory Ablavsky, "Empire States: The Coming of Dual Federalism," *Yale Law Journal* 128, no. 7 (May 2019): 1804–1808; see also Max Weber, "Politics as a Vocation," in *From Max Weber: Essays in Sociology*, ed. H. H. Gerth and C. Wright Mills (New York: Oxford University Press, 1946), 77, 78 (defining the state as a "human community that (successfully) claims the *monopoly of the legitimate use of physical force within a given territory*"). For an important exploration of the possibility that the Weberian model is inapposite for the analysis of American states even long after the Founding period, see William J. Novak, "The Myth of the 'Weak' American State," *American Historical Review* 113, no. 3 (June 2008): 752, 761–771.
8. See Ablavsky, "Empire States," 1795–1796, 1810–1811, 1815.
9. See Ablavsky, "Empire States," 1796.
10. *Records*, 1:483–484 (June 30, 1787) (Wilson, as rendered by Madison).
11. See, e.g., Bernard Bailyn, *The Ideological Origins of the American Revolution*, enlarged ed. (Cambridge, MA: Harvard University Press, 1992), 358; John Adams to William Tudor, June 28, 1789, in *DHFFC*, 16:870.
12. *Records*, 2:21 (July 17, 1787) (documenting the Convention's adoption of Resolution VI of the Virginia Plan). For more extensive discussion, see Chapter 3.
13. Consider in this connection the strategy adopted by the drafters of the Canadian Constitution, who worked eighty years after the Philadelphia Convention and who could draw on the lessons of the American experience. In Canada's Constitution, the text setting forth the legislative authority of Parliament—Section 91—contains a general statement of power "to make Laws for the Peace, Order, and good Government of Canada." That clause—the "POGG Clause"—is followed by an enumerated list of specific matters to which Parliament's legislative authority extends. And Section 91 expressly explains that the enumerated list follows "for greater Certainty, but not so as to restrict the Generality of the foregoing Terms of this Section" (i.e., the POGG Clause). In other words, the list of specific powers is provided to make certain that the particular subjects identified there—public debt, the regulation of trade and commerce, raising money by taxation, and so forth—fall within the broad grant of the POGG Clause, rather than taking the risk that subsequent decisionmakers might construe "Peace, Order, and good Government" narrowly enough to exclude the enumerated subjects.

14. An earlier version of the point made in these two paragraphs appears in William Winslow Crosskey, *Politics and the Constitution in the History of the United States*, vol. 1 (Chicago: University of Chicago Press, 1953), 410–428, 465–467.

15. See William Blackstone, *Commentaries on the Laws of England*, vol. 1, *The Rights of Persons* (Chicago and London: The University of Chicago Press, 1979) (first published 1765): 244–268. For an example of an important defender of the Constitution following Blackstone's analysis and attributing such powers to the king in the British system, see *The Federalist*, ed. Jacob E. Cooke (Middletown, CT: Wesleyan University Press, 1982), no. 69 (Alexander Hamilton), in which Hamilton argued that the president of the United States would be significantly less powerful than the king because he would not wield these powers. As some observers noted at the time, actual practice in the British system by the late eighteenth century made the king less powerful than Blackstone's list of powers would suggest: many ostensibly royal powers were by that time exercised in reality by ministers responsible to Parliament. See, e.g., Eric Nelson, *The Royalist Revolution: Monarchy and the American Founding* (Cambridge, MA: Harvard University Press, 2014), 218–228. But Blackstone's text was canonical, and that text associated those powers with the king.

    In an important study of executive power, and drawing partly on the writing of the early nineteenth-century British lawyer Joseph Chitty, Michael McConnell identifies a few other powers allocated to Congress in Article I, Section 8—including the power to establish post offices and post roads—as powers vested in the Crown in the British system. See Michael W. McConnell, *The President Who Would Not Be King: Executive Power under the Constitution* (Princeton, NJ: Princeton University Press, 2020), 30, 68, 368. For present purposes, it does not matter exactly which powers the Framers thought were liable to be associated with the king, and in any event it seems likely that different people would have answered that question differently. The point is simply that it was reasonable to think that some significant number of the powers allocated to Congress in Article I, Section 8, would have been subjects of this concern, such that the listing of powers in Section 8 can be understood as substantially animated by a desire to make clear that those powers would be vested in Congress rather than in the president.

16. Perhaps the Convention could have tried to solve the problem of allocating powers specified in the Articles among the branches of the new government by writing a general statement like "All legislative powers vested in the United States under the Confederation shall be vested in Congress, and all executive powers vested in the United States under the Confederation shall be vested in a president." But that solution would have been risky. Within eighteenth-century ways of thinking, it was not clear that all of the powers that the Framers wanted to allocate to Congress were in substance "legislative" rather than "executive." See Julian D. Mortenson, "The Executive Power Clause," *University of Pennsylvania Law Review* 168, no. 5 (September 2020): 1269, 1366–1367. Rather than reliably producing the specific allocation of powers that the Framers wanted, a statement assigning the Confederation Congress's legislative powers to Congress and the Confederation Congress's executive powers to

the president would have predictably set off squabbles about whether particular powers were properly understood as "executive" or "legislative." So if the Framers knew that they wanted Congress rather than the president to have power over regulating commerce, naturalizing aliens, coining money, regulating weights and measures, establishing courts, declaring war, issuing letters of marque and reprisal, and raising and regulating armies and navies, they were better off saying so with particularity rather than trusting to generalities.

17. See *Records*, 1:59–60 (May 31, 1787) (as rendered by Pierce).

18. See Daniel J. Hulsebosch, *Constituting Empire: New York and the Transformation of Constitutionalism in the Atlantic World, 1664–1830* (Chapel Hill: University of North Carolina Press, 2005), 221. See also, e.g., Richard Henry Lee to Edmund Pendleton, May 26, 1788, in *DHRC*, 9:878, 879; Richard Henry Lee to Samuel Adams, April 28, 1788, in *DHRC*, 9:765.

19. See, e.g., Richard Henry Lee to Edmund Pendleton, May 26, 1788, in *DHRC*, 9:879–880 (expressing the concern that the country would be too large for government to be representative and identifying the enumerated congressional power to tax as sufficient to render "resistance vain"); George Mason, speech at the Virginia Ratifying Convention, June 16, 1788, in *DHRC*, 10:1299, 1304.

20. See *Records*, 2:643–644 (September 17, 1787) (as recorded by Madison).

21. See, e.g., *Records*, 1:605 (July 13, 1787) (Butler, as rendered by Madison); *Records*, 2:95 (July 23, 1787) (C. C. Pinckney, as rendered by Madison).

22. Connecticut's Roger Sherman was the fourth. See *Records*, 1:54 (May 31, 1787).

23. See, e.g., Paul Finkelman, "The First Civil Rights Movement: Black Rights in the Age of the Revolution and Chief Taney's Originalism in *Dred Scott*," *University of Pennsylvania Journal of Constitutional Law* 24, no. 3 (June 2022): 704–705.

24. See, e.g., David L. Lightner, *Slavery and the Commerce Power: How the Struggle against the Interstate Slave Trade Led to the Civil War* (New Haven, CT: Yale University Press, 2008), 51–52, 59; William M. Wiecek, "Alvan Stewart," in *New York and the Union*, ed. Stephen L. Schechter and Richard B. Bernstein (Albany: State Commission on the Bicentennial of the United States Constitution, 1990), 739–740.

25. See William Wiecek, *The Sources of Antislavery Constitutionalism in America, 1760–1848* (Ithaca, NY: Cornell University Press, 1977). For Wiecek's definition of the "federal consensus," see page 16 of his book. See also Maeve Glass, "Slavery's Constitution: Rethinking the Federal Consensus," *Fordham Law Review* 89, no. 5 (2021): 1815, and sources cited at 1816n4.

26. See *Records*, 2:364–365 (August 21, 1787) (Charles Pinckney, as rendered by Madison). Delegates with other ideas forced a compromise under which Congress could prohibit the slave trade in or after the year 1808. See U.S. Const. art. I, § 9, cl. 1.

27. See *Records*, 2:306 (August 16, 1787) (Rutledge, as rendered by Madison).

28. *Records*, 2:360 (August 21, 1787) (Ellsworth, as rendered by Madison) (explaining that the debate over taxing exports was really only about a small number of taxable exportable commodities, namely tobacco, rice, and indigo); *Records*, 2:360 (August 21, 1787) (reporting that "Mr. Butler was strenuously opposed to a power over

exports; as unjust and alarming to the staple States," per Madison); *Records*, 2:364 (August 21, 1787) (Rutledge, as rendered by Madison) (noting the direct connection between the size of the slave population and the volume of exportable commodities). See also Michael J. Klarman, *The Framers' Coup: The Making of the United States Constitution* (New York: Oxford University Press, 2016), 279–280 (discussing the sectional nature of the export issue).

29. This text appeared as Article VII, Section 4, of that initial draft. *Records*, 2:183 (August 6, 1787).

30. See William Ewald, "The Committee of Detail," *Constitutional Commentary* 28 (2012): 197, 231.

31. See, e.g., *Records*, 1:605 (July 13, 1787) (Butler, as recorded by Madison); see also Mark A. Graber, *Dred Scott and the Problem of Constitutional Evil* (Cambridge: Cambridge University Press, 2006). But see George William Van Cleve, *A Slaveholders' Union: Slavery, Politics, and the Constitution in the Early American Republic* (Chicago: Chicago University Press, 2010), 103–142 (questioning this account). Whether that was a miscalculation depends on where one ends the story. Formally, Congress prohibited the slave trade in 1808. As a matter of practice, the slave trade continued, and prominently so through South Carolina, and the general government declined to stop it. See generally Jed Handelsman Shugerman, "The Louisiana Purchase and South Carolina's Reopening of the Slave Trade in 1803," *Journal of the Early Republic* 22, no. 2 (Summer 2002): 263; W. E. Burghardt Du Bois, *The Suppression of the African Slave Trade to the United States of America, 1638–1870* (New York: Longmans, Green, 1896), 89–93.

32. See generally Don Herzog, *Sovereignty, RIP* (New Haven, CT: Yale University Press, 2020) (arguing that sovereignty has ceased to be a useful category in political thought and had probably ceased to be so by the time of the Founding).

33. See, e.g., *Records*, 2:362 (August 21, 1787) (Mason, as rendered by Madison). On the origins of American colonies as corporations, and as exercising power under the constraints faced by other corporations, see Mary Sarah Bilder, "The Corporate Origins of Judicial Review," *Yale Law Journal* 116, no. 3 (December 2006): 502, 535–555. On the idea that states under the new Constitution might be conceived as corporations, see Bilder, 545–546, 546n241 (recounting articulations of this idea at the Convention and also outside the Convention in 1787).

34. See Herzog, *Sovereignty*.

35. *Records*, 2:25 (July 17, 1787) (Sherman, as rendered by Madison) (proposing that Congress should not be able to interfere in matters of "internal police" within the states).

36. *Records*, 1:59 (May 31, 1787) (Pinckney, as rendered by Pierce); *Records*, 1:354–355 (June 21, 1787) (William Samuel Johnson, as rendered by Madison); *Records*, 1:362–363 (June 21, 1787) (Johnson, as rendered by Yates). Franklin suggested proportional representation in the Senate except on cases implicating questions of state sovereignty, on which the states would have equal votes. See *Records*, 1:489 (June 30, 1787) (as rendered by Madison); *Records*, 1:507–508 (June 30, 1787) (Franklin's notes).

37. See, e.g., *Records*, 2:633 (September 15, 1787) (Elbridge Gerry, as rendered by Madison) (declining to sign the Constitution in part because of "the general power of the

Legislature to make what laws they may please to call necessary and proper"); George Mason, "Objections to This Constitution of Government," September 15, 1787, reprinted in *Records*, 2:637, 640 (warning that the Necessary and Proper Clause would permit Congress to "extend their powers <power> as far as they shall think proper"); Brutus I, *New York Journal*, October 18, 1787, reprinted in *DHRC*, 13:411, 413–414 (writing that the Necessary and Proper Clause gave Congress general jurisdiction); see also *DHFFC*, 14:403 (1791) (statement of Rep. John Laurance) (treating the Preamble as a broad grant of power). These readings are further discussed in Chapters 5 and 6.

38. See Centinel II, *DHRC*, 13:457, 460 (noting that the Articles of Confederation specified the principle expressly, so it was noteworthy and significant that the Constitution did not); Cincinnatus I to James Wilson, Esquire, November 1, 1787, reprinted in *DHRC*, 13:529, 531.

39. See Thomas Jefferson to James Madison, December 20, 1787, in *DHRC*, 14:482–483.

40. See *Records*, 1:291 (June 18, 1787) (Hamilton, as rendered by Madison); *Records*, 1:172 (June 8, 1787) (Wilson, as rendered by King); *Records*, 1:530 (July 5, 1787) (Morris, as rendered by Madison); *Records*, 1:324 (June 19, 1787) (King, as rendered by Madison); *Records*, 1:331 (June 19, 1787) (King, as rendered by King); *Records*, 1:492 (June 30, 1787) (King, as rendered by Madison); *Records*, 1:463 (June 29, 1787) (Madison, as rendered by Madison) (suggesting that "too much stress was laid on the rank of the States as political societies"); see also *Records*, 1:363–364 (June 21, 1787) (Madison, as rendered by Yates) (suggesting that it would be acceptable for the national government to swallow up the state governments, so long as it were done for the good of the whole). Yates was an unfriendly reader of nationalizing projects, and he may (or may not) have given Madison's words a more extreme meaning than Madison intended. But for present purposes, what matters is whether delegates eager to preserve the states as autonomous decisionmakers would have seen other delegates as contending for the contrary, regardless of whether that assessment was accurate.

41. *Records*, 1:263 (June 16, 1787) (Lansing, as rendered by King). In Lansing's view, as King recorded it, the Virginia Plan would have that effect even if the state legislatures selected senators. *Records*, 1:263.

42. See, e.g., *Records*, 1:155 (June 7, 1787) (Mason, as rendered by Madison); *Records*, 1:287 (June 18, 1787) (Hamilton, as rendered by Madison); *Records*, 1:357–358 (June 21, 1787) (Madison, as rendered by Madison).

43. *Records*, 1:492 (June 30, 1787) (Ellsworth, as rendered by Madison).

44. *Records*, 1:502 (June 30, 1787) (Ellsworth, as rendered by Yates).

45. See, e.g., *Records*, 1:34–35 (May 30, 1787) (Sherman, as rendered by Madison); *Records*, 1:53 (May 31, 1787) (Pinckney, as rendered by Madison) (reflecting the view that power given to Congress necessarily withdraws power from the states). See generally Alison L. LaCroix, *The Ideological Origins of American Federalism* (Cambridge, MA: Harvard University Press, 2010) (emphasizing the importance, in American thought up until the time of the Convention, of the idea that different legislatures had jurisdiction over different subject matters).

46. See, e.g., Smith v. Alabama, 124 U.S. 465 (1888); Hall v. DeCuir, 95 U.S. 485 (1877); Sherlock v. Alling, 93 U.S. 99 (1876); Crandall v. Nevada, 73 U.S. (1 Wall.) 35 (1867); Smith v. Turner (Passenger Cases), 48 U.S. (7 How.) 283, 408–410 (1849) (plurality opinion); Thurlow v. Massachusetts (License Cases), 46 U.S. (5 How.) 504, 582–583 (1847), *overruled in part by* Leisy v. Hardin, 135 U.S. 100 (1890); Mayor of New York v. Miln, 36 U.S. (11 Pet.) 102, 143 (1837); Wilson v. Black Bird Creek Marsh Co., 27 U.S. (2 Pet.) 245, 251–252 (1829); Brown v. Maryland, 25 U.S. (12 Wheat.) 419, 445–449 (1827).

47. For one good telling of important parts of this story, see Lawrence Lessig, "Translating Federalism: United States v. Lopez," *Supreme Court Review* 1995 (1995): 125. See also Chapter 7.

3. THE CONVENTION

1. The use of the word "delegates" to describe the men who attended the General Convention in 1787 is conventional, but it is not the word they used to describe themselves. The word they used was "deputies." See, e.g., *Records*, 1:1 (May 25, 1787). In this book, I use the word "delegates" because it is less jarring to the modern audience and nothing substantive—or at least, nothing substantive and also relevant to the argument of this book—turns on the difference.

2. For an excellent account of the nature and limits of Madison's journal, see Mary Sarah Bilder, *Madison's Hand: Revising the Constitutional Convention* (Cambridge, MA: Harvard University Press, 2015).

3. See, e.g., National Federation of Independent Business v. Sebelius (NFIB), 567 U.S. 519, 533–535 (2012).

4. See, e.g., Jack N. Rakove, *Original Meanings: Politics and Ideas in the Making of the Constitution* (New York: A. A. Knopf, 1996), 177–178; Richard Beeman, *Plain, Honest Men: The Making of the Constitution* (New York: Random House, 2009), 120–121, 288; Klarman, *Framers' Coup*, 147.

5. See, e.g., Beeman, *Plain, Honest Men*, 288 (describing the Committee of Detail as having accurately implemented the Convention's wishes by substituting an enumeration of powers for the broad language of Resolution VI). For a slightly different account, on which Resolution VI did call for giving Congress general legislative power but the Convention rejected that call and awarded only enumerated powers instead, see Carter v. Carter Coal Co., 298 U.S. 238, 292 (1936).

6. See Michael J. Klarman, "The Founding Revisited," *Harvard Law Review* 125, no. 2 (December 2011): 560 (reviewing Pauline Maier, *Ratification: The People Debate the Constitution, 1787–1788* [New York: Simon and Schuster, 2010]).

7. See *The Federalist*, ed. Jacob E. Cooke (Middletown, CT: Wesleyan University Press, 1982), no. 84 (Alexander Hamilton).

8. See, e.g., *NFIB*, 567 U.S. at 535.

9. *Records*, 1:53 (May 31, 1787) (per Madison).

10. *Records*, 1:53 (May 31, 1787) (per Madison), 1:59–60 (May 31, 1787) (per Pierce).

11. For prior scholarship arguing that the Committee of Detail's draft reflects the inten-tion to implement Resolution VI as a broad grant of congressional power rather than construing Resolution VI as a placeholder for a limiting enumeration or arguing that the committee substituted a narrow vision of congressional power for that of Resolu-tion VI, see Calvin H. Johnson, "The Dubious Enumerated Power Doctrine," *Consti-tutional Commentary* 22 (2005): 47–58; Jack M. Balkin, *Living Originalism* (Cambridge, MA: Harvard University Press, 2011), 141–149; John Mikhail, "The Necessary and Proper Clauses," *Georgetown Law Journal* 102, no. 4 (2014): 1071–1085.

12. *Records*, 2:131–132 (July 23, 1787).

13. For a good account of this problem and the ways in which various scholars have ap-proached it, see Jonathan Gienapp, *The People of the United States: The Lost Constitu-tion of National Popular Sovereignty* (forthcoming).

14. See Chapter 4. See also Mark A. Graber, "Enumeration and Other Constitutional Strategies for Protecting Rights: The View from 1787/1791," *University of Pennsylva-nia Journal of Constitutional Law* 9, no. 2 (2007): 377–379.

15. See, e.g., *Records*, 2:31 (July 17, 1787) (Mason, as recorded by Madison, noting that some delegates favored giving the national legislature "indefinite power").

16. The text in question, which the Framers called the Sweeping Clause, is the part of the Necessary and Proper Clause that gives Congress the power to make "all laws neces-sary and proper for carrying into execution" not just "the foregoing Powers"—i.e., the powers listed in Article I, Section 8—but also "all *other* Powers vested by this Constitution in the Government of the United States" (emphasis added). The Sweep-ing Clause is not an unambiguous endorsement of nonenumerated powers: "all other powers" might mean either "powers *not* enumerated in this document" or "powers enumerated *elsewhere* in this document" (or both). But at the very least, the clause contained a clear and well-understood ambiguity that left the possibility of nonenu-merated powers open. For further discussion, see infra Phase 3.

17. See Chapter 9.

18. See Chapter 4.

19. Mason to Mason Jr., May 20, 1787, in *Records*, 3:22–23 (May 20, 1787).

20. *Records*, 1:10–11* (May 28, 1787) (per Madison, describing conversation among Vir-ginia and Pennsylvania delegates); *Records*, 3:23 (May 20, 1787) (Mason, describing conversation among Virginia delegates). See also William M. Treanor, "Gouverneur Morris and the Drafting of the Federalist Constitution," *Georgetown Journal of Law and Public Policy* 21, no. 1 (2023): 8 (arguing that the Virginia Plan might be more ac-curately called the "Virginia-Pennsylvania Plan"); David S. Schwartz, "The Commit-tee of Style and the Federalist Constitution," *Buffalo Law Review* 70, no. 2 (April 2022): 811n91 (discussing the same suggestion).

21. *Records*, 1:21 (May 29, 1787).

22. *Records*, 1:33–34 (May 30, 1787) (as rendered by Madison), 1:41 (May 30, 1787) (as rendered by McHenry).

23. *Records*, 1:34 (May 30, 1787) (as rendered by Madison), 1:41 (May 30, 1787) (as ren-dered by McHenry).

24. One indication that other delegates had the same concern comes from the diary of New York's Robert Yates. In his notes for the day, Yates characterized Randolph's plan as calling for "a strong consolidated union, in which the idea of states should be nearly annihilated." *Records*, 1:24 (May 29, 1787). It is worth noting that historians tend to consider Yates's notes less reliable than most of the other sources recording the Convention's proceedings. See, e.g., Bilder, *Madison's Hand*, 227; James H. Hutson, "The Creation of the Constitution: The Integrity of the Documentary Record," *Texas Law Review* 65, no. 1 (November 1986): 12; Arnold A. Rogow, "The Federal Convention: Madison and Yates," *American Historical Review* 60, no. 2 (January 1955): 323–335. Moreover, Yates was among the delegates most skeptical of national power, and perhaps his skepticism led him to overread the centralization that the Virginia Plan proposed. Nonetheless, his characterization of the Virginia Plan suggests that Pinckney was not unique in wondering whether Randolph was proposing to eliminate the state governments.

25. *Records*, 1:34 (May 30, 1787) (Morris, as rendered by Madison).

26. See, e.g., *Records*, 1:172 (June 8, 1787) (Wilson, as rendered by King, arguing that the state could not be subject to the authority of the general government for some purposes but exempt for others); 1:172 (June 8, 1787) (Dickinson, as rendered by King, arguing that "[t]here can be no line of separation dividing the powers of legislation between the State & Genl. Govts. The consequence is inevitable that there must be a supreme & august national Legislature"); 1:287 (June 18, 1787) (Hamilton, as rendered by Madison, arguing that "the general power whatever be its form if it preserves itself, must swallow up the State powers, otherwise it will be swallowed up by them. . . . Two Sovereignties can not co-exist within the same limits").

27. *Records*, 1:34 (May 30, 1787) (Morris, as rendered by Madison).

28. In the first sentence of his notes on Randolph's presentation, Pierce described the Virginia Plan as calling for a "federal government," but in the next sentence he described the proposal as calling for a "national government." *Records*, 1:57 (May 31, 1787). Apparently he considered the terms interchangeable, or at least he was not scrupulous about a distinction.

29. *Records*, 1:53 (May 31, 1787).

30. *Records*, 1:53 (May 31, 1787).

31. *Records*, 1:162 (June 8, 1787) (Pinckney, per Convention *Journal*); *Records*, 1:144 (June 6, 1787) (Butler, as rendered by King).

32. *Records*, 1:60 (May 31, 1787) (Madison, Wythe, and King). The idea that Resolution VI was a preliminary statement of principles rather than a proposal for actual constitutional language might seem to accord with the conventional narrative's view of Resolution VI as a temporary placeholder. But the important question is not whether Resolution VI was a temporary placeholder. Like all the other resolutions in the Virginia Plan, it clearly was. The question is whether it was understood as a temporary placeholder *for a limiting enumeration of powers* or whether it might have been a temporary placeholder for a nonlimiting enumeration. On the basis of the surviving records, there is little reason for thinking that there was general agreement on the former interpretation.

33. *Records*, 1:53 (May 31, 1787).
34. *Records*, 1:59–60 (May 31, 1787).
35. *Records*, 1:53 (May 31, 1787).
36. As noted at the start of this chapter, one should be cautious about attributing too much significance to the specific wording of sources from the Convention. In the present case, where a delegate is recording his own thoughts, the specific wording may be more telling than in cases where delegates recorded the ideas of others: as a general matter, people are more likely to misdescribe other people's ideas than their own.
37. *Records*, 1:47 (May 31, 1787).
38. *Records*, 1:54 (May 31, 1787).
39. *Records*, 1:136 (June 6, 1787) (as rendered by Madison), 1:143 (June 6, 1787) (as rendered by King).
40. *Records*, 1:144 (June 6, 1787).
41. *Records*, 1:137 (June 6, 1787) (as rendered by Madison), 1:143 (June 6, 1787) (as rendered by King).
42. According to one school of thought, Mason favored a strong general government early in the Convention's proceedings but changed his mind and became a staunch opponent of centralized power when the Convention decided to allocate representation in the Senate equally among the states—a decision that greatly reduced the influence that Mason's home state of Virginia would wield in the new system. See, e.g., Joseph M. Lynch, *Negotiating the Constitution: The Earliest Debates over Original Intent* (Ithaca, NY: Cornell University Press, 1999), 3–4.
43. *Records*, 1:146 (June 6, 1787).
44. *Records*, 1:155–156 (June 7, 1787).
45. *Records*, 1:155–156 (June 7, 1787) (as rendered by Madison).
46. Mason to Mason Jr., May 20, 1787, in *Records*, 3:23 (May 20, 1787).
47. *Records*, 1:162 (June 8, 1787).
48. Madison, as rendered by Madison, Yates, and Lansing. *Records*, 1:165 (June 8, 1787), 1:169 (June 8, 1787), 4:60 (June 8, 1787) (respectively).
49. *Records*, 1:166 (June 8, 1787) (Wilson, as rendered by Madison), 1:172 (June 8, 1787) (as rendered by King).
50. *Records*, 1:42 (May 30, 1787) (as rendered by McHenry).
51. *Records*, 1:167 (June 8, 1787) (Dickinson, as rendered by Madison), 1:172 (June 8, 1787) (as rendered by King). In King's notes, Dickinson made his point about a process limit on Congress with specific reference to the issue of Congress taking control of the state militias. But the point seems to generalize.
52. *Records*, 1:163 (June 8, 1787).
53. *Records*, 1:173 (June 8, 1787).
54. *Records*, 1:163 (June 8, 1787).
55. *Records*, 1:4 (May 25, 1787) (per Madison), 1:6 (May 25, 1787) (per Yates), 1:37 (May 30, 1787) (Read, as rendered by Madison).
56. *Records*, 1:178 (June 9, 1787).
57. *Records*, 1:193 (June 11, 1787) (per Convention *Journal*), 1:201–202 (June 11, 1787) (per Madison).

58. *Records*, 1:202 (June 11, 1787) (as rendered by Madison). It is unclear whether Read thought this course of action reconcilable with his instructions not to agree to any arrangement that eliminated the system of giving each state an equal vote.

59. *Records*, 1:240 (June 14, 1787).

60. *Records*, 1:242–245 (June 15, 1787) (as rendered by Madison).

61. *Records*, 1:186 (June 9, 1787).

62. *Records*, 1:242 (June 15, 1787). See also Bilder, *Madison's Hand*, 90 (citing *Documentary History of the Constitution of the United States of America, 1786–1870* [Washington, DC: Department of State, 1901], 3:124).

63. *Records*, 1:255 (June 16, 1787).

64. *Records*, 1:265 (June 16, 1787).

65. *Records*, 1:269 (June 16, 1787). For further corroboration, see *Records*, 1:252 (June 16, 1787) (per Madison), 1:260 (June 16, 1787) (per Yates), 1:277 (June 16, 1787) (per Wilson).

66. *Records*, 1:263 (June 16, 1787).

67. *Records*, 1:249 (June 16, 1787).

68. *Records*, 1:313 (June 19, 1787) (per Convention *Journal*). See also *Records*, 1:322 (June 19, 1787) (per Madison).

69. *Records*, 1:322, 325 (June 19, 1787) (per Madison).

70. *Records*, 2:4 (July 14, 1787) (per Convention *Journal*), 2:26–27 (July 17, 1787) (per Madison).

71. *Records*, 1:322–323 (June 19, 1787) (per Madison), 1:328 (June 19, 1787) (per Yates), 1:330 (June 19, 1787) (per King).

72. *Records*, 1:323 (June 19, 1787).

73. *Records*, 1:335 (June 20, 1787) (as rendered by Madison).

74. *Records*, 1:336 (June 20, 1787).

75. *Records*, 1:334 (June 20, 1787).

76. *Records*, 1:345 (June 20, 1787).

77. *Records*, 1:340 (June 20, 1787).

78. *Records*, 1:357 (June 21, 1787).

79. *Records*, 1:357 (June 21, 1787).

80. *Records*, 1:357 (June 21, 1787).

81. *Records*, 1:360 (June 21, 1787).

82. *Records*, 1:364 (June 21, 1787) (per Yates).

83. *Records*, 1:492 (June 30, 1787), 530 (July 5, 1787).

84. See, e.g., *Records*, 4:158 (July 9, 1787) (per Dickinson), 1:144 (June 6, 1787) (Butler, per King), 1:463 (June 29, 1787) (Read, per Madison), 1:470–471 (June 29, 1787) (Gorham and Read, per Yates), 2:461 (August 30, 1787) (Carroll, per Madison), 1:462 (June 29, 1787) (Gorham, per Madison).

85. *Records*, 1:180 (June 9, 1787) (Wilson, per Madison); 1:183 (June 9, 1787) (Wilson, per Yates); 1:199 (June 11, 1787) (Franklin, per Franklin).

86. *Records*, 1:527–528 (July 5, 1787).

87. *Records*, 1:529 (July 5, 1787), 531 (July 5, 1787).

88. *Records*, 2:6 (July 14, 1787).

89. *Records*, 2:10 (July 14, 1787).

90. *Records*, 2:8 (July 14, 1787).

91. *Records*, 2:7 (July 14, 1787).

92. *Records*, 1:532 (July 5, 1787).

93. *Records*, 2:15 (July 16, 1787) (per Convention *Journal*).

94. *Records*, 2:17 (July 16, 1787) (as rendered by Madison).

95. *Records*, 2:18 (July 16, 1787).

96. *Records*, 2:19 (July 16, 1787).

97. *Records*, 1:229 (June 13, 1787) (per Convention *Journal*).

98. *Records*, 2:21 (July 17, 1787) (per Convention *Journal*).

99. *Records*, 2:21–22 (July 17, 1787) (per Convention *Journal*).

100. *Records*, 2:26 (July 17, 1787) (per Madison).

101. *Records*, 2:26 (July 17, 1787).

102. *Records*, 2:27 (July 17, 1787).

103. *Records*, 2:21, 24 (July 17, 1787) (per Convention *Journal*).

104. *Records*, 2:24 (July 17, 1787) (per Convention *Journal*).

105. *Records*, 2:21–22 (July 17, 1787) (per Convention *Journal*)

106. *Records*, 1:167 (June 8, 1787) (Bedford, as rendered by Madison); 1:173 (June 8, 1787) (Bedford, as rendered by Hamilton).

107. *Records*, 2:28 (July 17, 1787).

108. *Records*, 2:39 (July 18, 1787) (per Convention *Journal*), 2:47–48 (July 18, 1787) (per Madison).

109. *Records*, 2:48 (July 18, 1787).

110. *Records*, 1:53 (May 31, 1787).

111. *Records*, 2:17 (July 16, 1787).

112. According to Madison's notes, Rutledge spoke about Congress's assisting a state in putting down an insurrection, not Congress's putting down an insurrection unilaterally. *Records*, 2:48 (July 18, 1787). That wrinkle does not affect the analysis: modern enumerationist doctrine holds that the consent of state governments cannot add to Congress's powers. See New York v. United States, 505 U.S. 144, 182 (1992).

113. For a wonderfully painstaking and thoughtful account of the work of the Committee of Detail, see William Ewald, "The Committee of Detail," *Constitutional Commentary* 28, no. 2 (Fall 2012): 197.

114. *Records*, 2:181–182 (August 6, 1787).

115. See, e.g., *Carter*, 298 U.S. at 292; Randy E. Barnett, *Restoring the Lost Constitution: The Presumption of Liberty* (Princeton, NJ: Princeton University Press, 2004), 157–159.

116. See, e.g., Rakove, *Original Meanings*, 177–180; Beeman, *Plain, Honest Men*, 120–121, 227–228; Klarman, *Framers' Coup*, 147; Kurt T. Lash, "'Resolution VI': The Virginia Plan and Authority to Resolve Collective Action Problems under Article I, Section 8," *Notre Dame Law Review* 87, no. 5 (June 2012): 2147–2152.

117. See, e.g., *Records*, 1:60 (May 31, 1787) (Wythe, King, and Randolph, as rendered by McHenry), 2:17 (July 16, 1787) (Gorham, as rendered by Madison).

118. *Records*, 2:182 (August 6, 1787).

119. Mikhail, "Necessary and Proper Clauses." Mikhail speaks of three Necessary and Proper Clauses: one that gives Congress the power to make laws necessary and proper for executing the foregoing powers, one that gives Congress the power to make laws necessary and proper for executing all other powers vested in the government of the United States, and one that gives Congress the power to make laws necessary and proper for executing all other powers vested in particular officers or departments of that government. For present purposes, however, the second and third of those clauses can be bundled together as the "All Other Powers Clause."

120. Ewald, "Committee of Detail," 270; Mikhail, "Necessary and Proper Clauses," 1053.

121. See *Federalist*, no. 44 (James Madison). Hamilton offered the same view, sometimes. See *Federalist*, no. 33 (Alexander Hamilton).

122. See Mikhail, "Necessary and Proper Clauses," 1052–1055, 1097–1102; Ewald, "Committee of Detail," 269–272. Ewald speculates that Wilson may have been the committee member to introduce even the Foregoing Powers Clause and that that language's first appearance in a draft by Rutledge might mean only that Rutledge held the committee's pen at the time when Wilson suggested the wording.

123. *Records*, 2:177 (August 6, 1787).

124. Mikhail, "Necessary and Proper Clauses," 1128–1130.

125. Mikhail, "Necessary and Proper Clauses," 1122 (quoting Mansfield).

126. Pa. Const. (1776) § 9.

127. See Chapter 4.

128. See Chapter 9.

129. *Records*, 2:183 (August 6, 1787).

130. *Records*, 2:449–453 (August 29, 1787) (per Madison).

131. *Records*, 2:452–453 (August 29, 1787) (per Madison).

132. See Edmund Randolph, "Reasons for Not Signing the Constitution," December 27, 1787, in *DHRC*, 15:133. For a statement by a southerner of the sectional conflict over commercial regulations, see Harry Innes to John Brown, February 20, 1788, in *DHRC*, 8:386.

133. *Records*, 2:489 (September 3, 1787) (per Madison).

134. *Records*, 2:479 (August 31, 1787) (per Madison).

135. *Records*, 4:251 (August 31, 1787).

136. *Records*, 4:249 (August 30, 1787).

137. *Records*, 2:473 (August 31, 1787) (per Convention *Journal*). For Brearley's chairmanship of the committee, see, e.g., *Records*, 2:283 (August 14, 1787) (per Convention *Journal*).

138. See, e.g., *Records*, 2:489–492 (September 3, 1787), 499–502 (September 4, 1787).

139. See, e.g., *Records*, 2:483 (September 1, 1787), 497–499 (September 4, 1787), 505–509 (September 5, 1787).

140. Compare *Records*, 2:177 (August 6, 1787), with 2:590 (September 12, 1787).

141. See Gerard N. Magliocca, *The Heart of the Constitution: How the Bill of Rights Became the Bill of Rights* (New York: Oxford University Press, 2018), 26–27.

142. To say that eight states fell into this category is to make some decisions about what counts as a bill or declaration of rights (as would any other choice of number). For example, Georgia had not adopted anything labeled a bill or declaration of rights, but its

constitution included a preamble discussing the rights of freemen. For the present discussion, I have included Georgia among the states with bills or declarations of rights.

143. *Records*, 2:582 (September 12, 1787) (per Convention *Journal*).

144. See Bilder, *Madison's Hand*, at 141. For a more complete account of the material discussed here, see Richard Primus, "Sins and Omissions: Slavery and the Bill of
Rights," *Journal of American Constitutional History* 2, no. 4 (2024): 793–829.

145. *Records*, 2:587–588 (September 12, 1787).

146. On this view of constitutional rights among the Framers, see, e.g., Jonathan Gienapp, *Against Constitutional Originalism: A Historical Critique* (New Haven and London: Yale University Press, 2024), at 90–94; Jud Campbell, "Constitutional Rights
before Realism," *University of Illinois Law Review*, 2020 no. 5 (2020): 1436–1440.

147. Madison's notes for a different day do record one comment that might resonate with
the idea that the enumeration of congressional powers made a bill of rights unnecessary. On September 14, the Convention rejected a proposed clause stating that "[t]he
liberty of the Press shall be inviolably preserved." *Records*, 2:611 (per Convention
Journal). According to Madison, Sherman argued that the clause "is unnecessary—
The power of Congress does not extend to the Press." *Records*, 2:618. If we read Sherman's comment to mean that Congress had no enumerated power that would let it regulate the press, then his intervention might embody the idea that the enumeration of
powers made the affirmative specification of rights unnecessary. But that line of
thinking is problematic, in part because it is hard to imagine that Sherman thought
Congress's lack of power over the press was a function of the scope of its enumerated
powers. Congress's copyright power would authorize Congress to forbid or punish
certain publications. The power to tax could let Congress make paper or ink prohibitively expensive. The power to regulate commerce could let Congress restrict the
sale of newspapers. The plenary power to legislate for the capital city would let Congress impose any regulations whatsoever within that territory unless some affirmative prohibition blocked Congress from acting. So it makes sense to suspect Sherman
had something else in mind—and a less problematic reading is easily available. If
Sherman's exchange with Mason about a bill of rights on September 12 occurred as
Madison claimed, Sherman likely believed that some natural or common-law rights
would be enforceable against Congress whether codified or not. And as Jud Campbell has explained, some early Americans understood "the liberty of the press" as a
natural or common-law right that functioned whether or not it was codified in positive law. See Jud Campbell, "Natural Rights and the First Amendment," *Yale Law
Journal* 127, no. 2 (November 2017): 246, 269–270. Rather than arguing that Congress lacked an enumerated power sufficient to reach the press, Sherman was probably saying that a preexisting external limit on legislative power would block inappropriate censorship, whether or not the Constitution said so affirmatively.

　　Moreover, to take Sherman's September 14 statement as evidence for the enumerationist story about the Bill of Rights, one must believe that the Convention's
thinking about whether to make a declaration about the liberty of the press was interchangeable with its thinking about whether to include a bill of rights. For

modern Americans, those two issues might seem essentially similar: symbolically, the idea of a free press stands in for the whole First Amendment, and the First Amendment might seem like the core of the first ten, so an argument about the liberty of the press seems to suggest an argument about the Bill of Rights. But in 1787, the paradigmatic elements of a bill or declaration of rights were statements of principle about the basis or structure of government. To be sure, some Founding-era bills or declarations of rights included statements about freedom of the press. Section twelve of Virginia's Declaration of Rights, for example, described freedom of the press as "one of the great bulwarks of liberty." But the first seven sections described general principles about political morality, the foundations of governmental authority, and the structure of government. Only then did the declaration address any specific rights like the liberty of the press. To read an argument about a clause declaring the liberty of the press to suggest the same substantive argument about a bill of rights fails to appreciate how much more would have been at stake in one of those contexts than in the other. Certainly the Convention delegates differentiated between the two issues: the proposal for a clause declaring the liberty of the press was defeated only six states to five, but the proposal to draft a bill of rights was defeated ten states to none. Compare *Records*, 2:611 (September 14, 1787) (per Convention *Journal*) with *Records*, 2:588 (September 12, 1787) (per Madison).

148. Randolph seems to have advanced this point of view within the Committee of Detail, albeit in speaking about a "preamble" rather than using the term "bill of rights." See *Records*, 2:137; see also Jonathan Gienapp, "The Myth of the Constitutional Given," *American University Law Review Forum* 69, no. 5 (May 2020): 183, 200–201 (discussing Randolph's argument).

149. There is a large literature about slavery in eighteenth-century America, and much of it engages questions about the relationship between slavery and the adoption of the Constitution. But even scholars who have systematically analyzed the impact of slavery on the work of the Constitutional Convention have routinely neglected the possibility that slavery played a significant role in persuading the Framers not to adopt a bill of rights. See, e.g., Klarman, *Framers' Coup*, at 257–304 (describing various ways in which slavery affected the work of the Convention but not connecting the slavery issue to the omission of a bill of rights); George William Van Cleve, *A Slaveholders' Union: Slavery, Politics, and the Constitution in the Early American Republic*, 103–160, 166–172 (Chicago: The University of Chicago Press, 2010) (same); Beeman, at 341–344 (2009) (describing the Convention's decision to omit a bill of rights without any reference to slavery, despite giving considerable attention throughout the book to the role of slavery at the Convention); David Waldstreicher, *Slavery's Constitution: From Revolution to Ratification*, 72–105 (New York: Hill and Wang, 2009) (surveying many ways in which slavery permeated the Convention's work but drawing no connection to the omission of a bill of rights). Two exceptions—that is, scholars recognizing the likelihood of such a connection—are John Mikhail, "Does Originalism Have a Natural Law Problem," *Law and History Review* 39 (2021): 361, 364–365, and Ewald, "Committee of Detail," 239–240.

150. Ma. Const. Declaration of Rights, Article I (1780); Arthur Zilversmit, "Quok Walker, Mumbet, and the Abolition of Slavery in Massachusetts," *William and Mary Quarterly* 25, no. 4 (October 1968): 614, 615; see also *Legal Notes by William Cushing about the Quock Walker Case* (Massachusetts Historical Society, 1783), https://www.masshist.org/database/viewer.php?item_id=630&br=1 (https://perma.cc/5D3V-BELF).

151. N.H. Const. art. 1 (1783); Pa. Const. art. 1, § 1 (1776).

152. Delaware Declaration of Rights (1776) § 12; Maryland Declaration of Rights (1776), §§ XVII, XXI; North Carolina Declaration of Rights (1776) § XII, XIII; Georgia Constitution (1777) (Preamble).

153. See John E. Selby, *The Revolution in Virginia, 1775–1783* (Williamsburg, VA: Colonial Williamsburg Foundation, 1988), 106–108; *The Papers of George Mason, 1725–1792*, ed. Robert A. Rutland (Chapel Hill: University of North Carolina Press, 1970), 275; Edmund Randolph, *History of Virginia*, ed. Arthur H. Shaffer (Charlottesville: University Press of Virginia, 1970), 253.

154. Magliocca, *Heart of the Constitution*, 33.

4. RATIFICATION WITHOUT AGREEMENT

1. For an excellent narrative treatment of the discourse of ratification as a whole, see Pauline Maier, *Ratification: The People Debate the Constitution, 1787–1788* (New York: Simon and Schuster, 2010).

2. For other treatments of ratification-era disagreement about the meaning of the Constitution's texts addressing the extent of federal power, see, e.g., Joseph M. Lynch, *Negotiating the Constitution: The Earliest Debates over Original Intent* (Ithaca, NY: Cornell University Press, 1999), 31–49; Andrew Coan and David M. Schwartz, "Interpreting Ratification," *Journal of American Constitutional History* 1, no. 3 (Summer 2023): 449.

3. Randy E. Barnett, *Restoring the Lost Constitution: The Presumption of Liberty* (Princeton, NJ: Princeton University Press, 2004), 157. See also Missouri v. Jenkins, 515 U.S. 70, 126 (1995) (Thomas, J., concurring) ("When an attack on the Constitution is followed by an open Federalist effort to narrow the provision, the appropriate conclusion is that the drafters and ratifiers of the Constitution approved the more limited construction offered in response").

4. See, e.g., Raoul Berger, *Federalism: The Founders' Design* (Norman: University of Oklahoma Press, 1987), 70–71; see also 65 (arguing that a construction of the Constitution that empowers the federal government beyond the limits that the Federalists said would apply "constitutes a fraud on the Ratifiers"); Kurt T. Lash, "The Original Meaning of an Omission: The Tenth Amendment, Popular Sovereignty, and 'Expressly' Delegated Power," *Notre Dame Law Review* 83, no. 5 (2008): 1889, 1920 (describing the phenomenon as "reliance").

5. See Coan and Schwartz, "Interpreting Ratification," 449.

6. *DHFFC*, 14:371.

7. *DHRC*, 10:1353–1354 (Randolph discussing fears about the Sweeping Clause but explaining that he favors ratification anyway).

8. Silas Lee to George Thatcher, February 14, 1788, in *DHRC*, 7:1699.

9. On the distribution of Federalist opinion, see, e.g., Roderick M. Hills Jr., "Strategic Ambiguity and Article VII: Why the Framers Decided Not to Decide," *Journal of American Constitutional History* 1, no. 3 (Summer 2023): 410–416.

10. For example, at the Pennsylvania ratifying convention, Wilson acknowledged that the general government could exercise nonenumerated powers if those powers "result[ed] from the nature of the government itself," *DHRC*, 2:454, and also admitted that the Convention had found it "impracticable to enumerate and distinguish the various objects" of the federal government's jurisdiction. See *Records*, 3:140 (November 24, 1787).

11. *DHFFC*, 14:456–457, 460.

12. Maier, *Ratification*, 147 (Gerry was rejected as a delegate to the Massachusetts convention because he opposed ratification), 432–433 (Gerry's eventual support for ratification).

13. *Records*, 2:10 (July 14, 1787) (as rendered by Madison); *DHRC*, 13:341.

14. *Records*, 1:527 (July 5, 1787); *The Federalist*, ed. Jacob E. Cooke (Middletown, CT: Wesleyan University Press, 1982), no. 58 (James Madison).

15. Maier, *Ratification*, 258; *DHRC*, 9:902–903.

16. *DHRC*, 9:905.

17. For a survey of the surviving records of the ratifying conventions and their potential distortions, see Jonathan Gienapp, *The Second Creation: Fixing the American Constitution in the Founding Era* (Cambridge, MA: Harvard University Press, 2018), 424n9.

18. *DHRC*, 13:237.

19. *DHRC*, 13:237.

20. *DHRC*, 13:237.

21. *DHRC*, 13:237.

22. *DHRC*, 13:238.

23. *DHRC*, 13:235.

24. *DHRC*, 13:236, 275 ("Congress had never scrupled to recommend measures foreign to their constitutional functions, whenever the public good seemed to require it; and had in several instances, particularly in the establishment of the new Western Governments, exercised assumed powers of a very high & delicate nature").

25. *DHRC*, 13:337–338 (cataloging newspapers). The only state where no newspaper republished Wilson's speech was Delaware, where Philadelphia newspapers likely circulated widely enough to make local reprinting unnecessary.

26. United States v. Lopez, 514 U.S. 549, 592 (1995).

27. *DHRC*, 13:339–340.

28. *DHRC*, 13:340. Wilson's argument here about the liberty of the press calls to mind Madison's report—discussed in a footnote to Chapter 3—that at the Convention, Sherman said a declaration guaranteeing the liberty of the press would be unnecessary because the power of Congress did not extend to the press. As explained in Chapter 3, Sherman's argument (if he actually made it) was probably not about the internal limits of congressional power. Sherman was more likely arguing that the liberty of the press, as a natural or common-law right, would affirmatively limit congressional lawmaking whether or not it was expressly declared. Wilson, in contrast, could not have been ar-

guing that the liberty of the press would operate against Congress whether declared or not, because he conceded that Congress's power to regulate within the ten-miles-square district was a power that could control the press. He brushed that detail aside as minor, but his acknowledgment of the point shows that he did not think an uncodified liberty of the press would block congressional action taken under an enumerated power. Quite straightforwardly, Wilson's argument in Philadelphia was about internal limits.

29. See, e.g., *Lopez*, 514 U.S. at 592; "A Republican I," *New York Journal*, October 25, 1787, in *DHRC*, 13:477–479; Thomas Jefferson to James Madison, December 20, 1787, in *DHRC*, 14:482–483.

30. *Records*, 1:60.

31. Again, the solution cannot be that Wilson thought—as some Americans of his generation did—that the liberty of the press was a natural or common-law right that would be protected against legislative interference whether it was codified in positive law or not. That cannot be the solution because Wilson conceded that Congress's enumerated power to legislate generally for the district housing the seat of government would enable Congress to interfere with the liberty of the press within that district.

32. *Records*, 2:10 (July 14, 1787) (as rendered by Madison).

33. *DHRC*, 13:340.

34. Richard Henry Lee to Samuel Adams, October 27, 1789, in *DHRC*, 13:485.

35. Brutus II, in *DHRC*, 13:528.

36. Cincinnatus II, in *DHRC*, 14:11, 12.

37. Federal Farmer, in *DHRC*, 19:236.

38. Brutus II, in *DHRC*, 13:527.

39. Brutus I, in *DHRC*, 13:416.

40. Brutus II, in *DHRC*, 13:529.

41. Brutus V, in *DHRC*, 14:423.

42. Brutus V, in *DHRC*, 14:425.

43. Brutus V, in *DHRC*, 14:423.

44. Brutus V, in *DHRC*, 14:423.

45. Brutus XII, in *DHRC*, 16:74.

46. Brutus XII, in *DHRC*, 16:74.

47. See, e.g., An Old Whig II, October 17, 1787, in *DHRC*, 13:400–403; Letter from a Gentleman in Massachusetts, November 23, 1787, in *DHRC*, 19:293; Cumberland County Petition to the Pennsylvania Convention, December 5, 1787, in *DHRC*, 2:310; Federal Farmer Letter No. 1, October 8, 1787, in *DHRC*, 19:210; Federal Farmer Letter No. 3, October 10, 1787, in *DHRC*, 19:224–225.

48. James Madison to Edmund Randolph, October 21, 1787, in *DHRC*, 19:121 ("A new Combatant . . . strikes at the foundation").

49. See, e.g., Cincinnatus I, in *DHRC*, 19:162; An Old Whig II, in *DHRC*, 13:400; Centinel II, in *DHRC*, 13:460.

50. Federal Farmer 4, in *DHRC*, 19:233.

51. Jefferson to Madison, December 20, 1787, in DHRC, 14:482–483.

52. Maier, *Ratification*, 80.

53. *DHRC*, 2:386.

54. *DHRC*, 2:387.

55. *DHRC*, 2:387–388.

56. *DHRC*, 2:470 (emphasis added).

57. *DHRC*, 2:386, 392, 427.

58. Hartley, in *DHRC*, 2:430–431; Rush, in *DHRC*, 2:433; Yeates, in *DHRC*, 2:434–437.

59. *DHRC*, 2:441.

60. *DHRC*, 2:454.

61. *DHRC*, 2:482.

62. See John Mikhail, "The Necessary and Proper Clauses," *Georgetown Law Journal* 102, no. 4 (2014): 1045, 1129.

63. Maier, *Ratification*, 59–64.

64. Maier, *Ratification*, 63–64.

65. *DHRC*, 27:97.

66. *Records*, 2:334 (per Convention journal), 2:340 (per Madison). Because Madison's diary is especially unreliable for the last stages of the Convention, I would hesitate to assert that Pinckney moved for such a guarantee based on Madison's representation alone. But in conjunction with the record of the Convention journal and Pinckney's own January 16 statement that he had wanted such a guarantee in the Constitution, the representation seems likely to be true.

67. *Records*, 2:135.

68. *DHRC*, 27:158.

69. *DHRC*, 27:158.

70. John Mikhail, "*McCulloch v. Maryland*, Slavery, The Preamble, and the Sweeping Clause," review of *The Spirit of the Constitution: John Marshall and the 200-Year Odyssey of McCulloch v. Maryland*, by David S. Schwartz, *Constitutional Commentary* 36 (2021): 138–142.

71. *Records*, 1:605 (Butler, as rendered by Madison).

72. *DHRC*, 2:463, 499.

73. South Carolina Form of Ratification, in *DHRC*, 27:400.

74. At Virginia's ratifying convention, Patrick Henry warned that the enumerated powers of Congress could be read to warrant such a measure. *DHRC*, 10:1476.

75. *DHRC*, 27:124.

76. See William Wiecek, *The Sources of Antislavery Constitutionalism in America, 1760–1848* (Ithaca, NY: Cornell University Press, 1977). See also Maeve Glass, "Slavery's Constitution: Rethinking the Federal Consensus," *Fordham Law Review* 89, no. 5 (2021): 1815, 1816n4.

77. *Federalist*, no. 39 (James Madison).

78. *Federalist*, no. 40 (James Madison).

79. *Federalist*, no. 37 (James Madison).

80. *Federalist*, no. 38 (James Madison).

81. *Federalist*, no. 42 (James Madison).

82. *Federalist*, no. 44 (James Madison) (emphasis in original).

83. *Federalist*, no. 44 (James Madison).

84. *Federalist*, no. 45 (James Madison).

85. *Federalist*, no. 45 (James Madison).

86. See, e.g., *Lopez*, 514 U.S. at 552.

87. *DHRC*, 22:1955.

88. *DHRC*, 22:1955.

89. *Federalist*, no. 31 (Alexander Hamilton).

90. *Federalist*, no. 31 (Alexander Hamilton).

91. *DHRC*, 10:1325–1326 (Mason), 1328 (Henry).

92. *DHRC*, 10:1391, 1393–1395.

93. *DHRC*, 10:1321–1322.

94. *DHRC*, 10:1345–1346.

95. *DHRC*, 10:1329.

96. *DHRC*, 9:930.

97. *DHRC*, 9:936–937.

98. *DHRC*, 10:1476–1477.

99. *DHRC*, 10:1476–1477, 1504.

100. *DHRC*, 10:1483.

101. *DHRC*, 10:1483.

102. *DHRC*, 10:1353.

103. *DHRC*, 10:1353–1354.

104. *DHRC*, 10:1354.

105. *DHRC*, 10:1323.

106. *DHRC*, 10:1502.

107. *DHRC*, 10:1507.

108. *DHRC*, 10:1396.

109. *DHRC*, 10:1397.

110. *DHRC*, 9:998.

111. *DHRC*, 10:1503.

112. *DHRC*, 10:1503.

113. *DHRC*, 10:1542.

114. Both references occurred in *Federalist* 38. Halfway through that essay, in a list of more than a dozen objections to the Constitution that Hamilton presented as varied and often mutually contradictory, Hamilton mentioned that one such objection was the Constitution's "want of a bill of rights." Later in the same essay, he wrote as follows: "Is a Bill of Rights essential to liberty? The Confederation has no Bill of Rights." See *Federalist*, no. 38 (Alexander Hamilton). Apart from these mentions, nothing in the *Federalist* engaged the Bill of Rights issue until *Federalist* 84.

115. See *The Federalist: A Collection of Essays, Written in Favour of the New Constitution, As Agreed Upon by the Federal Convention, September 17, 1787* (New York: J. and A. McLean, 1788), 2:344–357.

116. See 2 The Federalist (1788) at vi, 344.

117. *DHRC*, 16:164, 168; *DHRC*, 16:163–164.

118. *DHRC*, 30:360.

119. *DHRC*, 30:360.
120. *DHRC*, 30:379–380.
121. *DHRC*, 30:380.
122. *DHRC*, 30:381.
123. *DHRC*, 30:381.
124. *DHRC*, 30:381.
125. *DHRC*, 30:381.
126. *DHRC*, 30:453–458, 461–462.
127. Federal Farmer 4, in *DHRC*, 19:233.

5. INTERNALIZED ARGUMENTS

1. For examples of constitutional law textbooks with different methodological and ideological orientations that present the bank debate this way, see Randy E. Barnett and Josh Blackman, *Constitutional Law: Cases in Context*, 3rd ed. (Boston: Aspen, 2018), 66–79; and Paul Brest et al., *Processes of Constitutional Decisionmaking*, 6th ed. (Boston: Aspen, 2015), 29–39. In so doing, they follow in a longer tradition of approaching the conflict over the bank in 1791 in this way. See, e.g., Bray Hammond, *Banks and Politics in America: From the Revolution to the Civil War* (Princeton, NJ: Princeton University Press, 1957), 115–119 (focusing on this same set of famous players).
2. See, e.g., Hamilton, *The Papers of Alexander Hamilton*, ed. Harold Coffin Syrett and Jacob E. Cooke (New York: Columbia University Press, 1965), 8:114. Whether Hamilton was moderating his own views so as to persuade Washington on the specific point at hand is a question on which I offer no view.
3. Hamilton, *Papers*, 8:100.
4. See William Wiecek, *The Sources of Antislavery Constitutionalism in America, 1760–1848* (Ithaca, NY: Cornell University Press, 1977). Wiecek's book, which initiated the use of the term, offered a succinct definition of the "federal consensus" at page 16.
5. Examples include Massachusetts, New Hampshire, Rhode Island, and New York. See *DHRC*, 6:1382; *DHRC*, 37:249; *DHRC*, 23:2331; *DHRC*, 37:276.
6. See *DHFFC*, 1:158–159.
7. *Records*, 2:615 (September 14, 1787) (per Madison); *Records*, 2:620 (September 14, 1787) (per McHenry).
8. See *Records*, 2:616 (September 14, 1787) (per Madison).
9. Jonathan Gienapp, *The Second Creation: Fixing the American Constitution in the Founding Era* (Cambridge, MA: Harvard University Press, 2018), 345–346n20.
10. *DHFFC*, 6:1608–1611.
11. *DHFFC*, 6:1610.
12. See Richard R. Beeman, *The Old Dominion and the New Nation, 1788–1801* (Lexington: University Press of Kentucky, 1972), 9–11.
13. See Noah Feldman, *The Three Lives of James Madison* (New York: Random House, 2017), 247.
14. Feldman, *Three Lives of James Madison*, 248–255.
15. *DHFFC*, 10:270.

16. *DHFFC*, 10:270.

17. *DHFFC*, 10:271.

18. *DHFFC*, 10:271

19. *DHFFC*, 10:271.

20. See, e.g., *DHFFC*, 10:273 (White, saying he did not "doubt [the] power of [the] house"); *DHFFC*, 10:275 (Sturges, "One body can supply an oath that will be uniform. On that principle, [I] am for it. . . . It appears we have [the] right to prescribe the form").

21. *DHFFC*, 6:1610.

22. *DHFFC*, 10:273.

23. *DHFFC*, 10:272.

24. *DHFFC*, 6:1611–1613.

25. *DHFFC*, 6:1612n2.

26. *DHFFC*, 10:481.

27. *DHFFC*, 10:481–482.

28. *DHFFC*, 10:484.

29. *DHFFC*, 10:486.

30. *DHFFC*, 10:482.

31. *DHFFC*, 10:486.

32. See Feldman, *Three Lives of James Madison*, 279; "Madison at the First Session of the First Federal Congress: 8 April–29 September 1789; Editorial Note," in *The Papers of James Madison*, ed. Charles F. Hobson and Robert A. Rutland (Charlottesville: University Press of Virginia, 1979), 12:52, 61–62.

33. See Feldman, *Three Lives of James Madison*, 309.

34. See generally Kenneth R. Bowling, *The Creation of Washington D.C.: The Idea and Location of the American Capital* (Fairfax, VA: George Mason University Press, 1991).

35. Act of Mar. 20, 1781, ch. 32, § 6, 1781 N.Y. Laws 40, 42.

36. See Act of Mar. 29, 1788, ch. 1334, 1788 Pa. Laws 443; Act of Mar. 1, 1780, ch. 870, 1780 Pa. Laws 492. See generally Edward Raymond Turner, "The Abolition of Slavery in Pennsylvania," *Pennsylvania Magazine of History and Biography* 36, no. 2 (1912): 129, 137–138. Pennsylvania's scheme exempted members of Congress, but the exemption did not extend to the federal government's executive officers.

37. Act of Mar. 1, 1780, ch. 870, § 10, 1780 Pa. Laws 492, 495; see Tobias Lear to George Washington, April 24, 1791, in *The Papers of George Washington: Presidential Series*, ed. Mark A. Mastromarino (Charlottesville: University Press of Virginia, 1999), 8:129, 130–132.

38. See Richard Primus, "'The Essential Characteristic': Enumerated Powers and the Bank of the United States," *Michigan Law Review* 117, no. 3 (2018): 415, 443.

39. *DHFFC*, 11:1415–1416.

40. *DHFFC*, 11:1463.

41. *DHFFC*, 11:1434–1443.

42. *DHFFC*, 11:1434–1443.

43. *DHFFC*, 11:1439–1441.

44. *DHFFC*, 11:1441.

45. *DHFFC*, 11:1471.

46. *DHFFC*, 11:1492–1494.

47. *DHFFC*, 11:1492–1494.

48. *DHFFC*, 11:1492–1494.

49. *DHFFC*, 11:1492–1494.

50. *DHFFC*, 11:1496.

51. *DHFFC*, 11:1497 (Smith), 11:1498 (Jackson).

52. *DHFFC*, 11:1498.

53. Feldman, *Three Lives of James Madison*, 277; "Madison at the First Session," in *Papers of James Madison*, 12:61.

54. See James Madison, "James Madison's Concurring Opinion," July 14, 1790, in *The Papers of Thomas Jefferson*, ed. Julian P. Boyd (Princeton, NJ: Princeton University Press, 1965), 17:199.

55. See One of the Gallery, "One of the Gallery on the Conduct of Madison, Page, and Carroll," *N.Y. Daily Advertiser*, July 15, 1790, reprinted in *Papers of Thomas Jefferson*, 17:200–201.

56. See Alexander Hamilton, "Treasury Dep't, Report on a National Bank," in *Papers of Alexander Hamilton*, 7:305.

57. Hamilton, *Papers of Alexander Hamilton*, 7:321.

58. See, e.g., Feldman, *Three Lives of James Madison*, 315.

59. See Stanley Elkins and Eric McKitrick, *The Age of Federalism* (Oxford: Oxford University Press, 1993), ch. 3; Feldman, *Three Lives of James Madison*, 315–318; Roderick M. Hills Jr., "Federalism and Self-Restraint: The Gentry, the Saints, and the Federal Republic in Nineteenth Century America" (unpublished manuscript, 2023), ch. 4, at 2–3 (forthcoming).

60. See Elkins and McKitrick, *Age of Federalism*, ch. 3; Hills, *Federalism and Self-Restraint*, manuscript ch. 4, at 3.

61. See *The Federalist*, ed. Jacob E. Cooke (Middletown, CT: Wesleyan University Press, 1982), no. 10 (James Madison).

62. Hills, *Federalism and Self-Restraint*, manuscript ch. 4, at 7; see also James Madison, for the *National Gazette*, in *The Papers of James Madison*, ed. Robert A. Rutland et al. (Charlottesville: University Press of Virginia, 1983), 14:137 (reprinting Madison's note on consolidation of December 3, 1791); James Madison, notes for the *National Gazette* essays, in *Papers of James Madison*, 14:157, 161–163 (concerning the "Influence of public opinion on Government"). Like the fear of debt, this concern about the power of financial networks at large scale was a staple theme in country-party thought. Hills, *Federalism and Self-Restraint*, manuscript ch. 4, at 7.

63. Hills, *Federalism and Self-Restraint*, manuscript ch. 4, at 9–10.

64. See Primus, "Essential Characteristic," 478–493.

65. See Act of July 16, 1790, ch. 28, 1 Stat. 130.

66. See, e.g., editorial note, in *Papers of Thomas Jefferson*, 17:452–453 (collecting opinion doubting that the planned Potomac move could be achieved).

67. *DHFFC*, 13:1651 ("[F]or the grave council of the United States, to pass a bill that the seat of government should be removed to that place, is a measure too ridiculous to be credited; few will suppose that Congress are serious. . . . You might as well induce a belief that you are in earnest by inserting Mississippi, Detroit, or Winnipipiocket Pond").

68. See, e.g., Edward Carrington to James Madison, February 2, 1791, in *DHFFC*, 21:660; Joseph Jones to James Monroe, January 27, 1791, in *DHFFC*, 21:557. Philadelphia was also home to the Bank of North America, to which a Bank of the United States would be a de facto and perhaps also a de jure successor. See Edward Carrington to James Madison, February 2, 1791, in *DHFFC*, 21:660.

69. George Thatcher to Jeremiah Hill, January 24, 1791, in *DHFFC*, 21:524, 525. For many more examples, see Primus, "Essential Characteristic," 487–488, 488n347.

70. For a more detailed explanation of Madison's writings during this time and the absence of this constitutional concern from them, see Primus, "Essential Characteristic," 445–447.

71. See Feldman, *Three Lives of James Madison*, 316–317; Madison, "Notes on Banks," in *Papers of James Madison*, 13:364; Madison, "Notes on the Bank of England," in *Papers of James Madison*, 13:367.

72. See *DHFFC*, 1:531–536 (describing Senate action on the bank bill between January 13 and January 20, 1791).

73. See *DHFFC*, 1:531–532, 535, 536.

74. *DHFFC*, 1:536.

75. See *DHFFC*, 9:359–366 (entries of January 10, 11, 13, 14, 17, 18, 19, and 20, 1791).

76. *DHFFC*, 9:362 (entry of January 18, 1791); *DHFFC*, 9:359, 361–362 (entries of January 11, 14, and 17, 1791); *DHFFC*, 9:361 (entry of January 14, 1791); *DHFFC*, 9:364 (entry of January 19, 1791).

77. *DHFFC*, 9:362 (entry of January 17, 1791).

78. *DHFFC*, 9:359, 361–362 (entries of January 11, 14, and 17, 1791).

79. *DHFFC*, 9:362–363 (entry of January 18, 1791).

80. *DHFFC*, 9:379 (entry of February 11, 1791).

81. *DHFFC*, 9:355, 361–362, 364 (entries of January 3, 14, 17, and 19, 1791).

82. *DHFFC*, 9:347 (entry of December 24, 1790).

83. *DHFFC*, 9:347 (entry of December 24, 1790).

84. Besides Maclay's diary entry affirming Congress's authority to charter a bank, the only writing by a senator of which I am aware that mentioned a constitutional question about the bank proposal prior to Madison's presenting his enumerated-powers objection in the House of Representatives is a letter from Pierce Butler to Georgia representative James Jackson, and the constitutional question it mentions is different from the one Madison later pressed. According to the letter, Butler was responding to Jackson's request for a description of the Senate's discussion of the bank. In two long paragraphs, totaling roughly nine hundred words, Butler described several policy arguments about the bank but nothing about the Constitution. Then at the end, he wrote this: "The exclusive privilege is considered as a violation of the Constitution—but the arguments adduced on this head need not be mentioned to

professional Gentlemen of your abilities." Pierce Butler to James Jackson, January 24, 1791, in *DHFFC*, 21:514–515. Butler thus related that someone in the Senate had raised the possibility that giving the bank a monopoly over the financial business of the general government ("exclusive privilege") might be unconstitutional. That objection, of course, is different from the objection that Madison would raise about a congressional power to issue charters of incorporation. Madison's objection was that nothing in the enumerated powers authorized Congress to issue corporate charters, and the argument Butler mentions was about a prohibition on monopoly concessions—a prohibition that would have doomed the bank bill, given its particulars, without denying Congress's power to charter any corporations whatsoever. It is also worth noting that a prohibition on monopoly concessions is more straightforwardly understood as an external limit than as a matter of internal limits: it is an affirmative rule about what may not be done. But one cannot be certain that Butler understood the proposition that way, rather than seeing the question as one about internal limits on the theory that Congress would have no power to grant monopoly concessions unless such a power were expressly specified in the Constitution. (To see matters the second way would have been an instance of internalization.) Similarly, whether Butler's statement that the arguments on that point "need not be mentioned to professional Gentlemen of [Jackson's] abilities" meant that the objection was trivial or that the arguments about that issue were well known is impossible to determine from this letter.

85. Feldman, *Three Lives of James Madison*, 246–247.

86. *DHFFC*, 9:359.

87. Unsurprisingly, Monroe was not to be outdone by Madison in his opposition to congressional powers. On February 7, one day after Madison made the second of his two major speeches against the bank in the House, Monroe for the first time (so far as I can tell) wrote that he objected to the bank bill as exceeding the powers of Congress as enumerated in the Constitution. But he hedged, writing that he was not certain of the correctness of that view. James Monroe to Nicholas Lewis, February 7, 1791, in *DHFFC*, 21:722. After another four days passed, Monroe was prepared to go all in, writing in a different letter that the bank was "absolutely unconstitutional" on enumerated-powers grounds, going into noticeably more detail about the argument, and seemingly presenting his constitutional objection as if it were a long-held conviction. See James Monroe to Zachariah Johnston, February 11, 1791, in *DHFFC*, 21:757, 758.

88. Virginia's other Antifederalist Senator—Lee—was not physically present in the Senate during the bank debate; illness seems to have kept him home in Virginia during January 1791. But he wrote to his colleague Monroe about the subject. In his letter, Lee gave several reasons why he thought the bank proposal was a bad idea. He said not a word about any potential constitutional problem. See Richard Henry Lee to James Monroe, January 15, 1791, in *DHFFC*, 21:437.

89. See *DHFFC*, 21:173–668.

90. Theodore Sedgwick to Peter Van Schaack, January 30, 1791, in *DHFFC*, 21:609.

91. See *DHFFC*, 3:702, 14:398–403. It also seems that Madison and Sedgwick had a personal falling out sometime in 1790, which again raises the possibility that

Sedgwick was disposed to think worse of Madison than Madison really deserved. See Theodore Sedgwick to Pamela Sedgwick, December 26, 1790, in *DHFFC*, 21:237, 238.

92. See *DHFFC*, 3:14–15 (describing the rules of proceeding on bills).

93. See, e.g., *DHFFC*, 11:894, 899–903, 1477, 1481–1485, 1485–1490; see also *DHFFC*, 3:14 (stating, as a rule of procedure, that opposition could be raised at the first reading of a bill).

94. *DHFFC*, 14:362, 366.

95. *DHFFC*, 14:366–367.

96. *DHFFC*, 14:367–368.

97. *DHFFC*, 14:369–375.

98. *DHFFC*, 14:472–477.

99. *DHFFC*, 14:369, 371, 375.

100. *DHFFC*, 14:374.

101. *DHFFC*, 14:369.

102. *DHFFC*, 14:368. He did not mention that he had voted in favor of enumerating such a power at the Convention. See *Records*, 2:615–616.

103. *DHFFC*, 14:369–373.

104. *DHFFC*, 14:369–370.

105. *DHFFC*, 14:370–371.

106. *DHFFC*, 14:474.

107. *DHFFC*, 14:475.

108. *DHFFC*, 14:371–374.

109. *DHFFC*, 14:374.

110. *DHFFC*, 14:374.

111. *DHFFC*, 14:374.

112. *DHFFC*, 14:371, 373.

113. *DHFFC*, 14:373, 375.

114. *DHFFC*, 14:373–375, 473.

115. *DHFFC*, 14:434–435 (Boudinot, regarding taxes); *DHFFC*, 14:364 (Laurance, regarding borrowing); *DHFFC*, 14:389 (Ames, regarding borrowing); *DHFFC*, 14:452 (Gerry, regarding borrowing); *DHFFC*, 14:388 (Ames, regarding commerce); *DHFFC*, 14:434–435 (Boudinot, regarding armies); *DHFFC*, 14:395 (Ames, regarding property); *DHFFC*, 14:434 (Boudinot, regarding debts); *DHFFC*, 14:389 (Ames, regarding the power to govern the ten miles square and other places of exclusive congressional jurisdiction).

116. *DHFFC*, 14:397 (Ames).

117. *DHFFC*, 14:437–438.

118. *DHFFC*, 14:400.

119. For example, Ames argued that the power to create a bank was inherent in Congress, *DHFFC*, 14:386–387, and he also argued that Congress could create a bank on the basis of its enumerated power to make needful rules for the property of the United States, *DHFFC*, 14:395, or its enumerated powers to borrow money and regulate trade, *DHFFC*, 14:388–389.

120. *DHFFC*, 14:472.

121. *DHFFC*, 14:393.

122. *DHFFC*, 14:393.

123. *DHFFC*, 14:393.

124. *DHFFC*, 14:393.

125. *DHFFC*, 14:393.

126. *DHFFC*, 14:393.

127. *DHFFC*, 14:393.

128. *DHFFC*, 14:393.

129. *DHFFC*, 14:393.

130. *DHFFC*, 14:472.

131. *DHFFC*, 14:423.

132. See, e.g., U.S. Term Limits, Inc. v. Thornton, 514 U.S. 779, 848 (1995) (Thomas, J., dissenting, joined by Rehnquist, C.J., O'Connor, and Scalia, JJ.) ("The Federal Government and the States thus face different default rules: Where the Constitution is silent about the exercise of a particular power—that is, where the Constitution does not speak either expressly or by necessary implication—the Federal Government lacks that power and the States enjoy it").

133. *DHFFC*, 14:446–447.

134. *DHFFC*, 14:447.

135. *DHFFC*, 14:399.

136. See, e.g., Herbert Wechsler, *Principles, Politics, and Fundamental Law* (Cambridge, MA: Harvard University Press, 1961), 52.

137. *DHFFC*, 14:393.

138. *DHFFC*, 14:457.

139. *DHFFC*, 14:438.

140. *DHFFC*, 14:438.

141. *DHFFC*, 14:403.

142. See *DHFFC*, 14:464 (Giles) (referring to the Preamble as the Constitution's "context"); see also "A Native of Virginia: Observations on the Proposed Plan of Federal Government," April 2, 1787, in *DHRC*, 9:661 (characterizing the first sentence of the Constitution as "The introduction").

143. *DHFFC*, 10:484.

144. Given the nonverbatim nature of the records, it is possible that Laurance did not actually use the word "declarations." But the underlying point does not depend on whether he used that particular word.

145. *DHFFC*, 14:425 (Stone).

6. IMPLIED POWERS

1. Jonathan Gienapp, "In Search of Nationhood at the Founding," *Fordham Law Review* 89, no. 5 (2021): 1783, 1802.

2. Thomas Jefferson, "Resolutions Adopted by the Kentucky General Assembly," in *The Papers of Thomas Jefferson*, ed. Barbara B. Oberg, (Princeton, NJ: Princeton University Press, 2003), 30:550.

3. See, e.g., David P. Currie, *The Constitution in Congress: The Jeffersonians, 1801–1829* (Chicago: University of Chicago Press, 2001), 95–107; Everett S. Brown, *The Constitutional History of the Louisiana Purchase, 1803–1812* (Berkeley: University of California Press, 1920); Dumas Malone, *Jefferson the President: First Term, 1801–1805* (Boston: Little, Brown, 1970), 311–332. According to one way of thinking, Jefferson's view was that when presented with an opportunity to take extralegal action that would achieve something important for the public good, an officeholder should violate the Constitution and then hope that the legislature would support the decision, thus ratifying and legalizing it retrospectively. See, e.g., Julian D. Mortenson, "A Theory of Republican Prerogative," *Southern California Law Review* 88, no. 1 (2014): 81n95; Currie, *Constitution in Congress*, 97–98. If so, Jefferson's attitude toward Louisiana would be a case of a decisionmaker's believing that the enumeration of federal powers did mark a boundary to what the federal government could constitutionally do and conceding that his desired course of action lay on the other side of that boundary, rather than a case of a decisionmaker's stretching the enumerated powers to justify the desired action. But it would not be an example of the enumeration's actually constraining federal action, because Jefferson's choice in the face of a perceived constraint was to ignore the rules. ("The less we say about constitutional difficulties respecting Louisiana," he wrote to Madison, "the better." Thomas Jefferson to James Madison, August 18, 1803, in *The Papers of James Madison*, ed. Robert J. Brugger et al. [Charlottesville: University of Virginia Press, 2000], 5:323.)

4. See Noah Feldman, *The Three Lives of James Madison: Genuis, Partisan, President* (New York: Random House, 2017), 612.

5. For Monroe's veto, see James Monroe, "Views of the President of the United States on the Subject of Internal Improvements," in *A Compilation of the Messages and Papers of the Presidents*, ed. James Richardson (Washington, DC: Government Printing Office, 1896), 2:713, 744. For the subsequent ideology of the Democratic Party, see, e.g., Roderick M. Hills Jr., "Federalism and Self-Restraint: The Gentry, the Saints, and the Federal Republic in Nineteenth Century America" (unpublished manuscript, 2023).

6. McCulloch v. Maryland, 17 U.S. 316, 405 (1819).

7. National Federation of Independent Business v. Sebelius, 567 U.S. 519, 534 (2012) (opinion of Roberts, C.J.); United States v. Lopez, 514 U.S. 549, 566 (1995).

8. *McCulloch*, 17 U.S. at 406.

9. *McCulloch*, 17 U.S. at 407. It may bear noting that no text in the Constitution contains words expressly authorizing the federal government to "conduct a war." Congress has the power to declare war and the power to raise and support armies and navies, and the president has the power to act as commander in chief, but the power to conduct a war might best be understood as implied rather than enumerated. That Marshall described it as enumerated might testify to the slipperiness of the categories "enumerated" and "implied."

10. *McCulloch*, 17 U.S. at 408.

11. *McCulloch*, 17 U.S. at 411.

12. Monroe, "Views of the President," 2:713, 744.

13. For the Vesting Clause of Article II, see, e.g., Youngstown Sheet & Tube Co. v. Sawyer, 343 U.S. 579, 610 (1952) (Frankfurter, J., concurring) (referring to presidential powers as "nonenumerated" after noting that "[t]he powers of the president are not as particularized as are those of Congress"); Myers v. United States, 272 U.S. 52, 128 (1926) ("The difference between the grant of legislative power under article 1 to Congress which is limited to powers therein enumerated, and the more general grant of the executive power to the president under article 2 is significant"). In a letter that Madison wrote to Jefferson during the debate over the Jay Treaty in 1796, Madison— arguing for a limited view of the treaty power that did not prevail—wrote that "the Treaty power is limited by the enumerated powers." That formulation suggests a view on which the treaty power itself is not an "enumerated" power, despite being expressly granted in the text of Article II. Madison to Jefferson, March 13, 1796, in *The Papers of James Madison*, ed. William T. Hutchinson et al. (Charlottesville: University of Virginia Press, 1989), 16:264.

14. See also, e.g., James Everard's Breweries v. Day, 265 U.S. 545, 558 (1924) (describing Congress's power under the Necessary and Proper Clause as not enumerated); see also Alison L. Lacroix, "The Shadow Powers of Article I," *Yale Law Journal* 123, no. 6 (2014): 2044, 2049 (describing the Necessary and Proper Clause as having an ambiguous status with respect to enumeration during the early nineteenth century).

15. In *Chisholm v. Georgia*, the Supreme Court described the Necessary and Proper Clause as part of the enumeration of powers even while noting that the power conferred by that clause differs from the powers conferred in the previous clauses by being general rather than specific. See Chisholm v. Georgia, U.S. (2 Dall.) 419, 432 (1793) ("[A]t the end of the special enumeration of the powers of Congress in the Constitution, is this general one: 'To make all laws which shall be necessary and proper. . . .'").

16. For a description of approaches to this question, see generally Julian Davis Mortenson, "The Executive Power Clause," *University of Pennsylvania Law Review* 168, no. 5 (2020): 1269–1367.

17. *McCulloch*, 17 U.S. at 409, 411–412 (explaining first that "the powers given to the government imply the ordinary means of execution" and then that "the constitution of the United States has not left the right of congress to employ the necessary means, for the execution of the powers conferred on the government, to general reasoning. To its enumeration of powers is added, that of making 'all laws which shall be necessary and proper, for carrying into execution the foregoing powers, and all other powers vested by this constitution, in the government of the United States, or in any department thereof'").

18. See, e.g., Gil Seinfeld, "Article I, Article III, and the Limits of Enumeration," *Michigan Law Review* 108, no. 8 (2010): 1389, 1430n208 ("Of course, the Article I powers (necessary and proper included) are enumerated in the text of the Constitution"); John Harrison, "Enumerated Federal Power and the Necessary and Proper Clause," *University of Chicago Law Review* 78, no. 3 (2011): 1101–1102; Erwin Chemerinsky, *Constitutional Law: Principles and Policies*, 3rd ed. (Boston: Aspen, 2006), 242 ("Article I, § 8, of the Constitution contains 18 clauses enumerating specific powers of Congress").

19. *McCulloch*, 17 U.S. at 417.

20. See the beginning of Chapter 7.

21. Act of February 12, 1793, 1 Stat. 302.

22. Prigg v. Pennsylvania, 41 U.S. 539, 618 (1842).

23. *Prigg*, 41 U.S. at 618.

24. *Prigg*, 41 U.S. at 615.

25. *Prigg*, 41 U.S. at 618.

26. Joseph Story, *Commentaries on the Constitution of the United States* (Boston: Hilliard, Gray, 1833), 1:§ 448, at 433.

27. Story, *Commentaries*, 3:§ 1232, at 109.

28. Story, *Commentaries*, 3:§§ 1119–1145, at 22–47 (postal power); §§ 1169–1174, at 62–65 (war power).

29. Story, *Commentaries*, 3:§ 1251, at 124; see also Alexander Hamilton, "Opinion on the Constitutionality of an Act to Establish a Bank," in *The Papers of Alexander Hamilton*, ed. Harold C. Syrett (New York: Columbia University Press, 1965), 8:100.

30. See generally Donald H. Kagin, "Monetary Aspects of the Treasury Notes of the War of 1812," *Journal of Economic History* 44, no. 1 (March 1984): 69.

31. See generally Kenneth W. Dam, "The Legal Tender Cases," *Supreme Court Review* 1981 (1981): 367.

32. As it happened, Chase had been the secretary of the treasury when the Legal Tender Acts were passed, and in that role he had been a leading architect of the paper-money innovation. See Dam, "Legal Tender Cases," 367, 372, 375. But when called on eight years later as chief justice to opine on the constitutionality of that money, Chase took a more skeptical view.

33. Hepburn v. Griswold, 75 U.S. 603, 616 (1870).

34. *Hepburn*, 75 U.S. at 615–618.

35. Knox v. Lee, 79 U.S. (12 Wall.) 457, 547 (1871).

36. *Knox*, 79 U.S. at 544–545, 547.

37. *Knox*, 79 U.S. at 529.

38. *Knox*, 79 U.S. at 545–546. Strong did not specify examples, but presumably he had in mind powers like the power to tax exports, which sovereign governments generally possess but which the Constitution expressly denies.

39. *Knox*, 79 U.S. at 534.

40. See *Knox*, 79 U.S. at 535. On the idea of "aggregate" powers, see also Robert J. Reinstein, "The Aggregate and Implied Powers of the United States," *American University Law Review* 69, no. 1 (2019): 3.

41. *Knox*, 79 U.S. at 535.

42. *Knox*, 79 U.S. at 533.

43. *Knox*, 79 U.S. at 536.

44. *Knox*, 79 U.S. at 540–541.

45. *Knox*, 79 U.S. at 534.

46. *Knox*, 79 U.S. at 536.

47. *Knox*, 79 U.S. at 554–555 (Bradley, J., concurring).

48. *Knox*, 79 U.S. at 555 (Bradley, J., concurring).

49. *Knox*, 79 U.S. at 556 (Bradley, J., concurring).

50. *Knox*, 79 U.S. at 564 (Bradley, J., concurring).

51. United States v. Curtiss-Wright Export Corporation, 299 U.S. 304, 315–316 (1936).

52. *Curtiss-Wright*, 299 U.S. at 316.

53. *Curtiss-Wright*, 299 U.S. at 318. That Sutherland's argument tracked core elements of Wilson's Founding-era thinking was no accident. In a book of constitutional theory published seventeen years before *Curtiss-Wright*, Sutherland had discussed and endorsed Wilson's thinking, drawing directly on Wilson's 1785 essay about the Bank of North America. See George Sutherland, *Constitutional Power and World Affairs* (New York: Columbia University Press, 1919), 38–39. See also John Mikhail, "James Wilson, Early American Land Companies, and the Original Meaning of 'Ex Post Facto Law,'" *Georgetown Journal of Law and Public Policy* 17 (2019): 93n71 (drawing the link between Sutherland and Wilson).

54. Burroughs v. United States, 290 U.S. 534, 544–549 (1934).

55. Mackenzie v. Hare, 249 U.S. 299, 311 (1915).

56. See Chae Chan Ping v. United States, 130 U.S. 581, 603–609 (1889). See also Ekiu v. United States, 142 U.S. 651, 659 (1892); Fong Yue Ting v. United States, 149 U.S. 698, 705, 711 (1893).

57. Jones v. United States, 137 U.S. 202, 212 (1890).

58. United States v. Kagama, 118 U.S. 375, 380 (1886).

59. *Kagama*, 118 U.S. at 379 (power does not derive from the Indian Commerce Clause or the Indians Not Taxed Clause), 384–385 (power arises from the logic of history and relationship). For further discussion of some of the cases mentioned in this paragraph, see Nikolas Bowie, "The Imaginary Immigration Clause," *Michigan Law Review* 120, no. 7 (2022): 1419; Sarah H. Cleveland, "Powers Inherent in Sovereignty: Indians, Aliens, Territories, and the Nineteenth Century Origins of Plenary Power over Foreign Affairs," *Texas Law Review* 81, no. 1 (2002): 1.

60. Specifically, *Curtiss-Wright* is remembered and invoked for its characterization of the president as "the sole organ of the federal government in the field of international relations." *Curtiss-Wright*, 299 U.S. at 320.

61. *Knox*, 79 U.S. at 561 (Bradley, J., concurring).

62. Story, *Commentaries*, 3:§ 1251, at 124.

63. Story, *Commentaries*, 3:§§ 1169–1174, at 62–65.

64. Story, *Commentaries*, 3:§ 1251, at 124.

65. Haaland v. Brackeen, 599 U.S. 255, 274, 278 (2023) (quoting United States v. Lara, 541 U.S. 193, 201 [2004]).

66. *Lara*, 541 U.S. at 201 (citing *Curtiss-Wright*, 299 U.S. at 315–322).

67. *Brackeen*, 599 U.S. at 318–331 (Gorsuch, J., concurring, joined by Sotomayor and Jackson, JJ.).

68. See Ralph Waldo Emerson, "The Problem," in *American Poetry: The Nineteenth Century*, ed. John Hollander (New York: Library of America, 1993), 1:260 ("He builded better than he knew").

7. CUMULATIVE COVERAGE

1. See, e.g., Arizona v. United States, 567 U.S. 387, 422 (2012) (Scalia, J., concurring in part and dissenting in part) (writing that the text of the Constitution had "no need to set forth control of immigration as one of the enumerated powers of Congress" because those powers are "inherent in sovereignty"); United States v. Comstock, 560 U.S. 126 (2010) (Post Office Clause); United States v. Lara, 541 U.S. 193, 201 (2004) (describing the federal government's early legislative authority with respect to Native Americans as resting "not upon 'affirmative grants in the Constitution,' but upon the Constitution's adoption of preconstitutional powers inherent in any Federal Government, namely, powers that this Court has described as 'necessary concomitants of nationality'") (quoting United States v. Curtiss-Wright Export Corp., 299 U.S. 304, 318 [1936]).

2. Haaland v. Brackeen, 599 U.S. 255, 296–333 (2023) (Gorsuch, J., concurring).

3. See *Comstock*, 560 U.S. at 166–172 (Thomas, J., dissenting). Thomas did not say that Marshall was wrong to read the Post Office Clause as implying the power to organize the Postal Service. But he took care to signal that Marshall's discussion might not be legally authoritative, either. Marshall, Thomas noted, was "discussing a hypothetical," and his analysis was "dictum." *Comstock*, 560 U.S. at 168n8 (Thomas, J., dissenting).

4. United States v. Morrison, 529 U.S. 598, 607 (2000).

5. National Federation of Independent Business v. Sebelius (NFIB), 567 U.S. 519, 535 (2012).

6. See Chapter 5.

7. See, e.g., oral argument at 4:52, United States v. Lopez, 514 U.S. 549 (1995) (No. 93-1260) ("If . . . Congress can reach under the interstate commerce power, what would be an example of a case which you couldn't reach?"), http://www.oyez.org/api/media /sites/default/files/audio/cases/1994/93-1260_19941108-argument.mp3 (http://perma .cc/J7YM-V5GJ).

8. *NFIB*, 567 U.S. 519 (upholding the Patient Protection and Affordable Care Act of 2010, Pub. L. No. 111-148, 124 Stat. 119 [2010] [codified as amended in scattered sections of 42 U.S.C.]); see Jeffrey Toobin, *The Oath* (New York: Doubleday, 2012), 272–282 (describing the role of the internal-limits canon in the struggle over the ACA).

9. David S. Schwartz, *The Spirit of the Constitution: John Marshall and the 200-Year Odyssey of* McCulloch v. Maryland (New York: Oxford University Press, 2019), 242.

10. *Lopez*, 514 U.S. at 564.

11. McCulloch v. Maryland, 17 U.S. (4 Wheat) 316, 405 (1819).

12. See, e.g., *Lopez*, 514 U.S. at 553, 566, 567 (quoting Chief Justice Marshall's language in *Gibbons* regarding the implication of Congress's enumerated powers three separate times); Bond v. United States, 572 U.S. 844, 877 (2014); *NFIB*, 567 U.S. at 534, 557 (2012) (Roberts, C.J.); David A. Strauss, "Foreword: Does the Constitution Mean What It Says?," *Harvard Law Review* 129, no. 1 (November 2015): 1, 45; Kurt T. Lash, "The Sum of All Delegated Power: A Response to Richard Primus, *The Limits of Enumeration*," *Yale Law Journal Forum* 124, no. 1 (December 22, 2014): 182.

13. Gibbons v. Ogden, 22 U.S. (9 Wheat.) 1, 14 (1824).

14. The language about commerce "with the Indian tribes" seems to have been a late addition to the text of the Commerce Clause. The Committee of Detail's draft would have simply given Congress the power "[t]o regulate commerce with foreign nations, and among the several states." *Records*, 2:181 (August 6, 1787) (per Madison). On August 22, a committee chaired by Rutledge recommended adding the words "and with Indians, within the Limits of any State, not subject to the laws thereof." *Records*, 2:367 (August 22, 1787) (per Journal). On September 4, the Convention approved the phrasing "and with the Indian tribes." *Records*, 2:493, 495 (September 4, 1787) (per Journal).

15. *Gibbons*, 22 U.S. (9 Wheat.) at 194 ("Commerce among the States, cannot stop at the external boundary line of each State, but may be introduced into the interior").

16. *Gibbons*, 22 U.S. (9 Wheat.) at 194.

17. *Gibbons*, 22 U.S. (9 Wheat.) at 194–195 (emphasis added).

18. See, e.g., Barnhart v. Peabody Coal Co., 537 U.S. 149, 168 (2003) ("As we have held repeatedly, the canon *expressio unius est exclusio alterius* does not apply to every statutory list or grouping").

19. *Gibbons*, 22 U.S. (9 Wheat.) at 195.

20. See, e.g., Houston, E. & W. Tex. Ry. Co. v. United States ("the Shreveport Rate Cases"), 234 U.S. 342, 351–352 (1914).

21. Ogden v. Saunders, 25 U.S. (12 Wheat.) 213 (1827). On the operation of state-level bankruptcy law at the time, see John A. E. Pottow, "Modular Bankruptcy: Toward a Consumer Scheme of Arrangement" (Law and Economics Research Paper Series 23.032, University of Michigan, August 31, 2023).

22. See, e.g., Passenger Cases, 48 U.S. (7 How.) 283, 391–392 (1849) (plurality opinion) (striking down state laws taxing alien passenger landings as unconstitutional encroachments on the federal power to regulate commerce); *Gibbons*, 22 U.S. (9 Wheat.) at 209 (describing the exclusive-power contention as having "great force").

23. See William J. Novak, *The People's Welfare: Law and Regulation in Nineteenth Century America* (Chapel Hill: University of North Carolina Press, 1996), 95–100, 115–131.

24. *Gibbons*, 22 U.S. (9 Wheat.) at 65.

25. In 1847, Justice John Catron argued against considering the commerce power to be exclusive by pointing out that a broad and exclusive commerce power would "expunge more State laws and city corporate regulations than Congress is likely to make in a century on the same subject." The License Cases, 46 U.S. (5 How.) 504, 607 (1847) (Catron, J., concurring).

26. The first court to do so was the United States Court of Appeals for the Fifth Circuit, in 1993, in the litigation that later became *United States v. Lopez* at the Supreme Court. See Lopez v. United States, 2 F.3d 1342, 1361 (5th Cir. 1993).

27. See United States v. Dewitt, 76 U.S. (9 Wall.) 41 (1869) (striking down a statutory section prohibiting the sale of naphtha as applied within states); Hepburn v. Griswold, 75 U.S. (8 Wall.) 603 (1870) (striking down the Legal Tender Act); United States v. Reese, 92 U.S. 214 (1876) (striking down sections 3 and 4 of the Enforcement Act of 1870); United States v. Cruikshank, 92 U.S. 542 (1876) (disallowing a prosecution

based on section 6 of the Enforcement Act of 1870); United States v. Fox, 95 U.S. 670 (1878) (striking down federal bankruptcy fraud prohibition); Trade-Mark Cases, 100 U.S. 82 (1879) (striking down the Trademark Act of 1870); United States v. Harris, 106 U.S. 629 (1883) (disallowing federal prosecutions under section 2 of the Enforcement Act of 1871); Civil Rights Cases, 109 U.S. 3 (1883) (striking down the Civil Rights Act of 1875). In *Reese, Cruikshank, Harris,* and the *Civil Rights Cases,* the enumerated powers most at issue were Congress's enumerated powers to enforce the Reconstruction Amendments. For reasons discussed in Chapter 8, cases about the limits of Congress's Reconstruction enforcement powers complicate the distinction between internal and external limits, and it is probably most accurate to say that federal laws struck down on the grounds that they exceed those powers are held unconstitutional for a combination of internal- and external-limit reasons.

28. *Civil Rights Cases,* 109 U.S. 3; *Harris,* 106 U.S. 629; *Reese,* 92 U.S. 214.

29. United States v. E.C. Knight Co., 156 U.S. 1, 14 (1895) (quoting Kidd v. Pearson, 128 U.S. 1, 21 [1888]). In *Kidd,* the Court upheld an Iowa law regulating the manufacture of liquor against the claim that it was preempted by Congress's exclusive power to regulate commerce. By way of explaining why the commerce power should not be construed broadly enough to preempt the Iowa law, the *Kidd* Court pointed out that such a construction would preempt state law on a catastrophic scale. In *E.C. Knight,* the Court took *Kidd'*s analysis not as a reason for upholding state law but as a reason for limiting the reach of federal law.

30. Employers' Liability Cases, 207 U.S. 463, 502 (1908).

31. Keller v. United States, 213 U.S. 138, 148, 149 (1909).

32. Hammer v. Dagenhart, 247 U.S. 251 (1918).

33. Child Labor Act of 1916, Pub. L. No. 164-249, 39 Stat. 675, *invalidated by* Hammer v. Dagenhart, 247 U.S. 251, 277 (1918).

34. *Dagenhart,* 247 U.S. at 276.

35. *E.C. Knight,* 156 U.S. at 14 (quoting *Kidd,* 128 U.S. at 21) (emphasis added).

36. *Employers' Liability Cases,* 207 U.S. at 502.

37. See, e.g., Cooley v. Board of Wardens, 53 U.S. (12 How.) 299, 318–319 (1852); Morgan's Louisiana & T.R. & S.S. Co. v. Board of Health ("Morgan's Steamship"), 118 U.S. 455, 465 (1886).

38. See, e.g., Sherlock v. Alling, 93 U.S. 99, 102–103 (1876); Smith v. Alabama, 124 U.S. 465, 474–475 (1888).

39. See, e.g., Lawrence Lessig, "Translating Federalism," *1995 Supreme Court Review* (1995): 160–161.

40. Six years after the *Employers' Liability Cases,* the Court made clear that state-level authorities could set rates for intrastate railroad shipping unless federal authorities issued contravening rules. See *Houston, E. & W. Tex. Ry. Co.,* 234 U.S. 342. In other words, the jurisdiction over intrastate shipping rates was concurrent.

41. *Dagenhart,* 247 U.S. at 273–274 ("The grant of power of Congress over the subject of interstate commerce was to enable it to regulate such commerce, and not to give it authority to control the states in their exercise of the police power over local trade and manufacture").

42. *Dagenhart*, 247 U.S. at 277 (Holmes, J., dissenting).

43. 37 Stat. 828, 847, c. 145.

44. See United States v. McCullagh, 221 F. 288 (D. Kan. 1915); United States v. Shauver, 214 F. 154 (E.D. Ark. 1914).

45. Missouri v. Holland, 252 U.S. 416, 432 (1920).

46. *Holland*, 252 U.S. at 433.

47. *Holland*, 252 U.S. at 432. A century later, Justice Scalia contested this part of Holmes's analysis by arguing that the Necessary and Proper Clause gives Congress only the power to make laws necessary and proper for the *making* of treaties, not the power to make laws necessary and proper for *complying* with treaties or carrying the treaties into execution. After all, Justice Scalia argued, the Necessary and Proper Clause says that Congress has the power to make laws necessary and proper for carrying into execution the "powers" of the federal government, not the obligations of the federal government. The Treaty Clause says that the president has the power to "make" treaties. So Congress has the power to make laws to help the president "make" treaties. But once a treaty is ratified, Scalia reasoned, the treaty "has been *made* and is not susceptible of any more making," so the Necessary and Proper Clause no longer has any bearing. To construe the Necessary and Proper Clause as giving Congress the power to make laws for doing something more than "making" the treaty would be to exceed its textually prescribed scope. See *Bond*, 572 U.S. at 874–876 (Scalia, J., concurring, joined by Thomas, J.) (emphasis in original). As a close reading of the Necessary and Proper Clause, Justice Scalia's argument has merit. But it is the same sort of merit that resides in the kind of close reading of the Post Office Clause that would interpret that clause as authorizing only the establishment of offices and roads rather than also authorizing Congress to develop and maintain a system for carrying and delivering mail.

48. Some treaties—called "self-executing treaties"—do not need enabling legislation to have the force of law. Their terms are legally effective on ratification. Carlos M. Vazquez, "The Four Doctrines of Self-Executing Treaties," *American Journal of International Law* 89 (1995): 695. So under *Holland*, it is possible for the federal government to create any law not prohibited by external limits with an exercise of the treaty power alone, even without the further step of legislation under the Necessary and Proper Clause. Legislation under the Necessary and Proper Clause was needed in *Holland* because the treaty in question—the Migratory Bird Convention—was not self-executing: by its terms, it required further legislation by the ratifying governments in order to become effective.

49. Mackenzie v. Hare, 239 U.S. 299, 311 (1915).

50. *Holland*, 252 U.S. at 433 (internal quotation marks omitted).

51. *Holland*, 252 U.S. at 433–434.

52. As noted in a prior footnote, understanding Holmes to have rested entirely on enumerated powers requires a willingness to read the Necessary and Proper Clause in a way analogous to the way constitutional law normally reads the Post Office Clause: as implying a responsibility and a power that goes a bit beyond its strict terms. If reading the Post Office Clause to authorize the creation and operation of the postal service

complies with the enumeration principle, then so, I think, does reading the Necessary and Proper Clause to authorize Congress to make laws fulfilling the obligations of treaties made pursuant to the power specified in the Treaty Clause. Readers who conclude that the Necessary and Proper Clause cannot be deployed in conjunction with the Treaty Clause to authorize Congress to make laws fulfilling treaty obligations might instead conclude that Holmes actually needed his underlying theory of implicit national power to make his analysis work. On that view, the real rationale of *Holland* was that the national government of the United States inherently had the power to make laws to fulfill its treaty obligations. With that point established, one might say that Congress had the power to make the Migratory Bird Treaty Act as an exercise of its power to make all laws necessary and proper for carrying into effect "all other powers vested by this Constitution in the government of the United States," including the power to fulfill its treaty obligations. But one could also skip that last step. If the power to make laws for the purpose of complying with treaty obligations is inherent, nothing further is needed.

53. For one excellent telling, see Jeff Shesol, *Supreme Power: Franklin Roosevelt vs. the Supreme Court* (New York: W. W. Norton, 2010). For different views, see Laura Kalman, *FDR's Gambit: The Court Packing Fight and the Rise of Legal Liberalism* (New York: Oxford University Press, 2022); Barry Cushman, *Rethinking the New Deal Court: The Structure of a Constitutional Revolution* (New York: Oxford University Press, 1998).

54. A.L.A. Schechter Poultry Corporation v. United States, 295 U.S. 495 (1935); Carter v. Carter Coal Company, 298 U.S. 238, 292 (1936).

55. Jones & Laughlin Steel Corp. v. NLRB, 301 U.S. 1 (1937).

56. United States v. Darby, 312 U.S. 100, 116-117 (1941) (overruling *Dagenhart*).

57. *Darby*, 312 U.S. at 114.

58. *Darby*, 312 U.S. at 110.

59. *Darby*, 312 U.S. at 118-119.

60. *Darby*, 312 U.S. at 119.

61. The Court in *Darby* concluded that the wage and hour regulations were constitutional even apart from their status as purported means for helping enforce the shipping regulations, because the wage and hour conditions themselves had interstate commercial consequences that Congress was entitled to address under the Commerce Clause. *Darby*, 312 U.S. at 122. So those regulations would have been upheld even without the fiction about their being means to the end of enforcing the shipping regulations. But the Court also did approve that fiction as another ground for its decision. *Darby*, 312 U.S. at 121-122.

62. *Darby*, 312 U.S. at 115.

63. Wickard v. Filburn, 317 U.S. 111 (1942).

64. *Wickard*, 317 U.S. at 114.

65. *Wickard*, 317 U.S. at 120; see also *Wickard*, 317 U.S. at 124.

66. *Wickard*, 317 U.S. at 125.

67. *Wickard*, 317 U.S. at 128.

68. *Wickard*, 317 U.S. at 114.

69. *Wickard*, 317 U.S. at 127–128.

70. See, e.g., Heart of Atlanta Motel, Inc. v. United States, 379 U.S. 241, 275 (1964) (Black, J., concurring) ("[S]ome isolated and remote lunchroom which sells only to local people and buys almost all its supplies in the locality may possibly be beyond the reach of the power of Congress to regulate commerce"). See also Maryland v. Wirtz, 392 U.S. 183, 196 (1968) (asserting that "the power to regulate commerce, though broad indeed, has limits").

71. See, e.g., Jesse H. Choper, *Judicial Review and the National Political Process: A Functional Reconsideration of the Role of the Supreme Court* (Chicago: University of Chicago Press, 1980).

72. *Lopez*, 514 U.S. at 567–568.

73. Gun-Free School Zones Act of 1990, 18 U.S.C. §§ 921–922 (1994), *invalidated by* United States v. Lopez, 514 U.S. 549 (1995); 136 Cong. Rec. 36930 (1990); 136 Cong. Rec. 36739 (1990).

74. Oral argument at 4:01, *Lopez*, 514 U.S. (No. 93-1260), http://www.oyez.org/cases/1990-1999/1994/1994_93_1260#argument (https://perma.cc/644J-9PPT).

75. Oral argument at 4:52, *Lopez*, 514 U.S. (No. 93-1260), http://www.oyez.org/cases/1990-1999/1994/1994_93_1260#argument (https://perma.cc/7ADT-2Q6X).

76. *Lopez*, 514 U.S. at 564.

77. *Lopez*, 514 U.S. at 552.

78. *Lopez*, 514 U.S. at 566.

79. *Lopez*, 514 U.S. at 552.

80. *Lopez*, 514 U.S. at 553, 566, 567.

81. *Lopez*, 514 U.S. at 564.

82. *Morrison*, 529 U.S. at 613.

83. 42 U.S.C. § 13981(c) (1995), *invalidated by* United States v. Morrison, 529 U.S. 598, 615 (2000).

84. *Morrison*, 529 U.S. at 615.

85. *Morrison*, 529 U.S. at 613.

86. *Morrison*, 529 U.S. at 613.

87. *NFIB*, 567 U.S. 519 (2012).

88. See Jonathan Cohn, *The Ten Year War: Obamacare and the Unfinished Crusade for Universal Coverage* (New York: St. Martin's, 2021).

89. See Amy Finkelstein et al., *Risky Business: Why Insurance Markets Fail and What to Do About It* (New Haven, CT: Yale University Press, 2023), 61, 64–65.

90. See Cohn, *Ten Year War*, 119–121.

91. See Cohn, *Ten Year War*, 141, 519–520.

92. *NFIB*, 567 U.S. at 549–552 (opinion of Roberts, C.J.); *NFIB*, 567 U.S. at 648 (Scalia, Kennedy, Thomas, and Alito, JJ., dissenting).

93. For one of my own efforts, see Richard Primus, "The Most Revealing Word in the United States Reports," *Green Bag*, 2nd ser., 22, no. 4 (Summer 2019): 333.

94. *NFIB*, 567 U.S. at 549–552 (opinion of Roberts, C.J.). See also Richard Primus and Roderick M. Hills Jr., "Suspect Spheres, Not Enumerated Powers: A Guide for Leaving the Lamppost," *Michigan Law Review* 119, no. 7 (May 2021): 1492–1495.

95. See, e.g., Lawrence v. Texas, 539 U.S. 558 (2003).

96. *NFIB*, 567 U.S. at 554 (opinion of Roberts, C.J.) (quoting *The Federalist*, ed. Jacob E. Cooke [Middletown, CT: Wesleyan University Press, 1982], no. 48 [James Madison]). When Madison in *Federalist* 48 warned of "[t]he legislative department . . . drawing all power into its impetuous vortex," he was writing about the relationships, in the 1780s, between the legislatures and the executive authorities of the various states. In other words, he was describing a dynamic of the separation of powers, not warning of a possible usurpation by the national legislature of powers properly belonging to the states.

97. *NFIB*, 567 U.S. at 652–653 (Scalia, Kennedy, Thomas, and Alito, JJ., dissenting).

98. *NFIB*, 567 U.S. at 655 (Scalia, Kennedy, Thomas, and Alito, JJ., dissenting).

99. See Gun-Free School Zones Act of 1996, 18 U.S.C. § 922(q) (1996).

100. See, e.g., United States v. Dorsey, 418 F.3d 1038, 1046 (9th Cir. 2005); United States v. Danks, 221 F.3d 1037, 1039 (8th Cir. 1999).

101. *NFIB*, 567 U.S. at 573 (opinion of Roberts, C.J.); *NFIB*, 567 U.S. at 589 (Ginsburg, J., concurring in part and dissenting in part, joined by Breyer, Sotomayor, and Kagan, JJ.).

102. *NFIB*, 567 U.S. at 661, 668 (Scalia, Kennedy, Thomas, and Alito, JJ., dissenting).

103. See Cohn, *Ten Year War*, 522–523.

104. *NFIB*, 567 U.S. at 616 (Ginsburg, J., concurring in part, concurring in the judgment in part, and dissenting in part).

8. FEDERALISM WITHOUT INTERNAL LIMITS

1. See Daniel Halberstam, "Federalism: Theory, Policy, Law," in *The Oxford Handbook of Comparative Constitutional Law*, ed. Michel Rosenfeld and András Sajó (Oxford: Oxford University Press, 2012), 586–588.

2. See Roderick M. Hills Jr., "Is Federalism Good for Localism? The Localist Case for Federal Regimes," *Journal of Law and Politics* 21 (2005): 187.

3. The classic account is Charles Tiebout, "A Pure Theory of Local Expenditures," *Journal of Political Economy*, 64, no. 5 (1956): 416. For an important challenge to these ideas, see Richard Schragger, "Federalism, Metropolitanism, and the Problem of States," *Virginia Law Review* 105, no. 8 (2019): 1592–1593 (showing that under modern conditions state-level governance produces less regulatory diversity than the classic model imagines and that better regulatory diversity would emerge if decisionmaking were shifted from the state to the municipal or metropolitan level).

4. See New State Ice Co. v. Liebmann, 285 U.S. 262, 311 (1932) (Brandeis, J., dissenting).

5. Youngstown Sheet & Tube Co. v. Sawyer, 343 U.S. 579, 610 (1952) (Frankfurter, J., concurring); Zivotofsky ex rel. Zivotofsky v. Kerry, 576 U.S. 1, 16 (2015); Bowsher v. Synar, 478 U.S. 714, 723 (1986); Clinton v. City of New York, 524 U.S. 417, 438, 448 (1998); Free Enterprise Fund v. Public Co. Accounting Oversight Bd., 561 U.S. 477, 500 (2010).

6. United States v. Lopez, 514 U.S. 549, 552 (1995) (emphasis added).

7. National Federation of Independent Business v. Sebelius (NFIB), 567 U.S. 519, 534 (2012) (opinion of Roberts, C.J.) (emphasis added). Roberts was partly quoting Marshall's statement in McCulloch that "[t]his government is acknowledged by all, to be

one of enumerated powers." McCulloch v. Maryland, 17 U.S. 316, 405 (1819). Marshall's statement did not use the phrase "federal government," but the government to which he was referring was of course the federal government.

8. See, e.g., Edward S. Corwin, "The Passing of Dual Federalism," *Virginia Law Review* 36, no. 1 (1950): 1; Ernest A. Young, "The Puzzling Persistence of Dual Federalism," in *Nomos LV: Federalism and Subsidiarity*, ed. James E. Fleming and Jacob T. Levy (New York: New York University Press, 2014).

9. See, e.g., Lawrence Lessig, "Translating Federalism," *Supreme Court Review* 125 (1995): 140–143.

10. See, e.g., Corwin, "Passing of Dual Federalism."

11. Once upon a time, Article I, Section 9, provided that Congress could not override state-level decisions about whether to continue the slave trade, and the First Amendment made states the exclusive decisionmakers on questions of religious establishments. Those affirmative reservations are now long gone, the former because Section 9's rule against congressional abolition of the slave trade expired in 1808 and the latter because the First Amendment has been interpreted to bar not just Congress but also the state governments from instituting religious establishments.

12. See, e.g., *Lopez*, 514 U.S. at 567–568 (citations omitted) ("The broad language in these opinions has suggested the possibility of additional expansion, but we decline here to proceed any further. To do so would require us to conclude that the Constitution's enumeration of powers does not presuppose something not enumerated, and that there never will be a distinction between what is truly national and what is truly local. This we are unwilling to do.").

13. Gonzales v. Raich, 545 U.S. 1, 42 (2005) (O'Connor, J., dissenting) (emphasis added). See also Haaland v. Brackeen, 599 U.S. 255, 377–378 (2023) (Alito, J., dissenting) (describing "the governance of family relations" as among "the States' reserved powers" and further explaining that "[t]his does not mean that federal law may never touch on family matters. . . . But we have never held that Congress under any of its enumerated powers may regulate the very nature of those relations or dictate their creation, dissolution, or modification. Nor could we and remain faithful to our founding.").

14. *The Federalist*, ed. Jacob E. Cooke (Middletown, CT: Wesleyan University Press, 1982), no. 45 (James Madison).

15. Examples of domains of complete federal preemption include the regulation of retirement savings accounts, see 29 U.S.C. § 1001, and the regulation of medical devices, see 21 U.S.C. § 360k. Note, however, that even the statute that prima facie preempts state regulation of medical devices permits the secretary of health and human services to permit concurrent state regulation that either (a) is stricter than the applicable federal law or (b) "is required by compelling local conditions" and would not cause affected medical devices to be in violation of federal law. 21 U.S.C. § 360k(b).

16. See United States v. Morrison, 529 U.S. 598, 659 (2000) (Breyer, J., dissenting).

17. Gregory v. Ashcroft, 501 U.S. 452, 460 (1991).

18. See Richard Primus and Roderick M. Hills Jr., "Suspect Spheres, Not Enumerated Powers: A Guide for Leaving the Lamppost," *Michigan Law Review* 119, no. 7 (May 2021): 1431, 1476–1480.

19. See Hammer v. Dagenhart, 247 U.S. 251, 272 (1918) (reserving regulation of "the production of articles," as opposed to their interstate transportation, to states exclusively, and holding such production immune from the effect of a regulation that formally regulated interstate transportation).

20. One might recast *Dagenhart* as a purely internal-limits decision if the Court's rationale had been that the commerce power authorized only legislation *aimed* at commercial regulation as such, rather than legislation that regulated commerce for some social or other noncommercial purpose. But even acknowledging the difficulty of distinguishing between commercial and noncommercial purposes, that characterization of *Dagenhart* cannot succeed, because the Court of that era often permitted Congress to wield its commerce power for purposes that were pretty clearly on the noncommercial side of the line. Indeed, the Court upheld several federal statutes that used exactly the same strategy as the Child Labor Act, prohibiting the interstate transportation of items (or people) in order to deter or prevent some underlying activity that Congress considered a social ill. See, e.g., Champion v. Ames, 188 U.S. 321 (1903) (prohibition of interstate transportation of lottery tickets); Hipolite Egg Co. v. United States, 220 U.S. 45 (1911) (prohibition of interstate transportation of impure foods and drugs); Hoke v. United States, 227 U.S. 308 (1913) (prohibition of interstate transportation of women for the purpose of prostitution); Weber v. Freed, 239 U.S. 325 (1915) (prohibition of interstate transportation of prizefight films, enacted to prevent widespread viewing of a championship prizefight in which an African American boxer knocked out a white boxer). That the statutes in these cases used the regulation of commerce as a means to a noncommercial end did not, in the Court's view, mean that the statutes were beyond the commerce power. But in none of these other statutes did Congress seek to regulate a domain that the Court regarded as affirmatively and exclusively a subject for state regulation. The Child Labor Act did exactly that, with the domain of manufacture. The result in *Dagenhart* was accordingly driven by an external-limit principle—that the states' exclusive power to regulate manufacture blocked a regulation otherwise within the commerce power—rather than by a theory of the internal limits of the commerce power.

21. United States v. Butler, 297 U.S. 1, 54–56 (1936).

22. *Butler*, 297 U.S. at 63–64.

23. *Butler*, 297 U.S. at 62, 64.

24. *Butler*, 297 U.S. at 66–67.

25. *Butler*, 297 U.S. at 68.

26. *Butler*, 297 U.S. at 68.

27. *Butler*, 297 U.S. at 68.

28. The Court's opinion in *Butler* also discussed the potential applicability of the taxing power: the statutory scheme imposed taxes, partly to deter hoarding and partly to raise funds to support the subsidy program. The Court concluded that the program was not a valid exercise of the taxing power, because its purpose was to regulate conduct (rather than to raise revenue). *Butler*, 297 U.S. at 58–61. Like its conclusion that the program was not a valid exercise of the commerce power because agriculture was not part of commerce, this ruling about the taxing power is reasonably understood as

a matter of internal limits. The key point, though, is that these internal-limit propositions would have been insufficient to block the federal program without the external
limit on agricultural regulation that the Court invoked to block the spending power.
Indeed, the Court's discussion of the taxing-power question further illustrated the
prominence of external limits in the Court's thinking. In reaching its conclusion that
the program was regulatory rather than revenue-raising, the Court described the operation of the subsidy program as coercive. *Butler*, 297 U.S. at 70–71. But the Court
also made clear that the unconstitutionality of the program did not depend on its coercive nature. Even if it were not coercive, the Court explained, it would be invalid
because "it is a scheme for purchasing with federal funds submission to federal regulation of a subject reserved to the states." *Butler*, 297 U.S. at 72. That is an external-
limit analysis.

29. New York v. United States, 505 U.S. 144 (1992).

30. Printz v. United States, 521 U.S. 898 (1997).

31. See Reno v. Condon, 528 U.S. 141, 149 (2000).

32. *Printz*, 521 U.S. at 924.

33. Murphy v. NCAA, 584 U.S. 453, 471 (2018).

34. Presumably because he understood that Congress can do things like charter corporations and ration the cultivation of wheat even though no enumerated power expressly authorizes those measures, Justice Alito offered a reason why the absence of
an express power to commandeer is different from those other absences. The power
to commandeer state officials, he argued, is not merely absent from the enumerated
powers: it is "conspicuously absent." See *Murphy*, 584 U.S. at 471. If the Framers had
meant to give Congress such a powerful tool, he argued, they surely would have
done so in writing, especially considering how controversial such a power would
likely have been. That they did not enumerate such a power accordingly reflects a
decision to withhold it. On its merits, this argument is problematic: the absence of a
specific delegation of power does not necessarily indicate that that power is categorically denied to Congress, even when the absence is "conspicuous." The power to
charter corporations was saliently contested at the Founding, and its omission from
the enumeration did not mean it had been withheld. But if the argument is valid, it is
an argument that presents the Constitution as embodying an affirmative decision to
prevent Congress from using a particular means for executing its powers. What the
absence of an express power to commandeer means, the argument runs, is not that
Congress can commandeer only when doing so is necessary and proper for the execution of some enumerated power. It means that Congress may never commandeer. In
other words, this line of reasoning entails the view that commandeering is affirmatively prohibited, even though it does not consciously or officially describe things
that way. Much as *Butler* and *Dagenhart* described themselves as internal-limits decisions but in substance struck down federal law on external-limit grounds, *Murphy*'s
internal-limits argument for anticommandeering doctrine actually points to the doctrine's status as an external limit.

35. The Nineteenth, Twenty-Third, Twenty-Fourth, and Twenty-Sixth Amendments also
have congressional enforcement clauses. Three of those amendments—the Nineteenth,

Twenty-Fourth, and Twenty-Sixth—create voting rights enforceable against state governments and accordingly could raise some of the same issues that arise in cases under
the Fourteenth and Fifteenth Amendments. To date, there are no cases in which the
courts have declared federal legislation unconstitutional on the ground that it exceeded
Congress's power to enforce the Nineteenth, Twenty-Fourth, and Twenty-Sixth
Amendments. But the question of whether such rulings would be best conceptualized
in terms of internal or external limits is in substance the same as the parallel question in
the Fourteenth and Fifteenth Amendment contexts, so this chapter's discussion of the
Reconstruction Amendments is applicable to these later amendments as well.

36. City of Boerne v. Flores, 521 U.S. 507 (1997); Shelby County v. Holder, 570 U.S. 529
    (2013).

37. Religious Freedom Restoration Act, 42 U.S.C. § 2000bb-1.

38. Garcia v. San Antonio Metropolitan Transit Authority, 469 U.S. 528 (1985); see also
    New York, 505 U.S. 144.

39. New York v. United States, 326 U.S. 572, 582 (1946).

40. Coyle v. Smith, 221 U.S. 559 (1911).

41. Texas v. White, 74 U.S. 700, 725 (1868) (describing an "indestructible Union, com-
    posed of indestructible States"); U.S. Const. art. IV, § 3.

42. *NFIB*, 567 U.S. at 579–582 (opinion of Roberts, C.J.); *NFIB*, 567 U.S. at 676–677,
    687–689 (joint dissent of Scalia, Kennedy, Thomas, and Alito, JJ.).

43. *NFIB*, 567 U.S. at 578 (opinion of Roberts, C.J.).

44. For a discussion of process limits that never worked the way the Founders imagined,
    see Larry Kramer, "Understanding Federalism," *Vanderbilt Law Review* 47, no. 5 (1994):
    1490–1491. For an example of a process limit that has been altered over time, consider
    the Seventeenth Amendment's conversion of the Senate from an assembly of agents of
    state governments into an assembly of popular representatives (though it may be more
    accurate to say that the amendment mostly ratified a conversion that had already taken
    place in practice, because for most of the nineteenth century state legislatures tended
    to elect to the Senate people who had campaigned successfully for the office among the
    general public). See William H. Riker, "The Senate and American Federalism," *Ameri-
    can Political Science Review* 49, no. 2 (1955): 463–464.

45. See, e.g., Jessica Bulman-Pozen and Heather K. Gerken, "Uncooperative Federal-
    ism," *Yale Law Journal* 118, no. 7 (2009): 1256; Kramer, "Understanding Federalism,"
    1543–1546.

46. "Cooperative federalism" is better understood as an umbrella term naming several
    varying arrangements rather than a single precise model of federal-state cooperation.
    See Abbe R. Gluck, "Intrastatutory Federalism and Statutory Interpretation: State
    Implementation of Federal Law in Health Reform and Beyond," *Yale Law Journal* 121,
    no. 3 (2011): 584–588. By the same token, cooperative federalism might be a species
    of process federalism, or it might be a separate phenomenon, or the two phenomena
    might overlap, depending on how one draws the boundaries of each concept.

47. See generally Abbe R. Gluck, "Federalism from Federal Statutes: Health Reform,
    Medicaid, and the Old-Fashioned Federalists' Gamble," *Fordham Law Review* 81, no.
    4 (2013). For examples, consider Social Security Act, 42 U.S.C. §§ 301–306; Clean Air

Act, 42 U.S.C. §§ 7543(b), (d), (e)(2); No Child Left Behind Act of 2001, 20 U.S.C. §§ 6304, 6311; Violent Crime Control and Law Enforcement Act of 1994, 34 U.S.C. § 60301; 23 U.S.C. § 148 (transportation).

48. See Gillian E. Metzger, "Federalism under Obama," *William and Mary Law Review* 53, no. 2 (2011): 575–579.

49. See Gluck, "Intrastatutory Federalism and Statutory Interpretation," 578.

50. See Roderick M. Hills Jr., "The Political Economy of Cooperative Federalism: Why State Autonomy Makes Sense and 'Dual Sovereignty' Doesn't," *Michigan Law Review* 96, no. 4 (1998): 868–870 (describing the practical limits on federal capacity that prevent federalization of policy areas at will).

51. See "Historical Tables," White House, accessed June 2024, Table 12.1, https://www.whitehouse.gov/omb/historical-tables/ (https://perma.cc/3GMA-TGCM).

52. See generally Bulman-Pozen and Gerken, "Uncooperative Federalism," 1256.

53. See generally Bulman-Pozen and Gerken, "Uncooperative Federalism," 1284–1294.

54. See, e.g., City of Arlington v. FCC, 569 U.S. 290, 305 (2013) (describing the question of the validity of a federal agency's construction of a statute specifying state obligations within such a system as one of "faux-federalism").

55. See, e.g., *Morrison*, 529 U.S. at 617–618 ("The Constitution requires a distinction between what is truly national and what is truly local"); *Garcia*, 469 U.S. at 580–581 (O'Connor, J., dissenting) ("The central issue of federalism, of course, is . . . whether any area remains in which a State may act free of federal interference").

56. See *Lopez*, 514 U.S. at 567–568.

57. Gluck, "Federalism from Federal Statutes," 1750–1751.

58. See, e.g., Bond v. United States, 572 U.S. 844, 857–859 (2014).

9. WHAT THE CONSTITUTION SAYS

1. See, e.g., Laurence H. Tribe, *American Constitutional Law*, 3rd ed. (St. Paul, MN: Foundation, 2000), 789 ("Article I, § 1 endows Congress not with 'all legislative power,' but only with the 'legislative Powers herein granted'").

2. Lawrence Lessig, *Fidelity and Constraint: How the Supreme Court Has Read the American Constitution* (Oxford: Oxford University Press, 2019), 75.

3. See John Mikhail, "The Constitution and the Philosophy of Language: Entailment, Implicature, and Implied Powers," *Virginia Law Review* 101 (2015): 1063, 1080–1081.

4. This is my conclusion based on searching, inter alia, the *DHRC* database for the term "herein granted" on May 31, 2019, and subsequently asking a research assistant to try to falsify my conclusion using a variety of search strings.

5. *DHRC*, 2:445; Cassius VI, "To the Inhabitants of This State," *Massachusetts Gazette*, December 18, 1787, in *DHRC*, 5:479; Cassius VI, "To the Inhabitants of This State," *Massachusetts Gazette*, December 25, 1787, in *DHRC*, 5:511. The two publications by Cassius are installments of a single essay.

6. See Chapter 4.

7. Again, the point is not that the enumerationist reading of the Vesting Clause was unthinkable. Indeed, it seems to have been offered at least once and perhaps twice dur-

ing the First Congress. According to Maclay's diary, Richard Henry Lee read the Article I Vesting Clause that way during the Senate's 1789 debate over whether the president had the power to remove executive branch officials. "Debate on the Foreign Affairs Act," July 14, 1789, in *DHFFC*, 9:485. The only other indication of which I am aware that any member of the First Congress ever offered the enumerationist reading of the Vesting Clause is from the records of a June 1790 debate about whether Congress would grant a loan to a glass-making merchant. In the course of that debate, in what was probably a reference to the Vesting Clause, Roger Sherman said that he understood Congress to "have the powers only herein granted." *DHFFC*, 13:1541. Sherman was speaking several months before the bank debate, so presumably many members of Congress at the time of that later debate had heard Sherman's comment. If so, the fact that nobody offered the enumerationist reading of the Vesting Clause during the bank debate might mean that, having heard it once, they did not find it persuasive. But the most significant thing about Lee's and Sherman's statements is how unusual they were. Given how many people spoke for how many hours about the extent of Congress's powers during the two years when the First Congress sat, and how many of those people had incentives to make whatever arguments were available for the proposition that Congress had only the powers the Constitution enumerated, it is telling that the enumerationist reading of the Vesting Clause was almost entirely absent.

8. Alexander Hamilton, "Pacificus No. 1," June 29, 1793, reprinted in *The Papers of Alexander Hamilton*, ed. Harold C. Syrett (New York: Columbia University Press, 1969), 15:33–43.

9. Hamilton, "Pacificus No. 1," 33–43.

10. See, e.g., Zivotofsky ex rel. Zivotofsky v. Kerry, 576 U.S. 1, 40 (2015) (Thomas, J., concurring in the judgment in part and dissenting in part) (invoking Hamilton's Pacificus argument); Eric A. Posner and Adrian Vermeule, "Legislative Entrenchment: A Reappraisal," *Yale Law Journal* 111, no. 7 (May 2002): 1665, 1675n26 (same); Saikrishna Bangalore Prakash, *Imperial from the Beginning: The Constitution of the Original Executive* (New Haven, CT: Yale University Press, 2015), 71–73 (same).

11. Joseph Story, *Commentaries on the Constitution of the United States* (Boston: Hilliard, Gray, 1833), 2:§§ 545–569, at 26–45.

12. Story, *Commentaries*, 3:§§ 1406–1423, at 278–291 (discussing Article II, Section 1); Story, *Commentaries*, 3:§ 1573, at 437, §§ 1584–1591, at 449–456 (discussing Article III, Section 1).

13. Kansas v. Colorado, 206 U.S. 46, 81 (1907).

14. For a discussion of the few occasions on which this idea appeared prior to the 1990s and a discussion of how it entered the discourse at that time, see Richard A. Primus, "Herein of 'Herein Granted': Why Article I's Vesting Clause Does Not Support the Doctrine of Enumerated Powers," *Constitutional Commentary* 35, no. 3 (2020): 305–307.

15. This ordinary-language reading does not establish a strong form of the nondelegation doctrine, because the fact that Congress is "vested" with a power is compatible with Congress's delegating that power to another decisionmaker. See Thomas W. Merrill, "Rethinking Article I, Section 1: From Nondelegation to Exclusive Delega-

tion," *Columbia Law Review* 104, no. 8 (December 2004): 2097; Julian Davis Mortenson and Nicholas Bagley, "Delegation at the Founding," *Columbia Law Review* 121, no. 2 (2021): 277 (adducing Founding-era support for the permissibility of Congress's delegating the exercise of its powers to other actors, provided that Congress retained the authority to end the delegation and exercise the relevant power itself).

16. See Pauline Maier, *Ratification: The People Debate the Constitution, 1787–1788* (New York: Simon and Schuster, 2010), 57, 151, 286, 365.

17. *DHFFC*, 11:868–869 (statement of Madison). See *DHFFC*, 11:1000–1001 (statement of Jackson) (explaining that the president obviously does not have all of the executive power under the Constitution).

18. Yes, this means that Justice Scalia was wrong about Article II's Vesting Clause in his rhetorically potent dissent in *Morrison v. Olson*, 487 U.S. 654, 705 (1988) (Scalia, J., dissenting) (insisting that the text of the Vesting Clause of Article II means that all executive power is vested in the president).

19. See Hayburn's Case, 2 U.S. (2 Dall.) 409, 410n (1792).

20. The account that follows is partly inspired by material discussed in John Mikhail, "The Necessary and Proper Clauses," *Georgetown Law Journal* 102, no. 4 (2014): 1045, 1100, 1104.

21. *Records*, 2:177 (August 6, 1787).

22. *Records*, 2:177 (August 6, 1787).

23. *Records*, 2:177 (August 6, 1787).

24. *Records*, 2:185, 186 (August 6, 1787).

25. Compare *Records*, 2:565 (text approved prior to the work of the Committee of Style), with *Records*, 2:590 (text as written by the Committee of Style).

26. National Federation of Independent Business v. Sebelius, 567 U.S. 519, 534 (2012) (opinion of Roberts, C.J.).

27. See, e.g., United States v. Lopez, 514 U.S. 549, 588–589 (1995) (Thomas, J., concurring).

28. Marbury v. Madison, 5 U.S. (1 Cranch) 137, 174 (1803).

29. Although I think such an argument should ultimately fail, it is possible to argue that the Counterfeiters Clause was not superfluous when written, even though it never added anything to the powers of Congress. On the model of exclusive jurisdiction, a clause specifying that Congress had the power to punish people who counterfeited federal securities and federal currency would signal that state governments were not permitted to enforce their own laws against such counterfeiting. If Congress's power to punish counterfeiters were implicit in the clauses authorizing Congress to borrow and coin money, then states would be prevented from enforcing their own laws punishing the counterfeiting of federal securities and federal currency whether or not the Counterfeiters Clause existed. But if in the absence of the Counterfeiters Clause Congress would have the power to punish counterfeiters only on the basis of the Necessary and Proper Clause, then state law on the topic would not be preempted. The Counterfeiters Clause would then not be superfluous: it would preempt state law that would otherwise be permissible. I suspect, however, that this thought process is more a dogged attempt to rescue Section 8 from redundancy than a real account of the significance of the Counterfeiters Clause. Marshall in *McCulloch* described the

power to punish mail thieves as implicit in the Post Office Clause itself rather than requiring the Necessary and Proper Clause, and by the same logic the power to punish counterfeiters should arise directly from the clauses granting Congress the powers to borrow and coin money. In the end, any exclusive-jurisdiction regime in which the states would be preempted from enforcing laws punishing the counterfeiting of federal securities and federal currency would probably function just the same with or without the Counterfeiters Clause.

30. For this phrase, I thank Ida Gorenburg.

31. Murphy v. NCAA, 584 U.S. 453, 471 (2018).

32. *DHFFC*, 11:1301 (August 18, 1789), 1310 (August 21, 1789).

33. Speaking in opposition to the first proposal to include the word "expressly," Madison noted that "the word 'expressly' had been moved in the convention of Virginia, by the opponents to the ratification." *DHFFC*, 11:1301 (August 18, 1789).

34. Christopher J. Tiedeman, *The Unwritten Constitution of the United States: A Philosophical Inquiry into the Fundamentals of American Constitutional Law* (New York: G. P. Putnam's Sons, 1890), 140–143.

35. Missouri v. Holland, 252 U.S. 416, 433 (1920) (internal quotation omitted).

36. As explained in Chapter 7, there are contexts in which saying that a power is "reserved" to the state governments might mean only that the state governments may exercise that power concurrently with the federal government, rather than that only the state governments may exercise that power. If the word were read that way in the Tenth Amendment, then the Tenth Amendment might make the most sense if "delegated" were read to mean "delegated exclusively." The Tenth Amendment would then be a statement distinguishing between those powers delegated exclusively to the federal government (like the power to declare war) and all other powers. The content of the rule would be that the powers not delegated exclusively to the federal government could be exercised by the states, though perhaps only concurrently. I do not claim that this is the best reading of the Tenth Amendment; all things considered, it seems to me that the conventional interpretation of "reserved" to mean "reserved exclusively" is, in this context, sensible.

37. New York v. United States, 505 U.S. 144, 155–157, 161 (1992); Alden v. Maine, 527 U.S. 706, 713 (1999).

38. *Alden*, 527 U.S. at 713–714; *New York*, 505 U.S. at 155–157.

39. Long ago, Karl Llewellyn described this phenomenon by saying that the clauses of the Constitution are like the drawers of a filing cabinet, and specific constitutional rules are filed where they seem to best belong. See Karl N. Llewellyn, "The Constitution as an Institution," *Columbia Law Review* 34, no. 1 (January 1934): 1, 4.

40. Lessig, *Fidelity and Constraint*, 75.

CONCLUSION

1. See Karl N. Llewellyn, "The Constitution as an Institution," *Columbia Law Review* 34, no. 1 (January 1934): 1, 15.

2. McCulloch v. Maryland, 17 U.S. 316, 405 (1819).

ACKNOWLEDGMENTS

So many people have helped me write this book that it seems impossible to identify them all. What follows is my best attempt to give thanks where it is due, and I am conscious that there may be others deserving of thanks whose names do not appear below. To them, I offer my apologies and a wry thought about the limits of enumeration.

My foremost thanks go to four colleagues at the University of Michigan Law School: Rich Friedman, Don Herzog, Eve Brensike Primus, and Gil Seinfeld. They gave immense amounts of time, energy, and intellectual firepower to help me make the book the best that it could be. I also thank my other Michigan colleagues who read chapters or full drafts and offered valuable feedback, including Nick Bagley, Elise Boddie, Evan Caminker, Dan Crane, Sam Erman, Daniel Halberstam, Scott Hershovitz, Ellen Katz, Julian Mortenson, Bill Novak, and Rachel Rothschild. Sam Erman merits a special thank-you for a suggestion about how to present Figure 7.1, and Scott Hershovitz merits one for the suggestion to include the FAQ section at the end of the book. My appreciation also goes to the broader Michigan Law community that engaged with the ideas of this book in a series of workshops and to the Law School's Cook Endowment, which provided financial support.

In the wider academy, many people read chapters, protochapters, or full drafts, and I benefited immensely from their reactions. I thank Tabatha Abu El-Haj, Jonathan Adler, Randy Barnett, Mitch Berman, Mary Bilder, Jud Campbell, Bill Ewald, Noah Feldman, David Franklin, Jonathan Gienapp,

Abbe Gluck, Rick Hills, Alison LaCroix, Sandy Levinson, Gerard Magliocca, John Mikhail, and David Schwartz. Within this group, I offer special thanks to John Mikhail for a suggestion about the book's title and to Rick Hills for a collaboration that profoundly shaped Chapter 8. (Rick is not responsible for the way the idea is argued in this book.) David Schwartz is due special recognition as the originator, to my knowledge, of the term "enumerationism."

I also had the benefit of feedback from a set of excellent readers beyond the academy. Tina Bennett gave generously of her time and expertise to help me think about the project after I had written an initial draft. In the final phases, Michael Farbiarz and Ida Gorenburg were superstars, reading revised chapters and making incisive suggestions for improvement in something close to real time. Sharon Fenick and Alan Promer volunteered to test-read the preface and the conclusion, and I'm grateful for their help.

Over the course of several years, I presented papers on the subject matter of this book at Notre Dame, Stanford, the University of Chicago, the University of Southern California, the University of Wisconsin, Vanderbilt, and Yale, as well as at the annual conference of the American Society for Legal History, the Works-in-Progress Conference of the Center for the Study of Originalism at the University of San Diego, and the Rehnquist Center's National Conference of Constitutional Law Scholars at the University of Arizona. (And while the pandemic raged, by Zoom to the faculty of the Pennsylvania State University and as part of a virtual symposium organized by the *Fordham Law Review* and the *Journal of American Constitutional History*.) I thank the organizers of all of these workshops for the opportunity to share my ideas, and I thank the participants for their productive and critical engagement. I also had the good fortune to have many valuable discussions outside the context of formal workshop exchange, both at Michigan and elsewhere. For those conversations, I thank Akhil Amar, Sam Bagenstos, Jack Balkin, Gary Bass, Jessica Bulman-Pozen, Kristina Daugirdas, Bruce Frier, Robert Gordon, Michael Grunwald, Monica Hakimi, Dirk Hartog, Dan Hulsebosch, George Kimball, Kyle Logue, Rob Lothman, Michael McConnell, Chris McCrudden, Adam Pritchard, Kim Roosevelt, Stephen Sachs, Margo Schlanger, and David Uhlmann.

Perhaps the greatest privilege of my professional life is the opportunity to work with Michigan's law students. Many of them helped refine the ideas presented in this book, some of them as research assistants and others as interlocutors in seminars or elsewhere. I especially thank Caleb Ashley, Scott

Bloomberg, Daniel Cowan, Ruby Emberling Giaquinto, Jennifer Fischell, Savannah Grice, Madeline Guth, Kelly Hagen, Katie Hurrelbrink, Hillary John, Tom Kloehn, Amy Lishinski, Claire Madill, Emily Minton Mattson, Leah Mintz, Jessica Morton, Caleb Nagel, Matt Rice, Haley Rogers, Kathleen Ross, Sam Rudman, Chris Schwartz, Anna Searle, Kenneth Sexauer, Audrey Springer-Wilson, Eli Temkin, Jessica Ullom-Minnich, Adam Wallstein, Tyler Washington, Rachael Westmoreland, Cali Winslow, and Dayna Zolle.

Michigan's faculty and its students are two of the communities that make Michigan such a wonderful place to work. Another is the professional staff. I offer special thanks to Virginia Neisler and Shay Elbaum, whose proficiency as research librarians is matched only by their eagerness to take on difficult projects; to Jenny Rickard, for overseeing a symposium on the work in progress; and, most of all, to Cheri Fidh, for doing more or less anything that needed to be done, and for doing it well and quickly, too.

At Harvard University Press, I thank Kathleen McDermott, who believed in the project, and Grigory Tovbis, who got it over the finish line, as well as an anonymous reviewer who provided feedback and encouragement. At Amnet ContentSource, I thank Jamie Armstrong for copyediting. I also thank *Constitutional Commentary*, the *Fordham Law Review*, the *Michigan Law Review*, the *University of Pennsylvania Journal of Constitutional Law*, and the *Yale Law Journal* for permission to incorporate in this book, in revised form, several ideas that initially appeared in their pages. More particularly, portions of Chapter 2 were first published in "Reframing Article I, Section 8," *Fordham Law Review* 89, no. 5 (2021): 2003–2032, and parts of Chapter 3 build on ideas first presented in that article. Portions of Chapter 5 were first published in "'The Essential Characteristic': Enumerated Powers and the Bank of the United States," *Michigan Law Review* 117, no. 3 (2018): 415–497. Chapter 7 builds on ideas first presented in "Why Enumeration Matters," *Michigan Law Review* 115, no. 1 (2016): 1–46, and "The Gibbons Fallacy," *University of Pennsylvania Journal of Constitutional Law* 19, no. 3 (2017): 567–620. Portions of Chapter 8 were first published in "The Limits of Enumeration," *Yale Law Journal* 124, no. 576 (2014): 578–642. This chapter also builds on ideas first presented in "Suspect Spheres, Not Enumerated Powers: A Guide for Leaving the Lamppost," coauthored with Roderick M. Hills Jr., *Michigan Law Review* 119, no. 7 (2021): 1431–1502. Portions of Chapter 9 were first published in "Herein of 'Herein Granted': Why Article I's Vesting Clause Does Not Support the Doctrine of Enumerated Powers," *Constitutional Commentary* 35, no.

3 (2020): 301–344. Again, my thanks to the editors of those journals, both for permission to use the relevant material and for their work in helping to formulate the articles that appeared in their publications.

My last round of thanks is reserved for my family. My parents, Chuck and Romana Primus, followed the progress of this book from the beginning, and they read pieces here and there and gave me valuable reactions. But their real contribution to this book is in their half-century of parenting. They taught me to think and to write, and they supported me in the study of my chosen discipline. I am deeply grateful. My siblings—Ida Gorenburg, Lisa Minsky-Primus, and Aryeh Primus—are the best lifelong peer group that anyone could ask for, whether for the purpose of talking about ideas or more or less anything else. My three children fill my life and my heart more richly than they can possibly understand. Indeed, it's safe to say that "Jessica Ruth, Jonathan Sigmund, and Talia Anne" is my favorite enumeration—and it's exclusive.

Finally, I thank my wife, my best friend, and my partner in all things: Eve Brensike Primus. Her contributions to this book have been enormous. She read an early draft, diagnosed its biggest problem, and told me how to fix it. It was the single most important piece of feedback I got in the entire process of writing the book, and I should have known it would come from her. Beyond that, she was a constant source of support, encouragement, and gentle prodding. She believed in this book both when I did and when I didn't. She encouraged me to keep going when it was hard to keep going, and she enabled me to see when the work was done. And she is, through her own work, a constant source of inspiration to me as an example of someone who believes the world can be made better through hard work and hard thinking in the field of law. But mostly I am grateful for all that she does, and is, beyond the realm of law and legal scholarship. The reasons why I am lucky to have her in my life cannot possibly be enumerated.

INDEX

Page numbers followed by *t* indicate a table. Page numbers followed by *f* indicate a figure.